LEGACY OF LOVE

"For the message of the cross is foolishness to those who are perishing, but to us who are being saved it is the power of God."
(1 Corinthians 1:18)

LEGACY OF LOVE
BIBLICAL WISDOM FOR FATHER-SON RELATIONSHIPS

Dr. David R. Blunt

CHURCH JUNCTION FOUNDATION
ChurchJunction.com
Wilmington, DE
2024

── DISCLAIMER ──

Readers are encouraged to use discernment, recognizing these pages are crafted as a representation of archetypal situations rather than specific instances. Any resemblance to actual persons or names is coincidental. Unless otherwise indicated, all names, characters, businesses, places, events and incidents in this fictionalized book are either the product of the author's imagination or used in a fictitious manner. The publisher, editor, and author are not providing professional advice or services. They expressly disclaim all responsibility for any liability, loss, or risk, personal or otherwise, incurred as a consequence, directly or indirectly, of using and applying any of the contents of this book. The author maintains a delicate balance between universality and practicality, employing a narrative style written in an abstract, content-oriented fashion to convey broader truths. This disclaimer underscores the focus on timeless principles derived from Biblical wisdom, using fiction for illustration. While diverse interpretations of Scriptural verses within the Christian conservative perspective exist, the book offers a mainstream viewpoint to illuminate themes relevant to father-son relationships. This interpretation is not absolute; however, it aligns with the rich theological tradition of this perspective.

Copyright © 2024 by Dr. David R. Blunt
All rights reserved. No part of this publication may be reproduced, distributed, or transmitted in any form or by any means, including photocopying, recording, or other electronic or mechanical methods, without the prior written permission of the publisher, except in the case of brief quotations embodied in critical reviews and certain other noncommercial uses permitted by copyright law.

For permission requests, write to the publisher at the address below.
CHURCH JUNCTION FOUNDATION
1207 Delaware Avenue, 3535
Wilmington, Delaware 19806
Email: support@churchjunction.com
Website: ChurchJunction.com
ISBN: 979-8-9899721-0-4
Printed in the United States of America
Cover design by Dr. David R. Blunt
First Edition: February 27, 2024

── DEDICATION ──

In recognition of the void left by an absent fatherly mentor, these pages stand as a tribute to the unyielding resilience of the human spirit. Within the intricate dynamics of father-son relationships, the inspiration to sow a legacy of love, wisdom, and fortitude transcends the limitations imposed by the emptiness of a distant earthly connection.

Amidst the silence, void of congratulatory voices, and echoes of fatherly compassion, the narrative of the book remains unwavering: let the paternal missteps cease here and initiate the journey of a new family legacy to be passed down to subsequent torchbearers.

This dedication extends a symbolic hand to those familiar with the untold chapters of a personal narrative, mirroring the profound odyssey of shaping a legacy. It is a homage to all fathers and their sons, an acknowledgment traversing temporal realms, weaving together the tapestry of collective humanity.

BIBLIOGRAPHIC RECORD

Library of Congress Cataloging-in-Publication Data:
Blunt, David R. (Dr. David R. Blunt)
Title of the Book: LEGACY OF LOVE
Sub Title: BIBLICAL WISDOM FOR FATHER-SON RELATIONSHIPS
Author's Affiliation: CHURCH JUNCTION FOUNDATION
p. cm. 15.24 x 22.86 cm
ISBN: 9798989972104
Library of Congress Control Number: 2024901428
Publication Date: February 27, 2024
Publisher: CHURCH JUNCTION FOUNDATION
Place of Publication: Wilmington, DE
Edition: First
1. Biblical Wisdom 2. Father-Son Relationships 3. Legacy of Love
I. Title.

HEARTFELT DEDICATION

Journeying through the whispers of time, it has been said, a young son embarks on three stages on his path to manhood. In the first, he gazes upon his father with admiration, perceiving him as the mightiest of beings, a superhero, mechanic, builder, coach, scout leader, and all along capable of assembling the most intricate toys, patching bicycle flats, mending wounds, defying gravity to retrieve elusive balls lodged in a tree, and everything else under the sun.

As adolescence unfolds into early adulthood, a son believes himself to be smarter, tougher, wiser, and a force to be reckoned with, often overshadowing the decades of silent sacrifice, sleepless nights, and the difficult choices made by a father during marital plights while in their youth.

Yet, within this journey, a revelation begins to dawn upon them as they evolve into manhood and even fathers themselves. They will come to recognize their fathers' tireless efforts were selfless acts of countless years of giving in an effort to impart life's lessons needed to surpass their own existence.

It is in this realization, the unique nature of fatherly love starts to become apparent. All the while, they begin to see their father's expressions as sincere and his directions firm, were set in place for a tough and difficult world, as the path ahead starts to materialize on the horizon of time.

At this juncture, father and son may cross life's path akin to each other, where a helping hand is hopefully extended for those who are starting to age out. In these moments, one imparts the wisdom garnered through trial and error, while the other grasps the importance of carrying forward the legacy of love.

It is a sentiment oft-repeated but ever profound: "There is no love on earth, greater than that of a father for his son." To my beloved sons, Joshua, Jonathan, and Jordan—you breathe life into my inspiration and embody the everlasting thread binding fathers to their sons. I am immensely proud of each of you and cherish the precious moments we share together.

With all my love,

Dad

──── BROTHERHOOD DEDICATION ────

In this heartfelt dedication to my brothers, Steven and Raymond, I want to express my sincere gratitude for the profound impact you have had on my life. Over the years, our shared experiences have forged an unbreakable bond, transcending time and distance.

Our diverse qualities have woven a rich tapestry of memories, each thread representing moments of laughter, support, and growth, strengthening our connection.

The unique gifts each of us brings to the table of life have not only enriched our individual journeys, but have also contributed to the depth of our brotherly bond. Your resilience, compassion, and unwavering determination inspire me, serving as a reminder of the loving strength within our family ties.

More importantly, witnessing the flourishing lives you both lead alongside your own families fills me with an immense sense of pride and joy. Seeing the love and devotion you pour into your relationships and the happiness you have found, brings warmth to my heart, reaffirming the importance of family and the void created without them.

As we continue to navigate the journey of life, I am grateful for the love and brotherhood binding us together. Through the highs and lows, I take comfort in knowing I have you both by my side, sharing in the good times ahead and challenges passing our way.

My prayers are with you always, guiding and supporting you in navigating the paths ahead.

With much love and appreciation,

Brother David

—— TABLE OF CONTENTS ——

TITLE PAGE	
DISCLAIMER – COPYRIGHT	
DEDICATION	v
BIBLIOGRAPHIC RECORD	vi
HEARTFELT DEDICATION	vii
BROTHERHOOD DEDICATION	ix
ACKNOWLEDGMENTS	xvii
AUTHOR'S NOTE	xviii
PREFACE	xix
PROLOGUE	xx
FOREWORD	xxi
INTRODUCTION	xxiii
Preparing for the Journey Ahead	xxiii
Exploring Love's Essence	xxv
Transformative Fatherly Love	xxvi
Eternal Melody of Fatherhood	xxviii
Nurturing Foundations of Love	xxix
Foundational Love in Fatherhood	xxxi
Love's Transformative Influence	xxxiii
Eternal Echoes of Love	xxxv
CHAPTER ONE	1
Legacy of Love	1
Patience a Pillar of Love	2
Unveiling Patience Through Empathy	4
Connecting Kindness and Compassion	5
Perseverance in Love	7
Tales of Reconciliation	11
John and Mark	12
Enduring Love and Transformation	13
Richard and Robert	13

Strength of Love	15
Michael and Ben	16
Weightiness of Separation	17
Walking in Your Father's Footsteps	**18**
Guidance Role in Fatherhood	20
Applying Proverbial Wisdom	23
Cultivating Fatherly Guidance	**26**
Wisdom's Compass in Mentorship	27
Gift of Understanding	28
Lessons in Fatherly Patience	31
Timeless Wisdom for Modern Fatherhood	**34**
Power of Open Communication	35
Empathy and Perspective-Taking	37
Resolving Differences and Conflict	38
Shared Values and Traditions	39
Passing Down Wisdom	40
Threads of Compassion and Unity	42
Moving Forward	**44**
CHAPTER TWO	**47**
Building a Strong Foundation	**47**
Love as the Lifeblood of the Family	48
Dynamic Role of Love	50
Attentive Listening as an Active Role	52
Sustaining Family Bonds	**54**
Core of Fatherhood	54
Integral and Irreplaceable Fatherhood	56
Resilience and Vitality of the Bond	57
Unconditional and Lifelong Love	60
Love as a Foundational Life Force	**62**
Building Mutual Respect	63
Nurturing Growth	66

Omnipresence of Love	69
Impact on Guidance and Support	71
Influence on Future Generations	74
Recognizing a Precious Gift	**75**
Nurturing the Legacy	76
Fostering Spiritual and Moral Growth	78
Gratitude and Reverence	**80**
Gratitude as a Transformative Emotion	80
Gratitude Beyond Joy	82
Gratitude as a Guiding Principle	83
Reverence for the Sacred Role	86
Humility in Fatherhood	87
Honoring the Significance of Fatherhood	87
Role of Godly Influence	89
Moving Forward	**91**
CHAPTER THREE	**93**
Lessons from Scripture	**93**
Foundational Principles for Exploration	95
Flexibility in Instructional Discipline	98
Imparting Spiritual Teachings	**100**
Instruction Grounded in Faith	103
Building Spiritual Growth	107
Moral Compass in Leading	109
Integrity in the Father-Son Bond	110
Fatherhood Beliefs in Understanding	112
Applying Practical Spirituality	114
Connecting to Relational Spirituality	**116**
Transformative Approach	120
Strength Anchored in Scripture	123
Building Deep Understanding	128
Spiritual Connections	131

Living Out Faith Together	133
Moving Forward	**136**
CHAPTER FOUR	**139**
A Father's Legacy	**139**
Divine Commandment	140
Legacies Through Divine Teaching	143
Driving Lessons of Love in Teaching	**145**
Love's Role in Legacy Building	148
Love's Steadfast Commitment	149
Shaping the Future Generation	**152**
Shapers of Character	156
Nurturing a Legacy of Virtue	159
Continuity of the Legacy	162
Guiding the Way	**164**
Modeling Excellence in Fatherhood	165
Living in the Present	167
Nurturing Values for the Future	168
Conveyance of Spirituality	171
Passing Down a Fathers Legacy	**173**
An Everlasting Legacy	178
Faith's Underpinning	180
Attributes of a Living Tradition	182
Legacy of Faithful Living	184
Moving Forward	**187**
CHAPTER FIVE	**189**
Embracing Love and Guidance	**189**
Exploring the Covenant	191
Drawing Divine Inspiration	193
Significance of Sacred Promises	196
Fathers as Earthly Representatives	198
Maintaining the Sacred Covenant	204

Counsel through Generations	205
Fathers Unwavering Commitment	207
Spiritual Character Development	213
Exploring Godly Spirituality	215
Dedication within Fatherhood	218
Guiding with Wisdom	**221**
Recognizing Individuality	223
Faith and Spirituality	225
Integrity and Honesty	227
Resilience and Perseverance	228
Enduring Parental Influence	230
Core Values as a Moral Compass	231
Practicality of Proverbs Wisdom	235
Moving Forward	**238**
CHAPTER SIX	**241**
Journey of Growth	**241**
Exploring the Father-Son Journey	242
Dynamic Generational Bond	246
Strengthening the Relationship	248
Transmission of Family Traditions	**250**
Shaping Character and Integrity	253
Emotional Impact on Well-being	258
Embracing Mental Perseverance	261
Nurturing Emotional Intelligence	**264**
Foundation of Fatherly Mentorship	265
Life's Profound Companionship	269
Bridging Generational Divides	271
Strong Father-Son Communication	273
Graceful Relationship Resolutions	279
Embracing Family Differences	283
Nurturing Dynamic Growth	285

Moving Forward	287
CHAPTER SEVEN	289
Everlasting Bond	289
Echoes of a Virtuous Heritage	291
Legacy of Living Wisdom	294
Legacy Narratives Past and Present	297
Passing the Torch	300
Torchbearer's Responsibility	301
Wisdom's Eternal Flame of Love	310
Honoring the Torch's Legacy	312
Influence on Future Generations	314
A Brief Reflection	317
Final Journey of Love	319
Reflecting on a Lifetime of Love	321
Closing Thoughts	329
EPILOGUE	333
AFTERWORD	334
SCRIPTURAL REFERENCES	335
DISCUSSION QUESTIONS	343
DISCUSSION QUESTIONS –	347
INSIGHTS FOR MODERATION	
BOOK CLUB GUIDE	351
BOOK CLUB GUIDE –	355
INSIGHTS FOR MODERATION	
INDEX	358
PUBLISHER RESOURCES	359
ABOUT THE COVER	360
NOTES	361

ACKNOWLEDGMENTS

Gratitude fills my heart as I extend my sincerest appreciation and thankfulness to those who have privately influenced the genesis of this book.

In countless moments of contemplation, I relied on my invaluable family members: Mom, Chuck, and Bob. Their unyielding presence served as both a sounding board and source of introspection, providing an opportunity for me to clarify the concepts as I vocalized them without reservation. I trust their ears have stopped ringing over the constant dialogue.

Dr. Zackery, thank you for your impromptu response and willingness to briefly lend your voice to my written words. It was an inspirational moment, as it spurred me to revisit these manuscripts and narrow my focus.

My absent paternal guide, though inadvertently, became a basis for this undertaking. Amidst the challenges of divorce, children bear the weight of this disruption. Inevitably, these young ones as they mature spend a lifetime of endeavors to prove themselves to those who were not present. It is a reminder, divorce, regardless of the reason, is never an opportunity to depart from a child's life.

Life's journey. The hard knocks of a failed relationship is an ever-present reminder, the best laid plans can still be disrupted by those you would least expect, and yet loved the most.

A special acknowledgment to the Church Junction Foundation for their constant financial support and trust. Their belief in the significance of this seldom-explored topic has been instrumental in bringing this project to fruition.

At the forefront, in gratefully acknowledging God for His instrumental guidance in these achievements, His unwavering support has been the driving force behind the fulfillment of these goals. Amidst the shift within a lifetime of hard work and dedication to those I have truly loved, His faithfulness has remained steadfast.

——— AUTHOR'S NOTE ———

In crafting these pages, the intention extends beyond offering mere words; it is a heartfelt invitation into the core of this exploration. As the architect of this narrative, solace and purpose is derived from sharing insights, reflections, and timeless wisdom drawn from sacred Scriptures.

This book transcends the mere impartation of knowledge; it is a dialogue between kindred spirits. Envision each word as a stepping stone, guiding one through the labyrinth of father-son relationships. Through these pages, the aspiration is to create a space where the echo of personalized experiences find resonance, and where the universality of love and guidance surpass the boundaries of the written word.

Within the author's notes, it is important to acknowledge the structure of the upcoming chapters. Each chapter stands independently, offering valuable insights on its own, while collectively contributing to a comprehensive narrative. Chapter 4 delves into a scholarly examination, meticulously exploring the intricacies of the father-son relationship. In contrast, Chapter 3 lays down a foundational understanding rooted in Biblical teachings, providing a solid framework for further exploration. Meanwhile, Chapter 2 places emphasis on the father's pivotal role in offering guidance and instruction.

Readers and listeners are encouraged to engage with the chapters in any order they prefer, allowing for a personalized journey through the themes presented. Whether one chooses to delve into a specific topic or revisit the text from the beginning, the aim remains to offer a rich and meaningful expedition into the father-son dynamics and Biblical insights.

May the reflections ahead serve as a companion on this personal odyssey, sparking contemplation, fostering connection, and illuminating the path toward a legacy of love.

PREFACE

In moments of quiet reflection, shared laughter, and the unspoken bonds between fathers and their sons, a timeless legacy emerges, a tapestry woven with threads of love, wisdom, and faith. Welcome to the *"Legacy of Love: Biblical Wisdom for Father-Son Relationships."* This is a personal invitation, for all to embark on a deep exploration, uncovering the profound connection in the realm of fatherhood, rooted in the truth of Scriptural understanding.

Throughout these chapters, insights gleaned from Biblical patriarchs and the power of their boundless love are revealed, shaping destinies and leaving an indelible mark on the hearts of familial bonds. Briefly illustrated by stories in ancient texts, such as Abraham and Isaac, a tale of faith and sacrifice, it serves as a reminder for fathers in their own journeys, instilling a sense of dedication and hard work while raising their sons in the likeness of God's commands.

The ultimate story of a father's love unfolds in the parable of the prodigal son, emphasizing forgiveness, unconditional love, and the joy of reconciliation. These timeless lessons serve as a beacon of hope for all who seek to strengthen their father-son relationship. As we explore these Godly truths and principles, each narrative mirrors our own experiences, hopes, and aspirations, inspiring us to strive for a closer connection with our sons.

Join us in opening your heart to the transformative power of faith and the wellspring of love flowing through these connections. Whether you're a father nurturing a legacy or a son embracing the inheritance of wisdom, this book affirms the significance of this bond and illuminates the path ahead. Let us explore this birthright together and uncover the Biblical mysteries guiding us on this sacred journey of leading our sons into manhood.

PROLOGUE

In the absence of a tangible father figure, this work emerges as a testament to the uncharted landscapes shaped by the void. From the echoes of a silent mentor yet to be heard, the quest for approval blossomed into a lifelong pursuit, molding the start of a meaningful imprint for the next generation.

This book serves as a timeless mirror into past generations, encompassing those who have missed opportunities to convey a heartfelt legacy to the next generation. Unbeknownst to some, fatherhood has a ripple effect, wherein inheritors of this precious gift often meander, seeking ageless wisdom yet to be bestowed. These insights serve as a testament to the immense impact fathers have on their sons and emphasize the significance of passing on this bequest.

In the intricate tapestry of these profound teachings, the chapters unfold as a journey through the sacred pages of Scripture, each revealing a layer of wisdom transcending time. For those who embark on this expedition, they are invited not merely to read or listen but to immerse themselves in the divine guidance having shaped the bonds between fathers and their sons for generations.

Through reflections on timeless verses and the exploration of practical insights, this journey aims not only to enlighten the mind, but also to touch the heart, fostering a deep understanding of the Godly connection between love, wisdom, and the intricate emotions shaping lives.

FOREWORD

Embarking on the journey of fatherhood, where the threads of love and wisdom intertwine, *"Legacy of Love: Biblical Wisdom for Father-Son Relationships"* stands as a guiding lighthouse. In this poignant exploration, the author peers into the ageless teachings of Biblical patriarchs, weaving a narrative transcending generations.

In beginning this odyssey, the resonance of universal truths echoes through the stories of fathers and their sons. This book extends a heartfelt invitation to reflect on the meaningful connections shaping familial bonds, drawing inspiration from the rich tapestry of Scriptural wisdom.

Within the upcoming pages, one discovers a harmonious blend of allegory and practicality, skillfully navigating the complexities of father-son dynamics. This work is not merely a book; instead, it is a compassionate companion on the sacred journey of nurturing legacies and embracing the divine wisdom passed down through generations.

May this step serve as an introduction to a narrative that illustrates, inspires, and celebrates the enduring legacy of love between fathers and their sons.

INTRODUCTION

Preparing for the Journey Ahead

Setting the thematic tone was a straightforward endeavor, drawn by the exquisite wisdom gathered in 1 Corinthians 16:14, "*Let all that you do be done in love.*" It is a calling to conduct every aspect of daily living in accordance with the guiding Biblical principles. This passage brightens the path toward understanding the central role of love in cultivating and sustaining a meaningful father-son connection.

Love is not a transient emotion but a deep commitment, transcending ordinary boundaries and becoming a conscious choice, a way of life nurtured and guided. It is the heartbeat of fatherhood, sustaining the bonds between generations with a flowing rhythm going beyond surface-level expression. It embraces the familial legacy, offering sustained support while cherishing the younger generation unconditionally. This commitment extends throughout every phase of their lives, demonstrating a strong dedication to their growth.

Fathers are encouraged to approach their role with both wisdom and compassion, led by these truths. Love is depicted as the divine momentum behind their interactions and guidance. It is an affection seeking the best interests in every decision and action, nurturing development, and providing a strong foundation.

The Corinthian passage serves as a reminder, the Divine embrace is the very essence of fatherhood. It is an effort expressed through words and actions, shaping an environment where one can flourish and bloom. Its essence extends beyond superficial displays of benevolence; instead, it embodies the lasting and transformative nature of true fatherly love.

The Scriptures foretell, love is more than a feeling but a way of life, a resident choice made to cherish, nurture, and protect the family. They inspire fathers to view their roles as opportunities to infuse tenderness into every moment, decision, and interaction.

INTRODUCTION

The challenge lies in the intentional fostering of a relationship where fatherly affection moves beyond the spoken word and is lived out daily, creating an atmosphere of familial warmth. Promoting an attentive bond within the family unit truly encapsulates the essence of love, reaching far beyond verbal expression and superficial displays. Instead, the nurturing atmosphere becomes a space where this attribute transcends a mere abstract concept, becoming an integral part of daily life. This dynamism reflects a deliberate commitment to ensure the expression of affection, not solely through verbal affirmations but in every interaction, decision, and experience within the domestic sphere.

Bringing this notion to life involves tangible acts of kindness moving to the forefront. In this sense, fatherly affection becomes a visible reality, something their sons can touch, feel, and rely on. Forming such a setting emphasizes the significance of a consistent, encouraging, and supportive role. In these roles, their harmonious emotions avoid sporadic occurrences and move beyond the temporal to an everlasting presence, constantly reassuring their sons they are cherished and valued. Their recognition begins by weaving this emotion into the very fabric of daily life, creating a safe and calming realm, and securing the knowledge they are unconditionally protected.

Consistency is key to fatherhood, extending beyond occasional acts of tenderness to being a reliable source of support and guidance. This reliability is integral to building trust, a fundamental element of the relationship. In this setting, love becomes the foundation upon which a trusting and meaningful connection is built, leaving a lasting familial legacy. While verbal expressions of devotion, such as saying "I love you," undoubtedly hold significance, they are just the beginning of the journey.

Deeds indeed speak louder than words when it comes to deep, fatherly affection. In simpler terms, creating an environment filled with love allows fathers to consciously and consistently show affection through their everyday actions. It involves exemplifying care, support, and warmth within the fabric of daily routines. Cultivating patience, understanding, and compassion, particularly during challenging moments, becomes an integral aspect.

Their commitment extends to making deliberate choices which prioritize the well-being and peace of the family. This involves creating a place where love transcends abstraction, evolving into a lived and tangible experience. This challenges fathers to be engaged in their roles, ensuring affection is not a passive sentiment but an active and guiding incentive in their relationships. The focus lies in establishing a compelling illustration of love's essence and guiding their sons to grasp the depth of affection, incorporating it into their personal interactions and relationships.

Exploring Love's Essence

Exploring the essence of love within the context of fatherhood and father-son relationships is a wonderful journey. To *"do everything in love"* is to make love a way of life rather than an occasional emotion. Fathers are called to infuse their interactions with warmth and understanding, allowing love to permeate daily routines, decisions, and conversations. In this relationship, it means prioritizing health, growth, and happiness, encompassing physical needs, emotional, psychological, and spiritual development, with love as the guiding principle.

It involves demonstrating compassion through actions and words, creating an environment where feeling cherished and valued is supported. Mentorship contributions demand intentionality, guided by Scriptural wisdom, while being attuned to the influence of words and actions in the nurturing connection. Strengthening compassion becomes a proactive catalyst, encompassing choices and decisions executed with meticulous consideration. In embodying these principles, fatherly role models illustrate the essence of unconditional love, patience, and kindness, prioritizing the well-being of others. This exemplar extends an invitation to cultivate a robust, enduring bond, forging a legacy defined by understanding and composure. It serves as a North Star, pointing the way to meaningful and fulfilling father-son relationships where love becomes an ingrained aspect of their connection.

In the vast expanse of parental affection, the concept of nurturing shines brightly. It manifests as a keen interest in a loved one's physical, emotional, and spiritual wellness. These are the opportunities to remain vigilant in discovering their joys and challenges, ensuring contentment and safety, and providing steady support. Compassion, another valuable facet, progresses deeper into the emotional domain. It is the embodiment of empathy, where those who offer solace and resonate with their loved ones' varied experiences. Whether it is a setback or a triumph, a loving presence is there, offering comfort during the storms and reveling in moments of sunshine. It is this deep emotional connection tightening the bond, making it unbreakable.

Consequently, the maturation process demands patience, with a steadfast presence offering wisdom and understanding of each lesson and experience as stepping stones toward manhood. Imposing timelines is avoided in favor of providing a comforting residence, assuring their protégés have a reliable hand to hold through life's difficulties. The pillar of selflessness prioritizes dreams and success, exemplifying boundless love through significant and subtle sacrifices with an inspiring focus.

By exploring these facets, fathers gain a comprehensive understanding of *"doing everything in love."* It goes beyond simple affection; it encompasses a holistic and Godly approach to nurturing and guiding. While these constructs, ideas, and viewpoints will be examined in greater detail throughout the chapters, this initial sojourn is a challenge to embrace love as an active and guiding stimulus, shaping the decisions, interactions, and the legacy fathers leave behind.

Transformative Fatherly Love

The Corinthian passage fundamentally urges fathers to perceive their roles as a call to action, propelled by love as the driving force. This perspective extends beyond basic ideology, and instead involves the deliberate process of decision-making, guidance, and engagement, all anchored in a heartfelt sense of love.

The inspired words also shed light on the art of nurturing, fostering an environment steeped in familial comfort, peace, value, and support. This process facilitates emotional, spiritual, and intellectual growth, underscoring the significance of being present during the ever-changing moments in life. Consequently, it cultivates an understanding of the father-son bond, with

PREPARING FOR THE JOURNEY AHEAD

love serving as its constant heartbeat, sustaining it through every season of life. Additionally, this connection is characterized by trust, knowledge, and a sense of belonging, forging a long-term relationship. This unified principle influences various supportive processes, encompassing a sustaining presence in moments of both joy and sorrow, active listening, validation of feelings, and providing a fortress of strength during personal struggles.

Ensuring unconditional support, it leaves behind a legacy rooted in values and statutes extending beyond their lifetimes. This legacy encapsulates wisdom, compassion, and understanding, passed down through generations yet to come. As a guiding influence, love forms the way fathers provide guidance, offer support, and establish their legacy, transcending the limitations of words and emotions.

Lived out on a daily basis, these essentials nurture strong and lasting relationships founded on understanding and compassion. It becomes a lived experience, a tangible embodiment of the everlasting connection between fathers and their sons. Through this intentional practice, a legacy is woven, one standing as a testament to the power of love in shaping familial bonds. The Apostle Paul, in the Corinthian writings, challenged fathers to extend their traditional roles beyond providing and enforcing authority; and instead, embrace Godly love as the standard in the journey of caregiving, becoming transformative and building perennial connections. This then permeates each facet of these interactions, forming the cornerstone upon which their relationships are constructed.

Fatherly embrace shapes their roles, revolutionizing the way they offer counsel. Instead of providing advice solely based on logic and experience, it infuses guidance with compassion and understanding. They can then use their instructions as a means of helping navigate life's complexities with empathy and wisdom.

In these verses, the multifaceted nature of this core tenet, including care, patience, and selflessness, is beautifully expounded upon, revealing its depth and richness. The Biblical words highlight the practical implications in the context of fatherhood as a challenge to be intentional in a domain where these powerful stimuli are not just spoken but lived out daily. This call to action emphasizes active and engaged commitment, whether in providing guidance, offering a lending hand, or building a legacy centered on love.

The insights from its transformative power are inspiring and perceptive, shedding light on the fatherly role beyond providership to focus on cultivating, guiding, and building their alliance. The loving bond, built by this sincere emotion, trust, and understanding, becomes the foundation for a legacy extending far beyond their lifetimes. This essence of mentorship offers various perspectives in the way it informs the relationship, direction, and future they create. It encourages them to embrace the wayward light in their journey and to recognize the significant impact on the lives they touch.

Eternal Melody of Fatherhood

The foundation of a strong father-son connection relies on the valuable concept of love, an incentive serving as the benchmark for all interactions, guidance, and legacies. It is not solely a rudimentary feeling but a commitment, a choice, and a way of being. Within this framework, every interaction in these bonds is infused with this powerful propellant, Godly in nature and divinely inspired. From providing guidance and discipline to offering comfort and encouragement, it serves as the motivation behind their actions. It is the underlying desire to witness growth and success while improving the quality of life.

Love permeates fatherly guidance, ensuring it is not a rudimentary set of instructions but is firmly rooted in compassion, understanding, and a deep yearning for the well-being and growth of those they care for. It tempers discipline with patience, offers wisdom with empathy, and embraces an environment in which loved ones feel secure and cherished.

The dynamics between a father and son, rich with lessons, shared experiences, and mutual growth, are eloquently orchestrated by the rhythmic pulse of love. It is the kind of emotion acting as both compass and anchor, guiding interactions and keeping them grounded, even amidst life's turbulent storms. This mood manifests in grand gestures as well as in everyday moments: the quiet understanding in a shared glance, the comforting embrace after a setback, or the joyous celebration of a milestone achieved.

These seemingly simple acts are imbued with abounding significance, each echoing a message of absolute care and sustaining support. Their affection evolves and matures over time, mirroring the changing seasons of life. In the early years, it is protective and nurturing, guiding the young steps with patience and anticipation. As the years advance, this love transitions into one of mutual respect and camaraderie, where wisdom is both given and received. In the golden years, it blossoms into deep gratitude and reverence for their memories and moments. Throughout this journey, it remains an unchanging constant, weaving tales of laughter, tears, triumphs, and lessons. In this eternal dance of fatherhood, love is the melody binding each step, twirl, and leap, creating a bond both timeless and precious.

Nurturing Foundations of Love

The concept of love being the foundational rock of strong and stable father-son relationships is certainly resonant. Love serves as the starting block upon which these connections are constructed, providing stability, warmth, and depth to the bond between fathers and their sons. At its core, love is a deliberate choice and a personal commitment. It represents deep-seated and consistent affection, extending beyond the boundaries of time and circumstance. In the framework of these connections, love finds expression in every interaction. It is the energy behind a father's desire to guide, nurture, and support his son.

Whether providing guidance, offering encouragement, or being a source of strength in times of need, love infuses these actions with genuine care and compassion. It models the direction provided and ensures it is rooted in wisdom, empathy, and a deep concern for their interest and growth. This isn't solely regarding material possessions but encompasses the values, ideologies, and deep love instilled. Extending beyond earthly lifetimes, this gift continuously shapes lives and influences the character and values of future generations within the family.

Emphasizing its transcending nature, the concept moves beyond idealized emotion; it is a substantial commitment supporting every facet of the relationship. Such a notion dwells deeply within the essence of fatherhood, leaving an unending legacy of love, guidance, and

INTRODUCTION

understanding. Within this realm, fatherly affection takes on a multifaceted nature, enriching the quality of the bond and encompassing a wide spectrum of actions, all of which contribute to building a strong and meaningful connection.

The concept of nurturing acceptance is indeed a powerful and transformative aspect of love. It signifies a fatherly bond transcending conditions and expectations, representing a permanent presence through all circumstances. This form of acceptance embraces the entirety of a person's being, recognizing strengths and vulnerabilities alike. It affirms one's worth is not contingent upon achievements, adherence to standards, and even missteps. Instead, it originates from the fundamental relationship itself. This dimension promotes a sense of security and belonging.

When one recognizes the steady and dependable nature of fatherly affection, it empowers their sons to authentically express themselves and confront life's impediments without fear of rejection. It cultivates a robust self-worth and confidence, underscoring the value of unconditional affection. This acceptance develops an environment of open and honest communication within the family relationship. When feelings are accepted unconditionally, regardless of actions or choices, open dialogue becomes more likely, addressing concerns, seeking answers, and acknowledging setbacks.

Their open exchange cultivates a solid basis for trust and comprehension, allowing instruction to be offered in a supportive and non-judgmental fashion. This facet exerts a lasting influence. Encountering these values often carries a significant sense of self-worth into future roles. Recognizing the significance of extending a similar level of love and acceptance to the next generation offers an attentive positive cycle spanning through time.

Acceptance stands as an influential element within familial bonds. It symbolizes sustained and permanent affection, independent of achievements or conformity to expectations. It cultivates security, open discourse, and self-value, with an impact extending beyond the immediate relationship and forming forthcoming generations. This serves as a poignant reminder of the vital role love plays in relational dynamics, urging an exploration of its intricate nature and far-reaching influence. At the core of this multifaceted affection lies love, an acknowledgment of the need for

PREPARING FOR THE JOURNEY AHEAD

nourishment and support, encompassing both the physical and emotional dimensions. Through the expression of a compassionate posture, a nurturing environment is established, providing fertile ground for growth. It is this support forming the foundation of strong family connections, especially when called upon to provide sustaining assistance, offering encouragement and guidance in various pursuits, including academic, spiritual, physical, or personal endeavors.

A supportive surrounding nurtures confidence and self-assurance, serving as the bridge to a deeper connection and wisdom. It's an invitation to engage actively, listen empathetically, and grasp thoughts and feelings. Through mutual understanding, bonds are fortified, emphasizing emotional presence. It is this reminder, seeking confirmation and appreciation, regardless of actions or accomplishments, is at the heart of these connections. This acceptance is the building block for trust and authenticity, facilitating growth.

The overarching message is clear: love, encompassing care, support, understanding, and unconditional favor, acts as the catalyst for eternal and meaningful relationships. It is an encouragement to recognize the importance of these qualities and actively embody them in their interactions. In doing so, this paves the way for a lasting bond infused with genuine and influential love, shaping future family legacies.

Foundational Love in Fatherhood

The central portrayal of love within the domain of fatherhood comes into prominence, highlighting its mark as more than an intangible attitude but as the foundational essence of these roles. The encouragement in recognition lies beyond the sheer cascade of internal emotion, finding its fundamental component in their seed-born identity.

Love serves as the conscription propelling acts of Godly nurturing, support, guidance, and unconditional devotion toward their offspring. This transformative perspective turns love from a passive emotion into an active and guiding influence shaping the father-son bond, standing as a monument embodying fatherhood itself. The notion of divine affection examples the cohesive element in sustaining connections between generations. Its timeless and enduring nature transcends temporal and age-related constraints, abounding in devotedness. It is a reminder, mutual affection in the present extends throughout the portal of time, shaping the eternal legacy left behind. The impactfulness of nurturing and fortifying these connections holds significant weight, highlighting their everlasting sway, molding values, and character carried forward. This rousing sentiment leaves a lasting impression, inspiring posterity and uplifting a broader perspective. It emphasizes their role as contributors to a larger, intergenerational narrative.

The transformative power of unconditional love is a significant and heartwarming quality, emphasizing transcending conditions or expectations, yet it is acutely capable of forming and fortifying familial bonds. Specifically, Agape love is similar in nature to nourishing soil where the seeds of trust, understanding, and growth can thrive. It encourages embracing loved ones for who they are, flaws and all, and steadfastly supporting them, regardless of circumstances. Their connection eliminates barriers, creates an atmosphere of trust and safety, and promotes round-table discussions.

When this form of unconditional love is present, it sends a powerful message beyond words. This type of love dismantles emotional barriers existing within relationships. It is a process of communication sending messages of trust, acceptance, and non-judgment, encouraging an attentive expanse for genuine emotional connections.

Trust is the foundation of healthy relationships, and its nature is vital in the cultivation of long-lasting bonds. Trust finds its place within the father-son dynamics, empowering a pathway toward conveying the innermost thoughts and emotions and seeking guidance without hesitation. Emotional safety is then cultivated, providing a haven where vulnerability and expression of concerns find solace. Their emotional sanctuary is indispensable for nurturing emotional strength and development. It instills confidence, value, and protection along the journey into adulthood. When trust and emotional security are cultivated, open communication thrives. It cultivates a relationship where thoughts, concerns, ambitions, and hurdles can be freely exchanged, promoting an atmosphere of open discourse and offering support, guidance, and knowledge.

Love's Transformative Influence

Within the complex framework of father-son relationships, love reveals remarkable transformative powers. A significant facet lies in its capacity to dissolve emotional barriers, often constructed within the human experience, hindering open and forthright dialogue. The process of dismantling these obstacles within love-infused connections is both powerful and life-changing. It creates an environment of willingness and freedom for open expression, where thoughts are freely realized, emotions are deeply felt, and acceptance is devoid of judgment.

Trust emerges as the foundation upon which robust familial bonds thrive. The steady support and acceptance stemming from Agape love creates an environment where it can truly flourish. Within the nurturing context, worth is recognized as intrinsic, unrelated to achievements or specific expectations. It is this unshakable virtue nurturing an atmosphere for genuine discussion.

Encouraged by such a supportive backdrop, a sense of empowerment emerges, allowing for the unveiling of the deepest sentiments and aspirations. This open communication, in turn, allows for genuine empathy, reinforcing the intricate emotional connections underlying their bonds. Emotional openness is more than a cathartic process, since it forges a bridge between corrective guidance and mutual respect.

In these enriched relationships, connections evolve into more than just guiding figures. They become strong allies, participating in common experiences and emotions. It is a newfound confidence moving beyond the internal world and radiating outward, elucidating their pursuits and ambitions with an unyielding determination. Such love doesn't simply offer comfort; it fortifies resilience. Furnished with the knowledge of having an unshakable support system in place, the path their sons navigate is a life's labyrinth with a fortified spirit.

Amidst heartaches, the choice of loneliness is dismissed, for a father assumes the role of a life preserver. In this capacity, he empowers his sons to overcome adversity, glean wisdom from life's encounters, and emerge with increased tenacity. The impact of this abundant love is unending. The safeguard provided becomes a lasting legacy, resonating across time and forming an unbroken thread of empathetic and understanding connections. Genuine altruism intricately weaves a tapestry of enduring memories, treasured throughout a lifetime. These are not fleeting instances but rather pillars of strength, solace, and inspiration.

Expressions of pure fatherly love transforms memories into defining moments, leaving an ineffable impression on their very identities and promoting an eternal sense of kinship. These memories serve as perpetual reminders, marvelous testaments to the unbreakable bonds shared with their fathers. It transcends cursory affection, forging a domain in which security is experienced and appreciated while girded with unyielding support. Within this nurturing space, they are poised to flourish personally and emotionally, facilitating their self-awareness and understanding of their family roles. This profound love contributes to individual growth and fortifies the intergenerational bond, building a legacy of compassion and mutual consciousness.

The fortification of their alliance is a multi-step process extending beyond the superficial aspects of a father-son relationship. The nucleus of this process involves the development of an intense emotional intercession beyond scant words and gestures. Their love establishes a stable and firm foundation for building such a connection, facilitating reliance and resilience.

Within this dominion, exploration is expressed through emotions and thoughts. It nurtures a deep level of shared understanding as fathers become attuned to their sons' needs, desires, and concerns, while their sons come to value the guidance and support provided. As this mutual understanding deepens, it nurtures personal growth for both. The older generation gains insight into their younger counterparts' unique qualities, aspirations, and mishaps, enabling them to offer customized guidance and support. In return, the youth glean wisdom from their seniors' life experiences and perspectives, contributing to their personal development.

This love bolsters the emotional bond between them, facilitating a dynamic process of growth and comprehension. It establishes an abode in which both can flourish individually and collectively, enriching their relationship and leaving behind a long-lasting legacy. It is evident, Agape love is unconditional, selfless, and sacrificial, and is not a docile emotion but an active, Godly impetus in the realm of nurturing their relationship, a goal to strive towards. It functions as the heartbeat sustaining and edifying the bonds between different generations, shaping interactions and promoting personal growth and understanding.

Eternal Echoes of Love

The concept of love, once sown in the heart of a father-son connection, transcends the present moment, initiating a sequence of endless echoes extending far beyond the present. When nurtured and cherished, it becomes their own legacy. Their affection is often characterized by its depth, constancy, and unconditional nature, which possesses the ability to transcend time. It evolves into an ageless motion, building familial bonds, values, and relationships for generations. The values and principles imparted through love continue to guide and inspire their offspring, who in turn pass on this inheritance. It is a cycle of affection and wisdom perpetuating itself, cultivating a family culture deeply anchored in the Godly virtues of love, integrity, and righteousness.

Essentially, this focus is not restricted to the present, it is a gift that keeps on giving, an eternal wellspring of strength and inspiration for fathers, their sons, and generations yet unborn. This serves as a prompt for the affection offered today, in holding the power to mold the character, values, and relationships of their family for tomorrow.

The deep-rooted concept of love, passed from one generation to the next, exerts an influence extending well beyond the present moment. It serves as the foundation upon which a family's values, traditions, and interconnectedness are built. Genuine and lasting affection leaves an indelible imprint on the family's narrative, weaving a legacy of care, support, and empathy. This fatherly affection forms both the lives of immediate descendants and the very essence of the family's identity. It sets the standard for family members' interactions, their approach to problems, and the cultivation of relationships. Their provision stands as a constant source of inspiration for the future, a testament to the power of fatherly love. It nurtures a sense of continuity and belonging, reminding each inheritor of the connection uniting them.

INTRODUCTION

Love transcends the confines of a single moment; it is a legacy spanning generations, a purposeful gift, leaving an indomitable impression on the family's heritage, values, and lasting connections. Love, guidance, and legacy-building are interwoven themes forming the essence of fatherhood. These elements are not motionless but continually evolve as connections grow and evolve together. Embracing the transformative power of affection, offering guidance as an act of love, and consciously building a lasting legacy are key aspects of nurturing strong and meaningful relationships spanning a lifetime.

In summary, this preparatory introduction briefly touched on several of the many theoretical concepts yet to be discovered. However, the primary intent was to lay the groundwork and, more importantly, establish love as the foundation for this journey. The focus remains "narrowly defined" and centered on the exclusive father-son bond. The tone is rooted in the living attributes and fruits of the Spirit, specifically love.

Chapter 1, titled "*Legacy of Love*," commences with 1 Corinthians 13:4-7, serving as the initial step in embracing the father-son connection. This bond, unique in its understanding, is scarcely addressed outside the journals of the Scriptures. Yet, it stands as a valuable and integral element in the continuity of male bonding, shaping boys into men and guiding them towards fatherhood.

Perhaps within the moments of growth and understanding lies the unspoken, echoing in a manner similar to Matthew 3:17, "*And a voice from heaven said, 'This is my beloved Son in whom I am well pleased!'*"

CHAPTER ONE

Legacy of Love

The Lord imparts a timeless lesson, urging his disciples to love one another as He has loved them. It is a divine commandment, characterized by selflessness and a resolute commitment, establishing a powerful precedent to follow, as exemplified in John 13:34-35, stating: *"A new command I give you: Love one another. As I have loved you, so you must love one another. By this everyone will know that you are my disciples, if you love one another."* This passage suggests love is not an abstract concept but an influential, Godly dynamism capable of transforming relationships and directing their trajectory.

The *"Legacy of Love"* is a journey broadening the depth and breath of love's attributes while embracing its nature, elements, and the components influencing the everlasting inheritance yet to be uncovered. Absorbing the impactful instruction of the divine command set forth by the Lord and seamlessly threading through the fabric of this bond, fathers and their sons embark on a journey of exploration into the very essence of love.

These lasting virtues are found in 1 Corinthians 13:4-7, *"Love is patient, love is kind. It does not envy, it does not boast, it is not proud. It does not dishonor others, it is not self-seeking, it is not easily angered, it keeps no record of wrongs. Love does not delight in evil but rejoices with the truth. It always protects, always trusts, always hopes, always perseveres."*

Love acts as a guiding light, casting its brilliance on the familial path they are about to traverse. The passage establishes the foundation for the pages ahead, where an exploration of the Godly-inspired connection between a son and his father unfolds. It carries a heartfelt message, reminding all, love transcends fleeting emotions, evolving into a meaningful and persistent presence providing solace, strength, and hope.

These Biblical instructions mark the initial steps taken together and serve as a foundational guide for reflection. The eternal values provide an operational understanding, as subsequent discussions on kindness, perseverance, empathy, and forgiveness illustrate the way these virtues manifest within the connection.

While the Corinthian text serves as a knowledge base, it is essential to recognize its unique function within the familial bond. This approach ensures love remains relevant and applicable to specific experiences, deepening insight, understanding, and the discernment of this vital theme. It further embraces the many attributes, including patience, while fostering trust and security, remaining constant and unwavering throughout their legacy.

Patience a Pillar of Love

Patience, often mistaken for passivity, plays a dynamic role. Instead of waiting without reacting, it actively engages with the challenges of the father-son relationship. It serves as a proactive and stabilizing action, enabling both to navigate their connection with calmness and understanding amidst high emotions and expectations. In James 5:7-8, the Scriptures share the importance of this virtue: *"Be patient, then, brothers and sisters, until the Lord's coming. See how the farmer waits for the land to yield its valuable crop, patiently waiting for the autumn and spring rains. You too, be patient and stand firm, because the Lord's coming is near."*

In this moment, the text encourages believers to be patient, drawing a parallel to a farmer's patience in waiting for crops to grow and stressing the importance of standing firm in faith while waiting for the Lord's return. Amidst this understanding, it serves as a guiding beacon, assisting both the father and his son in navigating the intricate landscape of emotions, conflicts, and personal development with grace and sensitivity.

This demeanor becomes a conduit for the spiritual fruits, as outlined in Galatians 5:22-23, *"But the fruit of the Spirit is love, joy, peace, forbearance, kindness, goodness, faithfulness, gentleness, and self-control. Against such things there is no law."* Through these attributes, observing others navigate challenging circumstances with grace and empathy builds a mutual understanding of the importance of self-control and awareness. This, in turn, leads to an engagement in profound dialogue, the expression of emotions, and conflict resolution with forbearance as the guiding principle. These dynamics nurture a sense of unity and trust, allowing for individual and collective growth. The proactive practice of patience equips them to approach the intricacies of their alliance with clarity, comprehension, and understanding, turning moments of tension into opportunities for personal development and the strengthening of their alliance. This sense of calmness becomes a cornerstone of their relationship, paving the way for everlasting love and companionship.

Within this realm, patience serves as a foundational element since it forms the bedrock upon which trust and intimacy are built. When fathers exercise this role, they communicate their love is steady and enduring, regardless of the circumstances. It is the willingness to listen attentively, even when faced with disagreements, and to provide support during times of trial. This commitment to understanding involves a genuine desire to grasp thoughts, feelings, and perspectives. It means taking the time to ask questions, actively listen, and empathize with each other's experiences. Being attentive in recognizing this consciousness creates a safe space for open and honest discourse. Nurturing this kind of understanding reveals a dedication to establishing valuable connections and bridging generational divides.

In these relational contexts, conflicts and misunderstandings are unavoidable. However, exercising self-restraint goes beyond steering clear of disagreements; it involves a readiness to extend forgiveness. When mistakes occur, an active display of calmness cultivates an environment where forgiveness and progress can thrive. This forgiveness is not merely a superficial gesture but instead a genuine recognition, acknowledging the imperfections within each other and realizing the potential for personal growth. It also serves as a pathway to understanding and empathy, transcending the limitations of individual experiences. This quality enables a deeper connection to the complex emotions and evolving perspectives of one another, free from the confines of personal biases. It forms the basis for meaningful conversations and mutual growth, a lasting pillar of strength for building relationships in times of adversity. Much like a fixed column supporting the pier at the oceanfront, it imparts stability and resilience, allowing them to resist life's rogue waves as a unified front.

CHAPTER ONE

Confronted with diversity, indifference, and difficulties, those who have nurtured this quality adeptly navigate roadblocks with poise and composure, avoiding the pitfalls of impatience and frustration. Rather than yielding, they depend on this foundation to navigate challenges with unwavering resolve. The significance of such endurance cannot be overstated; it is a Godly inspiration actively sustaining and enriching these relationships.

Unveiling Patience Through Empathy

Empathy plays a vital role in active patience. It requires individuals to step into the shoes of others, striving to comprehend their emotions and perspectives. This approach enhances one's ability to connect with the experiences and challenges faced by others, allowing them to view the world from a different vantage point. It provides valuable insights into the unique hurdles, fears, and aspirations encountered when navigating the complexities of life. Those who exhibit empathy gain a deeper appreciation for the intricacies and responsibilities associated with various life roles. In cultivating empathy, fathers construct a strong bridge of understanding, fortifying connections and enhancing their responsiveness to their family's needs. This empathetic approach goes beyond providing guidance; it also offers emotional support. Nurturing understanding and acknowledgment promotes open exchange, instilling trust, and cultivating a sense of security, ultimately reinforcing interpersonal bonds.

When sensitivity becomes the basis of interaction, a deep understanding of the complex roles at play begins to unfold. Those who perceive figures of authority, in their embrace of empathy, reveal the shared humanity within their family connections, where fears, challenges, and vulnerabilities are inherent. This revelation fosters equilibrium and respect within these dynamics. Not only do fathers exhibit heightened support, but they also extend a helping hand and a receptive ear in moments of adversity or stress faced by their loved ones.

Their support proves invaluable during critical life junctures, reinforcing the reciprocal nature of these relationships and laying a foundation of mutual understanding and assistance. This attribute transcends indifference; it is a dynamic and transformative Godly strength underlying their lasting connections. In the occurrence of such empathic understanding, a pathway to meaningful relationships unfold, prompting an exploration of mutual experiences, emotions, and perspectives. This transcends surface-level interactions, reaching into the core of shared struggles and joys.

The result of this compassionate exchange is a stronger, more open, and supportive father-son relationship. When this quality is present, there is a genuine sense of unity and understanding. They become allies in facing life's challenges, offering each other persistent encouragement and support.

There is an open channel of communication where thoughts and feelings are freely offered without the fear of judgment. In addition, this empathetic companionship nurtures mutual growth. They learn from each other's experiences, gaining knowledge and perspective only from such a close and meaningful relationship.

In the journey of exploring this fruit of the Spirit, the understanding emerges clearly: transcending mere virtue, it serves as a core pillar for the thriving of love. Beyond being just a virtue, this element constitutes an indispensable underpinning for the core essence of love. This realization is thought-provoking as it highlights the depth of its' role in nurturing their bond, serving as the basis upon which their relationship is built.

When fathers practice the values of patience, forbearance, and steadfastness, they create an environment where their sons feel heard, valued, and understood. This foundational synergy allows them to connect on a deeper level, bridging generational differences and creating a sense of unity.

Connecting Kindness and Compassion

Kindness and compassion stand as fundamental guideposts within the intricate realm of family connections. Their importance is vital, as they are not elementary virtuous traits but essential components breathing life and vitality into the bond shared between fathers and their sons. To begin, it is important to emphasize kindness and compassion go far beyond surface-level actions or gestures; they transcend the realm of mere deeds and touch the very center of the relationship. These qualities are a reflection of the genuine care and love they have for each other. They are manifestations of compassion, understanding, and a willingness to extend oneself for the well-being and happiness of others. In the context of this bond, kindness takes the form of supportive gestures, gentle words, and a readiness to offer help and guidance when needed. It is the act of being considerate of each other's feelings and perspectives, even in moments of disagreement. Kindness is the glue holding their connection together, building an atmosphere of warmth, acceptance, and mutual respect.

Compassion, on the other hand, embodies the capacity to deeply empathize with one another's experiences and emotions. It is the willingness to truly listen, not only to words but to the unspoken feelings lying beneath. It serves as the wellspring from which understanding flows, embracing a personal connection. This empowers fathers to navigate life's difficulties alongside their sons and encourages them to recognize the wisdom and love bestowed upon them.

These qualities function as the roots of a robust tree, nurturing and sustaining its growth. In these relationships, they offer the sustenance required for their bond to prosper and bloom. This cultivates an environment in which both experience safety, love, and understanding, creating a sense of unity and closeness persevering over time.

These are not simple options but essential elements enhancing and fortifying their connection. It embodies the vitality of their relationship, molding it into a source of love, trust, and companionship. The qualities exemplify the genuine care and affection residing at the core of their relationship, forging an unremitting and profoundly fulfilling bond. These deeds possess a remarkable ability to transcend time and become the basis of cherished memories shared between loved ones.

Their gestures, often appearing small in the moment, hold the power to create a lasting imprint on their connection, shaping it in various ways. It serves as a reminder of tireless commitment, along with memories accompanying individuals as they navigate life's twists and turns, becoming touchstones of reassurance and reinforcing the idea they have always been there for one another.

Similarly, acts of compassion create formidable memories, strengthening the alliance between fathers and their sons. When they sincerely listen to one another, offering empathy and understanding, these moments become milestones of connection. Family members remember the times when they truly felt heard and supported, and these memories shape their perception of one another as not just allies but as trusted companions. What is remarkable is these memories are not isolated instances; they accumulate over time, forming a rich collection of shared experiences.

A powerful example of compassion and love is the parable of the Prodigal Son (Luke 15:11-32). In this narrative, one observes a father's boundless compassion and forgiveness toward his wayward son. Despite his son's mistakes and poor choices, the father's steady love and mercy led to a dynamic reconciliation. This parable illustrates the way compassion, even in the face of disappointment and rebellion, can ultimately bring about redemption and restoration in a relationship.

In Genesis 22:1-19, another poignant example unfolds in the story of Abraham and Isaac. Within this narrative, a clear portrayal emerges of a father's willingness to sacrifice his beloved son out of obedience to God. While this story may initially seem counterintuitive to the theme of kindness and compassion, it highlights the depth of a father's faith and devotion. It serves as a reminder, a father's love and commitment can lead to acts of great sacrifice, demonstrating the impact of parental love on father-son dynamics.

These Biblical stories transcend specific eras and cultures; they are timeless narratives continuing to resonate with many today. Their everlasting relevance lies in the valuable lessons offered for contemporary father-son bonds. The parable of the Prodigal Son is a reminder of forgiveness and compassion bridging even the deepest divides. The story of Abraham and Isaac challenges reflection on the depths of fatherly love and devotion. These memories serve as a source of comfort during difficult moments, reaffirming they are cherished and supported. In essence, acts of kindness and compassion create a treasure trove of memories while building a footing with a strong and abiding father-son connection.

Perseverance in Love

Perseverance is a testament to love's perpetual essence and encapsulates an understanding of the intricate dynamics between commitment and love. The everlasting attributes of perseverance takes on a significant role,

CHAPTER ONE

signifying the unflagging steadfastness and determination to persist through the inevitable difficulties of life rather than succumbing to its adversity. It is not simply a demonstration of grit or stubbornness; it is a powerful reflection of love's durable character and signifies a deep and abiding commitment extending beyond the boundaries of momentary trials and tribulations.

Stories of persistence abound throughout the Scriptures. For example, Joseph's journey in Genesis Chapters 37-50, is marked by numerous trials. He faced betrayal by his brothers, who sold him into slavery. He was then falsely accused and imprisoned in Egypt. Despite these hardships, Joseph remained firm in his faith and trust in God. Through his steady resolve, he eventually rose to a position of power and influence in Egypt, becoming a trusted advisor to the Pharaoh. His ability to interpret dreams played a crucial role in Egypt's survival during a famine. Joseph's story exemplifies doggedness in the face of adversity. He endured years of hardship and injustice, yet he never lost hope and trust in God's plan. His story serves as a powerful reminder of the rewards of commitment, as he was ultimately reunited with his family and played a vital role in their survival and prosperity.

Another Biblical story surrounds the Apostle Paul, formerly known as Saul, who was a zealous persecutor of early Christians. While traveling on a road to Damascus, he experienced a dramatic conversion and became one of the most prominent figures in the early Christian church. Despite facing intense opposition, persecution, and numerous difficulties, Paul remained dedicated to spreading the message of the Gospel. Throughout his missionary journeys, he encountered various trials, including imprisonment, beatings, shipwrecks, and rejection. Even with these hardships, he persevered in his mission to preach to both Jews and Gentiles, writing numerous letters, which are now part of the New Testament, providing guidance and encouragement to early Christian communities and today.

Paul's life and ministry exemplify indefatigable sedulousness in the face of adversity. His commitment to faith and mission to share this message with others serve as a permanent example of determination and dedication, even in pressing circumstances. In the Corinthian passages, the Apostle Paul highlights a significant link between persistence and the timeless nature of love. This connection stands as a poignant reminder, when fathers and their sons face obstacles within their relationship, the capacity to persist through these difficulties serve as a compelling testament to the strength and depth of their affection for one another.

A valuable asset of perseverance is determination, since it provides strength and resilience in their alliance as it extends beyond simply lasting through or surviving trials; it represents a collective commitment to surmounting obstacles, a firm resolve to address disagreements, and a sustained dedication to grow together despite life's inevitable differences. Within this intersection, it transforms into the active expression of their love. The relationship between persistence, determination, and compassion in father-son connections is unique, serving as the pathway through which the continuing nature of love finds its expression. It signifies a commitment to withstanding adversity, solidifying their bond, and ultimately fulfilling a companionship built on resilience, love, and consistent zeal.

When fathers remain strong through difficulties, they demonstrate their unshakable dedication to the relationship they share. This quality showcases a willingness to endure and overcome obstacles, not as isolated acts but as an ongoing testament to their love and devotion. It speaks to the resilience of their connection, illustrating it can weather even the most formidable storm. In moments of difficulty, when perseverance is called upon, love serves as the spark, propelling both to stand together and face adversity head-on. Perseverance in love means they are willing to invest the time and effort required to navigate the complexities of the relationship. It involves actively seeking solutions rather than surrendering to conflicts, and a commitment to continuous growth and understanding, recognizing the journey is not without its share of hurdles.

In the face of challenges, whether stemming from differences in opinion, conflicts, or external roadblocks, their commitment underscores the unique nature of their love. It signifies their alliance is not easily shaken by adversity but is instead resilient, steadfast, and unyielding. This dedication reflects the persistent support for each other and their mutual relationship. It shows their readiness to invest the time and effort needed to resolve conflicts, bridge differences, and nurture their connection. It is a testament to their commitment in maintaining and strengthening their alliance, regardless of the issues they encounter.

CHAPTER ONE

In addition, there is a link between this commitment and long-lasting love, emphasizing their bond is deep-rooted in respect, care, and understanding. Navigating these differences is an acknowledgment: their relationship is worth the effort, and the love they embrace is meaningful and continuous. When they overcome these hurdles and missteps, it becomes a powerful declaration of the lasting nature of their affection, reinforcing the idea, their connection is unshakable and grounded in genuine, abiding care.

Within these bonds, love's promising composition envelops a sense of trust and security. It provides the assurance, regardless of external circumstances, their love for each other remains constant and steadfast. This sense of stability encourages open dialogue, vulnerability, and the willingness to work through difficulties together.

Their sustaining complexion is a testament to its far-reaching role, supported by a divine power transcending time and troubles, serving as the foundation upon which their relationship is built. It enriches their companionship, providing the strength and resilience needed to navigate life's trials and cherish the lasting alliance they share.

The connection between perseverance and its nature serves as a resounding affirmation; even in the face of hardship, love stands as the unbreakable thread weaving fathers and their sons together on their journey, holding immense significance as it highlights their inherent strength and resilience.

Throughout life's travels, conflicts, confrontations, and complications will inevitably arise, manifesting in various forms, including differences in perspectives and aspirations as well as external difficulties testing their mettle. In essence, perseverance, determination, and compassion form an inseparable bond within father-son relationships, fostering an enduring commitment to overcoming hardships and nurturing love transcending adversities, thereby solidifying their connection and enriching their journey together.

——— Tales of Reconciliation ———

The lifeblood of love becomes unmistakably evident, a defining moment of moral strength, spiritual firmness, and character resilience supported by a Godly determination. In these circumstances, this is not a quaint tolerance of hardship; rather, it is a dynamic response fueled by the spirit of love for one another. It signifies a mutual commitment to ride out the storms together, to stand side by side in the midst of distress, and to emerge stronger and more closely connected. When fathers and their sons choose to persevere, they send a clear message: their love is not a fair-weather emotion, subject to the whim of circumstances.

Instead, it mirrors the divine embrace described in Jeremiah 31:3, where the Lord declares: *"The Lord appeared to us in the past, saying: 'I have loved you with an everlasting love; I have drawn you with unfailing kindness.'"* This spirit remains single-minded and resolute, steadfastly anchoring them to one another with a love transcending time, echoing an eternal, inspired embrace.

It is an unbreakable thread keeping them devoted and bound together. As a constant reminder, their companionship is not fragile or easily severed but is rooted in deep, everlasting affection, signifying their passage is worth every effort, sacrifice, and step taken together. In times of trials, this everlasting love becomes their source of strength and motivation, providing a comforting embrace, a guiding light, and tireless support.

Tested and tried, their devotion emerges even more resilient, crafting an unbreakable bond enriched by their collective experiences. This constant, unyielding connection acts as a driving force, withstanding every challenge and embracing a spiritual link keeping them connected, devoted, and bound together. Love stands as a beacon of hope amid heartache, a powerful reminder laid before them; together, they can overcome all barriers and continue to build, cherish, and pass on their unique and sustaining legacy.

Within the realm of the father-son relationship, a tapestry of short stories unfolds, narratives steeped in compassion, durability, and sustenance, poised on the brink of discovery. They promise transformative insights into the potency of commitment and the lasting strength nestled in the heart of familial bonds. As each narrative is revealed, both father and son navigate their perspectives, mending, bonding, and faithfully maintaining their connection despite the seemingly insurmountable hurdles before them.

John and Mark

Consider the story of John and his estranged son, Mark. Their relationship was fraught with tension and misunderstandings, a familiar scenario in the intricate dynamics of father-son relationships. John, a steadfast and loving father, faced the formidable task of reconnecting with his teenage son. The discord between them arose from fundamental differences in personality and interests. Mark, a fiercely independent and headstrong teenager, frequently clashed with his father, leading to a breakdown in communication. Conversations grew strained, and the divide between them widened.

However, John refused to succumb to the prevailing discord. He saw beyond the surface-level conflicts, recognizing the persistent love he held for his son. With unrelenting determination, he embarked on a remarkable journey of patience and perseverance. His commitment to his son's well-being remained steady.

Understanding beneath the turbulent surface lay a bond waiting to be rekindled and refusing to let adversity define their relationship, he took a stand with resolve. Consistently reaching out to Mark, even in the face of resistance and reluctance, months turned into years, and though heartbroken, he maintained his relentless patience. Listening attentively, empathizing with his son's struggles, and offering support without judgment.

At times, it was challenging for John to embrace his son's perspectives, but his actions spoke louder than words, signaling to Mark his father's love was consistent and unshakable. As the years passed, the walls separating father and son gradually broke down. Mark, now in his mid-30s, experienced a shift in his outlook on life, moved by his father's unwavering commitment.

Eventually, their conversations deepened in meaning, and their interactions became more genuine. The healing process had begun. John's years of perseverance and love became the catalyst for transformation. Over time, both John and Mark set aside their differences for the betterment of the relationship and focused on the goodness they both brought to their loving familial bond.

Enduring Love and Transformation

Highlighting their short story stands as a powerful testament to the resilience of the father-son connection, revealing meaningful universal lessons. In the face of seemingly insurmountable differences and conflicts, it highlights the prevailing nature of love. John's untiring perseverance stands as a guide; demonstrating commitment and steadfastness can help mend the deepest rifts. Beyond their personal journey, John and Mark's story resonates as a universal narrative. It speaks to the potential for reconciliation and growth within every challenging family subtlety. The tale emphasizes the transformative impact of a father's love, marked by patience and perseverance.

It is a reminder, such qualities are capable of bridging the widest gaps and reigniting the deepest connections. In contemplating John and Mark's journey, an invitation arises to explore its broader significance, encouraging reflection on the value of patience, the lasting strength of love, and the possibilities for healing and growth amid strained relationships. Ultimately, the narrative serves as an inspirational story, offering hope and useful insights into the transformative impact, tireless commitment and love can have, transcending the intricate nuances of family dynamics.

Richard and Robert

The bond between father and son, Richard and Robert, proved unbreakable, a product of lifelong experiences and tireless love. However, their relationship faced an unprecedented challenge with Richard's recent dementia diagnosis. Years before this revelation, subtle signs manifested.

CHAPTER ONE

Once self-reliant, Richard now struggled with daily tasks, occasionally forgetting familiar faces and places. Prideful, he hesitated to admit needing help, straining their connection.

Seeking support in various forms, Robert connected with groups and sought professional advice on mental health. External resources emerged as vital lifelines, providing insights and camaraderie in shared struggles. Despite societal stigmas, Robert confronted misconceptions surrounding dementia. As an intermittent caregiver, he faced occasional difficulties balancing caregiving, a career, and personal relationships delicately. The increased demands took a toll on various aspects of his life, prompting moments of introspection and self-discovery. His resilience reflected a commitment to his father and personal growth despite adversity.

Amid the hardships, moments of unexpected joy arose. Richard, battling dementia, experienced infrequent clarity, sharing fleeting yet precious connections. As the dementia progressed, communication challenges intensified, adding a poignant layer to Robert's caregiving journey. Instances where Richard struggled to express himself or recognize his surroundings became emotionally charged. Robert grappled with the realization the man who shared countless conversations and memories was slipping away.

Facing a difficult decision, Robert ultimately chose to become his father's primary caregiver. This decision marked a crucial turning point in their journey. As he took on this role, the emotional and physical difficulties were daunting. Balancing his own life and responsibilities while tending to his father's needs became complex at times. The journey brought moments of frustration, exhaustion, and heartache. Yet, through it all, Robert stood fast, resolute in his commitment to providing his father with the best possible quality of life.

The process was transformative for both. In those challenging moments, Robert discovered untapped reservoirs of patience, empathy, and resilience within himself. The role of a primary caregiver became more than a duty; it became a sincere expression of love and dedication. Their journey wasn't defined solely by the trials of dementia but by moments of connection, understanding, and even laughter amid adversity. Richard, though battling with the difficulties of dementia, found solace and comfort in the consistent support of his son. The two forged a new kind of bond, one transcending the limitations imposed by the medical condition. As Richard's primary caregiver, Robert provided physical care and also created an environment filled with love, compassion, and dignity. The small victories became monumental in their significance, underscoring the power of resilience and the everlasting strength of their relationship.

In the face of the inevitable progression of dementia, Robert and Richard discovered a different kind of closeness, one going beyond the ability to recall names and faces. It was a connection rooted in the private moments of joy, understanding glances, and the unspoken language of love. In these moments, Robert found a deeper appreciation for the essence of his father, the person beyond the confines of memory loss, and the deepness of the father-son bond which still remained.

Strength of Love

In summarizing their story, it serves as a powerful testament to the eternal essence of love and perseverance. In the intricate balance of these familial bonds, love is often the thread holding everything together. It is a persistent position, transcending the challenges life throws its way. In this case, the adversity they faced was the prevalence of dementia, a condition incredibly difficult for both the person afflicted and their loved ones.

This disease brings a unique set of challenges as it gradually erodes memories, cognitive abilities, and even aspects of one's personality. Richard's diagnosis tested their relationship in significant ways. It was a situation neither of them had anticipated, and it required adjustments and sacrifices from both father and son. Robert's journey as his father's primary caregiver wasn't just about meeting physical needs; it was a testament to his loving commitment to maintaining the emotional connection they had shared for so long. It is in these moments of caregiving, the bond between them deepened. Robert's acts of love and perseverance, his readiness to embrace the problems, and his determination to offer the best possible care for his father showcased the remarkable strength of their connection.

CHAPTER ONE

Even in the face of an increasingly prevalent condition like dementia, where the path may be uncertain and the daily routines daunting, love and commitment can prevail. It emphasizes, father-son connections have the capacity to weather the storms of life and emerge even stronger. The sustaining power of their bond demonstrates the importance of cherishing and nurturing these precious relationships, regardless of the adversities encountered.

Michael and Ben

In a world filled with tales of fractured relationships, the story of Michael and Ben emerges as a testament to the power of love and the resilience of the human spirit. Their bond was once strong, but the turmoil of their family's divorce tore them apart, leaving behind a decade of estrangement. Misunderstandings and hurtful events fueled the chasm between them, deepening the wounds and leaving their relationship in shambles.

Yet, beneath the surface, both Michael and Ben carried the weight of the separation. The absence of a father figure in Ben's life left him yearning for guidance and connection, while Michael grappled with the pain of being distanced from his son. In moments of solitude, they both pondered if reconciliation was possible.

Then, one ordinary day, an extraordinary decision was made. Michael, with a heavy heart but determined spirit, picked up a pen and began to write a letter to his son. It was a heartfelt confession of regrets, an admission of mistakes, and a plea for understanding. As Ben received the letter, he was initially surprised and hesitant. The scars of the past still stung, and the pain of the family divorce lingered.

Amidst the emotions of anger and sadness, there was also a glimmer of hope as they both set out on a path of reconciliation. Their journey was fraught with emotional hardships, along with difficult conversations, moments of vulnerability, and the slow process of rebuilding trust characterizing their path forward. Both father and son had to confront the pain of the divorce and find a way to move beyond it.

As time passed, something beautiful began to happen. The love that had been overshadowed by the turmoil of the divorce started to resurface. It was a love transcending the scars of the past, a love with the power to mend broken hearts. In this heartfelt reconnection, Michael and Ben found solace, as their bond strengthened by forgiveness and understanding. Together, they embraced the opportunity to rebuild their relationship and create a new chapter filled with love and trust.

Weightiness of Separation

This narrative, entwined with others of its kind, serves as a touching reminder, love and commitment possess the transformative power to mend even the most protracted conflicts. Michael and Ben's ongoing journey stands as a living testament to the resilience of their bond. It illustrates, with perseverance and hearts laid bare, how deep wounds inflicted by time can begin to heal, allowing the most difficult connections to be revived.

The narrative unfolds as a tale imbued with hope, forgiveness, and awareness, emphasizing even in the shadows of a decade-long estrangement, reconciliation remains within reach. Their story resonates as a testament to the everlasting strength found in sincere confession, remorse, and a genuine plea for understanding. It underscores the truth: with the passage of time, commitment to healing, and an earnest desire to rebuild, relationships can evolve from fractured to fortified.

Michael's courageous act of penning a transparent letter became a symbolic turning point, a catalyst for transformative change. As the weight of separation began to lift, the narrative unfolded into a testament to the indomitable spirit of love, capable of transcending the barriers of hurt and time, ultimately paving the way for the restoration of a once shattered father-son bond.

The closing of these brief real-life stories encapsulates an important truth about the unique dynamics of love. They highlight the journey of fatherhood and sonhood is rarely without its share of trials and tribulations. However, what sets these portrayals apart is the resolute commitment persisting throughout their hurdles. It emphasizes the idea of love, coupled with perseverance, forms an invincible strength to conquer even the most daunting roadblocks. In these stories, one can witness fathers who refuse to let adversity define their relationships with their sons. Instead, they chose the path of perseverance, recognizing the sustaining nature of love provides the strength to weather any storm. These stories serve as powerful reminders, in the complex tapestry of family relationships, problems are inevitable, but they need not define the narrative.

The examples are not just isolated incidents but relatable anecdotes resonating with individuals from all walks of life. They highlight the idea, the power of perseverance is accessible to all, regardless of their unique circumstances. Whether it involves a father and his son navigating the complexities of dementia or reconciling after a decade of estrangement and distant relationships, these stories inspire hope and resilience.

More importantly, the tales provide a valuable lesson: perseverance is not merely a quality but a vital asset. It is a testament to the eternal power of love and commitment, demonstrating regardless of the challenges faced, there exists the capacity to strengthen and maintain these bonds. In moving forward, the next step is to connect with a passage in the Book of Proverbs and discover the Biblical importance of listening to a father's guidance. While the path is difficult and rocky at times, it provides an opportunity to cherish this relationship as they mature and grow together.

──── Walking in Your Father's Footsteps ────

In the quiet wisdom of ancient Scripture, deep truths frequently echo through the ages. These truths have a way of exposing the intricate qualities of life, revealing the ageless values bringing relationships into existence. In the heart of such sacred verses, the essence of love and the significance of fatherhood, a bond echoing through time are discovered. Within the texts of the Bible lies a powerful passage capturing the essence of a father's role in guiding and nurturing. Proverbs 4:1-4, states: *"Listen, my sons, to a father's instruction; pay attention and gain understanding. I give you sound learning, so do not forsake my teaching. For I too was a son to my father, still tender, and cherished by my mother. Then he taught me, and he said to me, 'Take hold of my words with all your heart; keep my commands, and you will live.'"*

LEGACY OF LOVE

This passage beckons all to listen, to pay attention, and to gain understanding. It is a universal plea, resonating through the ages, imploring all not to forsake the wisdom it imparts. As with generations before, fathers have cherished and guided their offspring, and these teachings and directions have become the cornerstone of their legacy. The sustaining nature of love is a potent and transformative aspect of this emotion. It persists even when confronted with the passage of time, the challenges of life, and the inevitable hindrances encountered in any relationship.

Within the father-son bond, love's ability to withstand these trials, which are often less discussed within family circles, underscores its strength and significance, as it remains among the most robust in humanity. In times of difficulty and vicissitude, love serves as the guiding light, sustaining their fellowship while navigating the intricacies of their relationship. Facing challenges, love's strength brings comfort and reassurance, reminding them of the unbreakable nature of their connection despite adversity.

The Book of Proverbs includes teachings and sayings attributed to various sages, including the legendary King Solomon. They offer guidance on a myriad of facets, from moral conduct to the pursuit of knowledge, representing the collective acumen of generations past, a heritage of insights passed down through time. Proverbs 4:1-4, and many other verses, reflect the eternal wisdom of those who understood the importance of imparting valuable lessons from one generation to the next.

Searching the Scriptures reveals this truth: within the sacred bonds of fatherhood, in the tender exchange of guidance and love, lies a heartbeat echoing through the ages. This heartbeat is not confined to these passages alone; it is a rhythm transcending cultures, eras, and creeds, resonating with the very essence of what it means to be a father, a son, and a bearer of love's eternal legacy.

Reading the unending love of the fathers for their sons in the previous stories of John, Mark, Richard, Robert, Michael, and Ben is a reflection of the compassion and guidance provided as guides, mentors, and instructors. The path towards fatherhood, as one will see at times, is difficult and challenging. It serves as a reminder of an old saying they once shared with their young sons: "There was a time when I was as smart as you." Thus, as the story goes, love becomes the binding connection leading their way towards maturity and adulthood, the path they tend to recount daily on their son's behalf. Perhaps as they age out, they too will recognize the value their fathers endeavored to impart, as told within the passages of Proverbs.

Guidance Role in Fatherhood

In early history, parental figures bore the weighty responsibility of imparting practical skills and serving as the primary educators and mentors for their offspring. Nowhere is this more vividly illustrated than in ancient Greece, where the duty of the patriarchs was of particular significance. These elders played a pivotal role in the education of their descendants, and their influence extended well beyond the confines of the family.

Their education was highly focused on the development of well-rounded individuals, with a strong emphasis on moral and intellectual virtues. Greek mentors, often well-educated themselves, were charged with imparting knowledge in subjects such as philosophy, ethics, and physical training. These leaders were revered as the architects of character, with the solemn purpose of instilling virtuous qualities and guiding the next generation throughout their lives.

One of the best-known examples of this tradition was the relationship between Socrates and his young disciple Plato. While not a biological father-son connection, it exemplified the mentorship and guidance highly valued in ancient Greece. Socrates, as a father figure in a philosophical sense, shaped the thinking and character of Plato, who would go on to become one of the most influential philosophers in history.

In contemporary societies, the role of fatherly figures has evolved in response to changing norms and expectations, but the lasting obligation of providing guidance and wisdom to the younger generation remains. Modern-day fathers continue to serve as essential role models, offering unremitting support, emotional nurturing, and the invaluable gift of life lessons. Historically, they shouldered an immense burden, with expectations deeply rooted in cultural and religious values. They played a central role in religious ceremonies and rituals, entrusted with upholding cherished traditions, including those related to faith and morality. This responsibility extended beyond the family, encompassing the preservation of ancestral legacies, which established them as the guardians of their family's Christian heritage. While specifics may vary, the core value of imparting wisdom, love, and instruction to the next generation remains at the forefront. In the contemporary landscape, the essence of fatherhood lies in passing down knowledge and nurturing relationships founded on tradition, shared experiences, and values. They play an essential role in shaping virtuous conduct and character, emphasizing empathy, respect, and the importance of love, righteousness, and family experiences.

In bygone eras, the wisdom transmitted by family mentors encompassed a comprehensive education, extending beyond the boundaries of formal schooling. Fathers played a pivotal role in equipping their sons with practical survival skills, instilling valuable moral and ethical teachings, and fostering a well-rounded upbringing. In practical terms, they often served as guides in various trades and crafts. For instance, in agricultural societies, essential farming techniques, from tilling the soil to planting crops, animal husbandry and crop rotation, were taught. In artisan families, skills such as blacksmithing, carpentry, or weaving ensured the continuation of vital trades from one generation to the next. These hands-on lessons were indispensable, as they not only empowered their descendants with practical skills but also secured the family's livelihood.

In addition, the responsibility of imparting moral and ethical values was assumed. Parables, stories, and life lessons were taught, transcending the transmission of knowledge. The moral teachings often revolved around Biblical principles of honesty, integrity, compassion, and respect for others. By weaving these values into the fabric of their upbringing, fathers sought to create a strong ethical compass, one guiding character and maturity, influencing their decision-making throughout life.

This holistic approach to learning was integral to the preparation for the practical challenges of life and the shaping of responsible and virtuous individuals. It reinforced their vital role in overall development, ensuring the legacy extended not only through the passing down of skills but also through the cultivation of moral strength and ethical integrity.

In contemporary society, fathers continue to play a central role in nurturing the development of the next generation. They bear the responsibility of imparting essential life skills, moral values, and emotional well-being. Serving as mentors and guiding their family through the complexities of the modern world, they offer vital support and contribute to emotional and intellectual growth, thus ensuring a lasting legacy of wisdom and guidance.

While societal dynamics may have evolved, the fundamental need for a strong and supportive father-son relationship persists. The wisdom, advice, and values passed on, stand as cornerstones of personal and familial development. Recognizing this pivotal role instills a profound appreciation for their influence. Whether in ancient times or the present day, fatherly instruction continues to play a critical role in instilling values, offering counsel, and nurturing the growth of the future generation, thereby leaving an invaluable impression on the legacy of love.

An element of fatherly guidance is the educational process, which prioritizes the installation of righteous and ethical principles such as honesty, integrity, kindness, and sensitivity, providing a lifelong moral directive. Empowering practical life skills spans from fundamental survival knowledge to the development of complex decision-making abilities, enabling them to confidently navigate dilemmas. Wisdom and self-control, drawn from life experiences, are shared, spanning domains such as relationships, career decisions, and personal development. This knowledge offers valuable tools to navigate complexities and make informed decisions as they mature.

A pivotal role is undertaken in cultivating emotional intelligence and awareness, imparting insight on understanding and managing emotions while sustaining the capacity to empathize with others. The significance of these teachings lies in their potential to nurture healthier relationships, promote emotional well-being, and prepare them with vital life skills.

In addition to emotional intelligence, valuable lessons often convey the importance of preserving family traditions and cultural heritage. These treasured teachings serve to connect to one's roots and instill a sense of belonging within the family and societal context. By passing down traditions, a connection is formed to appreciate the value of their heritage and the importance of preserving it for future generations. These cherished lessons align harmoniously with the soundness conveyed in Proverbs, offering immeasurable value to a father's instruction. The importance of heeding this guidance is emphasized, highlighting the Scriptural acuity passed down is not only for instruction but is deeply treasured for its transformative impact. In this way, the lessons imparted reflect the continuing and meaningful legacy of love, trust, and compassion advocated in the Biblical verses. The instructions serve a purpose in shaping their relationship. They act as a bridge connecting generations, creating a deeper connection and strengthening their bond. These cherished teachings create a reservoir of experiences and a sense of continuity within the family, enriching the familial fabric.

Applying Proverbial Wisdom

The opportunity to apply its timeless values emerges, embedding essential virtues such as honesty, integrity, and like-mindedness. These virtues serve as guiding principles, offering insights into human behavior and relationships. In the realm of emotional intelligence, this passage becomes fertile ground for valuable instruction. Understanding emotions, managing conflicts, and establishing meaningful connections find support. Exploring topics including anger management, forgiveness, and empathy through the Book of Proverbs enriches the emotional well-being of those in one's circle.

Practical guidance derived from these teachings becomes instrumental in the decision-making process. The text offers valuable advice on making wise choices, considering the consequences of actions, and seeking counsel in challenging moments. This practical application equips their sons with the necessary tools to navigate both personal and professional conflicts, ensuring the living legacy written in the Scriptures is confirmed.

The application of wisdom significantly contributes to nurturing personal growth. Cultivating a love for acquiring knowledge aligns with the emphasis placed. This approach inspires a lifelong commitment to curiosity, knowledge, and the pursuit of intellectual development. Engaging in various activities, such as exploring ideas, creating an unfaltering passion for continuous stewardship, and instilling a deep appreciation for diligence and responsibility, proves beneficial throughout one's life. The Scriptures underscore the importance of these tenets, emphasizing valuable qualities to impart. This encompasses the principles of hard work, accountability, and taking ownership of actions, extending to responsibilities both at home

CHAPTER ONE

and in broader contexts. The Biblical teachings introduce the concepts of respect and reverence, which find application in contemporary relationships. By serving as role models and demonstrating respectful behavior, fathers guide others to treat everyone with dignity and honor.

This approach encourages the development of strong interpersonal skills and an understanding of the value of respect in building positive and meaningful connections. Proverbs impart the importance of preserving family traditions and values, serving as an important guide in linking their sons to their familial heritage and cultural traditions. By heeding this insight, fathers nurture a sense of belonging and identity, enriching their understanding of their own roots and cultural legacy.

In addition, the application of this virtue extends beyond the present, leaving an eternal impact. This unique opportunity allows for shaping character and instilling persistent values, crafting a legacy of lasting foresight and goodness spanning a lifetime. The seamless integration of Godly-inspired knowledge into contemporary relationships becomes evident. By applying these teachings and providing invaluable tools for navigating the complexities of the modern world, this continues to honor the enduring legacy of Biblical truths passed down through the ages.

The timeless wisdom of fathers offers a rich source of insight with significant relevance in contemporary father-son connections. These insights can be applied in practical and meaningful ways in modern contexts. One such instruction emphasizes the value of wisdom as a virtue to be sought after and cherished. This Godly wisdom can inspire them to cultivate a love for knowledge and lifelong learning. Encouraging activities such as reading, critical thinking, and a commitment to education empowers them to make informed decisions throughout their lives.

Another vital lesson revolves around the virtues of honesty and integrity, repeatedly stressing the significance of truthfulness. Fathers can play a pivotal role in instructing their sons the importance of honesty in all facets of life, from personal relationships to professional pursuits. When leading by example, they can demonstrate the way integrity serves as a foundation of trust and forms the basis for building strong and meaningful connections.

Proverbs often provides practical advice for daily living, which can translate into valuable lessons on financial literacy, time management, and effective planning. These skills offer empowerment to confidently navigate the complexities of modern life, ensuring one is well-prepared to face its problems. The impact of words and speech within these verses is frequently found. Those who draw from these inspired words can visualize the value of thoughtful communication. Imparting the importance of kindness, empathy, and active listening develops effective communication skills indispensable for building strong and meaningful relationships in today's interconnected world.

Additionally, these verses contain teachings on virtues embracing humility, goodwill, and patience, offering direction in building a strong Christian character. Playing an instrumental role in nurturing these character traits contributes to personal growth and their ability to positively influence those around them. By drawing upon these axioms, fathers can help their sons become Godly men of substance, capable of making a lasting impact in their communities and society.

There are also valuable insights into the role of enlightenment and discipline in shaping character, emphasizing the importance of achieving balance. Applying these teachings, fathers can guide their sons in comprehending responsibility and accountability for their actions, employing appropriate discipline when necessary to reinforce these lessons. Moreover, it highlights the critical duty these mentors bear in instructing. They can wholeheartedly embrace this responsibility by actively engaging, offering consistent recommendations, and serving as positive role models. In doing so, a wholesome environment is created, generating a profound sense of security and belonging and encouraging their son's growth and development within a supportive and loving family structure.

Implementing these concepts to nurture and reinforce strong values such as respect, empathy, and gratitude is paramount. These values are instrumental in developing moral and ethical compasses, since they provide direction for making noble choices throughout one's life. This emphasizes the vital concept of passing down Biblical truth, knowledge, and Scriptural applications from one generation to the next. Leveraging this leadership brings to light the importance of family traditions, cultural heritage, and the continuity of values.

By doing so, a sense of belonging and connection is developed, ensuring understanding, discernment, and strong moral values endure. Ultimately, this promotes responsible, compassionate, and morally grounded individuals. It encourages the practice of paying attention and gaining knowledge. The emphasis on open discourse is particularly relevant in modern times, where active listening creates a safe environment for sharing feelings along with thoughts, concerns, and questions. It is an open exchange nurturing trust and cultivating a deeper emotional connection, strengthening their familial bond.

⸺ Cultivating Fatherly Guidance ⸺

Love molds a father's approach to mentoring, inspiring trust, respect, and receptiveness. This relationship promotes a sense of security and belonging, fortifying the bond. Expressing love through guidance transcends words and encompasses actions. Those who embody love, compassion, and empathy provide a powerful example, showcasing its practical application and underscoring the significance of the connection.

Fatherly affection plays a pivotal role in decision-making, as those who guide with care prioritize well-being and long-term resolve when offering advice, ensuring the choices made align with their sons' best interests. This affection-driven approach to decision-making aids in offering sound choices. In today's diverse landscape of mentorship, where relationships may manifest in various ways, the significance of providing guidance with compassion remains constant.

Regardless of their specific roles, fathers possess the ability to create a lasting impact by infusing their counsel with care, highlighting the timeless importance of this approach in contemporary alliances. When considering the role of emotional connection in mentorship, one discovers the meaningful influence of love on relationships. These emotional bonds fortify connections, individual development, and empower their sons to become self-assured and resilient. Those who offer instruction with compassion leave behind a lasting legacy of support and mentorship transcending generations.

Wisdom's Compass in Mentorship

Wisdom, resembling the radiance of the morning sun, functions as a valuable compass for mentors in their instructional roles. It goes beyond root knowledge, embracing the ability to wisely apply discernment acquired through diverse life experiences, education, and personal maturation across multifarious life scenarios. Fathers draw from their vast wealth of knowledge to offer valuable counsel to their protégés. This depth results from a fusion of accumulated knowledge from various sources.

It extends beyond theoretical understanding, involving practical insights into human nature and a commitment to righteous living. In essence, Biblical wisdom integrates divine principles with practical knowledge, emphasizing virtues such as humility, righteousness, love, and reverence for God in navigating life's complexities. They draw from this vast repository of knowledge to furnish pragmatic recommendations and insights, thoroughly equipping their family to confidently and lucidly traverse life's intricacies.

Wisdom, surpassing the confines of bookish knowledge, includes practical understandings and insights into human nature. These mentors, as stewards of such meaningful insight, dispense guidance going beyond theoretical abstractions, directly addressing the tangible challenges and dilemmas their sons may encounter. They convey these pearls of insight through a myriad of mediums, including engaging discourse, narrative elucidation, and embodiment through example.

By sharing personal experiences and the lessons derived from them, they create impactful avenues to transmit virtues, embracing a bond enriched with knowledge and understanding. Wisdom sustains the growth of critical thinking and serves as the foundation for ethical values and moral principles. Fathers play a vital role in this, urging their sons to meticulously analyze situations, weigh the consequences, and make informed decisions, instructing them to independently traverse the intricacies of life.

Simultaneously, their insightful leadership becomes a lighthouse, illuminating the vast seas of righteousness. In the ever-evolving landscape of this modern world, challenges continually transform, yet the adaptability of their wisdom stands firm. As role models, they are blessed with such keen insights and adeptly tailor their guidance to address contemporary dilemmas, leading their sons to make informed decisions in the intricate workings of today's society. Further, by valuing this timeless guidance, they ignite a spark, inspiring them to embark on an unending quest for knowledge and understanding. This dynamic consciousness nurtures a perpetual cycle of growth, learning, and mutual enlightenment. By embracing and internalizing their father's insights, their sons often metamorphose into sagacious mentors themselves, ensuring these invaluable understandings are passed down, echoing through generations.

This perpetuation of meaningful knowledge is beautifully encapsulated in the teachings of Proverbs. Such verses emphasize the quintessential role of wisdom in fatherly guidance and highlight the imperative of seeking understanding as benchmarks for navigating the myriad paths of life. Exploring the role of wisdom in guidance reveals it encompasses more than sheer knowledge; it involves practical insights, ethical values, and critical thinking. Fathers who infuse their guidance with such insight provide the empowerment to make informed decisions, navigate challenges, and build a strong moral compass. The legacy of meaningful insight they leave behind enriches relationships and shapes individuals into responsible, thoughtful beings who carry forward the mantle of wisdom to future generations.

Gift of Understanding

Understanding serves as the foundation of open and candid conversation. Fathers who fully embrace the depths of human thoughts, emotions, and concerns create an environment built on trust and security. In such settings, there is a sense of empowerment in expression, knowing their voice will be heard with receptivity. This understanding deepens when empathy is displayed, as those who actively seek to view situations from diverse perspectives open the door to richer and more meaningful interactions.

When fathers immerse themselves in the experiences and emotions of others, they facilitate more personal connections and impart a sense of trust. This communicates a powerful message: diverse viewpoints are not only heard but also genuinely valued and respected. Another facet of understanding is the acknowledgment of individualized emotions. When recognizing and affirming the feelings of those they engage with, there is a refuge of emotional security. This validation goes beyond mere kindness; it plays a crucial role in safeguarding emotional health. It provides a sense of recognition, which, in turn, nurtures self-confidence and a robust self-esteem.

However, understanding isn't solely centered on embracing joys and sharing sorrows. Its significance is most evident during periods of discord. Disagreements and conflicts arise in relationships, but how these are approached defines the relationship's resilience. Fathers well-versed in the concepts of understanding are better equipped to navigate disputes. By striving to grasp diverse perspectives, even when they diverge from their own, they lay the groundwork for collaborative conflict resolution. The result is agreements rooted in shared respect and mutual benefit fortifying the familial bond even in the face of challenges.

The art of active listening is central to true understanding. When fathers lean in and attentively listen, refraining from interruption, offering premature solutions, or passing judgment, they grant the space to fully articulate thoughts and emotions. Genuine listening demands both patience and a conscious presence. By setting aside distractions and dedicating uninterrupted time, they exemplify their commitment to comprehending and connecting. This dedicated time, combined with a loving understanding of their loved ones' personalities, passions, and dreams, allows them to weave a deeper bond.

Such a bond transcends surface-level interactions, espousing an unparalleled sense of belonging and intimacy. Understanding, while an anchor in the present, also shapes the path for the future. When fathers recognize and support their sons' ambitions, they strengthen the current relationship and empower their offspring to embrace their individuality and independence. Furthermore, this legacy of empathetic insight has a lasting impact. Having been recipients of such personal empathy, they are naturally inclined to echo this sentiment in their parental role, ensuring the perpetuation of this invaluable trait. Through these verses, mentors are beckoned to both seek and bestow understanding, appreciating its transformative power in crafting essential, meaningful bonds. The essence of these teachings stand as evidence in the significance of insight, impacting not only the dynamics between fathers and their sons but also all human connections. When examining the expansive influence of understanding, one recognizes its effects on communication, trust, and reciprocal respect. Fathers who actively cultivate this understanding contribute to a nurturing environment in which their offspring can flourish emotionally and intellectually.

This legacy of empathy enhances the relationship between them, guaranteeing the next generation inherits this valuable attribute, further nurturing meaningful connections and strengthening their bond. The concepts offered echoes in different facets, emphasizing the significance of nurturing the father-son relationship through various means. The core lies in embracing a deep and meaningful connection. Engaging in shared activities, be it sports, hiking, boating, or simple conversations, becomes a conduit for creating lasting memories and sustaining their alliance.

However, the essence of this connection extends beyond mere activities; it thrives in the realm of open and honest exchange. In their capacity, fathers can establish a foundation of trust, allowing their sons to openly share their thoughts, concerns, and aspirations. Within this space of trust and understanding, meaningful connections flourish, enabling both to peer into the depths of each other's hearts.

In addition, the narrative underscores the importance of discovering common enthusiasms as an additional avenue for bolstering their connection. Whether it be in the realms of music, art, or literature, embracing mutual passions contributes to the depth of their connection and opens up numerous avenues for growth. The intertwining of shared activities, heartfelt conversations, and common interests weaves a tapestry of a robust and lasting father-son relationship.

In this partnership, consistency plays a foundational role. Maintaining a regular presence, whether by attending pivotal events or simply being a constant source of support is essential. This commitment solidifies their dedication, weaving a lasting connection. In these experiences, encompassing reunions and milestones, while promoting autonomy remains crucial. Recognition and celebration of accomplishments, irrespective of magnitude, encourages self-esteem and embeds a sense of achievement. This coexists with the empowerment of those who are afforded the independence to assume responsibilities and make decisions.

Balancing the interplay of closeness and autonomy nurtures self-assurance while safeguarding the cherished connection uniting them. The strength of the relationship between fathers and their sons is not solely determined by the specific number of hours they spend together, but by the depth and significance of their interactions. Quality, in many instances, surpasses quantity. Short yet powerful moments, brimming with understanding and genuine connection, can carve a lasting imprint, fortifying their connection. Integral to this relationship is the embodiment of unconditional love. This unfaltering love lays the foundation upon which boundaries can be set with care and clarity. By establishing guidelines imbued with love and mutual respect, setting clear expectations, and cultivating an environment of trust and understanding, this intricately woven relationship, characterized by experiences and mutual regard, generates continuous ripples through time.

Those who have experienced this meaningful and persistent connection are naturally inclined to cultivate analogous bonds in their future relationships and as they assume roles as caregivers. This perpetuation guarantees the vibrancy of the legacy across generations. In this light, the teachings of Proverbs hold resonance. It underscores the pivotal role of a father's consistent presence and guidance in shaping a son's life, emphasizing the everlasting truth: nurturing these bonds is indispensable for personal and generational growth. Through engaging in activities, promoting open communication, and embodying love and support, both can establish a vibrant alliance.

Lessons in Fatherly Patience

The virtue of patience proves to be a crucible occurrence frequently encountered, especially when traversing the path of instructing and bestowing sagacity. Trials often arise from divergent perspectives, unique modes of communication, and the varying cadence at which knowledge is absorbed. Yet, precisely within these moments of heartache, internalized forbearance shines most brilliantly.

This approach considers the capacity to demonstrate aplomb and calmness, particularly in challenging or trying situations, whether on an outward or internal level. It involves the ability to maintain a sense of composure, restrain impulsive reactions, and persevere through difficulties without displays expressing frustration or irritation. This quality is one fathers cultivate within themselves, allowing for the navigation of various circumstances with a calm and collected demeanor, even when faced with adversity. It entails a disciplined approach to managing emotions and maintaining a composed state of mind in the face of disputes. Instances of instruction are abundant, with opportunities requiring the exercise of individualized great restraint.

Within these moments, they may find themselves revisiting directives, repeatedly clarifying uncertainties, or actively furnishing guidance as their sons embrace newfound skills. During such junctures, exercising tolerance in cultivating an environment, constructive and nurturing for the acquisition of knowledge becomes prudent. The spectrum of patience extends beyond typical instructional moments.

When guidance generates self-reliance, tolerance emerges as a leading principle. This entails allowing for errors, stumbles, and subsequent learning and resisting the impulse to shield from every misstep. This patient approach encourages autonomy and jump-starts development. Amid life's challenges, setbacks, and even failures, those under patient and supportive guidance cultivate resilience and perseverance, essential qualities for life's journey.

This domain of endurance transcends basic skill acquisition or self-sufficiency; it seamlessly transitions into the emotional sphere. As pillars of emotional support, fathers often function as havens for those seeking comfort, expressing joy, releasing frustrations, or simply communicating. Through attentive listening and empathy, they decode an array of emotions, strengthening trust and promoting open dialogue. This emotional strength is a key element of a lasting, solid, and compassionate father-son bond.

The intricate mosaic of emotional leadership is woven with many threads, among which temperance stands out as both vibrant and essential. Its rewards are manifold. Those immersed in the gentle glow of patient counsel invariably feel a sense of being understood and cherished. This, in turn, strengthens their connections, creating a bond rooted in mutual respect and trust. The significance of patience is often mirrored in tales and anecdotes. Many recount moments where sustained composure led to transformative breakthroughs in relationships, resulting in heightened trust and deeper understanding. To nurture this endurance, one often turns inward, seeking the calm anchors of mindfulness and self-awareness.

By recognizing and understanding the emotional triggers, individuals prepare themselves to approach others with heightened empathy, ensuring their reactions are both measured and understood. This practiced forbearance does more than smooth interactions; it builds resilience, allowing them to develop tenacity and sharpen their problem-solving acumen.

The lasting legacy of patience is deeply personal and possesses timeless significance. Those who have received such guidance tend to internalize this virtue, weaving it into their relationships. This ensures a legacy characterized by endurance, understanding, and wisdom persisting across generations. It is a concept aligning harmoniously with the highlighted Scriptural teachings, emphasizing the intrinsic spiritual values of sustained resolve as a central element of this journey. Through virtue, fathers enhance their personal interactions and ensure the forthcoming generations who inherit this valuable legacy have an opportunity to embrace the nuanced ideologies passed down. Recognizing the significance of these attributes in fatherly guidance reveals its key role in cultivating trust, resilience, and insightfulness. Practicing this important quality creates an environment in which growth, learning, and flourishing can take place.

The rewards of this approach extend far beyond immediate relationships, leaving behind a legacy of understanding and continuing to enrich their connections. The insights gathered thus far weave a complex tapestry, combining the emotional and pragmatic aspects of parental guidance within the broader framework of love, wisdom, understanding, and patience. At its essence, it emphasizes the emotional depth and the crucial role of a father's genuine desire for mutual understanding. Love consistently emerges as a central theme, portrayed not as a passive emotion but as an active spirit, shaping guidance and strengthening their bond.

Furthermore, it acknowledges this form of self-restraint surpasses mere quality, emerging as a central virtue in leading familial contexts. It recognizes the numerous instances when composure is tested, whether during academic endeavors or while supporting their son's aspirations for self-sufficiency. The reverberations of the Proverbs teachings are perennial; they exert a lasting influence, transcending the immediate family dynamic. This encapsulates the essence graciously, underscoring the legacy of strong relationships elegantly impacting not only current interactions but also resonating through future generations, weaving a legacy of valuable connections and intimacies.

Timeless Wisdom for Modern Fatherhood

The stage is set for a journey into the heart of the father-son relationship, an exploration grounded in the ageless wisdom of the Scriptures. This journey begins by recognizing its uplifting inspiration as a guiding force, leading towards a powerful understanding of the deep love a father holds for his son. It is a path of acquiring knowledge and the awareness to wield it by embracing legacies and opportunities, thereby perpetuating the rich history of the familial bond.

The Book of Proverbs stands as an everlasting light from the distant past, communicating truths both immortal and universal, escorting individuals through the ages while transcending temporal and cultural boundaries. The verses resonate with reciprocal experiences and aspirations, providing a plea for understanding transcending geography and history.

The Godly-inspired words move beyond historical relics, exuding contemporary relevance. The core principles, such as the importance of attentive listening, the pursuit of understanding, and the cherished role of guidance, have maintained their pertinence and enlightenment. This testament to timelessness vividly affirms the expansive connections cultivated and enriched by long-lasting wisdom. In the modern landscape, these relationships frequently face a myriad of challenges, often arising from evolving societal norms and the continuous march of change. Yet, within these inspired principles, an endless reservoir of rationale, prudence, and precision is discovered, ready to guide their relationships through the maze of contemporary complexities. The passages go beyond being simple echoes of a bygone era; they shine as a lamppost for the present, illuminating the pathway forward for those grappling with today's challenges.

Proverbs exceed their written form, emerging as an intense source of guidance and inspiration, serving as an encouragement for thoughtful reflection, with each perusal revealing deeper layers of understanding, offering fresh perspectives, and nurturing renewed connections.

At the heart of this pedagogy lies the intricate interplay between understanding and insight. Thus, the meaningful symbiosis of these two facets is recognized, reinforcing the quest for understanding as a pilgrimage with its trajectory mapped by timeless inspiration. This highlights the everlasting significance of the verses within the fabric of relationships.

It acknowledges their broad relevance, their concrete applicability in confronting present-day challenges, and their lasting role as sources of inspiration and direction. Progressing further, the foundation laid paves the path for an immersion into the practical avenues through which this age-old wisdom enhances and strengthens the insightfulness allocated in the contemporary framework.

Power of Open Communication

The fundamental role of open and honest communication is revealed. This form of interaction goes beyond simple verbal exchange; it acts as a bridge, connecting the depths of those involved and nurturing a vital connection. Within this space, a sanctuary of expression emerges, where both sides are free to reveal their thoughts, dreams, and fears without reservation.

Essentially, trust serves as the basis, interwoven with moments of vulnerability. When fathers and their sons engage in open conversation, they create a haven of security where vulnerability is transformed into a source of strength. This mutual trust leads to deeper emotional connections as they navigate the diverse landscapes of experiences, aspirations, and challenges, intertwining their emotional threads to understand nuanced perspectives.

Beyond the spoken word, the essence of communication often lies in the silent pauses and the intent with which listening occurs. This highlights the indispensability of active listening. It is a dance where both play specific roles, each lending an attentive ear, validating perspectives, and affirming

CHAPTER ONE

feelings. Their mutual reverence and respect enhances their bond and elevates understanding. But even in the most harmonious relationships, conflicts still arise. It is here the mettle of their communication is truly tested.

With the tools of open parley and mutual respect, they can navigate challenges, transforming disagreements into moments of learning and growth. Through such problem-solving, they find resolutions and discover invaluable insights about each other and their bond. In the pursuit of a deeper understanding within these relationships, it illuminates the transformative power of open communication. Central to this endeavor is the sense of belonging it fosters.

As fathers and their sons engage in genuine discourse, every word and expression stands as a testament to their cherished presence in one another's lives. The act of being truly heard, acknowledging and validating each other's emotions and thoughts, establishes the foundation of an unrelenting bond. The dynamics of this connection are not fixed; they evolve in all directions, adapting to their ever-changing personalities.

While navigating life's diverse paths, open communication serves as a channel for a common understanding and insight. It is a reciprocal exchange where narrated experiences and lessons create a crucible of mutual growth and enlightenment. Given life's inherent unpredictability, challenges are bound to arise. During these times, their commitment to open exchange furnishes them with the resilience to confront adversities directly. This forges a partnership where guidance, support, and determination transform challenges into opportunities for collaboration and growth.

At the heart of these multifaceted interactions lies the section's quintessential message: open communication is the essence upon which loving understanding is built. This is more than a medium of expression; it is the environment in which confidence begins its inflorescence and understanding blooms. It is an arrangement of trust, with its vulnerability and active engagement, where vocalizations lead to deeper emotional connections, problem resolutions, and mutual evolution.

Empathy and Perspective-Taking

Empathy and perspective-taking are foundational elements in the context of father-son relationships. These qualities are not only complementary but also essential. Empathy, the innate capacity to comprehend and resonate with another's emotions, forms the basis for a meaningful connection. By refining this skill and actively attending to narratives and emotions, fathers establish an environment rooted in genuine care and concern. The result transcends a common exchange of emotions; it bridges generational divides. Both can overcome barriers arising from differing experiences and viewpoints by harnessing the power of empathy and cultivating a unique connection characterized by sensitivity.

When emotions resonate with others, they inherently validate their experiences. This form of acknowledgment, particularly during life's troubles, offers solace and strengthens the bond. The robust connection, founded on understanding and mutual respect, encourages openness. Aware of the empathetic support received, it increases their son's inclination to share aspirations, fears, and dilemmas. In essence, empathy and perspective-taking are not elementary skills; they represent the lifeblood nourishing the connection, ensuring its vitality and growth. At the core of this relationship is the transformative act of perspective-taking. This unique ability, which entails seeing the world through another's lens, offers fathers a golden opportunity to understand their sons' viewpoints, feelings, and desires. Embracing this form of discernment builds mutual awareness and cultivates an environment where they feel a genuine sense of freedom to express themselves.

In such an atmosphere, they perceive their voices matter and they are truly heard, forming the basis upon which understanding thrives. The intertwined qualities of empathy and like-mindedness emerge as pivotal forces strengthening the familial bond. This sentiment, when recognized, acts as a catalyst for deepening trust and reinforcing mutual respect. In addition, when one exemplifies these qualities, they offer more than just values; they provide a toolkit of emotional intelligence, enabling adept navigation through complex, passionate landscapes and relationships. In moments of disagreement, this toolkit becomes invaluable. Those supplied with an understanding of diverse perspectives can engage in a form of mediation with empathy, facilitating solutions resonating with all parties involved. This illustrates how embracing these qualities catalyzes trust, nurtures openness, amplifies emotional intelligence, and serves as a cornerstone for harmonious conflict resolution. Through immersion in the art of empathy and awareness, one lays the foundation for an enriched, understanding-laden relationship, poised to flourish in depth and meaning.

Resolving Differences and Conflict

In the intricate web of father-son dynamics, difficulties and differences inevitably arise, presenting challenges and also opportunities for growth and deeper connections. Central to this discussion is the acknowledgment of conflicts within these relationships. However, while these disagreements are understandable, they also provide an avenue to support greater connections if approached with care and empathy.

Communication emerges as the focal point for addressing these differences. Through open and honest conversation, many conflicts begin to find resolution, encouraging one another to articulate their feelings and actively listen, ensuring a two-way street of understanding. Such conversations, when rooted in empathy, often lead to discovering common ground. By identifying values and aspirations, they can often bridge divides, crafting solutions catering to both their needs and feelings. This process of compromise is a testament to the strength and resilience of their bond. As significant as communication is, the manner in which it's conducted holds equal weight. It is a gentle reminder, regardless of the issue at hand, treating each other with love and respect remains vital.

At the heart of many conflicts is some type of misunderstanding. The focus of this growth lies in the transformative power of forgiveness. Through the practice of forgiveness, the constraints of past grievances can be transcended, opening the path to a renewed connection. This act of reconciliation is complemented by a continuous emphasis on maintaining the strength of the relationship. Even in the midst of disagreements, the sanctity of the bond remains a priority, upheld by mutual expressions of love and unyielding commitment. Every conflict, regardless of its intensity, holds valuable lessons waiting to be discovered. Through introspection and dialogue, one can derive insights from disagreements, using them as starting points for personal growth and relationship enhancement.

However, in the face of particularly complex conflicts, external avenues of resolution become invaluable. Seeking support, perhaps in the form of family Christian counseling, offers a neutral space for expression, enabling everyone involved to collaboratively unravel intricate issues. Ultimately, through forgiveness, communication, introspection, and additional support, these methods convey a hopeful perspective, demonstrating even in conflict, the potential for a deeper bond and enhanced connection exists.

Shared Values and Traditions

In the realm of these relationships, shared values and traditions emerge as influential elements, weaving bonds of understanding and alliance. These tenets, deeply ingrained within the familial fabric, provide the framework upon which the relationship is constructed. When values align, a natural absorption takes root, making pathways to mutual understanding more accessible and facilitating seamless communication. Beyond simple alignment, values and traditions serve a dual purpose: they form a palpable sense of unity and act as carriers of family identity.

By partaking in traditions, whether steeped in cultural practices, family rituals, or cherished beliefs, fathers and their offspring reinforce their bond and perpetuate a family identity transcending generations. These practices and values become a living legacy, a testament to the family's lineage and ethos. The most cherished gift offered is their uncanny ability to bridge generational divides.

In a world where these gaps can sometimes seem like vast chasms, these elements act as bridges. They facilitate conversations, nurture mutual respect, and enhance appreciation across the ages. The embrace of shared values and traditions becomes a unifying force, seamlessly melding the wisdom of the past with the promise of the future within their sacred bond. Deeply woven into the fabric of family relationships, they act as powerful pillars for strengthening their bond. It serves as a moment of communion where both can celebrate their heritage, bask in their mutual understanding, and reinforce the threads of connection linking their hearts.

Within these principles often lies a trove of wisdom, ethical tenets, cultural nuances, and invaluable life lessons fathers ardently wish to bestow upon their sons. These values become more than just principles; they transform into vibrant vessels through which generational wisdom seamlessly flows. While these merits are undeniably important, they should not overshadow the beautiful diversity of individuality, because a salient point becomes evident: true understanding does not demand uniformity but celebrates the harmonious blend of collective values and individual uniqueness. Psalm 139:14, valiantly articulates: *"I praise you because I am fearfully and wonderfully made; your works are wonderful, I know that full well."*

It is a verse encapsulating the uniqueness of individuality crafted by the hands of God, each possessing distinct qualities and attributes, thriving on the harmonious interplay of shared principles and their remarkable personality. Within this context, fathers and their sons find inspiration in co-creating traditions, fashioning new rituals reflecting the ever-evolving dynamics of their relationship, and the cherished values they hold.

Moving beyond mere interaction, there is practicality in introspection. Through thoughtful reflection on these traditions, a deeper understanding emerges, unveiling a more keen appreciation for the values serving as the bedrock of their relationship. This journey of introspection aligns seamlessly with the timeless Scriptural wisdom promoting a celebration of the unique and wonderful qualities inherent in each individual. By reflecting on these traditions, they can search deeper, unearthing a richer appreciation for the values anchoring their relationship.

Passing Down Wisdom

The journey of fatherhood encompasses more than just provision and protection; it entails the deep-seated responsibility of imparting wisdom and guiding the next generation through life's intricate mazes. At the heart of this duty is the role fathers play as educators, as inferred in the Book of Proverbs. Far removed from the confines of traditional classrooms, these lessons are imparted in the sacred classroom of life. They are not just protectors or providers; they emerge as life's primary teachers, paving the way with the rich soil of their experiences. Through the narration of their trials, tribulations, victories, and lessons, they make the abstract tangible. These personal stories, rich with emotion and real-world experiences, become reference points, making complex teachings both accessible and memorable.

However, it is equally vital to listen. By supporting an environment where questions are celebrated and curiosity is nurtured, they create an atmosphere for active, engaged learning, encouraging an in-depth understanding, as the most influential lessons are not those spoken aloud, but those lived out.

Keep in mind, family observers absorb not only words but actions, often watching intently as they observe the choices, behaviors, and responses of their mentors. Unknowingly, fathers frequently impart wisdom through their conduct, values, and principles. The most lasting instructions are those lived; showcasing wisdom is as much about actions as it is about words.

In the intricate realm of fatherhood, imparting practical skills is of paramount importance. Beyond just the theories of life, fathers bear the immense responsibility of outfitting their sons with tangible abilities, including problem-solving, resilience, and effective decision-making. It becomes crucial to bequeath the timeless insights of past generations while simultaneously ensuring their direction remains relevant and adapt to the ever-evolving tapestry of time. Recognizing the uniqueness of each person becomes foundational in this instructional endeavor.

Those with experience understand a one-size-fits-all approach is seldom effective. Instead, fathers are encouraged to tailor their guidance, factoring in the distinct personalities, dreams, and challenges. This personalized approach paves the way for a deeper, more intimate connection, ensuring the imparted insights resonate and stay. Alongside these methods, there is an imperative to cultivate a spirit of inquiry and ignite the flame of critical thinking. By urging their sons to question, evaluate, and ponder, they are not simply sharing knowledge but demonstrating how to think, fostering a lifetime habit of introspection and analysis.

In life's journey, milestones, moments of triumph, and transformative events punctuate the path. These instances offer golden opportunities for bonding, sharing insights, and celebrating together. Whether it is an academic achievement, a work-related breakthrough, or overcoming a significant hurdle, these moments are the arenas where love, pride, and valuable teachings intermingle. Qualities such as honesty, empathy, and integrity become the guiding stars in the vast universe of experience. These values, consistently reinforced, form the character and essence of their being. In the end, the act of passing down knowledge is not just a transfer of information but an intense journey of shaping souls, building character, and nurturing loving bonds.

Threads of Compassion and Unity

In the intricacy of close relationships, the everlasting birthright of empathy stands as a testament to the sturdy influence of this bond. Understanding, as life unfolds, is not an impermanent emotion; it leaves a lasting impression reverberating through time, touching the immediate connection while echoing through subsequent generations. The undulating effect of this knowledge is life-changing, molding family dynamics in a manner stimulating trust, open communication, and harmony.

These qualities, once ingrained, become the stanchion of a family, crafting an abode filled with support and positivity. Its influence extends to the decision-making processes within these relationships. Decisions cease to be unilateral and evolve into collaborative endeavors. It serves as the driving momentum guiding families to make considerate and reflective choices, encompassing collective needs and perspectives. Furthermore, this legacy becomes a conduit for the perpetuation of knowledge. Those who have been privy to fatherly instruction, wisdom, and insight often find themselves inclined to cherish these attributes, seeking their depths and in turn, passing them down to subsequent heirs.

In essence, it becomes the golden thread, moving through the fabric of time, bridging generations, and constructing a legacy of insight, unity, and compassion. This postulate within the family unit plays a pivotal role in contributing to societal well-being. Families nurtured with care cultivate an unyielding spirit of compassion and responsibility shaped by the connections woven into their familial bonds. The miracle of compassion forms a lasting connection between fathers and their sons, a bond remaining constant in the face of life's shifting landscape.

Their relationship, founded on mutual respect and understanding, emerges as a beacon of strength and a steadfast pillar of support. Families endowed with this quality exhibit remarkable resilience during tumultuous times. In the face of adversity, they stand united, drawing strength from their bond and collectively navigating difficulties with fortitude. The legacy of this attribute sheds light on its meaningful cascading influence. This influence extends its reach, molding generational narratives, anchoring core values, and reinforcing family ties lasting a lifetime. Beyond the confines of the family, this legacy becomes a launching pad for broader societal harmony, weaving threads of unity, common purpose, and compassion throughout the church and Christian communities.

Emphasizing the creation of an environment nurturing understanding is essential. This environment acts as fertile soil where effective communication and mutual respect can thrive, thereby strengthening their connection. A setting filled with openness, trust, and receptiveness becomes the nurturing ground, providing the conditions for understanding to take root, grow, and flourish. Yet, in this carefully crafted setting, it is not just about creating a conducive atmosphere but actively participating in the dance of dialogue. Effective discussion emerges as the linchpin, the centerpiece supporting and enhancing understanding. It's through these lenses this virtue truly blossoms. This type of intellect transcends inadequate expressions and embraces the art of experiencing one another's perspectives. It is a journey continuously unfolding with a willingness to embrace the roles of both guide and explorer. Just as a captain charts a course through uncharted waters, reasoning is similar to navigating the unexplored territories of each other's thoughts, emotions, and aspirations. It is finding receptivity in the uncharted terrain and venturing into the depths of their unique, ever-evolving worlds.

Awareness, perception, and discernment encompass the capacity to read the various road maps of life, extending a hand of empathy and curiosity, similar to an archaeologist carefully uncovering the layers of buried history. The terrain of discernment is not shiftless; instead, it is ever-evolving, molded by a continuous exchange of ideas and emotions. This dynamic process opens the door to mutual growth and enriches the bonds defining their connection.

Venturing into the unexplored, fathers and their sons cultivate an attachment going beyond words and into the realm of communal experiences and emotions. Within these associations, conflicts and disagreements are inevitable landmarks. In addressing this reality, the importance of resolving differences with grace is emphasized, ensuring the spirit of communion and mutual respect remains intact even amidst discord. Embracing these common markers, participating in cherished rituals, and revering Godly beliefs can bridge potential generational chasms, weaving a blanket of unity and mutual appreciation.

Beyond the exchange of words and experiences, there is an important transmission of wisdom taking place. This does not necessarily involve recounting tales or sharing knowledge; rather, it pertains to imparting the deeper insights encapsulated within life's lessons, helping to decipher the nuances and grasp the broader context of their inherited revelation. When progressing through these moments, it recognizes the echoes of understanding are not confined to the present. They spread outward, forging a permanent legacy, fortifying their contemporary bond, and leaving an indelible imprint.

—— Moving Forward ——

The theme explored thus far pursued the significance of gaining an awareness of the fundamental elements of the father-son relationship, emphasizing the various roles essential for strengthening their connection. An underlying lesson was the building of a strong bond reaching beyond the creation of personal moments or memories; it involved developing a dimension of mutual respect, open communication, and a recognition where their interdependence could flourish. Understanding was portrayed as a guiding light leading both on their combined travels, promoting harmony and unity. While underscoring the importance of establishing a foundation of openness and receptivity, it enabled a genuine exchange and mutual respect as an opportunity to thrive.

The verses noted were not just ancient words; they resonated with timeless truths, remaining as pertinent then as they are today. By weaving the Scriptural insights into the broader narrative of family dynamics, this connection established a bridge between ageless wisdom and contemporary challenges, ensuring the legacy of understanding, comprehension, and awareness continued to guide and inspire fathers and their sons in this modern era.

LEGACY OF LOVE

In the symphony of this relationship, open communication struck a resonant chord, echoing the fundamental importance of genuine dialogue and heartfelt expressions. The pivotal role of transparent dialogue was discussed, painting a vivid picture of the myriad advantages stemming from an environment where both could freely articulate their thoughts and feelings.

This realm facilitated a smoother flow of ideas and developed an ambiance ripe for growth, bonding, and mutual respect. Journeying deeper into the heart of these constructs, the spotlight shifted to the intertwined virtues of empathy and perspective-taking. Their qualities were subtle and emerged as instrumental in nurturing a common understanding. For fathers, cultivating a sense of empathy was more than an act of compassion; it was a conscious commitment to emphasize their son's role, appreciating their unique worldviews, feelings, and aspirations.

Drawing inspiration from the wonderful verses of 1 Corinthians 13:4-7, the intricate gifts of love were unraveled, showcasing virtues such as patience, kindness, and perseverance. Guided by John 13:34-35, the puissant directive of Jesus was recognized as a timeless instruction to love selflessly. These beacons of Scripture illuminated the understanding: love is not in the sense of a transient emotion; instead, it was a steady presence blanketing individuals, granting solace, fortitude, and optimism.

In closing this chapter, Proverbs 4:1-4, summoned a resonant echo from the past, highlighting the rich tapestry of wisdom and fatherhood. This powerful passage underscored the quintessence of a father's role, stressing the vitality of imparting knowledge, understanding, and above all, love to the next generation. It became a clarion call, urging all to heed, comprehend, and embrace the perennial legacy handed down.

Standing on the precipice of Chapter 2, titled: *"Building a Strong Foundation,"* one embarks on the exploration of the abundant messages conveyed in 1 John 4:7-8, specifically the command to love one another. This love transcends mere sentiment; it is a pulsating momentum, an ageless essence defining the very heart of fatherhood. Much like a heartbeat, which signifies vitality and life, love flows through the channels of the father-son connection, infusing it with energy and vibrancy. Within the embrace of love, fathers discover their truest calling.

CHAPTER ONE

The quest for deeper insight into the timeless, inspired teachings intensifies, with the ultimate aim of sourcing wisdom and contributing to the laying of a robust groundwork and foundation for father-son relationships. As one ventures forth, reliance on the Scriptures serves as a navigational tool, guiding towards the forging of bonds capable of withstanding life's tempests. The invitation is extended to pause, reflect, and then move forward into this pivotal phase, initiating the fortification of these connections and ensuring they stand resiliently against the sands of time.

CHAPTER TWO

Building a Strong Foundation

In the diverse landscape of human emotions, love stands out as the vibrant and sustaining lifeblood of the family. This hallmark is not a halfhearted emotion but a powerful Godly effect, an ageless essence defining the very soul of fatherhood. Just as a heartbeat signifies vitality and life, love flows through the channels of the father-son relationship, infusing it with energy and vibrancy.

It is in this embrace, fathers find their truest calling, echoing the words of 1 John 4:7-8, *"Dear friends, let us love one another, for love comes from God. Everyone who loves has been born of God and knows God. Whoever does not love does not know God, because God is love."*

The text highlights the connection between love and divinity, extending beyond a perceptive choice. It is depicted as a divine inheritance, a unique gift granted to fathers as they set forth on their quest of nurturing, guiding, and forging an unbreakable bond with their sons.

In the pilgrimage ahead, love emerges as a dynamic and life-affirming momentum rather than a static emotion. It emanates from a Heavenly source, bestowed as a gift from the Sacred. Within the realm of fatherly roles, it takes on the form of a constant and nurturing presence, reminiscent of the reassuring rhythm of a heartbeat.

This love represents the foundational essence of fatherhood, acting as the pedestal upon which all aspects of this relationship are built. It sustains the connection between fathers and their sons, ensuring the unceasing flow of emotional bonds, comprehension, and support. Similar to the unwavering nature of divine love, the affection within this familial bond remains untouched by the passage of time.

CHAPTER TWO

Love as the Lifeblood of the Family

In this exploration, the journey travels through the vibrant corridors of fatherhood, where it assumes a dynamic and life-giving role, infusing strength and vigor into the very essence of this cherished relationship. Considered as the heartbeat of the fatherly bond, love transcends simple sentimentality, challenging its stagnancy. Instead, it stands as vitality, continually fueling the familial connection, moving with unwavering persistence, ensuring the special bond remains spirited and resolute.

Serving as a poignant reminder, it is not a momentary or one-time expression but rather an ongoing, pulsating spark, breathing life into the relationship and infusing every moment with its undeniable presence. In nurturing this companionship, the emphasis shifts towards the abstraction of an essential element, transcending individuals, be they fathers or sons. When this influence assumes the role of a heartbeat within the context of fatherhood, it embodies a vigorous and dynamic presence. Its pulse is an unwavering rhythm, maintaining a constant cadence and safeguarding the resilience and vivacity of the connection between them. As it embraces its beating form, it evolves into a sound, enduring influence, defining and sustaining their bond.

It transcends singular expressions and fading emotions, evolving into a lasting, rhythmic energy, infusing vigor into their connection. This perpetual reminder underscores the link they share is not idle but continuously nurtured and rejuvenated by the ever-present influence of the Godly spirit. Recognizing this dynamic role becomes pivotal in building their companionship; motivating both to actively engage in its cultivation and acknowledging its liveliness depends on their mutual efforts. This prompts fathers to consistently convey their affection and encourages their sons to receive it with open hearts, recognizing its life-affirming essence.

By perceiving love as a dynamic entity, both become better equipped to appreciate its significance in their shared journey. Much like a ceaseless heartbeat, the loving bond remains ever-present. It signifies the continuous flow of emotions, care, and father-son affection between them, a reminder their alliance is not fragile but lasting and resilient. This concept is vital because it underscores love transcending the passage of time and changing

BUILDING A STRONG FOUNDATION

circumstances. It is not a finite resource diminishing with each expression; instead, it resembles a waterfall continually renewing itself. In nurturing their companionship, the grasp of this insight becomes first and foremost, urging them to acknowledge the perpetual presence of love, undeterred by the vicissitudes of existence. Analogous to the pulse sustaining the corporeal vessel, love operates as the life coursing through their bond, safeguarding its vigor and resilience. The perspective instills in them an abiding commitment to the sustenance and cultivation of their relationship, perpetuating the regular expression of closeness and warmth.

This focus captures the essence of a nurturing role, featuring the inherent capacity for care and support as intrinsic attributes. From this standpoint, love serves as the basis upon which all aspects of caregiving are built. Whether one imparts guidance, offers support, or engages in the process of legacy development, the intense emotional connection remains the central driving force behind these endeavors.

It highlights the fervent roots of their emotional bond within the role, rendering it as an indispensable and inseparable aspect of their responsibility. This insight challenges the perception of fatherly affection as just one facet of caregiving, asserting the emotional connection resides at the very core of their existence, shaping and defining every aspect of the role. It is responsive and adaptive, evolving as they themselves grow and develop.

This awareness motivates the active nurturing of the relationship, enabling it to evolve in harmony with changing needs and experiences. By emphasizing this transformative power, the concept brings to light its influence on their bond. It acts as a stimulus for change, capable of reshaping the dynamics of relationships, with the potential to mend wounds, bridge divides, and cultivate mutual understanding.

The transformative aspect of a deep connection encourages fathers to intentionally harness its potential, using it as a tool to build a more robust and lasting bond. This approach cultivates a purposeful and meaningful style, firmly grounded in the dynamic role of their emotional tie. The emotional connection is not a dormant feeling in the background, waiting for a special occasion for expression.

For instance, when fathers encounter challenging situations with their sons, whether in school, work, or beyond, a devoted father does not offer a one-time word of encouragement and then ignores it. Instead, they consistently provide support, actively engage, attentively listen, offer guidance, and demonstrate a consistent commitment to help navigate through the difficulties. This ongoing care and support exemplifies love in action, illustrating it as a persistent and dynamic manifestation rather than a passive one.

Further, active engagement in significant life events and challenges remain of paramount importance. It involves frequent participation in various events and activities, demonstrating love and commitment through a persistent presence. This not only highlights the significance of being actively involved in one's responsibilities but also provides reassurance and support within a close and cherished relationship. These consistent displays affirm it is not occasional but an ongoing, tangible spirit enriching their connection. Through practical instances such as sustained support, unwavering presence during important moments, and daily gestures of tenderness, one can observe God's love as a powerful and formidable lifeblood continually shaping and sustaining the connection between fathers and their sons.

Dynamic Role of Love

While emphasizing the active role of love, it does not remain dormant as an emotion but is depicted as an energetic and dynamic energy, akin to a powerful current of a flowing river. This force actively shapes and enhances all aspects of their father-son interaction, molding the landscape, be it in tranquil moments or during challenging times. Holding significant implications in these roles, it encourages active expression, going beyond the internal emotion to demonstrate it through words and actions.

Love is not solely an inner feeling; it is a divine power evident in everyday interactions, calling for intentional engagement and nurturing. It involves consistently showing compassion, offering guidance, and maintaining a presence, encouraging the building of meaningful and enduring connections through ongoing engagement. The message in 1 John 4:7-8,

BUILDING A STRONG FOUNDATION

encourages a commitment to nurturing and sustaining relationships, emphasizing the continuous attention love demands. This involves actively expressing affection, providing guidance, and maintaining a consistent presence. Additionally, the emphasis on its dynamic nature serves as a reminder to fathers of its life-affirming qualities. This depiction encourages the revitalization of relationships, infusing them with strength and significance. Essentially, devotion becomes a motivating and sustaining driving factor, enhancing their connection. It is a reminder the emotional bond isn't idle but evolves, contributing to its growth and depth. Viewing love as an active, integral part requires attention. This involves maintaining a presence, expressing love through deeds, and remaining receptive to the potential growth and deepening as the relationship matures.

Understanding love as dynamic and life-giving sets the stage for a more useful discussion of the ways it moves into a position of resilience and promotes the longevity of the father-son bond. Embracing love as a dynamic and evolving presence prepares both to navigate life's obstacles and changes, demonstrating the enduring strength prevailing like an oasis in the ever-shifting winds of the Sahara. When it engages, continuous nurturing transcends escaping emotions, evolving into a binding essence.

This scheme asks those to recognize the bond between fathers and their sons is not placid; instead, it is dynamic and ever-evolving, forming the foundation of a strong relationship. Continuous nurturing emphasizes the daily actions and small gestures build a resilient relationship. The strength and depth of this connection avoid the sole reliance on grand displays of affection but rather on the consistent and often subtle acts of guidance, support, and love. Understanding these qualities nurtures an ongoing and dynamic connection, inspiring and humbling in nature, while recognizing the relationship is a lifelong commitment.

The concept of continuous nurturing places significant emphasis on the notion, love is an ever-present and dynamic connection continuously feeding and nurturing their relationship. This can indeed feel overwhelming because it underscores it is not solely responsible for initiating the bond but also for its maintenance and strengthening over time. It emphasizes the daily acts of affection, support, and understanding fathers provide for their sons, breathing life into the alliance.

These consistent gestures of love keep the bond vibrant and thriving. This perspective challenges fathers to perceive it as an ongoing commitment rather than a one-time occurrence. It prompts them to consider whether they recognize this and are willing to embrace it as an integral part of their role.

Within the framework of continuous nurturing, daily actions emerge as a striking theme. These actions are not limited to monumental gestures but extend to the routine interactions shaping the father-son bond. It is about being present in everyday moments, such as assisting with important life decisions yet to be made, engaging in meaningful conversations, or simply spending quality time together.

Attentive Listening as an Active Role

In the context of continuous nurturing, attentive listening and open discourse play a crucial role. It is not just about physically being there; it is also about being emotionally available. This availability implies a state of vulnerability, openness, and honesty. It means a father trusts his son and is willing to engage in meaningful, soul-stirring exchanges. Being emotionally available involves having the willingness to be vulnerable, revealing their true selves, and sharing their emotional experiences.

At the core of emotional availability is trust. This readiness is a fundamental aspect of nurturing. It entails being truthful about feelings and reactions. If something is bothering a father, sharing it with his son in an honest and respectful way can lead to meaningful conversations and a deeper connection. Both must trust each other to share their emotions openly and honestly, since it is built through consistent exchanges and a sense of reliability. It does not mean letting their sentiments run rampant and unchecked. It involves healthy heart-rendering expressions, where both learn to communicate their feelings constructively and positively.

Furthermore, fathers who recognize this state of being are comfortable with their own emotions and those of their sons. They understand their varying feelings are a natural part of life and are not to be disguised but embraced and managed in a healthy way. In this process, they can create a safe and trusting space for their sons to express themselves openly. These

BUILDING A STRONG FOUNDATION

are instances in everyday life where they have the opportunity to impart values, share wisdom, and offer guidance with emotional checks and balances in play.

Another significant facet of attentive listening is the expression of affection. At times, this can be especially difficult within a historical framework. Old school dynamics are easily set in motion involving strictness, heavy-handedness, unwarranted discipline, and rules with narrow or little leeway. Love offers temperance and emotional availability, allowing fathers to balance former traditional hierarchical standards appearing rigid and less flexible. Modest yet significant actions, such as a hug, a gentle word, or a friendly pat on the back, carries a long-lasting and loving meaning. They reinforce the emotional connection, providing a sense of security and offering warmth in love.

When recognizing the diverse nature of growth and development, continuous nurturing underpins the significance of emotional adaptability. This perspective brings into focus the importance of adjusting approaches to meet evolving requirements while maintaining a steady foundation of love and support. Such adaptability is vital to nourishing a strong and enduring bond through various life stages. This nurturing plays a central role in understanding family relationships. Since it centers around love as an ever-present influence, daily actions, open communication, teachable moments, displays of affection, emotional vulnerability, and adaptability are essential elements for building profound and lasting bonds.

While it is acknowledged this can be a challenging task, concentrated, attentive listening and nurturing can enable their bond to thrive, mature, and endure over time. Emotional openness, within the context of continuous care, seeks to create an environment where they can openly share their emotions, thoughts, and experiences. This environment promotes values such as vulnerability, honesty, and trust, allowing for the establishment of a deep and meaningful connection in strengthening their relationship. It is an approach encouraging a constructive and healthy means of understanding and managing feelings, ultimately contributing to the resilience and longevity of their bond.

CHAPTER TWO

────── **Sustaining Family Bonds** ──────

In the realm of fatherhood, love serves as the very heartbeat, acting as the element uniting the father-son bond. This analogy draws a parallel to the unwavering pulse of life, as their dedication ensures an unceasing flow of emotional connection, understanding, and support. It stands as a perpetual assurance, guaranteeing the relationship is cultivated even in the midst of adversity and life's inevitable transformations. This viewpoint serves as a reminder, Godly love is a resilient and nourishing influence. It is a dimension remaining constant, offering solace and stability in a world filled with uncertainties, providing a sense of security and continuity, ensuring both their connections endure regardless of the trials they may encounter. Fathers are challenged to recognize their role in nurturing, as it does not diminish with time; instead, it intensifies, building a deeper and more resilient bond. It is about embracing affection as a continuous journey requiring unwavering care, attention, and commitment.

The inseparable nature of love establishes a fundamental truth: it is not an optional or peripheral component but rather its very essence. It brings to light, this is not something one can choose to engage with or set aside; instead, it is an intrinsic and inseparable part of life. This emphasizes love is not an accessory or an add-on; it is at the core of what it means to be nurturing and caring. Love serves as the foundational basis upon which all aspects of their relationships are built. Whether offering guidance, providing support, or engaging in the process of building a legacy, it serves as the fundamental core driving these actions and signifies the role itself is rooted in this deep-seated essence, making it integral and irreplaceable.

Core of Fatherhood

The core of fatherhood emphasizes an inherent truth: within its' essence resides the natural ability to love and nurture, establishing it as an essential and defining characteristic. This role is often described as a deep and transformative experience, and the concept reinforces this perspective. It asserts the ability to love and nurture as not simply an optional attribute but a fundamental aspect of the fatherly role, contrary to historical social expectations. This is not something fathers can choose to engage with or disregard; instead, it is an intrinsic quality defining and enriching their identity. In practical terms, the perspective challenges fathers to recognize and embrace their innate capacity. It highlights the inherent qualities and abilities they possess without requiring external influence or learning. This suggests the capacity to love and nurture is part of an inherent nature, instinctual makeup, and DNA. It is not something to be acquired or learned; instead, it is already present within them from the beginning.

Affirming this axiom and echoing God's words, *"Let us make man in our image, in Our likeness,"* in Genesis 1:26, carries a heartfelt significance with broader implications. This suggests a shared spiritual and moral quality akin to those of the Divine, such as reason, morality, creativity, spirituality, and love. The likeness signifies a unique relationship between their father and the Creator, entrusting them with the responsibility to care for and have a Godly influence. Furthermore, being created in this image underscores an inherent capacity for meaningful relationships, especially as a father, transcending at times, their ability to create connections of love and purpose. These God-given principles can inform and enrich their understanding, offering valuable insights for those on their nurturing journey.

In reflecting on Psalm 78:4, which declares: *"We will not hide them from their descendants; we will tell the next generation the praiseworthy deeds of the Lord, His power, and the wonders He has done,"* an enlightening realization emerges. As fathers engage in thoughtful contemplation, acknowledging, comprehending, and embracing their innate potential, they affirm not only their ability to love and nurture, but also fortify their responsibility in safeguarding the spiritual legacy of the family. The act of passing down the admirable events to the succeeding generation, as emphasized, signifies an expression of this inherent potential. It symbolizes an aptitude to construct connections of love and purpose in more dynamic manners. The alignment between these inherent traits and the act of storytelling resonates, affirming their love as instinctual and loyal.

Regardless of societal expectations, one can find solace in understanding the nurturing nature of fathers, which is deeply embedded within their identity. This empowerment validates their roles as spiritual leaders, mentors, and caregivers, passing down the generational legacy of nurturing through faith, love, hope, and joy, guided by the enduring and timeless essence of this responsibility. In a world where social constructs sometimes undervalue the role of fathers, it remains essential to highlight their indispensable contributions to familial development. Their capacity for love, guidance, and nurturing transcends stereotypical, ever-changing societal norms and is firmly rooted in their identity, not shaken by the washed-down meaning of manhood.

Fathers are not merely capable but possess a distinct and invaluable capacity for nurturing their children, particularly their sons. Their innate qualities are a precious resource for enriching and guiding them toward responsible adulthood. This perspective encourages a more inclusive and supportive view of fatherhood, emphasizing the crucial role played by their influence on the well-rounded development of the family. It aligns with Biblical principles and recognizes the enduring and timeless nature of a father's responsibility in nurturing their boys to become men while passing down the legacy awaiting them.

Integral and Irreplaceable Fatherhood

Fatherhood is a vast trek securely rooted in an enduring and unconditional connection. It's an affection-defining character and shapes the essence of this unique relationship. From an alternative position, the concept of guidance undergoes a significant transformation. It emerges as a deeply personal and emotional expression of sustained commitment. This viewpoint transcends everyday solutions, exploring the domains of nurturing critical thinking, encouraging independence, and fortifying resilience. It's a dedicated guide who walks alongside, providing knowledge, unwavering support, invaluable wisdom, and genuine care throughout the intricate journey.

Within this unique relationship, the act of guiding transcends the simplicity of a straightforward exchange of information; it becomes an intense expression of their shared bond. When these invaluable qualities are passed on from one generation to the next, it is a testament to the powerful influence of love and commitment. Love transforms the act of mentoring

BUILDING A STRONG FOUNDATION

into an intricate expression of their common connection, an essence unreplicable by straightforward directives. Therefore, the emotional support, encouragement, and care fathers provide originate from a well of love flowing through these bonds. The support surpasses the boundaries of material assistance and empty words; instead, it embodies an irreplaceable presence felt at the core of a son's heart. In the realm of legacy-building, it becomes evident, these values, traditions, and teachings passed down constitute more than just a legacy of knowledge; they create a legacy of eternal affection.

This stance emphasizes the lasting and significant influence these bonds have on relationships, firmly rooted in the foundation of love. It positions it as an intrinsic and defining element, inviting recognition of its significance in shaping connections not only familial but also transcending into the very core of their human experience. It is within the embrace of these deep and meaningful bonds where the true essence of fatherhood is revealed, an essence never replaceable.

Resilience and Vitality of the Bond

In the intricate orchestration of life, love assumes the role of a conductor, guiding the harmonious composition of the father-son relationship. This love is not a quaint performance but a symphony of emotions, each note resonating with the depth of their connection. It is the melody lingering in their hearts, a timeless composition transcending the boundaries of elementary words. The sonata of love is not a solo act but a duet, with each participant adding their own unique tune, creating a masterpiece of familial bonds. As the conductor, love ensures every instrument in this orchestra of connection plays in harmony, nurturing a melody touching their souls. When a masterpiece is expertly crafted and harmonious, it signifies the artistic expression is in tune, ensuring a melodious experience.

In a similar vein, the presence of love within this alliance indicates the vitality of the relationship. It is viewed as an active and dynamic rhythm promoting their well-being. Just as a finely-composed musical opus ensures a harmonious experience, love infuses this relationship with energy and vibrancy. It breathes life into their connection, making it more than a casual existence; it becomes a source of growth and fulfillment. Godly love within the father-son bond, similar to the wisdom spoken of in Proverbs 8:17-21, sets vitality as prominent, signaling the relationship is far from dormant. It is continually evolving into position, drawing closer to a cohesive connection, just as this divine wisdom declares, *"I love those who love me, and those who seek me find me. With me are riches and honor, enduring wealth and prosperity. My fruit is better than fine gold; what I yield surpasses choice silver. I walk in the way of righteousness, along the paths of justice, bestowing a rich inheritance on those who love me and making their treasuries full."*

In the light of this wisdom, one can glean personal insight into the nature of love, breathing life and vigor into the union and making it thrive and flourish. This is more than just a lifeless emotion, but rather an energetic and festive dynamic progressing towards the likeness of God. In their quest, the father-son bond demands dedication, diligence, and a willingness to explore its depths. A deliberate choice unfolds to nurture and cherish the relationship, akin to seeking purity in the connection, bringing forth riches and honor.

Embracing fatherly love through the Spirit of God transforms the relationship into a testament to the values of righteousness and justice. This bond overflows with wealth, surpassing the value of mere material riches. Just as the fruits of divine wisdom are described in Proverbs as better than gold or choice silver, the fruits of love within this connection are immeasurable in their worth. They include kindness, patience, selflessness, and forgiveness, qualities enriching and fostering a harmonious and just connection.

Love, often compared to a flame, is a vibrant and dynamic element requiring continuous care and nourishment, not something applied once and forgotten. Similar to a flame needing a constant supply of fuel to keep burning, this relationship necessitates ongoing attention and nurturing to thrive. The flame is not a roaring blaze but a gentle, constant glow, a source of warmth permeating every interaction. Actively nurturing this deep connection through all dimensions, they consistently express affection and support.

BUILDING A STRONG FOUNDATION

This approach encourages fathers to recognize their intrinsic value and the essential need for continual investment. It challenges them to view love not solely as an emotion but as a verb, an action, and a significant commitment. Rather than passively assuming their cherished status, proactively demonstrating their affection and support is a requirement. They are not distant observers but invested participants in their sons' lives, consistently expressing care through meaningful gestures. The promise of granting an inheritance to those who love, as outlined, finds a parallel strengthened by Godly compassion.

This embrace fills the treasures of their hearts, and in doing so, it strengthens the very foundation of their bond. The love within their relationship mirrors the honorable principles of knowledge and wisdom, highlighting it as a divine gift nurtured and upheld, leading to a father-son connection growing in vibrancy, drawing them closer to each other and to the spiritual essence of love itself.

Irrespective of condition, situation, and circumstance, love functions as the agglutinate, maintaining, strengthening, and bringing them together. It is a constant, everlasting strength while gathering their embrace and ensuring a continuous flow of emotional connection, understanding, and support. Remember, love ever-present in the father-son relationship embodies its reliability and steadfast nature. It signifies love is not conditional or situational but has an everlasting spiritual essence, enriching their connection. This understanding deepens their fellowship, creating a resilient and nurturing alliance.

The resilience of the father-son bond emphasizes love's vital role in maintaining a strong alliance. It highlights the capacity to endure difficulties, with love serving as the binding source holding their relationship together, supplying emotional strength and support. The concept highlights the relationship's durability. Instead of fragility, it possesses a remarkable ability to bounce back from adversity. Love stepping up when times get tough is a testament to the strength and depth of this connection. Similar to a sturdy bridge supporting travelers over turbulent waters, it serves as a secure pathway, offering support and solace during difficult times.

CHAPTER TWO

Unconditional and Lifelong Love

The courtyard of fatherly love, reminiscent of heartfelt expressions, conveys an expanse and boundless essence. Unaffected by events and changing circumstances, love maintains its resolute and focused presence amidst trials. Its resilient nature reinforces an unbreakable bond, serving as a perpetual source of strength and support. Love embodies a constant and reliable connection, reflecting the consistent rhythm of the waves, undisturbed by daily fluctuations.

This highlights the steadfastness of their relationship, free from the variations seen in fair-weather emotions. Their affection remains straightforward and firm, an implicit commitment transcending the tides of life. Within this relationship, the shore break moves beyond achievements, appearances, or behaviors and thrives on an inherent connection surpassing situational factors. This lifelong love underscores the steady nature of their bond, which spans generations from father to son and beyond. As they both age, this commitment will remain a constant presence, offering strength and a reminder of their unbreakable connection.

This concept portrays a timeless and sustained love not weakening with age or circumstances. An active and dynamic presence, love continually recharges and nourishes the bond between fathers and their sons. Similar to a reliable compass guiding their personal journey, the presence of love within this bond serves as a clear indicator of its total passion. This approach questions the notion that the quality of the connection relies solely on outside events or observable gestures.

Instead, it suggests love itself is a powerful measure of the bond's strength. When present, it signifies the emotional connection, understanding, and support are vibrant and robust, extending active nurturing and cultivation of affection for each other. Just as one would take steps to maintain personal well-being, prioritizing love's presence within this union is key. Thus, one can further emphasize a father-son connection cannot remain stagnant or stale. The focus is on love and its power to infuse the bond with energy, vibrancy, and vivacity. Imagine a dynamic and thriving relationship filled with life and enthusiasm. It is a connection where they both actively engage with each other, involving a constant

BUILDING A STRONG FOUNDATION

exchange of emotions, understanding, and support. Here, love plays a central role in this dynamism. Fathers are encouraged to continually nurture their affection for their sons, not only cherishing these feelings in their hearts but actively expressing them through their words and actions.

This accentuates affection as an infinite resource in a dynamic and thriving relationship, emphasizing its potential to grow stronger and more vibrant as they continue their journey together. Love, seen as the heartbeat of fatherhood, is not just one-way but rather a reciprocal and mutually beneficial embrace enriching their lives together. It is a source of nourishment for the soul. Just as a healthy diet contributes to physical well-being, it enhances emotional, spiritual, and psychological health.

Fathers benefit from the love they feel for their sons, as it brings joy, fulfillment, and a sense of purpose to their lives. This provides them with the opportunity to nurture and guide the next generation, imparting wisdom and values. In contrast, their sons thrive in this environment, establishing a strong emotional foundation and bolstering their self-esteem and resilience. It builds a sense of security and belonging, which is integral for growth and development, emphasizing the positive contributions extending beyond the emotional realm with tangible effects on the overall well-being of both generations.

For fathers, a loving presence reduces stress, improves mental fitness, and enhances their quality of life. As for their sons, this leads to improved academic performance, healthier relationships, and increased self-confidence in a rigorous work environment. The positive contribution emphasizes its powerful role in personal growth and enjoyment, enriching their lives in meaningful ways.

Within the dimension of a meaningful connection, it signifies a thriving, dynamic relationship, holding deep significance. This driving energy, far from being stationary or inert, fuels ongoing growth and development within their unique bond. The alliance is like a lush garden, with love as the rich soil nurturing their connection. Just as gardens need sustenance, care, and attention to thrive, this connection flourishes under the influence of this unique essence. It furnishes the vital elements, ensuring its vibrancy and health. In a practical sense, this encourages one to actively nurture and cultivate their emotional, physical, and spiritual ties. This devotion demands committed care, much like a gardener's attention to their flowers. These actions mirror the maintenance and nurturing of the garden, preserving its lasting well-being and beauty. The concept of growth and flourishing suggests the maturation process is not a stationary entity but one evolving with patience, understanding, and wisdom.

Love fuels this transformation, as their sons transition into manhood, their needs, interests, and challenges evolve. This adjustment and development to meet shifting circumstances build a resilient and enduring relationship. Essentially, it highlights the importance of not taking the responsibility of cultivation for granted. It requires ongoing attention, care, and effort. The rewards are significant, as a nurtured connection becomes a source of joy, strength, and fulfillment for both. This signifies the bond is not just alive but thriving, continually growing, and gaining more significance over time.

—— Love as a Foundational Life Force ——

Describing love as the heartbeat of fatherhood beautifully conveys its continuous and ever-present nature throughout their relationship, infusing it with life, meaning, and depth. This powerful metaphor, like a perpetual cascade, emphasizes its consistent nature and provides a flowing path for recognizing its role in their journey. The emotion flows continuously and cannot be halted or diverted. It is an integral component of their shared existence, a constant, unceasing stream. This dispels the misconception it only intensifies during extraordinary natural events or when situations demand it. Instead, it presents itself as a lasting and ever-present element, similar to an unceasing force permeating every facet of their connection. Their spirit is there in moments of joy and celebration, just as it is during times of challenge and adversity, like an ever-flowing stream.

For instance, think of the imagery in Solomon 8:7, *"Many waters cannot quench love; rivers cannot sweep it away. If one were to give all the wealth of one's house for love, it would be utterly scorned."* Just as many waterfalls cannot extinguish love and riches cannot purchase it, this continuous connection remains a constant and invaluable source of their relationship, regardless of circumstances or occasions. It reinforces this emotion as not something to be halted or redirected but rather a perpetual and priceless gift flowing through every aspect of their bond.

Similar to a sturdy structure relying on a stable footing to endure external pressures and challenges, these relationships depend on this unshakable strength to support their growth. It forms the solid ground upon which fathers and their sons establish trust, understanding, and closeness, becoming the bedrock of their bond. It provides the stability required for the relationship to remain resilient, even in troubling times. Their affection sustains the connection over the years, helping both navigate complexities, nurture connections, and cultivate significant ties. Fathers are encouraged to recognize the importance of this element in their relationship, prompting them to nurture it intentionally.

Love as the foundation plays a crucial role in weathering life's storms and ensuring an ever-lasting alliance. This footing is solid ground, offering a stable platform where trust, understanding, and closeness can flourish. Their compassion serves as the cornerstone, imparting stability and empowering the relationship to thrive even in adversity. It becomes the unbreakable bond holding fathers and their sons together, serving as a straightforward source of support. This perspective stands as a testament to its depth and enduring nature, serving as a potent influence sustaining the connection.

Building Mutual Respect

Mutual respect, an essential trait of virtuous living, finds its essence in the teachings of the Scriptures. The Bible offers a multifaceted viewpoint applicable to various human relationships. It transcends specific gender roles and serves as a basis for harmonious interactions. Guidance emphasizes its importance, as seen in Romans 13:7, *"Give to everyone what you owe them: If you owe taxes, pay taxes; if revenue, then revenue; if respect, then respect; if honor, then honor."* The theme brings to light its value where due. The concept of respect is interwoven throughout the New Testament, as in 1

CHAPTER TWO

Peter 2:17, *"Show proper respect to everyone, love the family of believers, fear God, honor the emperor,"* which further reinforces the universal call to respect, irrespective of any other distinction.

Another example can be found in Leviticus 19:32, *"Stand up in the presence of the aged, show respect for the elderly, and revere your God. I am the Lord,"* emphasizing the significance of respecting the elderly, adding depth to this foundational virtue. This principle extends to all, transcending age or status and forming the bedrock of ethical and loving relationships.

Exploring the diverse instances of respect offers deeper insights into this virtue and its role in nurturing harmonious connections in life. Mutual respect is a fundamental element in building bonds and facilitating the exchange of wisdom. It serves as a pathway within relationships, enabling individuals to communicate, collaborate, and share experiences. The exchange of these events is a valuable form of mentorship, passing on wisdom from one generation to the next.

Love, seen as the heartbeat of fatherhood, is not one-way, but a reciprocal and mutually beneficial embrace enriching their lives together. It transcends the boundaries of father-son specific roles, promoting unity and growth. Embracing respect within these connections acknowledges the intrinsic worth of each individual, building relationships built on trust and empathy. This standard encourages an environment where knowledge and life's wisdom flow freely, forming the foundation for lasting bonds.

It calls upon fathers and their sons to uphold the dignity of fellow human beings, recognizing their intrinsic worth. This truth aligns with Biblical teachings, such as Genesis 1:27, which states: *"God created mankind in His own image,"* highlighting the inherent worth and dignity of humankind. This universal truth finds relevance in various settings, from father-son relationships to community bonds and society at large. It nurtures an environment where individuals from diverse backgrounds come together in unity, promoting understanding and cooperation, as Galatians 3:28, reminds believers: *"There is neither Jew nor Gentile, neither slave nor free, nor is there male and female, for they are all one in Christ Jesus."*

The implications of recognizing mutual respect as a universal truth are far-reaching. They promote a society where one coexists with understanding, empathy, and compassion, mirroring the teachings of Colossians 3:12, which encourages individuals to: *"Clothe themselves with compassion, kindness, humility, gentleness, and patience."* In such a society, the exchange of knowledge and experiences is encouraged, leading to shared growth and interconnectedness, reflecting the wisdom of Proverbs 27:17, *"As iron sharpens iron, so one person sharpens another."*

By recognizing mutual respect as a Godly truth, they contribute to building a world where every person's inherent worth is celebrated, enhancing inclusivity and harmony in society, in line with the teachings of Matthew 22:39, which implores individuals to: *"Love your neighbor as yourself."* This unique bond commences with fathers consistently expressing love towards their sons, conveying a message of care and fondness. It establishes a benchmark of trust and understanding between them, cultivating a robust and respectful bond.

Mutual respect encompasses various actions, including demonstrating care, offering support, and actively engaging in each other's lives. These tangible expressions of affection and support are vital. It deepens their sense of trust and appreciation, establishing a strong foundation of care and support through these gestures. Love creates an atmosphere of emotional safety and security. When their sons feel genuinely loved, they are more likely to engage in open and empathetic communication, expressing their thoughts and emotions.

This candid and compassionate dialogue is a crucial component, enabling both to gain a deeper understanding of each other and to genuinely value each other's unique perspectives. Fathers can actively nurture mutual respect by consistently demonstrating love through their words and actions, providing guidance, showing affection, and being unwavering sources of support to strengthen their foundational connection.

Nurturing Growth

The comparison of nourishing soil for a sturdy tree beautifully conveys the belief, love is essential for nurturing the growth of the father-son bond. Imagine a young sapling planted in rich, fertile soil. The soil provides the nutrients, stability, and support the sapling needs to grow into a strong and vibrant tree. Similarly, love acts as the nourishing soil for the relationship, creating an environment promoting growth and flourishing.

One key aspect to consider is how it enables both to flourish individually. Just as a tree's roots reach deep into the ground to draw nutrients and water, it allows for the exploration of their individual identities, values, and aspirations. This gives them the confidence and security to be themselves and pursue their own personal growth and development. Their compassion promotes mutual development within a relationship.

As a tree's branches reach out and provide shade, shelter, and beauty, there is an encouragement for them to connect, communicate, and support each other in their respective journeys. It strengthens the bonds of understanding and empathy. This nurturing atmosphere is akin to a safe and loving domain where they can grow together. It is a space where they can share their dreams, fears, and experiences without judgment, knowing their connection is deeply rooted and accepted.

Their proclivity plays a significant role in nourishing growth. It creates a nurturing environment where both individuals can thrive while also supporting each other's development. This atmosphere allows them to explore their identities, values, and aspirations within the safety of their bond. It provides a foundation for their family to feel secure in expressing themselves and pursuing personal growth. It instills confidence they can be true to themselves while knowing they have steady support.

For instance, a son may feel comfortable discussing his dreams and ambitions because he knows his father's caring nature offers a safety net. This growth is integral for their ongoing evolution as individuals. Beyond this development, their partnership encourages a dynamic exchange within the relationship, promoting open communication and mutual learning. For example, through honest conversations, fathers can gain a deeper understanding of their sons' generation, while their sons can tap into their wisdom and life experiences. They can apply this concept by actively engaging, showing genuine interest in their pursuits, and being open to learning from them. Likewise, their sons can reciprocate by valuing their guidance and experiences. This reciprocity of learning and growth strengthens the bond and allows the relationship to evolve harmoniously.

Love offers a haven to delve into understanding who they are as individuals, building a sense of acceptance and value for their true selves. This safe and loving space allows them to embrace their unique qualities without fear of judgment. Within this dimension, one can explore their values and beliefs, engaging in discussions about what matters most to them and why.

Guiding these discussions are influential mentors who share their own values and listen to different perspectives. This exchange broadens their connection and helps them solidify their moral compass. Love is the inspiration to dream and aspire to be the best version of themselves. Whether aiming to excel academically, pursue specific careers, or become well-rounded individuals, love reinforces the belief these aspirations are not only valid but fully supported.

In real terms, creating a safe and nurturing environment involves attentive listening, constructive feedback, and active engagement in each other's interests and concerns. This reciprocal exchange strengthens their bond, creating a space where growth and self-discovery are cherished and nurtured. It is the binding agent keeping them together, constructing a sense of belonging, security, and intimacy at the core of their existence. Just as a solid foundation keeps a building securely connected to the ground, Godly love acts as the tether keeping fathers and their sons deeply connected to each other's hearts.

At its essence, this concept emphasizes the way love surpasses simple friendship, shaping a sense of belonging. This sense of belonging helps them develop a strong bond through their experiences and expressions of tenderness. In such a relationship, there is an unspoken understanding, a sense of security, and a feeling of being truly known and accepted. It is a personal connection, allowing them to share their innermost thoughts, joys, sorrows, dreams, and fears without reservation. Fatherly love serves as a source of belonging and security. It is portrayed as the anchor keeping them deeply secured and protected from the rough seas of life. Imagine a father and his son when they share a strong bond. Both feel they truly belong to each other; their connection is not just circumstantial but fundamental to their identities. This sense of belonging is a powerful source of comfort. In addition, it creates an environment of security. It is a protective shield surrounding them, guarding them from the uncertainties and troubles of the world.

In the presence of love, they feel safe to express themselves and to be vulnerable. This sense of belonging and security means they can navigate life's interruptions with a strong support system. When they face difficulties and uncertainties, they can turn to each other, knowing their love is a constant, reliable presence. It allows them to weather storms together and find solace and comfort in each other's company. This emotional anchor strengthens their relationship and enriches their lives with a sense of connection and security.

Again, envision a father and his son whose relationship is deeply rooted, this is not a surface-level emotion; it is the foundation upon which their bond is built. It creates a space where intimacy thrives. In this connection, intimacy does not refer solely to physical proximity but to emotional closeness as well. Love allows both to be vulnerable to each other. This emotional closeness enhances the meaningfulness of their connection. They can confide in each other, knowing their receptiveness is a constant source of support and understanding.

Love infuses their interactions with an immense sense of meaning. Every moment they spend together, whether a heartfelt conversation or a simple shared event, carries significance. It deepens their understanding of each other, enriches their lives with common memories, and adds purpose to their relationship. This encourages them to prioritize emotional closeness and vulnerability. It suggests open and honest communication is the key to creating an intimate and meaningful bond. It is about actively engaging with each other's emotions, attentively listening, and being present in each other's lives.

Omnipresence of Love

Love's omnipresence saturates every facet of fatherhood. Rather than being merely one element among many, it serves as the thread weaving through the entire connection, building interactions, influencing legacies, and enriching their relationship. This pervasive presence actively guides their approach, providing advice and direction to one another. Infusing guidance transforms it into a nurturing and supportive experience, transcending simple directives or instructions.

This quality ignites motivation, enabling them to navigate life's challenges with a foundation of care and understanding. It serves as the motivating presence behind a person's commitment to being there for their family in times of need, transcending surface-level care and molding into a genuine desire for their success and happiness. This form of support is both practical and emotionally significant, fortifying their connection.

Driven by deep affection, fathers impart meaningful lessons, values, and experiences, creating a legacy positively influencing the lives of their sons. Everyday interactions are immersed, emerging in shared laughter, communication styles, and an underlying current of love flowing through these exchanges.

It functions as an imperceptible influence, raising ordinary moments to a higher plane and infusing everyday conversations with significance. This prompts acknowledgment in the impact of the connection on responsibilities, motivating the intentional infusion of every facet of relationships with love, whether in instruction, support, legacy-building, or everyday interactions. It is recognizing its transformative influence in fashioning their bond into something genuinely exceptional.

In nurturing relationships, their compassion serves as the unifying element, sustaining and fortifying connections. It stands as an enduring presence, strengthening the bonds uniting them and building a sense of belonging transcending coexistence, becoming an integral component within the intricate web of human relationships. Love's presence resembles a constant undercurrent, a salient yet compelling energy preserving these bonds, much like a river's flow sustains surrounding ecosystems.

CHAPTER TWO

This consistency ensures the zest and longevity of their alliance, acting as a foundational element guiding both through the complex dynamics of connection and providing a deep sense of unity and purpose in their interconnected lives. The influence of this connection serves as a foundational linchpin for nurturing meaningful interactions and establishing the groundwork on which genuine relationships are built. This enables the exchange of experiences, knowledge, and wisdom in an environment characterized by trust and understanding, acting as a bridge facilitating meaningful dialogue, collaboration, and growth. When fathers and their sons treat each other with sincere regard, they create an environment where personal and collective experiences can be openly exchanged.

This exchange of experiences represents a valuable form of loving mentorship, where the knowledge and wisdom gained through life's journey are passed on to those embarking on their own paths. This alliance is not limited to a specific type of relationship; instead, it functions as a universal principle applicable to all interactions. Whether in familial bonds, friendships, or otherwise, it serves as the common thread promoting understanding and cooperation, transcending the confines of specific family positions, and promoting unity and maturity.

By embracing these efforts in their interactions, they recognize each other's inherent worth, paving the way for harmonious relationships founded on trust and sensitivity. The concept of this connection transcends boundaries, serving as a primary truth applicable to all individuals, irrespective of their positions and relationships. This influential principle extends widely, nurturing unity, shared growth, and harmonious interactions among all, emphasizing its universality, and guiding virtuous living.

Encouraging each other to honor the dignity of their fellow human beings and acknowledging the intrinsic worth of every person lays the foundation for ethical and compassionate interactions. Recognizing this value holds significance in various settings, from family relationships to community bonds, and even within the broader scope of society, promoting an environment where those from diverse backgrounds and walks of life can come together in unity. The common value of the father-son connection serves as a mutual thread, bridging differences and fortifying the alliances uniting everyone. The implications of this focus as a guiding principle are significant, since it encourages a society where individuals coexist with understanding, empathy, and compassion, fostering an environment where the exchange of knowledge and experiences is encouraged, resulting in growth and enlightenment. It exemplifies the Godly power of this relationship to transcend boundaries, nurturing a sense of interconnectedness and uplifting humanity as a whole. Recognizing this universal truth contributes to building a world where the inherent worth of every person is celebrated, leading to a more inclusive and harmonious society.

Impact on Guidance and Support

Love's influence extends beyond the realm of emotions, evolving into a guiding principle shaping the provision of counsel and support. When infused with love, it bestows significant meaning upon the guidance provided with heartfelt empathy and understanding. It involves not just giving counsel but also evolving into mentors who are genuinely concerned about the health of those in their care. Love empowers the navigation of the delicate balance between sharing knowledge and wisdom while allowing the acquisition of experiential learning.

This influence promotes open and honest communication, establishing a safe space for seeking guidance without the fear of judgment. Support, significantly influenced by love, transcends material assistance, encompassing a strong source of emotional wellness. Within the realm of fatherhood, nurturing goes beyond physical needs, encompassing emotional, psychological, and spiritual well-being.

It reflects an attunement to emotional states and the provision of nurturing driven by love and compassion. Guiding the way to active presence, attentive listening, and the offering of subsistence encourages a sense of connection and belonging, thus creating a lasting bond.

In practice, this concept urges fathers to acknowledge its impact on their instruction and advice, encouraging them to intentionally infuse these aspects of their role with warmth and affection, recognizing these qualities as active currents transforming their interactions. This involves becoming mentors, pillars of support, and caregivers who lead with love, thus shaping

CHAPTER TWO

their relationship defined by trust, empathy, and a deep connection. Love ultimately enriches and elevates the father-son dependence to extraordinary heights. First and foremost, it imbues their connection with depth and emotional richness. It adds layers of vibrant colors to their relationship canvas; each stratum represents a common experience, a moment of laughter, or a heartfelt conversation. It infuses these moments with a unique warmth and intensity, making their relationship a series of interactions and a cascade of shared memories and emotions.

In addition, it acts as a bridge to new heights while connecting their hearts on a more intimate level, cultivating an understanding of transcending words, enabling fathers and sons to communicate in a way reaching far beyond the surface. At this level of understanding, a sense of unity blossoms, akin to sharing a clandestine language comprehensible only to them. This depth enables genuine insight into each other's perspectives and emotions, fortifying their kinship.

Love's presence is also manifest in their mutual values and co-crafted legacy. As fathers instill these values, anchored and intertwined with kindness and compassion, they bequeath not only a moral compass but also an enduring legacy. This legacy serves as an unwavering wellspring of guidance for their sons as they traverse life's trials and make character-defining choices.

It stands as a testament to love's perpetual influence, eternally molding their lives. In everyday interactions, love radiates through small gestures and displays of affection: a friendly smile, a thumbs-up, a man-hug, their unique father-son handshake, or words of encouragement. These seemingly ordinary acts collectively embody the father-son affinity, warmly embraced after a long day at school or work. It elevates these everyday moments into cherished memories, emphasizing their relationship thrives not through grand gestures but through daily expressions of love and devotion.

BUILDING A STRONG FOUNDATION

They follow the Biblical principle found in 1 Corinthians 16:14, *"Let all you do be done in love."* These values build the father-son connection, acknowledging love as a constant gift from God and enhancing the depth and quality of their relationship with intimacy, mutual values, and countless precious moments. It acts as an invisible guide, steering their journey together and ensuring their propinquity remains resilient, long-lasting, and meaningful. This concept signifies its pivotal role in molding not only the present connection but also the future of the family lineage. Love's legacy is not confined to the boundaries of time but stretches across generations, leaving an indelible mark on the family's values, principles, and traditions.

It serves as the soil from which the father-son relationship grows, much like the rich earth nurturing a blossoming flower. This soil is infused with the natural nutrients of affection, life, and compassion, providing the essential elements for the relationship to flourish. Just as a flower draws sustenance from the earth, fathers and their sons draw strength and guidance from love forming the very essence of their closeness.

Moreover, affection offers unyielding support, sustaining the relationship over time. It resembles the sturdy foundation of a building standing through the ages. This support is unwavering, providing a stable platform upon which fathers and their sons can build their connection. Through life's storms and trials, this support remains firm, ensuring the relationship's endurance and strength. Most remarkably, their legacy of care and devotion has had an impact on the family for generations. It is a symbolic torch passed from one generation to the next, carrying the flame of connected values, principles, and love.

When fathers instill warmth in their relationships, they are not just nurturing a connection for the present; they are shaping the future of their family. The values of compassion, respect, and tenderness become part of the family's DNA, passed down like a treasured heirloom. In essence, the lasting legacy signifies the association between fathers and their sons is not fleeting but everlasting, leaving an imprint on their history and future. It is the life pulse sustaining, supporting, and enriching their lives, ensuring the connection between them remains unbreakable, resilient, and intensely meaningful.

CHAPTER TWO

Influence on Future Generations

Love's influence transcends the immediate connection, emphasizing its lasting legacy as it forms the lives of future generations within the family. Visualize this affection as a torch passed from one generation to the next. When they cultivate a connection deeply rooted, they effectively ignite this torch, ensuring its flame continues to burn brightly in the hearts of their descendants. This concept highlights these values and principles are not confined to the current relationship but become an integral part of the family's heritage.

When their sons witness the immense care and respect their fathers have for them, they are more likely to carry forward these similar values in their own roles as fathers. This establishes a cycle of warmth and respect perpetuated through the family lineage. When they mature in an environment where this love serves as the guiding light, they are more likely to emulate this in their own relationships, passing on the legacy of this affection to their future generations.

In essence, the durable legacy of this allegiance has a generational impact, forming the current relationship and the family's culture and values. It is a testament to the sustaining power within the context of father-son relationships, ensuring its influence is felt by generations within the family lineage. The analogy between love's constant legacy and a solid foundation supporting generations emphasizes love serving as the bedrock upon which the family's growth and continuity depend.

Similar to a stable foundation providing durability to an edifice over time, it ensures the values, principles, and emotional bonds nurtured within the father-son relationship endure and prosper. In this likeness, love emerges as an unshakable cornerstone persisting through the ages. Just as a well-constructed footing withstands the test of time, the long-standing legacy remains a lasting influence, guiding their values and connections. This comparison emphasizes the long-lasting strength, highlighting its significant role in building the legacy in a perdurable manner. Furthermore, the analogy of a robust foundation also conveys, like a well-built structure, a family rooted in deep love can withstand the storms of life. It acts as a support system, aiding the family in navigating struggles and changes with

BUILDING A STRONG FOUNDATION

resilience. It signifies the values and associations formed through this formidable connection are not easily eroded but remain fixed, contributing to the family's lasting power, longevity, and unity.

—— Recognizing a Precious Gift ——

Psalm 127:3, *"Children are a heritage from the Lord, offspring a reward from Him,"* beautifully highlights the divine origins and importance of the next generation, emphasizing their intrinsic worth as a spiritual heritage. This passage serves as a compelling reminder for those entrusted with guiding this legacy, prompting a sense of gratitude and reverence. Fatherhood is depicted as a divine gift, shifting perspectives from seeing it as a burden to recognizing it as a blessing.

The Scriptures serve as inspiration to contemplate the impact on future generations. This encourages a commitment to nurturing and cultivating wisdom within their relationships, embracing a continuous quest for learning and the application of timeless Biblical wisdom. Essentially, it calls for reflection on the legacy one aspires to create and a dedication to weaving these teachings into daily life. This view reshapes perceptions, urging recognition of innate worth and distinctiveness. It emphasizes responsibility in nurturing and guiding, instilling obligation and reverence.

Fatherhood evolves into a spiritual and moral calling, with heirs seen as their divine gifts. This shift transcends biology, underscoring the stewardship of a spiritual legacy. The transformation highlights the significant connection between this role and Godly spirituality, morality, and the offspring's unique individuality and destinies. This realization motivates cherishing and guiding with a sense of duty extending beyond physical needs. It drives investment in time, love, and knowledge, molding character, and values. Additionally, it inspires imparting knowledge, wisdom, and virtues with a clear sense of purpose. This change awakens fathers to their son's significance as inheritors of a divine legacy, motivating reverence, dedication, and lasting impact.

CHAPTER TWO

Love, as the lifeblood of a family, forms the basis for nurturing future generations. It is a divine gift, emphasizing the sanctity of this role in forming their futures. This shift elevates the significance of parenthood, moving beyond the physical to encompass spiritual and moral dimensions. Fatherhood becomes the stewardship of a spiritual legacy, with a commitment to values, righteousness, and faith. This transformative perspective instills a sense of purpose, reshaping their role into a multifaceted, meaningful one.

The recognition of their offspring as inheritors of a divine legacy stirs reverence, duty, and lasting impact. This idea highlights intrinsic worth and individuality, transcending the notion of simple extensions. The fatherly duty extends to holistic well-being, encompassing emotional, ethical, and spiritual development. This realization transforms fatherhood from a one-dimensional task into a deeply meaningful journey, marked by guidance, mentorship, and nurture. It reveals the evolutionary power of recognizing the precious inheritors and invites embracing the meaning and purpose therein.

Further, welcoming love and guidance as the foundations of a sacred legacy is a journey of intense significance. This pathway leads to a transformative connection, emphasizing the timeless wisdom within the Biblical teachings. It reframes the understanding of fatherhood from a fundamental biological function to one of spiritual mentorship. This function transcends simple physical care to encompass nurturing the soul, guiding with wisdom, and instilling core values. As fathers adopt this strong sense of duty, they enable the next generation to inherit a legacy enriched with love, knowledge, and spiritual growth. It is a cycle of nurturing, as these attributes perpetuate across time, intertwining the past, present, and future.

Nurturing the Legacy

The Psalms set into place the preciousness of the next generation while emphasizing the responsibility born in nurturing this sacred legacy. Fathers are entrusted with the task of providing not just for the physical needs of their sons and the family but also for their emotional, moral, and spiritual

BUILDING A STRONG FOUNDATION

fitness. It is an emphasis on fatherhood as a multifaceted purpose extending beyond material provisions. It calls for action and active participation in shaping the character, values, and destiny of their descendants in a holistic manner. This verse transcends the conventional concept of meeting physical needs, gathering a broader perspective highlighting valuable responsibilities.

While offering an invitation to embrace the health of the younger generation, it emphasizes the creation of a nurturing and supportive environment where emotions can be freely expressed. Attunement to these needs establishes a foundation of security and trust within these relationships. Additionally, this holistic view extends to moral development, calling for male Christian role models to guide the younger generation in the principles of Godly living. Recognizing this role is at play means acknowledging many-sided responsibilities and active engagement in creating all aspects of maturation. It calls for creating a harmonious blend of emotional, ethical, and spiritual upbringing in nurturing a strong and enduring bond.

Recognizing this holistic view reshapes the concept of fatherhood, emphasizing their involvement in developing emotional and spiritual growth, not just as providers. It underscores the various responsibilities fathers hold, extending beyond material provisions to encompass health, moral guidance, and spiritual mentorship. This perspective transforms fatherhood into a purpose-driven role actively engaging in nurturing a strong and loving bond. By understanding this holistic role, they play a pivotal part in forming values, beliefs, and overall development, ultimately contributing to well-being and future success.

They are called upon to invest their love, time, and wisdom into the upbringing of their sons, recognizing the impact these investments can have on their development. This investment means more than displaying affection; it signifies a close and long-lasting personal connection. It creates a safe and nurturing environment in which they can flourish. Fathers who invest their love in this way demonstrate their commitment to nurturing a sense of security and belonging within the family unit.

CHAPTER TWO

Wisdom is a vital element of the holistic duty of fatherhood, embodying the moral and spiritual guidance shaping the paths of the next generation. It encompasses the transmission of invaluable life lessons, core values, and ethical principles, which serve as guiding lights for promoting sound decision-making and nurturing responsible character. Fathers who invest in this wisdom pass down their personal experiences and provide a guiding compass, offering a clear sense of direction and purpose. This guidance plays an integral part in molding character and instilling the readiness to confront life's myriad challenges and opportunities.

Within this framework, the function of fatherly leadership goes far beyond simply providing physical comforts. They become mentors and role models, actively engaging in forming values and beliefs. By embracing this responsibility and investing in emotional, moral, and spiritual development, they profoundly contribute to the growth and well-being of the succeeding generation. This investment enriches the intergenerational connection and prepares the next lineage for a life enriched with purpose, meaning, and cherished values. Through values in action, they can impart a strong moral direction, aiding in navigating life with integrity and virtue. This sets into place its vital pattern of behavior for nurturing spiritual health. It involves introducing the younger generation to faith, values, and beliefs, providing a sense of purpose and meaning in life. In leading by example, they demonstrate a commitment to their own spiritual journey and encourage exploration of spiritual paths.

Fostering Spiritual and Moral Growth

The central theme of fatherhood focuses on the cultivation of spiritual and moral growth. It accentuates the unique role played in instilling essential values, faith, and ethical principles. Fatherhood encompasses a broad range of responsibilities beyond providing physical provisions and protection; it entails nurturing a solid foundation of spirituality and morality. Spirituality encompasses the promotion of inner moral values, a belief system, and a connection to God. It is a continuous exercise in guidance, developing a sense of spiritual awareness, enlightenment, and a keen understanding of life's hidden mysteries within the Scriptures.

BUILDING A STRONG FOUNDATION

By engaging in conversations about faith, morality, and the significance of Godly beliefs, fathers can help form a solid ethical compass, guiding their sons toward manhood. Expanding on this notion, they are the spiritual guides in the family, and play a central position in the lives of the younger generation by sharing their own journeys and experiences.

This exchange of wisdom creates a bond transcending generations, drawing from Biblical insights in an effort to encourage the exploration of beliefs, ask questions, and seek a clearer understanding of the Divine. These conversations nurture spiritual growth while also strengthening the connection between them.

In addition, by setting an example, they demonstrate living a life guided by ethical tenets through faith. Through daily interactions and choices, practical applications of moral values are demonstrated, underscoring the significance of these principles in the real world. Cultivation in Christian growth is a chief ingredient, extending beyond mere words and aiding fathers in serving as guides, mentors, and living examples while instilling values, trust, and virtuous statutes. The intertwined journey forges a lasting bond and prepares the next generation with essential tools to navigate life's confrontations with integrity and compassion.

Moral growth, in this context, pertains to the cultivation of ethical guidelines and values. This intricate process involves imparting a sense of integrity, honesty, compassion, and empathy, demonstrating these values through both actions and words. Emphasizing the commitment to nurturing these aspects of an individual's development underscores this is certainly an ongoing journey, not a singular effort.

It necessitates active engagement in the lives of those under their influence. By fostering spiritual and moral growth, there is a substantial contribution to the formation of character, providing them with the tools essential for making responsible decisions and leading lives imbued with meaning and purpose.

CHAPTER TWO

——— Gratitude and Reverence ———

The themes of gratitude and reverence continue to draw inspiration from the endless wisdom of Psalm 127:3, a verse encapsulating the essence of parenthood. Acknowledging the concept of divine blessings instills a sincere sense of appreciation. It transcends the simple joys and embodies a significant, Godly gratitude for the privilege of nurturing and guiding. This sense of appreciation extends beyond the tangible aspects of fatherhood, encompassing the intangible, forging a heartfelt connection reaching beyond specific relationships, and holding the potential to reshape one's perspective on fatherly responsibilities. Reverence, as the second theme, broadens the understanding of the sacred responsibilities. The approach to parental duties takes on an aspect of humility, recognizing the trust placed in them. This reverence transforms daily interactions into acts of devotion and honor. When gratitude and reverence unite, they become influential forces, enriching their connection and shaping the perception of divine gifts entrusted to their care.

Gratitude as a Transformative Emotion

Gratitude, as an influential factor, possesses the unique capability to reshape the essence of fatherhood. It evolves into a perpetual awareness of the gift of nurturing and to navigate the complexities with resilience. This empowerment supports a Godly attitude, reinforcing commitment to their transformative journey. It becomes a recognition of its significance. The heightened sense of gratitude extends its embrace, encompassing the inevitable challenges and sacrifices accompanying this path.

These difficulties are no longer burdens but opportunities for growth for the family. In essence, this power lies in its ability to create a transformative shift in hearts, allowing them to see their role as more than just parenting. It is a journey enriched by a heightened awareness, enabling fathers to nurture, guide, and cherish their sons in ways transcending the ordinary, leaving a legacy of love and appreciation. In their youth, sons as they mature, embody innocent curiosity and boundless energy, mirroring the marvels of life itself. Each day spent with them offers a chance to view the world anew, embracing often-overlooked simple joys. This sense of wonder, ignited by their presence, serves as a catalyst to slow down, observe, and engage in life's small yet profound moments. Fathers who acknowledge their sons as living testaments to life's mysteries naturally nurture this sense of wonder. They actively participate in exploratory and curious activities, whether it involves a visit to the local museum, an excursion in nature, or simply stargazing while camping on a clear night. These shared adventures bolster their bond, cultivating a lifelong passion for learning and discovery.

Embracing the significant role of the family's heirs as testaments to life's wonders carries a substantial responsibility. This awareness extends beyond meeting basic needs; it includes the duty to instill values, knowledge, and a sense of purpose. Fathers, who are guides, mentors, and role models become not only providers but also assistants, aiding their sons in navigating daily complexities. This sense of responsibility shapes the parenting journey, motivating them to be present, engaged, and nurturing, with a deep commitment to their prosperity.

It embraces the difficulties and sacrifices fatherhood inevitably involves, transforming them into opportunities for growth and learning. Fathers who embrace this attribute discover the power to navigate the difficulties with resilience and an affirmative attitude. They view these problems not as burdens but as stepping stones towards personal and collective development.

Appreciation serves as a catalyst, cultivating a fuller personal bond among family members. It communicates the fundamental values of love and thankfulness, establishing a strong foundation of trust and security. This connection reinforces the sense of being valued, cherished, and deeply loved, creating a nurturing and safe environment for the growth of the collective unit. Thankfulness not only serves as a guiding principle in fatherhood but also molds a father's perceptions and responses to the joys and difficulties of nurturing the next generation. It transforms parenthood from a primary obligation into a fulfilling and purpose-driven journey, laying the groundwork for a legacy of gratitude and love within the familial bond.

CHAPTER TWO

Gratitude Beyond Joy

In an extraordinary moment, life events take on a unique encounter. It is a perspective in bringing the seeds of a dream into reality, a miracle gift hearing the breath of life as it surpasses the depths of imagination. The birth of a son becomes an extraordinary life-changing event, a profound experience transcending the boundaries of speechless happiness. It's a movement in the hands of time when the path leads from manhood to fatherhood, witnessing the arrival with a cry from the womb, a legacy undeniably blessed through the eyes of a living God.

In this raw and unadorned moment, a newborn son in hand, not yet cleansed from the event, exudes an exhilarating and deeply felt beauty washed over the heart. It is a bond beyond words, a love-defying description, and an experience revealing the bountifulness of the soul. The tears of gratitude are but a small acknowledgment of this initial joy being just the beginning, a prelude to a lifelong journey filled with both peaks and valleys.

As daily fatherly duties ascend, understanding dawns upon the realization: appreciation extends beyond celebratory moments. It permeates the late-night responsibilities, the challenges, the moments of support, and the countless small acts of care and compassion yet to be discovered. Gratitude in the realm of parenthood transcends the initial joy of becoming a father. It extends to encompass the privilege of guiding and nurturing in the journey of fatherhood. This enduring sense of appreciation is not confined to passing moments of happiness; rather, it becomes a constant and guiding presence throughout the various stages of life.

It is appreciating the lessons learned from mistakes, the wisdom gained from experiences, and the strength emerging from overcoming obstacles. Beyond the joy, there is the realization: fatherhood is a journey, not a destination. This perspective infuses fatherhood with purpose and resilience, encouraging them to be present and engaged throughout their sons' lives. It is the recognition of the privilege of parenting, extending beyond the moments of happiness and embedded in the entirety of the father-son bond.

Engaging in reflection is pivotal to cultivating heartfelt gratitude. Taking the time to appreciate the unique qualities and experiences entering their lives becomes a reflective process transcending elementary acknowledgment. It involves thorough and thoughtful contemplation of the individuality each one brings. First and foremost, fathers can consider their son's distinct personalities, since each individual possesses a unique combination of traits, talents, and quirks, making them one-of-a-kind. By actively observing and appreciating these characteristics, a deeper understanding of their personalities and preferences can develop. This reflection builds a sense of wonder and thankfulness, enriching their lives with a diversity of qualities.

Furthermore, one can explore the experiences and milestones they've shared, as these moments, whether substantial or minute, craft indelible memories and form connections. Contemplating these mutual experiences enables a fuller appreciation for the depth of their relationship and the voyage they have embarked upon together. It reinforces the concept, underscoring each moment as a precious Godly gift.

Fostering a heartfelt sense of appreciation through reflection is a transformative process. It is not superficial or obligatory, but rather a deep and genuine indebtedness for the role in their lives. This is born from the recognition of this unique and irreplaceable bond. When reflecting upon these qualities, experiences, and challenges accompanying fatherhood, understanding the depth of this relationship begins. It is a relationship going beyond mere duty; it is a sacred connection shaping both father and son.

Gratitude as a Guiding Principle

Embracing gratitude as a guiding principle in the father-son relationship wields the power to direct decisions, actions, and interactions, ultimately nurturing a more meaningful and connected bond. When at the forefront, fathers approach each day with a sense of appreciation, as each morning unfolds with a heart brimming with thankfulness and the presence of their sons. The sense of companionship guides their decision-making process, leading them to choices resonating with Godly values and beliefs. It instills intentionality, inspiring them to create a conducive environment stimulating emotional, intellectual, and spiritual growth. In these deliberate actions, there is a display of heightened attentiveness and engagement, actively seeking opportunities to express love and affection. It guides them towards patience and understanding, even during difficult moments, as they discern the inherent value of the relationship. Their expressions of appreciation extend beyond the spoken word, encompassing their presence and actions, developing into attentive listeners, finely attuned to their sons' needs and emotions.

Such expressions encourage candid and open dialogue, nurturing trust and strengthening the bond. It acts as a guiding compass, directing them throughout their daily journey in parenthood, shaping their decision-making, imbuing their actions with love, and enriching their interactions. This guiding principle establishes a more interconnected relationship, founded upon love, appreciation, and a sense of the precious blessing of fatherhood. Cultivating genuine thankfulness transforms a father's overall perspective on parenting. It forms their view, infusing it with optimism and enhancing their journey, even when confronted with difficulties.

Through the active cultivation of gratitude, fathers undergo an intuitive shift in their view of parenthood. They begin to perceive their role not as a humdrum responsibility but as a divine privilege along an extraordinary path. This shift in perspective is extensive and far-reaching, yielding notable effects, including the development of a more positive and hopeful worldview. It enables them to concentrate on the joys of fatherhood rather than dwelling on difficulties or setbacks. They grow in resilience when facing challenges, recognizing them as opportunities for personal growth rather than insurmountable hilltops.

This optimistic outlook fosters a more harmonious and fulfilling parenting experience, thereby enriching perspectives through the cultivation of gratitude resulting in a heightened appreciation for the small, everyday moments of family life. The practice leads to treasuring the simple joys of spending time with loved ones, engaging in meaningful conversation, and witnessing growth and development. These seemingly mundane moments become sources of fulfillment and contentment. It also enhances the ability to connect on a deeper level, encouraging one to be fully present in life and

BUILDING A STRONG FOUNDATION

savor each moment. This heightened presence strengthens the bond between generations, creating a sense of closeness and trust. Cultivating gratitude's impact reaches far beyond the immediate, with the potential to create a lasting and positive influence. Fathers, through the active cultivation of a thankful attitude, initiate a dynamic and lasting effect on their family relationships.

As a result, the father-son bond strengthens, growing more resilient and persistent even during challenging tasks. The influence spreads through generations, imparting not only the value of gratitude but also the importance of cherishing the blessings in their lives. This legacy is then handed down from one generation to the next, developing a family culture of thankfulness and appreciation.

Wholeheartedly embracing these attributes in everyday life-changing practice deeply enriches the bond within a family and enhances the overall experience of familial connections. This practice transcends the benign acknowledgment of life's blessings; it involves actively nurturing this attitude in everyday interactions and routines. One practical way to achieve this is through reflection, dedicating a few moments each day to contemplate the unique interactions shared, which encourages the appreciation of the present and the recognition of beauty in the ordinary.

Another valuable approach is to express it openly and sincerely, communicating genuine appreciation for one another. Simple acts such as expressing love and admiration or saying "thank you" for their efforts contribute to creating a positive and affectionate atmosphere. Incorporating these actions into family routines is essential. Family rituals provide opportunities for each member to express their daily appreciation. This practice establishes open conversation and underscores thankfulness as a shared family value. Engaging in activities promoting mindfulness and gratitude, such as keeping a journal, can be a powerful means of cultivating a focus on the important and Godly aspects of life. It is a simple yet effective tool for nurturing a sense of acknowledgment.

Furthermore, leading by example inspires others to adopt a similar mindset. Narrating thoughts and feelings and explaining why admiration is felt for certain experiences or moments helps others understand and internalize their values. Embracing a thankful viewpoint in everyday life is a practice that has a positive impact on relationships and family dynamics. By reflecting on special moments, openly expressing appreciation, incorporating thankfulness into daily routines, keeping a gratitude journal, and leading by example, an environment imbued with respect, adoration, esteem, reverence, love, and a Godly energy can be cultivated.

Reverence for the Sacred Role

Acknowledging parenthood as a divine calling is a fundamental aspect of fostering reverence for fatherhood. This recognition transforms the perception of the role, elevating it from a mere duty to a sacred responsibility. The shift encompasses various key dimensions influencing the way fathers approach their responsibilities. Primarily, viewing fatherhood as a divine opportunity emphasizes the sacred nature of the role. They begin to see themselves as custodians of a precious gift from God. This awareness instills an overwhelming sense of honor and reverence for their responsibility in guiding and nurturing. It transcends the fulfillment of misguided societal expectations, evolving into an inspired call to actively participate in their son's spiritual and moral development. The understanding of fatherhood as a divine calling, infuses fathers with a Godly purpose, transcending the ordinary aspects of parenting.

It encompasses the significant responsibilities of instilling values, imparting wisdom, and cultivating spiritual growth. This purpose-driven perspective becomes the driving force behind their unwavering commitment to the well-being and maturity of their sons. Recognizing fatherhood as a calling emphasizes the weight of the responsibility they carry. Fathers grasp they are stewards of a precious life, entrusted with the weighty task of nurturing and guiding in alignment with Scriptural principles and values. This heightened sense of responsibility cultivates a commitment to making choices and decisions prioritizing the best interests of their family. Consequently, they approach their calling with depth, honor, and reverence, guided by an immense understanding of the sacred nature of their role in shaping the lives entrusted to them.

Humility in Fatherhood

Reverence in fatherhood leads to humility as fathers come to understand the Godly trust placed upon them. This humility is a meaningful aspect of cultivating reverence and influences their approach to responsibilities. They comprehend they've been entrusted with a tremendous task extending beyond their own abilities and capabilities. This awareness encourages a sense of modesty and meekness, as fathers realize they are not the ultimate authority but rather stewards of a precious gift. Humility manifests in several ways. First, it encourages them to approach their responsibilities with an open heart and mind. They become receptive to learning and growing because there is no one-size-fits-all approach to parenting. Each son is unique, and the challenges and joys of fatherhood require a willingness to adapt and evolve.

Second, humility leads to a recognition of the importance of seeking guidance and support. Fathers understand this journey is not meant to be traveled alone. Consequently, they become more willing to seek advice from experienced fathers, mentors, and other trusted sources. This readiness to learn from others and acknowledge their own limitations contributes to their individual growth. Humbleness in fatherhood results in a sincere sense of respect for their sons as individuals. They recognize mentorship is not about control or dominance but rather about guidance and nurture.

In this process, there is respect for autonomy while encouraging their sons to develop their own unique qualities and potential. Essentially, humility is the outcome of cultivating reverence. It stems from recognizing trust and the responsibility it entails. This view shapes fathers into more empathetic, open-minded, and respectful mentors, encouraging them to approach fatherhood with a sense of modesty, constantly seeking to learn, grow, and provide the best possible guidance and love.

Honoring the Significance of Fatherhood

Reverence in the realm of guiding the next generation instills a deep appreciation for the importance of shaping lives. This recognition prompts fathers to transcend conventional expectations and embrace multifaceted responsibilities as mentors, guides, and models for those on the journey of life. When this veneration is directed toward recognizing the spiritual calling and the unique essence of each individual, it carries the weight of immense responsibilities. This transformative perception leads to a shift in how they perceive themselves as guardians of well-being. This view molds their approach to interactions, promoting intentionality and mindfulness in every action as the impact on the path of others is acknowledged.

Proactively, opportunities are sought to provide knowledge, wisdom, values, and life lessons, recognizing their important impact on character and development. Honoring the significance of parenthood encourages fathers to be actively present in their sons' lives, emphasizing the time spent together is a valuable investment in their future. Prioritizing quality time, engaging in meaningful conversations, and participating in activities to build bonding and growth characterizes their approach.

Reverence also fosters an environment of love and respect within the family. By leading by example, fathers demonstrate the importance of treating others with kindness and compassion. Nurturing an atmosphere where safety, value, and support are paramount for healthy emotional, psychological, and spiritual development. Honoring the significance of fatherhood under the influence of reverence is a cathartic experience. Recognizing their power to shape character, values, and the future is a pivotal realization. This awareness encourages them to approach their role with dedication, love, and a profound sense of purpose.

Cultivating reverence within fatherly roles initiates a transformative shift in perspective, enabling a fresh outlook. This redirection moves the focus from daily safekeeping tasks and duties to recognizing the heartfelt impact on their lives. Initially, this mission may seem like a sequence of routine responsibilities, concentrating on meeting essential needs such as food, shelter, and education.

While these aspects are undeniably crucial, reverence prompts a broader view, considering the long-term effects of these actions. As the Godly calling of fatherhood and the gift of a son become evident, the primary significance of this mission becomes apparent. The influence extends beyond material provisions, encompassing the molding of character, values, and the future legacy. This change in perspective motivates a purposeful approach to responsibilities, building intentionality in actions and decisions for their development. In the pursuit of wisdom transmission, value inculcation, spiritual enlightenment, and emotional and moral nurturing, fathers actively seek opportunities for personal wellness. These evolving perspectives prompt a deep appreciation for every moment of life. Everyday interactions are no longer perceived as routine but as valuable chances for connection and self-improvement. This heightened presence and engagement with life's experiences lead to a sense of fulfillment and the cultivation of meaningful relationships.

Additionally, this sense of reverence encourages introspection into one's own journey. Contemplating the legacy to be passed on to future generations becomes a powerful motivator for action and a commitment to personal maturity. Cultivating reverence transforms the perspective on life from being centered on the mundane to focusing on the long-term impact on the world, leading to a more intentional and purpose-driven approach to living.

Role of Godly Influence

The concept of fatherhood as a blessing is closely linked to the recognition of a Godly influence. It emphasizes this role as a purposeful choice rather than a random assignment, adding depth to its reverence. By acknowledging the Divine's involvement, fathers come to understand it as a deliberate and purposeful selection by the Spirit rather than a matter of chance. This realization instills a sense of humility, gratitude, and purpose as they understand their mission.

Belief in a Heavenly choice underscores fatherhood as extending beyond a basic biological process, emphasizing its spiritual, moral, and transcendent nature. Seen as part of a Holy plan and exclusive to their relationships, it nurtures the respect they hold. This recognition inspires a commitment to live up to the trust placed in faith.

The pursuit of a Godly presence in nurturing is marked by seeking guidance and wisdom directed by the principles of faith and acknowledged through the insight of Philippians 4:6-7, which advises: *"Be anxious for nothing, but in everything by prayer and supplication, with thanksgiving, let your requests be made known to God; and the peace of God, which surpasses all understanding, will guard your hearts and minds through Christ Jesus."* This reminder emphasizes how peace transcends anxiety, leading to a serenity beyond comprehension in their intention to impart moral and ethical values and cultivate purpose and meaning within their lives.

The presence of Biblical beliefs in fatherhood is viewed as a dedicated mission, deepening the reverence for this calling. This recognition reaffirms their chosen status, lending a spiritual dimension to the journey. It inspires humility, gratitude, and a purpose-driven approach, impacting not only their own lives but also the lives of the next generation in a meaningful, spiritually enriched manner. Cultivating reverence yields eternal benefits, with its impact extending far beyond the immediate moment.

One of the most significant long-term effects is on the father-son relationship. A stronger and more resilient bond is created by developing respect and honor for their responsibilities, along with reverence for their duties. This fortifies the relationship, transforming it into a source of stability and emotional support.

It establishes a secure foundation from which they can confidently explore the world, build their self-esteem, and form healthy relationships with others. The notion of reverence instills trust within the father-son bond, allowing them to confide, seek guidance, and share their joys and challenges. This involvement profoundly influences character development, nurturing responsibility, empathy, and moral grounding.

The overflowing effect of reverence, contributing to the betterment of society as a whole, strengthens their bond, providing a source of stability and support throughout their lives. Virtuous and righteous individuals emerge as leaders and contributors to their Christian and social communities. Cultivating an understanding for the spiritual gift of guidance impacts their relationship and overall well-being and development. It empowers the growth of morally grounded and empathetic individuals who, in turn, positively influence the world around them.

——— Moving Forward ———

The essential principles of this chapter nurtured a robust father-son bond centered on the foundational roles of love, wisdom, and faith. Love emerged as a dynamic and vital force within fatherhood, sustaining the emotional connection and fostering a nurturing environment for mutual growth. Wisdom and faith played integral roles in constructing a holistic approach to their son's development, encompassing physical, emotional, moral, and spiritual well-being.

The spiritual foundation for these concepts was provided by 1 John 4:7-8, Psalm 127:3, and others. The introduction of gratitude and reverence, inspired by key Scriptures, became fundamental to understanding these principles. Gratitude was portrayed as a transformative emotion, shaping a perspective on fatherhood and leading to an appreciation for the unique qualities and experiences in life. Reverence was presented as an attitude of deep respect and honor, recognizing a Godly calling, and instilling a sense of duty.

The conclusion emphasized the significance of mindful parenting in enhancing the connection within the father-son relationship, offering insight into the nurturing of gratitude and reverence. Ultimately, this approach strengthens their bond and aligns with the wisdom found in the Scriptures.

In Chapter 3, wisdom stands at the forefront, aiming to enrich the understanding of the father-son relationship. At the outset, a reflection on Colossians 3:21, reveals valuable insights into providing guidance and instruction while nurturing the father-son connection to maturity.

CHAPTER THREE

Lessons from Scripture

Continuing this discourse commences with a reflection from the inspired pages of Scripture, unveiling an abundance of invaluable instruction and insight to enrich the father-son relationship. Directed by wisdom, their bond takes them to particular verses where Godly insights illuminate their path, serving as a lighthouse to lead their progress. Under the guiding beacon of faith and the timeless inspiration, the focus shifts to Colossians 3:21, *"Do not come down too hard on your children, or you will crush their spirits."*

In this passage, a key principle stands out: fathers who are nurturing their sons are encouraged not to incite anger but to offer counsel through discipline and instruction, firmly grounded in the teachings of the Lord. The Colossians verse serves as a reminder: love, while essential, is not the sole element of fatherhood. It requires responsible advice to steer their sons toward a righteous path.

In this endeavor, fathers come to understand their actions have significant meaning for their spiritual and emotional goodness. A key insight is the capacity to discipline in a manner which, instead of being harsh or provoking, creates a loving and supportive environment conducive to growth.

The concept of discipline rooted in love highlights a transformative approach, drawing inspiration from Ephesians 6:4, which urges one not to provoke but to bring them up in Godly discipline and instruction. It serves as an encouragement to recognize discipline is not synonymous with strictness or severity but can be a tool for teaching and nurturing. As Proverbs 13:24, aptly points out: *"The one who loves their children is careful to discipline them."*

CHAPTER THREE

Discipline, when intertwined with love and guidance, builds an environment of support encouraging learning through actions, reflecting the wisdom of guiding them onto the *"right path,"* as recommended in Proverbs 22:6. Addressing misbehavior or mistakes with empathy and understanding creates a secure space for personal growth, character development, and the strengthening of the connection between them.

Hebrews 12:11, serves as a reminder, discipline, although not enjoyable in the moment, can yield a harvest of righteousness and peace for those who undergo it. These sacred teachings lay the groundwork for addressing the complexities of instruction and structure, emphasizing the importance of maintaining a Godly and compassionate relationship.

The Scriptures propose such guidance can serve as a tool for growth and character development when administered with care and intention, while encouraging a loving directive rooted in a sincere concern for the well-being of those under guidance. This approach acknowledges the significance of boundaries and structure, while simultaneously recognizing it can be implemented with empathy and understanding.

The significance of love as the foundation upon which effective discipline is built cannot be over emphasized. Fathers are encouraged to approach it with genuine care and affection, creating an atmosphere where this becomes an act of love meant to positively guide and shape character rather than to be used as a punitive measure.

In highlighting their role as guides through the challenges and mistakes inherent in development, they can provide direction, support, and wisdom during these moments, while drawing inspiration from Proverbs 3:12, which is a reminder: *"The Lord disciplines those He loves."* This path aids in navigating difficulties and deriving lessons from experiences. It reframes the concept as an avenue for growth and learning rather than mere correction.

The emphasis lies in its role as a platform for imparting valuable life experiences and instilling important virtues, morals, and spiritual guidelines. By clarifying the reasons behind it and its link to broader life opportunities, they provide empowerment for making wiser choices in the future. Nurturing growth through this approach corrects behavior and has the potential to strengthen the father-son bond. When administered with love

LESSONS FROM SCRIPTURE

and understanding, discipline reinforces trust, as their sons learn it originates from a place of care, further strengthening their relationship. In the journey of fatherhood, balancing firmness with compassion can be a difficult task.

Fathers have the privilege and responsibility to set clear expectations and consequences, while always holding the torch of compassion and understanding, mirroring the Lord's embrace for those who fear Him, as noted in Psalm 103:13-14. This balance creates a caring environment where their sons feel safe to explore, make mistakes, and learn. It is within these moments of learning they build resilience and grow into the best versions of themselves.

Trust and respect are the basis of strong relationships. When discipline is rooted in love and genuine concern, it becomes a powerful tool for building these foundations. Understanding the guidance stemming from a place of deep embrace, their sons recognize the respect for wisdom and place trust in judgment. This underpinning forms the basis of open dialogue and a bond spanning a lifetime. In emphasizing the importance of creating healthy and lasting relationships, the central message running through their discussions is underlined: the balance between firmness and compassion, along with a loving approach to discipline, serves as the impetus for real-world and thriving connections.

Foundational Principles for Exploration

Colossians serve as a foundational benchmark for the exploration of nurturing father-son relationships, underscoring their multifaceted role. It signifies the importance of discipline and instruction rooted in Biblical wisdom, guiding them in fulfilling their duty as both loving caregivers and responsible mentors. This reminder extends beyond affection; it encompasses the vital task of providing ethical and spiritual leadership. By adhering to the Scriptures, fathers instill values, moral principles, and a strong sense of faith, ultimately directing their sons toward a righteous path. As a guiding light, it illuminates the way for cultivating meaningful and enduring relationships where love, discipline, and instruction converge to nurture spiritual growth and character development. When introducing the concept of discipline in the context of guidance, it advises avoiding actions inciting frustration, as this could diminish enthusiasm. This approach highlights its application with care, empathy, and sagacity rather than resorting to severe or inequitable methods.

The significance lies in conscientious and loving mentorship, encompassing the establishment of boundaries, the provision of guidance, and the bestowal of valuable insights, all while developing a loving and supportive connection. This promotes a harmonious approach to behavioral correction, seeking to nurture character and cultivate a strong bond.

Effectively applying correction in harmony with Scriptural teachings and fostering growth and development represents a delicate yet crucial aspect of mentorship. At its core, discipline in these relationships is firmly grounded in love. Fathers who are leading are urged to ensure their approach is founded in a heartfelt dedication to the well-being of those under their care. This idea serves as a powerful reminder, emphasizing the need for Godly mentors to prevent the arousal of resentment or disillusionment. It is a call to refrain from strong measures driven by anger or frustration and instead employ it as a tool for direction and instruction, transcending oblique punitive measures.

In doing so, the establishment of lucid and rational boundaries for behavior becomes an integral element in their sons' character development. Fathers are then encouraged to draw insight from the sacred texts, utilizing them as a guiding compass to set ethical and moral standards within their environments. Clear rules and expectations are paramount, as they empower their sons to grasp and internalize the principles they are called to uphold.

This step imbues them with an accountable understanding of the moral consequences of their actions and inspires them to make choices aligned with these guiding truths. Recognizing the importance of consistency and fairness emerges as a fundamental element. Since unjust or overly severe consequences can lead to dissatisfaction, as discipline extends beyond buoyant repercussions; it also encompasses the provision of motivation and milestones for personal growth. Welcoming these moments as

LESSONS FROM SCRIPTURE

opportunities to redirect toward improved choices and highlighting statutes of repentance, forgiveness, and reconciliation holds significance. This is due to the idea that open and honest communication establishes a fundamental foundation for fostering a healthy relationship, particularly in creating a supportive atmosphere where candid discussions are embraced, even in the presence of mistakes. In this manner, it cultivates a continuous cycle of guidance, mutual understanding, and growth.

Leading by example goes beyond being a mere suggestion; it acts as a powerful source of inspiration. Encouraging the embodiment of desired behaviors not only showcases authenticity but also strengthens moral lessons. Additionally, seeking divine instruction through prayer and the Scriptures aligns seamlessly with the theory of relying on Godly strength in the sacred journey. Restrictive measures should be a loving, instructive, and redemptive process, aiming to instill values, build character, and ultimately contribute to spiritual and moral growth in a manner reflecting the divine teachings of righteousness.

One key aspect of this significance is the establishment of a moral foundation. Biblical instruction provides a solid moral grounding, imparting values such as honesty, compassion, forgiveness, and humility, which are essential for building strong character. By establishing these teachings, it ensures the values are not cultural or situational but rooted in eternal divine wisdom. Beyond moral values, it provides a deep understanding of faith, the teachings of Jesus Christ, and the importance of a personal relationship with the Divine. This spiritual dimension is crucial for guiding toward a righteous path, as it instills a sense of identity as children of God.

The use of Biblical stories and parables can help navigate complex moral dilemmas and ethical choices, providing invaluable wisdom in a world filled with transgressive acts. These instructions instill a sense of purpose by helping them understand they are part of a larger narrative of faith, encouraging them to live their lives in alignment with God's plan, and serving as a powerful motivator for making righteous choices. By imparting knowledge and wisdom, they create a sense of continuity and belonging within the Christian faith, conveying their beliefs are not isolated but part of a broader heritage. Character building is another significant outcome of disciplinary instruction. It involves learning virtues such as patience, kindness, and self-control, all emphasized in Godly living and essential for a solid, virtuous lifestyle. By setting an example, one can gain tools to navigate life's challenges and trials, understanding the importance of prayer, faith, and a reliance on God. This builds spiritual resilience as a source of strength on the righteous path.

This instructive process deepens the connection, creating a shared journey of learning and growth. The appreciation for the wisdom and guidance provided, forms a lasting alliance, building a loving father-son relationship encompassing strong moral values, spiritual development, guidance, purpose, tradition, character building, resilience, and a strengthened bond.

Flexibility in Instructional Discipline

The significance of Biblical instruction in molding character, developing spiritual growth, offering counsel in decision-making, instilling purpose, connecting to tradition, building resilience, and strengthening the bond between generations is evident. Fathers who impart these teachings play a vital role in building the future and contributing to a legacy of faith, love, and righteousness. Striking a balance between discipline and guidance is a delicate art. Recognizing love provides an unwavering foundation; this creates a safe and nurturing environment for growth. Love serves as the basis from which trust, understanding, and connection flow.

Counsel should always be rooted in love, aimed at directing and teaching rather than imposing punishment. This entails establishing clear boundaries, clarifying consequences, and consistently upholding guidelines while maintaining a loving and empathetic approach. When experiencing unconditional love, their sons become more receptive to receiving disciplinary correction.

Love fosters an environment conducive to effective communication, enabling the imparting of knowledge, values, and life lessons without fear of judgment. Discipline, when administered with compassion, becomes a means for character development, instilling responsibility, self-control, and ethical decision-making.

LESSONS FROM SCRIPTURE

Consistency in this approach, with clear rules and equitable consequences, is essential. Yet, recognizing the uniqueness of each son and their specific needs calls for flexibility. By modeling these qualities in their own lives, fathers can effectively harmonize love and discipline, embodying the values they seek to instill. This equilibrium builds an atmosphere of trust, respect, and mutual understanding, contributing to the growth and development of their sons into responsible, ethical, and compassionate beings. Love, as the keystone of lasting connections, creates an environment where growth thrives amidst the delicate balance of guidance and direction. Mastering this balance creates both personal development and the strengthening of bonds across generations.

The sacred duty, as articulated in these timeless principles, transcends a simple obligation, evolving into a Godly commitment. It resides in the capacity to guide loved ones along a Christian walk, an entrusted duty met with sincere reverence and dedication. This responsibility involves setting ethical boundaries and nurturing the ability to discern between right and wrong. As exemplars, they illuminate the path with the values they aim to impart, empowering individuals with the tools for proper decision-making and life navigation with relentless integrity.

At the heart of this special relationship lies the nurturing of Godly principles, deeply anchored in faith and upstanding values, forming the cornerstone of character. Virtues such as love, compassion, forgiveness, humility, and uprightness stand as strong pillars, guiding the journey towards Christian living. Faith, serving as the leading light, provides wisdom, and teachings, functioning as a compass for the path to honorableness. In this shared voyage, the journey encompasses generational bridges, with the transmission of spiritual guidance drawing from fatherly experiences. These spiritual journeys aid not only in comprehending beliefs but also in understanding one's place within the broader tapestry of Christian centered communities.

One of the most potent methods of fulfilling this inherent duty is leading by example. By embodying faith and values, a profound and lasting influence is established. Love, empathy, kindness, and a commitment to morality become the embodied lessons. Embracing sacred responsibilities become a transformative odyssey, leaving a remarkable and indelible mark.

CHAPTER THREE

Those who approach their role with the utmost seriousness and reverence guide their sons towards honor and honesty, fortifying the family bond. In turn, their sons glean the significance of responsibility, faith, and moral guidelines through this leadership, fulfilling the inspired duty of guiding the next generation towards a sense of integrity. Those raised with responsible guidance and a solid virtuous foundation are more likely to carry forward these values, thus ensuring the perpetuity of this legacy. The teachings of Colossians serve as a poignant reminder of their duty to provide responsible mentorship, instill values, and nurture faith. This responsibility is not to be taken lightly, as it fashions the character and moral compass of the next generation.

——— Imparting Spiritual Teachings ———

In the practical application of Scriptural teachings within everyday scenarios, it is essential to effectively put into practice the principles of nurturing, discipline, and instruction. One facet of this approach is active involvement. Nurturing with patience transcends mere presence; it involves actively immersing oneself in the world of those under their care. This entails making a deliberate effort to spend meaningful time and participating in activities igniting interests. By doing so, not only does it communicate the significance of the passions within the next generation, but it also exemplifies patience by allowing them to explore and develop at their own pace.

Another important element is direct listening and understanding. It is intricately linked with the capacity to listen and empathize. Creating an environment where feelings are heard and validated is of utmost importance. This involves being fully present when expressions occur, demonstrating empathy, and refraining from passing judgment. When their sons recognize these concerns and perspectives are genuinely understood, they become more inclined to seek guidance and openly share their thoughts, deepening the quality of the relationship.

LESSONS FROM SCRIPTURE

The idea of patience extends beyond waiting; it touches on the realm of emotional support. It involves being prepared to offer comfort and advice in times of difficulty. In the context of intellectual pursuits, complex relationships, and personal challenges, a patient and empathetic father creates an atmosphere where ideas can flow freely and solutions can be sought collectively. They serve as the bedrock for healthy father-son relationships. This emotional sustenance assumes a pivotal role in generating emotional fortitude and self-assurance, thereby making a substantial contribution to one's holistic welfare.

A fundamental aspect of this endeavor is the acknowledgment of individual growth. This entails refraining from imposing rigid expectations and fixed timelines while celebrating their unique journey and offering guidance when necessary. Such an approach promotes a sense of autonomy and self-discovery, which are essential components of personal maturity and development.

Fathers play a significant role through their actions, transcending verbal communication to influence conduct. When they confront hardships with resilience, persistence, and a composed demeanor, their actions serve as instructive models. This observational learning process cultivates understanding, as they are not solely virtues but practical and indispensable qualities for navigating life's intricacies.

In retrospect, the application of nurturing, training, and instruction in real-life scenarios entails a proactive involvement, empathetic listening, emotional support, recognition of individual growth, and the pivotal role of modeling a composed demeanor in fatherly interactions. Integrating these nuanced approaches into their relationships within the role of mentorship, they can effectively nurture, thus molding a robust foundation based on love, trust, and understanding, aligning with Biblical principles, and fortifying intergenerational bonds.

This perspective nurtures development and spiritual growth, preparing them to confront life with grace. Employing love-infused discipline is a vital element in effective relationships between mentors and those under their guidance. Founded in love and empathy, it serves as a powerful tool for building character and behavior. This approach includes the establishment of clear boundaries, elucidating expectations, and considering the consequences of one's actions. Explaining the rationale behind these boundaries and their corresponding consequences nurtures comprehension rather than instilling apprehension.

Fatherly mentors also aid in making improved choices, gleaning insights from their errors, and evolving into responsible and empathetic individuals. By using discipline as a means to impart valuable life lessons, they vividly express their love and commitment to growth, fortifying the connection between them. This approach resonates with Christian values, emphasizing empathy, forgiveness, and guidance, mirroring the way in which God steers His children with love and compassion. Integrating instruction into everyday moments emerges as a valuable method for embedding faith-based values and teachings. By seamlessly incorporating insights from the Biblical text, engaging in discussions about ethical dilemmas, and providing instruction on how to apply faith to life's trials during routine activities, mentors weave a multifaceted understanding into the lives of those they guide. This highlights its significance and practical application.

Those under guidance come to perceive it as an integral element in their daily lives, shaping their choices and actions. This method imparts knowledge and wisdom, cultivating a sincere and meaningful understanding of their faith, making it a natural and indispensable part of their lives. Setting an example stands as a core element of effective leadership. This role transcends temporal instruction; it assumes the position of a role model, and actions communicate volumes. By embodying the values and truth intended to be imparted, including faith, love, and humility, a formidable influence is established.

When their sons witness these values exemplified in daily interactions, it serves as a compelling testament to the relevance and authenticity of these directives. This demonstration inspires those they guide to walk a similar path, reinforcing the teachings espoused under the guidance of Colossians, in a tangible and meaningful manner. It strengthens the connection between mentors and their protégés as they jointly commit to living out their life in practical and visible ways, forging a shared and purposeful commitment.

LESSONS FROM SCRIPTURE

Developing an environment of love and support within the domain becomes essential for nurturing a strong and lasting connection. In the current context, the act of fatherly guidance plays a pivotal role in shaping emotional maturity, good mental health, and spiritual well-being. When cultivating a setting characterized by compassion and support, a stable foundation is provided for exploring belief, and addressing life's challenges.

This domain encourages open and meaningful conversations where thoughts, questions, and concerns can be freely expressed. Trust and mutual respect are built within this framework, serving as fundamental components for a lasting bond. Being attentive listeners, showing empathy, and understanding the experiences and perspectives of those under counsel strengthens the alliance and reinforces values of compassion and faith-rooted love. Ultimately, creating such a habitat in the present lays the groundwork for a lifelong alliance built upon trust.

Instruction Grounded in Faith

Fathers embrace a multifaceted role, extending far beyond conventional provider and protector to become spiritual guides. Their responsibility reaches beyond material support, encompassing the task of leading by example, particularly in matters of love, conviction, credence, trust, and belief. Through actions and words, one seeks to possess the power to emphasize the significance of a genuinely lived faith, moving beyond mere profession. Central to this guidance is the act of passing down timeless insights, including the teachings from the sacred Scriptures, to the next generation.

Family mentors have the privilege and duty of introducing ageless wisdom, helping their sons understand the values and instructions it contains. By doing so, they impart knowledge and sow the seeds of faith, which can flourish into a profound and enduring spiritual allegiance. Guiding in this manner is an ongoing journey of spiritual development. It creates situations where prayer, worship, and conversations regarding Biblical applications become interwoven into their lives. This includes collective worship, attending alternative church gatherings, and engaging in discussions about the Scriptures and its implications.

CHAPTER THREE

Additionally, there is an opportunity to promote a personal connection with God, helping them navigate their spiritual path through its highs and lows. Nurturing spiritual transcendence involves instilling a deep sense of reverence for the Biblical truths and inspiring those to seek the vast and unimaginable depths in their limited understanding, even as Romans 11:33, declares: *"Oh, how great are God's riches and wisdom and knowledge! How impossible it is for us to understand His decisions and ways."*

When consistently witnessing these merits in practice, it reinforces their importance and provides tangible examples of using them in various life situations. Shared-life experiences become powerful illustrations of faith's significance, learning not only from success but also from moments of struggle and doubt. During these vulnerable times, it becomes evident, this fruit of the Spirit doesn't rest on perfection but instead centers on a persistent trust in spiritual guidance and a willingness to learn and grow through the daily challenges. These conversations strengthen bonds as they collectively navigate intricacies, forming a foundation of spiritual fortitude, emotional maturity, power, and resilience for a lifetime.

Promoting open and enriching discussions within the family resembles the careful cultivation of fertile soil where spiritual growth flourishes. Within this nurturing ambiance, fathers actively extend invitations to their sons, encouraging them to embrace their Christian beliefs and explore intricate questions. This establishes a safe haven where doubts and uncertainties are greeted with empathy and motivation rather than judgment, making them keen listeners while acknowledging these reciprocal conversations offer opportunities for mutual enlightenment.

Together, they contemplate life's enigmas and ponder the hidden mysteries of the Scriptures. These dialogues bolster an understanding of their beliefs and contribute to the fathers' own spiritual journey while witnessing their sons' burgeoning spiritual growth and inquisitiveness. Through this mutual exploration, a more robust bond is forged, and the connection evolves into a sanctuary of trust and resolution. The tireless display of Biblical values involves the embodiment of faith, transcending isolated moments to become an intrinsic facet of character and decision-making.

LESSONS FROM SCRIPTURE

At the juncture of both success and adversity, whether in professional arenas or the familial sphere, the resolute commitment to their Scriptural faith remains a constant. This dedication embodies a belief system, imparting the understanding that it extends beyond a basic set of doctrines and becomes an integral way of life. It functions as a street lamp, shining a light on the direction through life's diverse situations and triumphs. Through its observable steadiness in action, their sons not only acquire knowledge of Christian tenets, but also witness a tangible example of wholeheartedly and authentically embracing it.

A prominent theme revolves around the transmission of spiritual wisdom from one generation to the next. It highlights a unique role in the conveyance of insight, transcending the boundaries of conventional knowledge to explore the depths of these teachings. This guidance, beyond the mere exchange of facts, aims to instill core values, spiritual principles, and a comprehension of the Godly tenets. Within this journey, there exist opportunities for discussing Biblical narratives, unraveling intricate theological concepts, and engaging in thought-provoking dialogues, all of which contribute to the cultivation of spiritual maturity.

The instruction anchored in the Scriptures extends far beyond religious rituals and canonical teachings; it encompasses the practical wisdom of life and divine insights. Everyday scenarios serve as valuable platforms for instilling virtues, manifesting kindness, forgiveness, and humility in real-life illustrations, illuminating the significance of prayer and worship. In doing so, a bridge emerges between the spiritual and the practical, enabling a perception of the divine relevance across every facet of life.

Nurturing Christian principles within the family dynamics involves playing a pivotal role through actions and discussions. Acts of kindness serve as a canvas for imparting the significance of loving one's neighbor, harmonizing these deeds with the teachings of love attributed to our Lord. Incorporating these values into daily life extends to modeling modesty and meekness through the acknowledgment of mistakes and the willingness to apologize when warranted. This practice imparts the virtue of humility and the recognition of human imperfection.

CHAPTER THREE

The inclusion of family prayer as part of the daily routine highlights its significance and the pursuit of Biblical instruction. Instances of disappointment, disruptions, and difficulties present occasions for engaging in conversations regarding maintaining a healthy outlook and placing trust in God's plan, even when circumstances deviate from expectations. The regular study of the Scriptures, with a focus on passages and stories relevant to everyday life, further strengthens the integration of their beliefs into the routines of daily living. This concept can be further stimulated by motivating engagement in voluntary service, thereby reinforcing the Biblical idea of selfless devotion to others. Amidst the ordinary routines of life, moments of collective gratitude through prayer can be initiated, nourishing a spirit of appreciation and a heightened awareness of the blessings bestowed.

Drawing guidance from the framework of relationships, particularly echoing the wisdom found in Ecclesiastes 11:1,*"Cast your bread upon the waters, for you will find it after many days,"* illustrates the essence of generosity, emphasizing the reciprocity emanating from selfless acts, reinforcing the values of giving and helping others. It establishes a solid foundation from which a resilient and Godly trust takes root. This underpinning goes beyond a superficial understanding of doctrine; it creates a meaningful and personal connection. The task is to function as spiritual guides, walking alongside them on their journey.

In fulfilling this responsibility, fathers impart an understanding of Christian beliefs and the pragmatic facets of living out one's faith. This includes imparting the importance of spiritual practices such as meditation, Bible study, and acts of service. Prayer and mediation serves as a conduit for connecting with the Creator, enabling a pursuit of guidance, strength, and solace amid life's problems. Engaging in an exegesis of the Holy Scriptures unfolds a gateway to insightful comprehension of God's word, facilitating the extraction of wisdom and insights steering daily life. Acts of service, embodying the essence of selflessness, mirror the Christian principles of love and service to others. Within these spiritual disciplines, a meaningful connection to God is cultivated, transcending inheritance alone to become a personally embraced mission. This guidance, grounded in love, provides the essential tools for constructing resilience in the face of life's uncertainties. The role of spiritual mentors within fatherhood extends beyond the conveyance of beliefs, encompassing the building of an enduring living trust. This legacy surpasses verbal transmission, immersing into the realm of experiential wisdom, an invaluable gift transcending generations. As a result, it enriches the spiritual journey and fortifies the bonds within their relationship.

Building Spiritual Growth

Leading as a spiritual escort is a vital element of mentorship within the domain of fatherhood, especially when shouldering the responsibility of cultivating faith and imparting an understanding of the sacred directives. This progenitorship extends beyond casual instruction; it encompasses the unique art of modeling behavior firmly grounded, exemplifying the significance of Godliness in everyday living. The role of Biblical teachings is undeniably paramount in the relationship between fathers and their sons. This connection between spiritual guidance, mentorship, and familial bonds finds resonance in the Scriptural narrative of the Apostle Paul and Timothy, his young protégé.

The Apostle Paul, an empowered servant of Jesus Christ in early Christianity, served as both a spiritual mentor and a fatherly guide to Timothy. Their relationship exemplified the everlasting importance of passing down spiritual wisdom and teachings from one generation to the next. 2 Timothy 3:14-15, offers a reflection of this mentoring relationship: *"But as for Timothy, he continued in what he had learned and had become convinced of because he knew those from whom he learned it and how from infancy he had known the Holy Scriptures, which were able to make him wise for salvation through faith in Christ Jesus."*

Paul, as the spiritual mentor, played a significant part in Timothy's growth by nurturing his understanding of the inspired scrolls from a young age. This tale highlights the memorable impact of the Biblical teachings within father-son relationships, emphasizing the significance of learning from those who have walked the path before them. In exploring the intrinsic values of these Scriptural insights, a multifaceted connection is uncovered.

CHAPTER THREE

First, it nurtures a sense of shared identity as fathers and their sons engage with the sacred passages, exploring its narratives, parables, and commandments together. This experience strengthens their spiritual bond and creates a sense of continuity within the family, connecting past, present, and future generations through a common faith.

Second, it instills a strong moral compass, providing guidance in making ethical choices grounded in the teachings of Christ Jesus and the wisdom of the Scriptures. This foundation becomes a firm anchor, helping to navigate the complexities of life with clarity and integrity. Last, it empowers them with spiritual resilience, preparing them to face life's complexities and adversities with unyielding fortitude.

By drawing from these writings, it provides a fountain of strength, hope, and peace in times of difficulty, creating a spiritual resilience as a legacy while leaving an impact not only on their lives but also on those they encounter. It is a reminder, fatherly mentorship goes beyond the casual; it weaves a tapestry of shared identity, moral strength, and spiritual power. This reflects the timeless wisdom of passing down faith from one generation to the next, drawing inspiration from patriarchal personas such as Paul and Timothy.

The inspired messages are not distant and abstract ideas but rather living principles intertwined with the core of faith. It becomes essential for one to illuminate how these Scriptural guidelines align harmoniously with the foundational tenets of Christianity. This process of connection brings the knowledge of the Bible to life and makes them relevant and applicable to the daily lives of believers. Consider for instance, the Golden Rule, a simple yet deeply impactful concept found in Matthew 7:12, *"So in everything, do to others what you would have them do to you, for this sums up the Law and the Prophets."*

Fathers can explain this concept, embodying the essence of Godly-inspired love and compassion. By treating others as they would wish to be treated, the value of empathy and selflessness in their interactions with the world is learned. The importance of forgiveness, a central theme in Christian theology, is illuminated through Biblical teachings. They can be guided to passages such as Matthew 6:14-15, where Jesus said: *"For if you forgive other people when they sin against you, your heavenly Father will also forgive you.*

LESSONS FROM SCRIPTURE

But if you do not forgive others their sins, your Father will not forgive your sins." This emphasizes the importance of forgiveness and encourages embracing its transformative power in the father-son relationship.

Moral Compass in Leading

The intrinsic value of humility, as exemplified in the life and examples of Christ our Lord, holds remarkable significance in the realm of relationships and spiritual development. A pivotal passage encapsulating this principle is found in Philippians 2:3-4, urging adherence to humility: *"Do nothing out of selfish ambition or vain conceit. Rather, in humility, value others above yourselves, not looking to your interests but each to the interests of others."*

This instruction serves as a foundational basis for the review of the essence of humility and its application in daily life. It invites reflection on the divine message conveyed. Stepping into humility reveals it as more than a brief absence of arrogance; it is an active practice of prioritizing the needs and interests of others over one's own.

In abstract terms, it's an opportunity to present theoretical examples and scenarios, highlighting the transformative power within. The discussion of hypothetical situations where choosing selflessness over selfish ambition leads to positive outcomes adds layers of depth to the understanding of this Biblical instruction. These narratives breathe life into the abstraction, making it relatable and tangible.

Additionally, an invitation extends to participate in open discourse, cultivating a lived journey where reflection on character formation and the impact on interactions within the broader community can unfold. This approach aims to create a place for contemplation where thoughts, questions, and contemporary challenges can be explored. By instilling these values, there is an intentional effort to provide an ethical directive, guiding individuals through the intricacies of life.

This principle emerges as a leading force, influencing the way they navigate relationships, make decisions, and respond to the unfolding trials. Ultimately, the incorporation of Biblical doctrines within the father-son relationship serves as a transformative and loving legacy. It imparts wisdom and instills an understanding of the importance of valuing others and placing their interests first. This familial heritage becomes a source of strength and guidance, aiding in the growth of compassionate and empathetic individuals who carry the light of this principle into the world. By connecting these Scriptural ideals with their beliefs, fathers can empower their sons with a righteous directive leading their actions and decisions. It transforms the Bible from a historical artifact into a living guide for life, reinforcing the idea, faith is not a simple Sunday ritual but a Godly strength permeating every aspect of life.

Integrity in the Father-Son Bond

This integration of faith within the father-son bond creates a meaningful and important legacy of virtues carried with them throughout their lives. Therefore, instruction grounded in Biblical doctrine serves as the cornerstone for cultivating a strong moral domain. It provides them with the tools and direction to discern right from wrong, make ethical decisions, and uphold the values of Godliness. This foundation of moral integrity is of utmost importance, especially in a world presenting numerous righteous dilemmas and ethical challenges.

Fathers, in their role as spiritual guides, mentors, and instructors, carry the responsibility of imparting these virtues. They can draw upon the various Biblical scrolls and parchments to illustrate the importance of morality and ethics in the Christian walk. For example, a helpful instruction referenced in Micah 6:8, declares: *"He has shown you, O mortal, what is good. And what does the Lord require of you? To act justly, to love mercy, and to walk humbly with your God."*

By exploring such passages, fathers can share the deep connection between belief and moral conduct, emphasizing these virtues are not confined to the walls of an edifice but extend into every facet of life. These values rooted in Biblical teachings provide a reliable and staunch ethical compass, guiding their sons in the decision-making process.

In a broader context, a framework emerges where discussions regarding ethical dilemmas and moral choices encompass both hypothetical scenarios and real-life situations. This engagement encourages the development of critical thinking and personal reflection, prompting consideration of the implications inherent in various measures. Through this process, there is empowerment to evolve into decision-makers firmly grounded in values derived from a Godly perspective. In addition, there is an opportunity to exemplify these values through daily actions; recognizing these moments often resonate more strongly than words. The emulation of ethical behavior witnessed becomes a natural outcome, connecting the incorporation of Scriptural values, such as honesty, compassion, and integrity, in the lives of those involved.

Within this holistic approach, rooted in instruction and grounded in Biblical truth, provides a moral compass to confront the ethical challenges prevalent in the contemporary world with confidence and conviction. This moral foundation, serving as a source of strength and guidance, contributes to the development of responsible, ethical, and compassionate individuals who actively contribute to their communities. Consequently, the pivotal role in providing grounding through Scriptural instruction proves invaluable in shaping the character and conduct of the succeeding generation. In the endeavor to provide the future heirs with a robust framework for spiritual understanding, a fundamental aspect of parental guidance is revealed. This framework acts as the stable scaffolding upon which the spiritual journey is constructed, comprising essential elements forming the foundation of trust.

Fundamental to this sacred foundation is a deep understanding of Scriptural tenets. It serves as the cornerstone in ensuring families acquire a fuller understanding of these essential truths, including the nature of the Heavenly Father, the divine essence of Christ, redemption through faith, and the vital importance of the Spirit of God. With this knowledge at their disposal, they are empowered to confront doctrinal inquiries and overcome obstacles encountered along their spiritual path.

Grasping the essence of the divine becomes a vital aspect of this Biblical framework. Within this viewpoint, fathers as spiritual guides assume a crucial role in describing the attributes as depicted in the Bible. This entails navigating intricate concepts such as omnipotence, omniscience, and omnipresence. Through this exploration, a more expansive understanding of immanence, being present in all things, and transcendence, beyond human comprehension, emerges. It is the foundational understanding laying the groundwork for cultivating an immense and meaningful father-son relationship.

Fatherhood Beliefs in Understanding

At the very essence of Christian doctrine lies the recognition of Jesus as the Son and the Savior of humanity. Family leadership holds the responsibility of imparting this knowledge regarding His earthly existence, teachings, sacrificial crucifixion, and triumphant resurrection. This knowledge forms the basis upon which a personal connection with Him is established. Within this narrative, the opportunity to convey the concept of salvation through faith, emphasizing it as a divine gift, not a reward earned through good deeds, is placed at the father's foothold. It becomes imperative to underscore the role of grace, along with the necessity of repentance and faith in Him, as pivotal elements for experiencing the gift of redemption.

Additionally, exploring the indispensable role of the Holy Spirit in the life of a Christian reveals a divine presence acting as a guide, counselor, and source of empowerment. Insight into the Spirit's work, including conviction, instruction, empowerment, and transformation, aids in understanding the significance of being filled for a life characterized by spiritual growth and service.

Finally, as maturity occurs in faith, their sons inevitably encounter theological questions and challenges. Encouraging exploration of these inquiries and seeking answers from Scripture, trusted theological resources, and mentors within the church and Christian community can cultivate a robust and resilient faith capable of withstanding the complexities and uncertainties of the spiritual journey.

When fathers impart a solid framework for this understanding, they establish the groundwork for a lifelong path of virtuous living. This comprehensive formation reiterates the vital elements of doctrinal knowledge, an exploration of the nature of the Divine, recognition of the divinity of Jesus Christ, understanding salvation through faith, acknowledgment of the Holy Spirit's role, and guidance in navigating theological questions and queries. These elements collectively construct a spiritual foundation, supporting growth in faith and the capacity to embrace and embody the teachings of Scriptural tenets.

Beyond doctrinal knowledge, nurturing Biblical literacy is another vital aspect of building spiritual growth and comprehension. This dimension encompasses several essential components, with a central emphasis on reading and interpreting the Bible. Encouraging a holistic understanding involves guiding and fostering engagement with entire passages and parables during regular reading. This approach goes beyond mere perusal; it includes learning to interpret the inspired text by considering its historical and cultural context and recognizing various literary styles, metaphors, and symbolism employed within its pages.

Additionally, cultivating Scriptural literacy involves nurturing critical thinking skills. By inhabiting an environment where exploration and questioning are encouraged, one can engage with the text, extracting meanings and considering its applications to life. This process aids in developing a deep and personal connection and understanding of God's plan. Embracing the historical context of the Scriptures then becomes valuable for accurate interpretation. Insights into the historical settings of Biblical events and the patriarchs enable an appreciation of the narratives' significance.

Further, recognizing and navigating cultural variations becomes an essential aspect of scriptural insight. Guidance in understanding the ways societal differences impact the interpretation and application of Biblical principles in diverse contexts is vital to leading to a more robust understanding of the Word of God. The aim of Scriptural knowledge is to nurture a rich connection with the inspired scrolls, acting as a lasting source of sustenance and offering insights into navigating faith within an ever-evolving world. Conveying theological understanding establishes a robust foundation, addressing the challenges of fatherhood with confidence, knowledge, and wisdom.

Cultivating a meaningful bond with these texts provides the tools needed to engage in a transformative way, allowing the application of spiritual principles in daily lives and a deepening relationship. Embedding moral and ethical values drawn from Biblical teachings is a pivotal aspect of establishing a sturdy framework for conceptualizing spirituality. In the role of Godly leaders, mentors, and guides, those in these positions play a vital part in imparting truth, honesty, and essential values.

For example, Proverbs 12:22, emphasizes the importance of honesty, stating: *"The Lord detests lying lips, but he delights in people who are trustworthy."* This core virtue is further reinforced by the teachings of Jesus, noted in Matthew 5:37, *"Let your 'Yes' be 'Yes,' and your 'No,' be 'No.' Anything more comes from the evil one."* This underscores the unshakable commitment and consistency between one's beliefs and actions, aligning with the values each seeks to instill.

Understanding the concept of justice and righteousness, as found in the teachings and the messages of the prophets, helps develop a sense of fairness and equity. Service, rooted in Jesus' humble acts and ministry, should be an integral part of values, motivating all to engage in acts of service and charity. In addition, recognizing the responsibility to care for God's creation and be responsible stewards of the resources entrusted reflects a commitment to these principles in their daily lives.

By imparting these moral and ethical ideals, one develops a strong virtuous orientation rooted in Scriptural insights. This orientation guides character development, shapes relationships, and influences decision-making in a manner aligned with Christian values. It ensures the spiritual framework is not just theoretical but practical and applicable to daily life.

Applying Practical Spirituality

Practical spirituality is a vital component of providing a solid framework for Biblical competence, with prayer playing a crucial role in understanding the significance of communication with God. An important facet of spiritual dialogue is meeting with the believers. However, engaging in communication through worship goes beyond attending specific services; it is about expressing continuing reverence and adoration. When leading by example, fathers can demonstrate the importance of worship through their own acts of devotion, whether through song, prayer, or contemplation. Recognizing worship as a way to connect with God expresses devotion and

LESSONS FROM SCRIPTURE

nurtures a spiritual practice, enriching the faith journey through acts of giving. Encouraging active engagement in acts of service, charity, and kindness reinforces the Christian axiom of love in action, providing a practical expression of faith. It also imparts the values of selflessness and the joy of making a positive impact on the lives of others. Integration into daily life stands as a core tenet of practical spirituality, extending beyond specific religious rituals or settings; instead, it permeates every aspect of life.

Modeling beliefs influence daily decision-making, relationships, and interactions with others. Understanding Biblical axioms as a guiding compass for behavior, ethics, and worldview is essential. Whether at home, school, work, or in the community, the commitment is to live out these values consistently. Spiritual disciplines provide valuable tools for growth, introducing practices such as fasting, meditation, prayer, and studying the Scriptures. These disciplines broaden the connection to God and offer avenues for personal growth and an understanding of one's values. Recognizing the expansive nature of these disciplines beyond religious obligations, they serve as pathways to personal enrichment and a more intimate faith experience.

Involvement within the church and Christian communities represents another dimension of practical spirituality. Understanding the importance of being part of a faith community where one can grow spiritually, receive support, and contribute to the well-being of others becomes crucial. It is within these communities where active practice of faith through fellowship, worship, and service reinforces the bonds of trust and nurtures a sense of belonging. When fathers instill practical spirituality in the upbringing of their sons, it ensures faith, trust, and truth can transcend the realm of abstract concepts, and instead transform into a lived experience.

The practical dimension within this framework helps navigate life's mishaps, make ethical choices, and build a meaningful and fulfilled relationship. Reinforcing this notion, a dynamic practice becomes embodied in daily life rather than just a belief. Developing a strong and thoughtful approach necessitates the cultivation of critical thinking and discernment, pivotal elements in building a deeply meaningful and personal connection. Questioning and doubt, rather than being feared, are embraced as integral parts of a growing understanding. Creating a safe and open environment where exploration is encouraged, fathers cultivate an atmosphere where inquiry is comfortable, asking questions and expressing doubts about their Biblical understanding. Through this dialogue, a thoughtful exploration of spiritual concepts takes place, encouraging personal understanding and conviction rather than relying on traditional and unquestioning acceptance.

Examining Scripture with a discerning mind is an important aspect of critical thinking. Encouraging exploration of the Holy Bible, analyzing its passages, and seeking to understand their relevance in contemporary life is essential. Guidance in studying the historical and cultural context helps build a connection and enables the application of its teachings. Therefore, welcoming this engagement with theological concepts is vital; embracing the diversity of perspectives within Christianity, and encouraging a critical evaluation of these ideas for the formation of a personal Biblical view, guided by the Holy Spirit through reasoned reflection and individual conviction is paramount. This exploration aids in helping understand the diversity of thought within the faith and brings unity in the father-son connection.

—— Connecting to Relational Spirituality ——

Promoting respectful dialogue is essential to nurturing critical thinking. Engaging in discussions with mutual respect, even when holding differing views, teaches the value of listening to others' perspectives, appreciating diverse viewpoints, and engaging in constructive conversations. Reason and faith are encouraged, emphasizing their non-mutual exclusivity and complementarity. Critical thinking empowers, enabling exploration of the intellectual aspects while maintaining a Godly relationship. This integration enriches the journey, enabling thoughtful responses to inquiries and questions.

Ultimately, examination and discernment lead to personal exploration. Encouraging ownership of beliefs and seeking an authentic and deeply meaningful perspective is valuable. Providing guidance and support in this process, emphasizing it is an intimate journey of discovery and growth where critical thinking and insight serve as invaluable companions, intellectually engaged and personally significant. This approach ensures it is not passive or based on quaint tradition but is an active and thoughtful relationship with God. It empowers them to face the complexities of the modern world with a perspective resilient enough to withstand challenges and grow stronger through reasoned reflection and personal conviction.

Relational spirituality serves as a vital pillar in nurturing a holistic and meaningful Godly bond. A foundational aspect lies in its direct relationship with the Divine. Teaching the importance of cultivating a personal and intimate connection plays a pivotal role. This involves instilling the significance of prayer, worship, and spiritual discipline as a means of communicating with God. Understanding faith in the daily Christian routine is more than a casual set of beliefs and enactments; rather, it is a living relationship with a loving, caring, and gracious Creator.

Another facet of this construct involves family dynamics. Modeling loving and respectful family interactions and exemplifying Christian acts of compassion, forgiveness, and humility play an instrumental role in the cohesiveness of the father-son bond. By nurturing a harmonious and Christ-centered family environment, there is an impartation of the practical application of faith within this context. It becomes the connective substance, serving as a guiding influence throughout the interactions with family members, promoting unity and love, while also highlighting it is not an isolated pursuit but an integral part of their connection.

It integrates community engagement as a foundational element. Encouraging active participation in the community, whether at the local church or within a broader religious circle, assumes a critical role. Involvement in communal activities, collective gatherings, and altruistic endeavors provides an edifying experience of shared worship and service. Emphasizing participation transcends individual efforts, evolving as a collective journey among believers.

Through these interactions, a sense of interconnectedness and spiritual unity emerge in the father-son bond. When embracing a complimentary viewpoint, it becomes clear, service and compassion are central components; encouraging engagement in acts of hospitality, both within the familial and broader community contexts, facilitates a deeper understanding of the practical manifestation of Jesus' teachings on love and compassion.

Embedding a sense of responsibility for the comfort of others reinforces the concept of fatherhood in finding expression through actions, especially in the treatment of those in close proximity. Assuming roles as mentors and leaders in discipleship plays a valuable part in walking alongside their sons. The mentoring relationship emphasizes trust, confidence, and reliance as a mutual and evolving experience in creating an environment of open dialogue, essential to these relationships.

Promoting honest discussions regarding Scriptural doctrine builds an openness where spiritual freedom is expressed through questions, doubts, and experiences. Open conversation supports shared learning and deepens understanding, reinforcing the idea, complete confidence is not rigid but a dynamic and evolving relationship with others.

Incorporating this concept into the familial dynamics enriches this dimension of the bond, aiding in recognizing, it is not confined to rituals but permeates every aspect of life and relationships. Through these connected experiences, a deeply personal and interwoven bond emerges, embracing love, compassion, and community, reflecting the teachings and examples of Biblical virtues.

Preparation for crises within the domain of spiritual growth emerges as a valuable aspect of embracing fortitude. This readiness enables the confrontation of life's inevitable events with resilience and perseverance. Confronting adversity becomes a fundamental part of crisis preparedness, emphasizing the importance of cultivating a belief system capable of withstanding adversity.

Learning confidence is not confined to celebrating the good times; it also involves finding strength and hope in the face of hardship. Illustrating inspiring stories from Biblical patriarchs who faced adversity with untiring resolve provides tangible examples of how faith can serve as a source of resilience and courage. Demonstrating the application of Biblical concepts to real-life challenges helps their sons recognize the enduring relevance of trust in crisis situations. Resilience and reliance become integral to crisis

LESSONS FROM SCRIPTURE

preparedness; emphasizing such challenges is not a shield against hardships but a source of inner strength, enabling perseverance. Underlining the significance of seeking support from the Christian community in times of crisis becomes integral.

It is important for fathers to encourage their sons to seek reliance on the church, family, friends, and other established networks of care and assistance. Facing these upheavals alone is unnecessary; depending on the support and prayers of the community emerge as a vital aspect of preparedness. Establishing a foundation of trust as the overarching goal of crisis readiness can ensure a unique, authentic, and personal relationship with God while functioning as an anchor in turbulent times.

This foundation involves engaging in daily spiritual practices, understanding core beliefs, and committing to a consistent expression of conviction. It prepares fathers and their sons to navigate difficulties with resilient and sustained support. Integrating crisis readiness into the cultivation of spiritual growth equips them with the tools and mindset to confront life's difficulties with courage and resilience.

Reinforcing this notion is not confined to favorable moments but is a constant companion, providing guidance and strength. Even in the midst of calamity, they can lay hold onto their faith from a wellspring of hope and assurance, empowering them to navigate storms with grace and unwavering trust. Establishing a solid framework for spiritual understanding involves imparting doctrinal knowledge, building scriptural literacy, instilling moral values, teaching practical spirituality, encouraging critical thinking, emphasizing relational aspects of faith, and preparing individuals for life's challenges.

This comprehensive approach prepares them to understand faith and live it out authentically and meaningfully. It nurtures a meaningful and personal connection, guiding them in their Christian life and journey. This preparation enables them to embrace their commitment and live it out authentically and meaningfully in all aspects of life.

CHAPTER THREE

Transformative Approach

At the core of generational connections lies a timeless legacy transcending eras, a heritage of love and trust symbolized as a torch of wisdom brightening the way of common values. This torch prepares them with the knowledge to make informed decisions, avoid pitfalls, and overcome obstacles, serving as a constant source of guidance derived from insights and lessons. Most significantly, the legacy establishes a continual connection, transcending physical distance and time itself. In addition, the transmission encompasses not only faith and trust but also the wisdom derived from life experiences.

Through these teachings and values, there is a meaningful presence in the lives of successive generations, offering counsel, encouragement, and support, providing a sound and lasting bond between eras. Primarily, this legacy stands as a testament to the profound love given across successive generations. It showcases the immense affection guiding individuals to bestow the most invaluable gift within their possession: the gift of faith.

This act echoes through the ages, fortifying an unbreakable bond. Similar to a brightly lit path guiding those through rough and uncertain terrain, their legacy shines on the journey for successive heirs amid life's complexities. It operates as a beacon, directing them toward spiritual growth, moral integrity, and a purposeful relationship with common values, reminiscent of a lighthouse aiding navigation through stormy seas.

The lasting legacy serves as evidence of the influential power of father-son relationships, guiding them through life's journeys and linking them to the wisdom and love of preceding generations. When grounded in Biblical teachings, the impartation of moral values transcends rudimentary knowledge, involving the installation of statutes guiding actions and decisions in everyday life. This approach aligns with Christian ideology, that is, establishing a sense of what is right and just. A moral needle is provided within the legacy, playing a pivotal role in instilling a deep understanding of the ethical values underpinning trust and commitment. It goes beyond teaching right or wrong to help develop a strong foundational belief.

LESSONS FROM SCRIPTURE

This guides them in making ethical decisions and upholding their values even in the face of moral dilemmas, serving as an essential tool in navigating the complexities of life. Constructed upon the lasting pillars of faith, love, and hope, this legacy stands as an everlasting bridge, connecting across the expanse of time.

It represents a heritage of conviction and credence, functioning as a structure enabling travelers to overcome barriers and reach common destinations. Safeguarding continuity beyond the ages, the legacy unfolds as a transformative continuation spanning epochs. This bridge serves multiple roles: a bridge of trust, an illuminated path, a torch of wisdom, a perpetual connection, and, above all, a testament to eternal love. Its resilience ensures, wisdom and guidance persistently influence successive family links, acting as a pathway for shared teachings and values to seamlessly transmit into the next era.

In this way, the legacy becomes a timeless force, shaping the course of generations with enduring principles. During this upbringing, the practical application of Christian ethics is learned, including values such as honesty, integrity, compassion, forgiveness, and humility. These values are not abstract concepts but practical guidelines for how to treat others and conduct oneself in the world.

Equipped with a moral framework, one is informed in interactions, decisions, and responses to ethical breaches and injustice. A model of precepts is embodied, becoming a living example of moral virtue and demonstrating through actions and choices the values they impart. It reinforces the importance of living a life in alignment with Scriptural convictions. When witnessing firsthand the impact of these guidelines on character and relationships, it provides a powerful illustration of what it means to live out faith.

Developing an understanding of Christian standards accompanies the growth in the capacity to live them out authentically. This empowerment ensures carrying forward the legacy of moral beliefs into their own lives and continuing to pass it on to future generations. A gentle fluctuation of goodness is the ultimate outcome of imparting moral values within the legacy of faith. Guided by the ethical compass provided through their mentors, they become agents of positive social change. They carry with them the knowledge of ethical guidelines and the commitment to live by these values. This gentle wave in motion extends far beyond the mentoring relationship, influencing communities and society as a whole as individuals model the values bestowed upon them and contribute to a legacy of goodness.

Under the auspices of a Godly framework, mentors who provide grounded Biblical teaching impart moral values, offer an ethical framework, model virtue, empower ethical living, and create a gentle wave in motion of goodness in their lives and the broader community. This approach is more than just teaching morals; it is about shaping their sons into individuals who embody values in their actions and choices. It functions as a rectitude pointer, a virtuous architecture, an integrity scaffold, empowerment for ethical living, and a tidal effect of righteousness.

Certainly, this approach unfolds as an opportunity to provide guidance and fortify fathers and their sons with the tools essential for navigating the complexities of the modern world while adhering to their faith. It represents a proactive stance in addressing potential conflicts and moral dilemmas that may surface along their journey. Encounters with adversity become occasions for them to draw from the wellspring of wisdom and guidance inherent in foundational truths.

Engaging in meaningful discussions serves as a path in connecting the teachings encapsulated in timeless principles with the nuanced barriers posed by contemporary existence. By exploring the ways Biblical stories and ideas offer insight and guidance in navigating adversity, fathers empower their sons to draw strength, wisdom, and moral clarity.

This process enriches their understanding of the Scriptures and prepares them with the tools to face adversity with resilience and a strong commitment to their beliefs. In doing so, they empower each other to make informed and morally sound decisions, even when societal pressures may suggest otherwise. It is a reminder, Christian values are not just theoretical but practical guidelines for living a meaningful and virtuous life.

LESSONS FROM SCRIPTURE

Strength Anchored in Scripture

Engagement with the Scriptures together strengthens the bond and fosters a context where trust, respect, and open communication flourish. Through this transformative journey, a heightened connection is forged, nurturing an understanding of faith and enriching the relationship with spiritual depth and sustaining love. The influence of Biblical wisdom has the power to sustain the spiritual journey of relationships across generations. It is not solely about possessing knowledge of the words in the Bible; it involves living those words, embodying the teachings of Christ Jesus, and perpetuating them in one's own life.

It is the understanding, Biblical truth transcends mere knowledge; its transformative potential extends to relationships. Through active engagement with the teachings of the Scriptures, the internalization of embedded words, values, and principles occur. This transformation manifests in actions, choices, and interactions. For instance, embracing the commandment to *"Love your neighbor as yourself"* (Matthew 22:39), cultivates empathy and kindness, fortifying the bond between them.

Turning to the Scriptures for insights on moral dilemmas and personal growth creates a resource acting as a decision-making roadmap and a source of comfort in uncertain times. The Bible underscores resilience in adversity, exemplified in stories similar to the confrontation between David and Goliath (1 Samuel 17), showcasing courage and faith in daunting circumstances.

Fathers and their sons can draw inspiration from such accounts, learning to confront hurdles with faith and determination. This collective journey toward building resilience deepens their bond and instills confidence in each other's capabilities. The power of Biblical wisdom within these relationships lies in its transformative, guiding nature, contributing to the creation of a formidable legacy. It serves as a living guidebook for navigating complexities, cultivating resilience, and establishing a strong and continuous spiritual connection across generations.

Encouraging a reliance on the Scriptures and personal belief in the face of difficult choices is vital. Emphasizing the strength derived from unyielding conviction is part of this empowering process, preparing to

CHAPTER THREE

withstand hardships and yet influence change through living out faith with integrity and compassion. This transformative journey extends beyond the conventional roles of relationships; it forms a partnership where both explore spirituality, confront uncertainties, and celebrate revelations together. Here, one can find illustrative instances of navigating profound inquiries while delving into their Godly faith.

Essential questions within the realm of theology often arise, such as grappling with the existence of suffering in a world created by a loving God. To address this, passages from the Book of Job, specifically Job 1:20-22, or the Psalms, such as Psalms 23, may be explored. When searching these themes of suffering and drawing solace and wisdom from Biblical stories, these passages offer unique insight and comfort in times of questioning and adversity. Through these discussions, a discovery unfolds, faith grounded in the Word of God can provide both comfort and resilience, even in the face of misfortune.

Another vital aspect of their journey involves the exploration of morality and ethics. Examining intricate dilemmas presented in the Bible, such as Abraham's willingness to sacrifice Isaac, allows for deep conversations about the essence of morality, obedience to God's will, and ethical decision-making. These exchanges generate critical thinking and contribute to the development of a nuanced understanding of the way faith influences their moral bearing.

Within the contemporary societal landscape, the interplay of science and faith often manifests as an intricate conundrum. The appearance of a lack of harmony among scientific discoveries and Biblical truths tends to emerge as a focal point in this dynamic scenario. This necessity becomes increasingly apparent as societal dynamics evolve toward injurious moral dilemmas and convoluted images of identity.

In this evolving landscape, there is a pressing need to address adverse Scriptural diversity. Society contends with misnomered ethical technological complexities diverging from divine truths. The juxtaposition of scientific advancements and spiritual principles may create a tension requiring thoughtful consideration and understanding. As societal dynamics continue to unfold, navigating this cross-way becomes indispensable for maintaining

LESSONS FROM SCRIPTURE

a balanced perspective amid the complexities of contemporary life. Within this realm, inquiries often arise concerning Christianity's relationship with other faiths. The implications of pertinent passages take precedence, nurturing an environment of comprehension and reverence toward individuals embracing varied beliefs. It is crucial to recognize that the core of reconciliation with God lies in the sacrificial redemption offered through Christ Jesus, irrespective of the diverse perspectives and worldviews prevalent across humanity.

Delving into the intersection of Christianity with other faith traditions necessitates a commitment to dialogue and comprehension. Guided by relevant scriptures, this exploration underscores the significance of acknowledging and valuing the array of beliefs present. At its heart lies the unwavering truth that reconciliation with the Divine is deeply rooted in the sacrificial redemption provided by Jesus Christ our Lord.

Moreover, it is important to recognize that while Christianity maintains its distinctiveness, engaging in meaningful dialogue with adherents of other faiths is encouraged. Such interactions, grounded in respect and understanding, serve to enrich one's own faith journey while fostering mutual appreciation and cooperation amidst diversity. The interconnection of faith, truth, and reason, is encapsulated in Proverbs 25:2, *"It is the glory of God to conceal a matter; to search out a matter is the glory of kings,"* invites a reflective journey. This passage, rich with metaphorical depth, implies that the divine essence resides in concealed knowledge.

Exploring these hidden truths is akin to the majesty attributed to kings when unraveling mysteries, initiating a thoughtful exploration into the intricate tapestry of wisdom within the realms of faith and reason. The essence of this passage extends beyond the mere act of searching; it calls for the acknowledgment of the divine glory inherent in unraveling the intricacies of Biblical truth and scientific understanding. This summons initiates a contemplative journey, encouraging confidence in the knowledge and truth of Scriptural wisdom while concurrently delving into the concealed insights within the domains of both faith and reason.

CHAPTER THREE

This call prompts the recognition of an important connection between the pursuit of understanding and the acknowledgment of the Divine. It emphasizes the inherent glory in the exploration of both revealed and concealed aspects of truth. As one engages in the thoughtful unraveling of mysteries, there is an invitation to appreciate the majestic interplay between faith and reason, recognizing the pursuit of knowledge is not merely an intellectual endeavor but a journey infused with divine significance.

In Philippians 2:3-4, the call to embrace values of humility, compassion, and selflessness extend beyond these ethical imperatives; it acts as a transformative spiritual presence, constructing bridges in nurturing a fuller, more complete understanding across a diverse array of religious boundaries. As such, this is characterized by its inherent simplicity, advocating for virtuous conduct, and a fundamental shift in personal perspective: *"Do nothing out of selfish ambition or vain conceit. Rather, in humility, value others above yourselves, not looking to your own interests but each of you to the interests of others."* These inspired words encourage an embodiment of virtues within the confines of ethical obligations and radiate outward while connecting hearts and minds in an understanding surpassing the limitations imposed by religious differences.

The essence lies not just in practicing humility, compassion, and selflessness as ethical duties but in recognizing them as universal designs binding humanity together, transcending the boundaries and creating a divide. Thus, as Jesus said in John 8:12, *"I am the light of the world. Whoever follows me will not walk in darkness, but will have the light of life,"* He also declares in John 14:6, *"I am the way and the truth and the life. No one comes to the Father except through me."* This is a valuable reminder as Christians come into knowledge of the Scriptures and the mysteries they behold, the true guiding light in the navigation of life through the intricacies and intersections of faith held steady with a spirit of openness, empathy, and shared humanity within the body of Christ.

The wisdom encapsulated in Romans 1:20, unveils an embracing perspective on the relationship between faith, reason, and the natural world, declaring: *"For since the creation of the world, God's invisible qualities, his eternal power and divine nature, have been clearly seen, being understood from what has been made so that world is without excuse."* This revelation beckons all to engage in thoughtful contemplation, recognizing the magnificence of the created world as a manifestation of God's eternal power and divine nature. The interconnectedness of faith, reason, and the natural world is intricately woven into the fabric of this message, urging a harmonious understanding of these elements attesting to God's greatness. The call is not merely to acknowledge the natural world but to understand it as an inspired reflection of the Divine, inviting a personal connection between faith and reason. Its implications are clear; through the observation of the natural world, insights into the invisible qualities of God are revealed.

The practical application of this insight in the father-son connection of science and faith becomes evident as adherents navigate the complexities of the modern world. It encourages a balanced perspective where scientific inquiry and appreciation for the natural world coexist with unwavering Biblical truth. By acknowledging the Divine fingerprints on creation, scientific discoveries become additional windows into the eternal power and inspired nature revealed in Scripture.

This passage becomes a guiding light into the reconciliation of science and faith, emphasizing the study of creation as a means to deepen the understanding of God's attributes. This insight necessitates a harmonious relationship between reason, faith, and the observation of the created order, establishing a solid foundation for those to engage with the scientific realm without compromising their spiritual convictions.

Proverbs 14:15, as part of the exploration into the interplay between science and faith, highlights the essence of discernment. It communicates: *"The simple believe anything, but the prudent give thought to their steps."* This revelation urges a thoughtful approach in the face of the nuanced challenge where scientific discoveries may appear discordant with Biblical truths. It prompts navigating this intricate terrain with careful consideration; emphasizing simplistic acceptance may not be sufficient.

Instead, it encourages deliberate and contemplative engagement, guiding each to thoughtfully address the complexities inherent in reconciling scientific insights with Scriptural teachings. In this nuanced exchange, the encouragement of open discourse becomes pivotal. The examples provided illustrate the potential of engaging in meaningful discussions, jointly confronting challenging questions and uncertainties, using navigational tools to address the complexities, and cultivating an environment where prudence and wisdom guide the collective journey.

Building Deep Understanding

Nurturing a comprehensive understanding within the academic contexts anchored in faith assumes a valuable role, signifying a unique evolution in the dynamics of their father-son relationship. The focus extends beyond the conveyance of Biblical doctrines or ideologies as factual information for rote memorization; instead, it centers on substantive discussions, enhancing understanding of faith at an increased level. This transparent exchange serves as a path across generations, facilitating the sharing of personal experiences, beliefs, and uncertainties while encouraging reciprocal engagement.

Within these dialogues, opportunities emerge for fathers and their sons to pose questions, express uncertainties, and seek enlightenment on matters in the hidden wonders of the Word. This atmosphere of openness nurtures a collaborative learning process where insights from life experiences and wisdom are drawn, gaining fresh perspectives from a newer and distinctive worldview. It offers an exchange of ideas and experiences proving instrumental in influencing an authentic and personal connection to their spiritual beliefs.

Elevating the discourse beyond basic memorization becomes imperative as it encourages critical thinking and prompts a broader understanding. Rote memorization may enable the recitation of religious texts or ideas, but it often falls short of instilling a genuine understanding of their meaning and significance. True comprehension emerges through contemplation of the myriad questions posed, reflection on its applicability to daily life, and active engagement with the tenets and values it encapsulates. By encouraging exploration and questioning, one can not only cultivate a deeper connection but also empower oneself to have a personal and relevant faith. It involves nurturing a relationship, transcending tradition, and evolving into a personal and transformative experience.

LESSONS FROM SCRIPTURE

Thus, faith-grounded instruction within these relationships is the essence of meaningful discussions. The exchanges embody a dynamic and reciprocal transfer of thoughts, beliefs, and experiences, providing fertile ground for the growth of understanding. In this realm, insightful articulations transcend one-sided lectures, offering opportunities for a convergence of perspectives, questions, and a collective journey. Such conversations instill a sense of collaboration and respect, reinforcing the idea of a mutual experience within the family.

The intergenerational nature of these dialogues enhances their richness, with each contributing life experiences, wisdom, and insights and bringing forth unique perspectives and questions reflective of the evolving world around them. This mutual influence allows for comprehensive insight, encompassing the revisitation of traditional beliefs and addressing contemporary challenges. Importantly, these conversations extend beyond the boundaries of Biblical texts and citations, peering into broader aspects of life, morality, and spirituality. Those involved in the discourse can explore how their faith influences decisions, relationships, and responses to life's challenges, engaging in conversations around ethical dilemmas, sharing personal anecdotes of spiritual growth, and providing mutual emotional support during moments of doubt.

Through these meaningful discussions, the opportunity arises to nurture a safe and open space where thoughts can be expressed, challenging questions posed, and guidance sought. In these dialogic moments, connections form and cognitive correlations blossom. During such times, faith bears witness to the truth, as it is intricately woven into the fabric of life. The insights gained into Scriptural beliefs and Godly experiences solidify the bond between those engaged in the discourse.

Ultimately, these conversations play a connective role in molding the development of a more intimate and personal embrace of their spiritual beliefs. This serves as a catalyst for critical thinking, self-reflection, and spiritual growth. As such, meaningful exchanges are not simply conduits for imparting knowledge; rather, they serve as pathways to wisdom, empathy, and a greater understanding of the role their personal conviction plays in shaping lives.

CHAPTER THREE

Encouraging questions within the context of faith-based instruction is foundational for cultivating a rich and dynamic learning experience within the father-son bond. Rather than avoiding inquiries, questions are actively welcomed and embraced as opportunities for exploration, discovery, and the deepening of understanding. Acting as powerful tools for engaging with complex Biblical concepts, clarifying doubts, and seeking direction on matters of spirituality and Scriptural understanding, questions serve as gateways to knowledge.

Creating an environment where raising inquiries feels safe and respected is valuable to encouraging questions. Recognizing inquiries indicates a genuine interest in understanding; addressing these queries can lead to meaningful conversations and spiritual growth. Dialogues can take various forms, from straightforward theological questions to nuanced colloquiums about the application of insights in daily life. It creates an environment where all are free and encouraged to delve into the depths of their spirituality, navigating the intricate landscape of their beliefs and values.

This involves searching through theological concepts, engaging with sacred texts, and pondering the mysteries and complexities of the Scriptures. The process is not linear or one-size-fits-all; rather, it is deeply personal and can take on various forms. Those engaged may struggle with challenging moral dilemmas, seek to understand how their faith informs ethical choices, or wrestle with philosophical questions about the nature of God, the existence of evil, or the purpose of life.

Through this process of exploration, a more intimate connection to God and the messages of salvation and redemption develop, understanding faith as a dynamic and evolving aspect of their identity. The role of fatherly mentors is to guide and support through this process, providing a safe space to voice questions and uncertainties and offering insights and perspectives gained from their own experiences.

The mentors' willingness to engage in these discussions with humility and openness sets a powerful example. This connection strengthens the bond, becoming a shared spiritual quest. It is not just about passing down a set of beliefs but about embarking on a path of discovery together, sharing the joys and struggles. Therefore, encouraging the process within this

LESSONS FROM SCRIPTURE

relationship is an integral aspect of instruction grounded in the Word, nurturing spiritual growth, and helping to develop a deeply rooted and authentically lived experience. It is a journey of self-discovery and spiritual enlightenment, and fathers have the privilege of guiding their sons along this transformative path.

Spiritual Connections

The ultimate aim of faith-based instruction within the father-son relationship is to nurture a genuine connection through salvation, redemption, and a personal relationship with God through Jesus Christ. This connection transcends mere adherence to religious practices or traditions; instead, it symbolizes an inner journey of encouragement to authentically embrace the Christian faith with conviction. Thorough exploration, meaningful discussions, and questioning are integral aspects of this path, contributing to spiritual development.

This faith evolves from an unquestioning inheritance to a personal journey of discovery and understanding through the Scriptures, guided by the Holy Spirit, and grounded in their own convictions and insights. The personal connection to the Divine goes beyond ritualistic practices or mere church attendance; it transforms into a guiding principle informing every aspect of life.

Instead of compartmentalizing this experience, it shapes decisions, molds values, and influences interactions with others. The development of a personal connection to God, nurtures a sense of ownership and authenticity. Those who actively engage with their faith, making it uniquely their own, discover a significant sense of fulfillment and purpose in their spiritual lives. Playing a vital role in this process involves creating an environment encouraging exploration, welcoming inquiries, and meaningful discussions. Their spiritual guidance is not about dictating belief but providing wisdom, support, and a loving presence on the journey of faith.

As living examples of an intimate connection, fathers model a life of genuine belief. By exemplifying their Christian commitment in decisions, relationships, and actions, they inspire others to forge their own authentic, Godly spiritual path. The development of a genuine and personal divine

CHAPTER THREE

connection represents the culmination of instruction grounded in Biblical truth. It signifies a spiritual identity is deeply meaningful and genuinely lived. This transformative journey is one, each has the privilege of traveling, ultimately strengthening the bond within relationships.

Teaching rooted in Biblical precepts involves a journey aimed at cultivating a clear understanding of Godly principles. Meaningful conversations take center stage, creating an environment of genuine and personal connections to spiritual understanding. This approach transcends rote learning, inviting a more personal engagement with Scriptural tenets and encouraging not only the possession of knowledge but the true comprehension and embrace of it.

Dynamic conversations in the father-son alliance replace one-sided lectures, creating an atmosphere where generations within the family can freely share thoughts, questions, and insights. Such exchanges provide fertile ground for the growth of understanding, enabling both to learn from each other's perspectives. The important role of fatherhood becomes a keystone in navigating intricate theological concepts and ethical dilemmas while crafting a spirit of inquiry and exploration.

In addition, promoting questions plays a vital role in influencing understanding. Encouragement, rather than mere acceptance, empowers them to burrow into their faith, wrestle with intricate spiritual concepts, and actively seek answers. It is through this exchange, fathers serve as guides, mentors, and teachers within an intellectual and spiritual odyssey, offering considerate and insightful responses igniting further Biblical explorations.

The concept of freely exploring Biblical views holds paramount importance for spiritual development, allowing freedom to navigate theological intricacies, confront complex moral dilemmas, and seek spiritual truths. This exploration transcends prescribed teachings, extending to personal introspection and self-discovery. It allows them to forge a connection with Scriptural beliefs, strengthen their faith, enhance a sense of spiritual identity, and develop a closer relationship with their earthly father and God.

LESSONS FROM SCRIPTURE

Living Out Faith Together

Shared engagement in Biblical practices, encompassing prayer, worship, and acts of service, serves as a foundational element in strengthening their connections within the father-son connection. This collaborative journey fashions growth and deepens relationships, underscoring the communal nature of their conviction. Prayer, in particular, transcends religious ritual, evolving into an immensely intimate and personal experience. In these moments, both can openly share hopes, fears, and gratitude with God, cultivating vulnerability in each other's presence. This vulnerability strengthens emotional bonds, teaching faith as a collective pursuit where family support and love are fundamental.

Praying together becomes a powerful model for approaching God with reverence, humility, and sincerity. Witnessing genuine conversations with the Divine instills not only words but also the authenticity and depth of meaningful communion. These common experiences provide insight into the Heavenly world, enabling valuable guidance and support. Communal worship aligns hearts and minds with Scriptural teachings, nurturing a sense of belonging within the larger faith community. Private worship encourages personal and reflective expressions, sparking deeper discussions about its meaning and significance. This unity in worship creates lasting memories and strengthens their spiritual connections.

Engaging in these practices of compassion, kindness, and generosity become a tangible expression of beliefs and values. These actions go beyond mere deeds, actively demonstrating commitment to living out faith in practical ways. Volunteering together provides a visible testament to principles of empathy and altruism, encouraging a continued devotion to service.

Opportunities for meaningful conversations on the virtue of selflessness arise, deepening understanding of underlying values and inspiring a sense of purpose. These selfless acts become a living embodiment of shared beliefs. Through them, they are impacting their community, strengthening their Godly connections, and cultivating a sense of purpose deeply rooted in faith. This loyalty to service leaves a lasting legacy of love, compassion, and resolution within their relationship.

CHAPTER THREE

The role of fathers in guiding spiritual growth through common Biblical practices holds deep significance. As mentors and exemplars, their active engagement in prayer, worship, and acts of community service molds the trajectory of their sons' spiritual journey. Observing their fathers seek guidance, find solace, and express gratitude through prayer inspires the development of an authentic and heartfelt relationship. Prayer experienced collectively transforms into an instructive spiritual force with sincerity and devotion serving as a guiding illustration, establishing a personal connection with God.

The depth of prayer as a means of communication extending beyond common ritual is emphasized. Recognizing the potency of prayer during crises becomes crucial for preparedness. It goes beyond a simple temporal ritual; teaching prayer transcends into a source of solace, guidance, and strength gains significance. Sharing personal experiences of prayer, providing comfort and clarity during difficult moments, offers practical insights into navigating the complexities of life. Through active participation in common religious practices, fathers not only embody living examples of Christian values but also engage in experiential learning, which nurtures and strengthens their bond. This walk of faith, inspired and guided by their actions and devotion, transforms into a lasting legacy of love, seamlessly carried forward into their own lives and thoughtfully passed on to future generations.

As fellow believers, they walk together on a path illuminated by the Holy Spirit. They form a unique connection, weaving through the highs and lows of their growth in spiritual maturity. This navigation adds depth to their relationship, forming a sense of camaraderie and mutual support. The collective experience becomes a powerful testament to their communal nature, creating ties with a larger spiritual family throughout history. During this togetherness, their connection deepens, promoting spiritual growth and leaving a legacy transcending time. Their Christian faith emerges as a powerful force, shaping the dynamics within familial relationships. It serves as a homing device, drawing paths of nurture, instruction, and bond strengthening towards itself. Within the realm of Biblical faith, wisdom, values, and principles become the aiming forces, shaping responsibilities and connections.

LESSONS FROM SCRIPTURE

Scripture plays a multifaceted role, providing a foundation for leadership, a framework for moral and ethical guidance, and a well of inspiration amid the complexities of familial bonds. Operating as a moral guide, it becomes instrumental in steering fatherly roles, offering a foundation of values and tenets for ethical decision-making. Amidst a world marked by shifting moral landscapes, Godly values provide an unchanging set of principles for navigating diverse situations, ensuring moral guidance remains steadfast.

The role of these values as an ethical way-finder extends beyond stability, offering consistent standards for virtuous behavior. Rooted in Biblical beliefs, these principles become a timeless guide, crucial for navigating diverse situations. They serve as a fountain of wisdom and guidance during encounters with intricate moral dilemmas in parenting. Turning to this foundation, they find answers aligning with core values, facilitating ethical decision-making.

In the transmission of ethical codes rooted in faith, proponents lay the groundwork for robust moral foundations. Instilling practical virtues such as honesty, kindness, compassion, empathy, and integrity, advocates provide guiding principles for decision-making. Biblical values, functioning as a moral directive, equip adherents with tools and principles vital for navigating complexities while fostering a strong sense of morality. These transmitted values align with such beliefs, emphasizing virtues from teachings such as love, empathy, forgiveness, and humility.

Within the Christian framework, love expands beyond casual affection, embodying selflessness and sacrificial attributes reflective of divine love. They convey the impact of love in relationships, building trust and genuine affection. Compassion, as exemplified by revered religious patriarchs, entails empathy and a dedicated commitment to alleviating the suffering of others, instilling a sense of responsibility toward the less fortunate. The virtue of forgiveness, pivotal in Biblical teachings, imparts the liberating power of pardoning wrongs, contributing to personal healing and reconciliation. Anchoring values in these beliefs cultivates sustaining connections and prepares individuals for lives guided by faith, love, and ethical living.

These virtues, firmly grounded in teaching, function as a moral compass, directing interactions and life pursuits. Faith takes on tangible expressions in daily life, moving beyond abstraction. Embodying Scriptural principles through action provides a powerful example for observation and emulation. Love is expressed through affection and kindness, while compassionate actions, such as aiding those in need, underscore empathy and selflessness. Integrity, a core principle, manifests through honesty, transparency, and commitment to ethical behavior, teaching the value of truthfulness and reliability.

—— Moving Forward ——

Chapter 3, titled *"Lessons from Scripture,"* opened with a contemplation of the sacred pages within the Bible, emphasizing the diverse role fathers played in their sons' lives. Colossians 3:21, served as a foundational principle, highlighting the indispensable aspect of responsible guidance and discipline in fatherhood. The exploration extended to the practical application of this teaching in everyday scenarios, highlighting the broader role of fathers as providers and spiritual guides.

These insights culminated in a focus on imparting wisdom, transcending practical knowledge to inquire into the heartfelt teachings of Biblical faith. The chapter underscored the holistic nature of fatherhood, weaving together the threads of guidance, discipline, and Scriptural mentorship. It illuminated the significance of fathers as more than figures of authority, emphasizing their pivotal role in shaping the practical aspects of their sons' lives along with influencing their growth and understanding.

In *"Nurturing Spiritual Growth,"* fathers were implored to recognize their Biblical role as mentors, kindling their sons' faith while imparting profound insights into the abiding principles outlined in 2 Timothy 3:14-15. The review of humility, derived from the life and teachings of Christ Jesus, unfolded within the intricate dynamics of the father-son bond. The encouragement of critical thinking emerged as a catalyst, building a deep connection with the inspired texts, along with the promotion of respectful exchange. The transformative approach of passing along a legacy of love and faith through the ages was accentuated, underpinning the anchoring of formative strength in the ancient scrolls along with the deliberate nurturing

LESSONS FROM SCRIPTURE

of spiritual growth. This emphasized the intentional act of instilling faith as a robust foundation, ensuring the legacy of love, trust, and belief became an everlasting beacon guiding successive lineages on their Christian walk.

Turning the page to Chapter 4, "*A Father's Legacy,*" the narrative peers even deeper into the ageless and prolonged birthright fathers leave for their cherished sons. It is an odyssey and invitation into the impact of imparting wisdom and love to the next generation, drawing inspiration from the classic examples set by the Biblical passages. It reinforces the compelling role of contemporary mentorship in molding positive legacies resonating through the corridors of time and enriching lives. Chapter 4 promises to be a poignant continuation of the journey of faith, love, and the eternal bonds between fathers and their sons.

CHAPTER FOUR

A Father's Legacy

The revealing significance of leaving behind a lasting legacy tilts forward and continues to navigate the importance of passing on wisdom and love to subsequent generations. This legacy gathers its inspiration and movement from the timeless examples set by the Biblical stories. Serving as a spirituous reminder, the transmission finds its role in shaping familial legacies reverberating through the annals of time. Guided by the inspired insights found in the Scriptures, the traversed path unveils the essence of the father-son connection, uncovering layers of responsibility, love, and the immense impact echoing within their bond.

Recognizing these legacies extend far beyond the immediate bequeaths, it emphasizes the importance of present-day actions. Relationships are nurtured with values of love, trust, and wisdom, acknowledging their life-changing influence of the preceding procreations.

Throughout this passage, the focus remains on fatherly guidance through Scriptural instruction, as further highlighted in Deuteronomy 6:6-9, *"These commandments that I give you today are to be on your hearts. Impress them on your children. Talk about them when you sit at home, when you walk along the road, when you lie down, and when you get up. Tie them as symbols on your hands and bind them on your foreheads. Write them on the door frames of your houses and on your gates,"* emphasizing the importance of God's commands residing in the hearts of those who guide the way for their families.

This serves as an everlasting axiom, bringing to focus the Godly duty of passing down Biblical clarity, which strengthens and fortifies these legacies. It underscores the responsibility borne in forming the hearts, minds, and souls for generations.

In the exegesis of the text and within the application of the father-son relationship, this brief road map offers a useful path for consideration. First, the internalization of the verse: *"These commandments that I give you today are to be on your hearts."* The decree should be deeply ingrained in one's heart, indicating a personal commitment to live by them. Second, parental responsibility: *"Impress them on your children."* Fathers have the responsibility to impress these directives on their sons, signifying a duty to pass down spiritual values and teachings. Third, the instructions are meant to be a continual topic of conversation within the family, fostering an ongoing conversation about faith and values: *"Talk about them when you sit at home and when you walk along the road, when you lie down and when you get up."*

Fourth, everyday application: *"Tie them as symbols on your hands and bind them on your foreheads."* Discussions about these commandments should occur in various life situations, whether at home, on the road, during bedtime, and upon waking up, demonstrating the relevance of faith in all aspects of life. Fifth, informal setting: *"Write them on the door frames of your houses and on your gates."* The setting for these discussions is not limited to formal or structured environments, emphasizing the importance of casual, everyday conversations about spiritual matters.

Keep in mind, this discourse moves beyond verbal instruction, promoting interactive learning through meaningful dialogue, probing questions, and active engagement. When embracing these fundamental precepts, the familial bond transforms into a living testament, embodying the abiding strength derived from faith and beliefs.

Divine Commandment

Derived from the wisdom enshrined in the Book of Deuteronomy, precious insights emerge for the guidance of subsequent generations. One notable lesson surfaces, accentuating the imperative of diligently embedding spiritual teachings within the core of family connections. This heightens the significance of cultivating a boundless and straightforward connection to timeless tenets within the familial rondure. Furthermore, the notion conveyed in Psalm 78:4, *"We will not hide them from their descendants; we will tell the next generation the praiseworthy deeds of the Lord, his power, and the*

A FATHER'S LEGACY

wonders he has done," emphasizes the transmission of a family legacy and resonates strongly. The encouragement lies in the act of sharing the intricate array of collective experiences, which serves as a reservoir of guidance for the forthcoming descendants.

The essence of Deuteronomy's message echoes in the metaphorical act of *"passing the torch,"* articulated in 2 Timothy 2:2, *"And the things you have heard me say in the presence of many witnesses entrust to reliable people who will also be qualified to teach others."* The passage signifies a statutory responsibility to impart wisdom and knowledge, stimulating an unbroken chain of spiritual heritage. This process ensures the perpetual radiance of the flame of faith and righteousness across successive epochs. The directives gleaned transcend father-son partnerships, mandating intentional custodianship of spiritual and moral principles for the benefit of subsequent generations. These instructions represent guiding theories and authoritative insights, conveying a sense of obligation and direction.

The faithful transmission of a legacy becomes central in forming collective character and convictions, furthering a timeless bond spanning through the continuum of time. The calling is clear: adhere to these foundational principles, offer guidance into moral behavior and conduct, make prudent choices, and contribute to the continuity of faith and righteousness. This method of passing on the directives ensures perpetual illumination in the flame of faith and nobleness across successive eons, creating a legacy resolute through the ages.

This route begins by considering the significance of embedding God's commands within the hearts of those entrusted with guiding their families. The timeless wisdom abridged in these tenets hold deep-seated meaning by sifting through the focus on the intricacies and insights within the Scriptures, linking them to the overarching thematic approach. Fundamentally, the passage underscores the essential role mentors play in leading as spiritual educators.

The emphasis is on internalizing God's commands and allowing them to take root, symbolizing a step beyond the passive absorption of religious teachings towards a deliberate and active embrace of Biblical insight. A call to embody these instructions allows faith to mold character and actions, forming the basis upon which robust relationships are constructed. This necessitates a persistent commitment to personal spiritual growth, engaged continually with trust and belief to comprehend and internalize its virtuous standards. Through this internalization, faith is genuinely communicated, reaching a connection deeply rooted in common beliefs.

Reflecting on the ramifications, this legacy is passed down, serving as models and spiritual mentors. When embodying these principles, there is a palpable demonstration of faith in motion. Observing commitment to God's commands happens not only in words but in deeds, fostering a genuine sense of reverence and appreciation, as observed.

First, the call to diligently impart wisdom suggests a continuous and intentional process of instruction. Engaging in frank and meaningful dialogue involves providing not only the letter of the law but the spirit behind it. Through these exchanges, there is a comprehensive understanding of faith and its relevance to living the Christian example.

Second, in building robust connections, this commandment promotes candid exchange, trust, and mutual respect. Mentors then have the opportunity to offer guidance in navigating life's moral and spiritual intricacies. Third, in turn, one learns to rely on their father as a trusted source of knowledge, wisdom, and guidance. The inspired enlightenment embedded speaks to a timeless bond, emphasizing its extension beyond familial ties to a unique spiritual connection.

Last, by embracing their obligation as spiritual instructors, fathers, who are the mentors and leaders of the family, carry tremendous weight in their guiding capacities, wielding the influence to shape an understanding of faith, character, and spiritual belief. Accepting this legacy with receptivity and an open heart transforms it from a set of fundamental rules into a lasting connection with those who lead by their faith, embodying a robust relationship firmly rooted in divine guidance.

Legacies Through Divine Teaching

The mentorship directive transcends conventional rule-setting, anchoring itself as the foundation upon which the spiritual inheritance bestowed by fathers upon their sons is constructed. It traverses a perfunctory list of prescribed actions and restrictions, establishing a spiritual basis and molding the inner refuge of an individual's identity and values.

This Scriptural directive serves as the nucleus upon which the entire legacy is built, carrying the weight of generations to come. In this pivotal moment, fathers transcend the role of basic instructors, transforming into living vessels of God's teachings. Their lives become a reflection of Biblical truths, tangibly expressed through actions. Through a sustaining commitment to the fundamental precepts, they illuminate the practical application of faith, making it tangible and relatable in the daily walk of life.

The core ideals, drawn from these passages, become the compass, guiding actions and decisions in relationship-building and problem-solving processes. This dynamic interplay between mentorship, lived faith, and adherence to guiding tenets forms a cohesive narrative, illustrating the enduring legacy built on the solid foundation of spiritual values.

Together, the elements create a seamless continuum, a timeless bond resonating across generations, serving as a guiding light in the intricate journey of their family spiritual heritage. The emphasis lies in entrusting stewards with Heavenly wisdom, moving beyond conventional transmission of knowledge to seamlessly embody divine teachings in life. Lives transform into living testaments to values intended for inheritance, becoming a reflection of the sacred commands they carry. A guiding role emerges, shedding light on the path toward a life centered on Christian living and the moving essence of the Divine.

This embodiment instills authenticity into relationship dynamics, urging an alignment of beliefs with actions and ensuring a seamless fusion of faith in every aspect of existence. The privilege evolves into a solemn responsibility, connecting to the spiritual birthright of the past and empowering the continuity of this inheritance into the future. For the guiding tenet, it serves as a gateway to a loving legacy of faith, recognizing the spiritual heritage transmitted through generations. It transcends the simple conveyance of information, nurturing a deep connection with a vibrant and living faith. Witnessing a dedication to beliefs, steady adherence to divine commands, and the embodiment of values such as love, justice, and mercy leave a lasting imprint, shaping character and molding values. Within the context of legacy construction, this foundational aspect transforms architects of character, laying the groundwork for a moral directive and instilling guidelines to forward life choices and interactions.

Furthermore, this transformative process, inspired and guided by the Spirit of God as exemplified in ancient truths, finds resonance in the Biblical texts. Just as the Scriptures reveal in Proverbs 20:27, *"The spirit of man is the lamp of the Lord, searching all his innermost parts,"* suggesting fathers are bestowed with divine illumination. The Spirit becomes the guiding force, navigating the intricate terrain of familial mentorship. The Scriptural support extends to Galatians 5:22-23, where the fruits of the Spirit are outlined: *"love, joy, peace, forbearance, kindness, goodness, faithfulness, gentleness, and self-control."* The Spirit works to cultivate these virtues, building emotional connections and enriching the sense of continuity within the family.

Drawing on the promise in John 14:26, *"But the Helper, whom the Father will send in my name, he will teach you all things and bring to your remembrance all that I have said to you."* The Spirit becomes the unseen hand, forming a spiritual odyssey across generations. Inheritors, then, receive not just convictions but witness firsthand the manifestation of the Spirit's guidance, strengthening their connection to a legacy diligently cultivated under the influence of a Godly path.

Going beyond factual transfers, passing this inspired gift evolves into an art form, intentionally imparting life lessons, ethical principles, and spiritual guidance. Assuming the role of mentors, fathers meticulously shape and convey essential aspects of life to their sons.

The intentional process of this inspired insight draws upon personal life experiences, encompassing successes, failures, and challenges. Distilling valuable insights becomes a guide through life's complexities. It is the utilization of Biblical wisdom emphasizing the significance of God's commands as guiding tenets. This practical application connects historical instructional wisdom to contemporary life, highlighting its relevance for ethical decision-making and virtuous living. Prioritizing values then takes precedence, portraying these commands as a calling for building purposeful, meaningful, and integral lives.

The important behest of wisdom transfer is portrayed as a continual practice fortifying the bond between generations. Fathers are perceived as reservoirs of wisdom, unwavering fountains of guidance, persisting throughout life's journey. Embracing Biblical wisdom becomes an act of humility and respect, acknowledging the rich insights acquired through years of experience. This practice goes beyond conveying knowledge; it instills values, nurtures understanding, and forges robust relationships. With the privilege of imparting Scriptural instruction, they ensure the seamless continuity of a familial legacy rooted in ageless insights and irreplaceable love, transcending the boundaries of time and resonating through generations.

—— Driving Lessons of Love in Teaching ——

The foundational role in the creation of family legacies, inspired by the wisdom in Deuteronomy, aligns seamlessly, emphasizing the connection between mentorship, spiritual guidance, and the assembly of a lasting endowment. In exploring the concept, the guiding influence is not simply a sentiment but a vigorous factor propelling meaningful action. Embodying such influence naturally inclines one to express it through acts of compassion, understanding, and guidance, particularly within the context of imparting divine commands.

This guiding element becomes the driving force behind the lessons shared, emphasizing the essential nature of reciprocity. The experience of this influence is more likely to meet on common ground, deepening the bond and forming the essence upon which trust, respect, and meaningful relationships are constructed. Within its confines, affection takes on a transcendent quality, evolving from an abstract concept into a tangible reality. Divine directives extend past fundamental notions, encapsulating both instruction and compassion. This foundational element steers individuals toward a purposeful, integral, and passion driven life.

CHAPTER FOUR

Expressions of benevolence, empathy, and understanding foster an environment where all feel valued, nurturing open and meaningful communication.

Within this context, inquiries are embraced, uncertainties are addressed, and discussions yield fruit. Through these dynamic interactions, the teachings come to life, searching for the spiritual and moral dimensions inherent in these commands. Deeds of goodwill and compassion leave a lasting impression on many hearts and minds. The recollection of love and guidance reverberates long beyond those moments, transforming this into an enduring gift continuing to mold the essence of relationships and the trajectories of generations.

The lesson is clear: kindness surpasses emotion; it is a dynamic spirit shaping destinies. The expression of compassion and guidance extends well beyond its origin, emerging as a wellspring of inspiration for the ongoing journey. It carries forward not only wisdom but also faith. When influencing the essence of a legacy, love manifests its impact through the transmission of moral beliefs. Cultivating relationships steeped in this affection concurrently imbues the moral compass, ethics, and principles into the fabric of their connections. These ingrained values seamlessly integrate into the very makeup of one's identity, guiding decisions, actions, and character over a lifetime. The emotional bonds forged then build a sense of belonging and continuity within the family.

Over time, those who have experienced such interactions carry the torch of emotional security into adulthood and fatherhood, influencing those they touch. The impact of this influence on the legacy extends far beyond familial boundaries, weaving into the broader inter-workings of community and society as a whole.

Nurtured in an environment of such support, this becomes a natural inclination toward contributing positively to their Christian and social communities. The compassionate and empathetic contributors actively seek to make a difference, perpetuating the spirituality of these connections beyond their family confines. This embodies a legacy characterized by values, emotional bonds, and constructive contributions.

A FATHER'S LEGACY

Aware of the immeasurable impact their connections have on the family legacy, fathers recognize this role extends beyond the present, influencing the lives of the immediate generation and those of the future in meaningful ways. The abundant influence extends beyond the confines of the moment, setting in motion a resonating impact through time and sculpting a loving heritage. This essence becomes a key element, infusing it with qualities transcending generations and contributing to its lasting impact.

At the heart of this concept embodies a transformative presence. Cultivating a relationship centered on this meaningful conceptualization involves sowing the seeds of virtues, righteousness, and love, which successive family members then carry forward. These ingrained values become part of the family's inner workings, passed down from one generation to the next.

Within the framework, the formulation forms the foundation upon which values and ideals are constructed. It is a narrative of compassion, empathy, and kindness, defining the character of those who come after. This important influence extends beyond family boundaries into the broader Christian community and society.

Those raised in an environment imbued with such a spirit are naturally inclined to contribute positively, carrying with them the values of care and support. Their empathetic and responsible nature seeks to make a favorable impact on the lives of others, perpetuating the cycle of positive values and character traits. This is a legacy of merit, character, and an understanding extending far beyond the present, molding the lives of their sons, grandsons, and future generations.

It is a powerful reminder of the central role of father-son relationships, transcending surface emotions and highlighting the significant impact it has on every aspect of these connections, from day-to-day interactions to the lasting imprint left behind. As noted, it portrays the basis upon which strong and meaningful bonds are built, encompassing a treasury of qualities, including care, support, understanding, and unconditional acceptance.

CHAPTER FOUR

Love's Role in Legacy Building

The central role of love in constructing a lasting legacy is of paramount importance, constituting its very essence. When consistently expressed, it evolves into a guiding influence defining actions and decisions, extending beyond the present moment to influence the lives of descendants. Love molds their perception of family figures, the values they inherit, and how they navigate relationships and responsibilities. Transforming into a timeless thread weaving through the makeup of a family's history, love nurtures these lasting bonds, trust, and emotional well-being, carried forward through generations.

This crafted legacy is a cherished and personal gift, leaving an everlasting impression on the family lineage. It signifies love as a lasting and transformative spirit transcending time. This affection becomes the foundation upon which family values, bonds, and relationships are constructed, extending its influence far into the future and influencing the lives of descendants. Consistent expressions of care and support set a precedent for the way love should be experienced within the family. This demonstration of affection instills values such as compassion, empathy, and unconditional acceptance, which are carried forward in their lives and relationships. It forms the basis for robust family bonds, cultivating trust, fostering open communication, and nurturing physical, mental, and spiritual health.

The influence of this love extends beyond the immediate family, creating echoes through time and molding the character and values of future heirs. The legacy becomes a timeless and purposeful contribution, persistently impacting family dynamics, traditions, and the way future descendants approach their roles as fathers and sons. This contribution embodies a heritage marked by values, emotional connection, and personal family bonds transcending time, enriching the lives of successive eras.

The effects of building a lasting presence transcends the simplicity of an emotion; it emerges as an active and essential spirit, molding values, principles, and character. When consistently demonstrated in actions, words of love and guidance, each imparts an essence of compassion, empathy, and unconditional acceptance. This extends its reach to their own relationships as they carry forward the lessons of support and understanding. It initiates a momentum effect, building and extending lives for descendants. Essentially, it serves as the foundation for family bonds, influencing values, and making a lasting impression on their hearts and minds. This essence continues to enrich and fortify the family line.

Through their unrestricted care, fathers become impressionable teachers and mentors. This guidance, driven by profound affection, extends beyond emotions, imparting vital life lessons, instilling moral values, and igniting a sense of purpose. Leading with love demonstrates the significance of empathy, kindness, and resilience in navigating life's events. Leaving behind a legacy is not just a collection of memories but a wealth of wisdom and principles carried forward.

The instructions serve as the gateway for pointing in the direction of righteousness, empathy, and integrity while building respectful, responsible individuals. In this way, the impact transcends material possessions or worldly achievements; it reaches into hearts and minds, framing character and influencing choices. It forms a history resonating with values, morals, and purpose, establishing a family culture rooted in wisdom.

Love's Steadfast Commitment

Portraying faithfulness, loyalty, allegiance, and love as a persistent and sustained construct, it stands resolute in the face of provocations. This devotedness ensures the reliability of a stable and caring presence, embodying a promise of perseverance through life's twists and turns. When it emerges as a source of strength, trust, and security, the relentless commitment fortifies lifelong connections. Emphasizing such devotion forms the very nature of meaningful relationships, offering stability and assurance, regardless of circumstances. It is a consistent partnership positively contributing to emotional wellness and development, serving as a daily practice and defining lasting bonds.

Acknowledging the transcendence of this love goes beyond words; it is exemplified through actions and the daily choices prioritizing well-being and happiness. As evident in the consistent provision of guidance and support, this persistent loyalty forms a resilient bond. The depths of nurturing a robust relationship lie in the essence of dedication, extending beyond verbal expression to manifest in actions. It highlights an authentic alliance, not confined to verbal declarations but is integrated into the canvas of everyday life.

Actions materialize in the choices made on a daily basis, stemming from a sincere commitment. Through these focused behaviors, their decisions convey a sense of reliance and build a secure and nurturing environment where an important understanding and value are established. Upon reflection, it is acknowledged, the choice to love is an active, daily decision in order to prioritize peace and prosperity. This resilience is exemplified through deeds such as spending quality time, attending significant events, and building open conversation, which contribute to the formation of a secure bond, strengthening the relationship.

The concept of commitment as a lasting influence extending beyond passing emotions stands as a powerful perspective on fatherhood. It calls for embracing this influence as more than an ephemeral feeling, progressing into a firm and resolute dedication to care for and support the family, irrespective of circumstances. As one internalizes this truism, understanding of its constancy arises, independent of behavior or achievements. Their faithful dedication establishes a secure and nurturing foundation for the family bond, functioning as the source of stability and reassurance.

Illustrating this concept involves navigating challenges or disagreements and consistently providing instruction and support, which at times can be difficult, especially without withdrawing affection based on temporary conflicts. Consistent care conveys a powerful message of value and cherishment, regardless of obstacles encountered.

Encouraging reliability as a source of support cultivates a sense of trust in the father-son dynamic. Such a perspective emphasizes the sustaining nature of fatherly care and its transformative impact on their lives. The statutes become a driving impetus behind actions, transcending emotional fluctuations and ensuring faithfulness in the roles of supporter, advisor, and mentor.

Embracing this connection means being there through thick and thin, offering solid support during challenging times, and providing unshakable assistance in the face of difficulties. Its steady presence becomes a reliable pillar of strength, providing a sense of security and stability. This dedication extends to cherishing loved ones wholeheartedly and valuing them for who they are, with all their unique qualities and imperfections.

The message of love transcends worldly standards and expectations; it is a perpetual and constant presence empowered by the Spirit of God. Following the lead of Romans 12:2, which urges: *"Don't copy the behavior and customs of this world, but let God transform you into a new person by changing the way you think, then you will learn to know God's will for you, which is good, pleasing, and perfect."*

This love expressed aligns with God's good, pleasing, and perfect will. The transformative spirit fashions a depth going beyond societal norms, echoing the divine will in the connections and relationships within the world. It is an approach to establishing a resilient and lasting bond capable of weathering life's setbacks, nurturing growth, and ensuring well-being throughout a lifetime. Undoubtedly, embracing the message of love transcends the immediate moment. This extension goes beyond the specific father-son relationship, permeating time and influencing the broader structure of values, character, and connections within the family unit.

Central to this lasting extension are the values passed down through generations. The demonstration of love as a firm commitment becomes a model for essential values such as loyalty, perseverance, and resilience, ingrained in the family's cultural history. This consistent devotion significantly influences the dynamics of connections, values transcending generations, personal character, and interactions with the world. It stands as an enrichment, molding lives and resonating through those who follow in its path.

These lessons are learned from the experience undergone, serving as a valuable teacher, developing an understanding of the true meaning, and guiding the navigation of future relationships. Persistent displays of commitment send a powerful message of love. Teaching this involves being reliable, supportive, and dedicated to the goodness of others. Consequently, this enhances the likelihood of carrying forward these lessons into relationships, recognizing the significance of commitment, trust, and reliability in developing generational connections. This positive influence on values extends beyond specific bonds, impacting the broader dynamics of personal interactions within the Christian community.

Moreover, having experienced this devotion increases the likelihood of embodying and cultivating similar dedications. Acknowledging the impact of significant influences, there is a pursuit to replicate this essence in relationships, perpetuating a cycle of lasting and affectionate connections across time. Essentially, the exhibited commitments imprint a far-reaching understanding, leaving a heartfelt impression on future heirs, thereby establishing a legacy woven into the broader societal framework.

The impact, characterized by trust, transcends earthly emotions, providing a solid foundation stable in all human aspects, surpassing the Phileo love relationship. This emphasis is of divine origin in the legacy-building dimension, influencing current relationships and the values and connections passed down to subsequent generations within the Biblical context.

—— Shaping the Future Generation ——

In the vast expanse of existence, a weighty responsibility rests on the shoulders of those who build the narrative of generations to come. This solemn duty transcends the temporal and touches on the very essence of fashioning the ever-evolving trajectory of humanity. It acknowledges a deep responsibility entrusted to the architects of what is to come. The fountain of inspiration, a timeless source from which wisdom flows, draws from the essence of Biblical texts.

Without dwelling on the intricacies of specific verses, the essence of this entrusted role summarizes the spirit found in Deuteronomy. It acts not as a guide but rather casts a radiant glow on the sacred responsibility bestowed upon fathers, the custodians of the family heirs.

A FATHER'S LEGACY

The essence of this inspiration acts as the winds in a sail, guiding toward credos transcending the boundaries of time. Within this odyssey of influence and responsibility, fathers emerge as stewards, not only of immediate well-being but as designers of lasting development and character formation. The acknowledgment is akin to recognizing them as keepers of the very fabric weaving the intricate patterns of generations. As conservators, their influence extends beyond the realm of daily routines, resonating at the very core of character development and building a surviving legacy reverberating through the ages.

In the passage of abstract concepts, the emphasis shifts towards a more heavenly dance of responsibility and influence. This becomes a contemplation on the universal themes of fatherhood echoing through time, where responsibility transcends the confines of personal identity and the essence of wisdom is distilled from the collective genre of human experience. The perception of the far-reaching consequences gathers an understanding of the intricate web woven by a father's influence.

Beyond the immediate sphere of the family connection, this perception searches the depths within the interconnectedness of human relationships and societal dynamics. It is a recognition of the impact of one's values, choices, and principles extending beyond personal boundaries, resonating in the broader medley of existence.

This acumen emphasizes the intricate interplay of influence and the subtle yet potent threads connecting families, communities, and the collective consciousness. The collective consciousness embodies the reservoir of values, Godly constructs, and interconnected narratives uniting individuals in a web of common understanding, nurturing a sense of belonging and identity within the broader human experience.

In pursuing this intricate script, one contemplates its indirect contribution to forming the larger societal fabric. It involves an acknowledgment of the influence wielded is not restricted to a direct, observable transformation but rather manifests in the subtleties of human interaction, community dynamics, and the cultural ethos. The indirect contribution is akin to a gentle breeze carving the landscape over time, leaving an imprint on the shared beliefs without imposing a visible, immediate alteration. It focuses on the unique nature of influence, operating silently yet weaving its essence into the very fabric of societal evolution. Guided by the timeless wisdom of Deuteronomy, there emerges a directive to impart meaningful values transcending the confines of rigid rules.

This directive prompts contemplation on the nature of ideals and values going beyond common regulations and, thus, resonates with the deeper currents of human existence. It invites an exploration of values, similar to perennial streams flowing through the landscape of life, nourishing the roots of virtue, justice, compassion, and love. The Mosaian guidance beckons one to contemplate the essence of everlasting values, understanding them not as restrictive mandates but as guiding stars illuminating the path toward virtuous and harmonious living.

Highlighting the ever-evolving process prompts contemplation of the dynamic nature of the imprints left on the canvas of existence. This challenges the notion of legacy as a static entity and invites a shift in perspective toward a continuous, unfolding narrative. It suggests the family story is not bound to a singular moment or a defined set of values; instead, it is a fluid and evolving tale woven through the threads of time. This encourages a reevaluation of the conventional understanding, transcending the limitations of a linear progression and embracing the idea every interaction, every lesson, and every act of love contributes to the ongoing tale, shaping their heritage.

Within the concept of heritage-building, there emerges a unique recognition of the active role fathers play in crafting this narrative. It is an acknowledgment, in the transmission of values which is not a passive inheritance but a deliberate and intentional creation. Sculpting this ongoing portrait through interactions signifies a conscious engagement with the unfolding story of existence. Each interaction becomes a stroke on the canvas, contributing to the vibrant hues of the continuing tale. Lessons cease to be only scant instructions but transform into histories of wisdom inscribed in the chronicle. Love, in its varied expressions, becomes the foundation binding these chapters together, infusing the ongoing story with a timeless and loving essence.

A FATHER'S LEGACY

As the account of their birthright unfolds, there is an invitation to embrace future roles as fathers and mentors. This invitation is not a predetermined screenplay, but an open-ended curtain call to participate actively in the ongoing creation of the inheritance. It prompts contemplation on the contributions made in the larger scheme of human experience, recognizing the potential for each person to be a steward of values, an overseer of wisdom, and a shaper of the narrative extending beyond the personal boundaries inhibiting growth. Embracing these future responsibilities signifies a recognition of the interconnectedness of human stories, acknowledging the legacy framed today resonates in tales extending to tomorrow's pages.

The emphasis on the transformative potential of the fathers' sway reveals a meaningful understanding of the subtle yet powerful impact they can have on the fabric of human existence. This calls for a contemplation of influence as a catalyst for transformation. It suggests every nuance of instruction possesses the inherent ability to develop perspectives, instill virtues, and contribute to the ongoing evolution of the collective human consciousness within the Christian domain. In this light, these cooperatives become a dynamic movement from the Spirit, transcending the immediate and resonating across the vast expanse of generations.

As virtuosity is created, this contributes to a legacy transcending the boundaries of time, representing not just a collection of skills or talents but a state of moral and ethical excellence tested against the Word of God. It becomes an embodiment of the essence of wisdom, compassion, and justice, constituting the foundational pillars upon which the legacy stands. This process is an act of craftsmanship, where every intentional stroke adds layers of depth and resilience to the father-son bond. It is a recognition the legacy extends beyond the individual, becoming a testament to the collective pursuit of a higher moral ground echoing through the corridors of eons.

Therefore, sageness becomes a timeless gift passed down from one heir to the next. It is not a static accumulation but a dynamic reservoir of insights, lessons, and experiences. Even in the midst of this transmission, the responsibility to perpetuate the legacy becomes a sacred trust; acknowledging this keenness, perceptiveness, and insightfulness is not meant to be hoarded but shared, cultivated, and expanded upon. This inheritance carries with it a powerful responsibility to navigate the complexities of life with discernment and to contribute to the ongoing story of spiritual growth. It is an acknowledgment that the legacy is a living entity, sustained and enriched by the continuous flow of Biblical enlightenment.

Shapers of Character

The responsibility for character arc extends beyond traditional roles, emphasizing a wider societal impact. The essence lies in the intricate connection and the foundational principles developing personal growth. This recital transcends immediate relationships, portraying a dynamic interplay between molding and broader considerations. Unfolding as a testament to its influential role in sculpting virtues, the focus extends beyond the conventional understanding of ties, situating character-building as a universal societal contribution.

The alignment approach serves as a guiding principle, emphasizing collective responsibility for nurturing values beyond personal relationships. This broader perspective encourages a shift from a narrow focus on roles to a more expansive view of Christian growth. In the realm of character building, it reveals the interplay between personal responsibility and collective themes, emphasizing this character development extends beyond isolated instances and is connected with broader considerations. In this role of builders, they represent a virtuous society guided by overarching principles extending beyond relationships. This emphasizes the intricate connections between personal responsibility, thematic alignment, and the collective effort of nurturing virtues resonating across societal dimensions.

In the philosophical realm of personal design, the guidance emanating from Deuteronomy serves as an ageless well of wisdom. It transcends individuality, providing a conceptual framework for navigating the complexities of moral and ethical choices. The teachings encapsulated offer Biblical postulates illuminating the path toward virtuous living, surpassing simple prescriptive paradigms. This guidance, drawn from Scripture, transforms into a source of inspiration leading individuals through the landscapes of moral contemplation, emphasizing the universal relevance of these statutes. In addition, within functional growth, the power of modeling emerges as a transformative force. It transcends the limitations of direct instruction, manifesting as a congruent abstract with implications. Exampling becomes the salient language through which ideas are communicated, illustrating actions speak louder than words. This discourse on modeling highlights the intricate motion between influence and perception, emphasizing the impact of a virtuous model extending beyond the tangible realm, leaving a discreet impression on the hive mind of collective consciousness.

In learning, this encourages a shift from a narrow emphasis on parental relationships to gaining a broader understanding of influence. As learners, their sons engage in a process of observing, internalizing, and emulating the behavior modeled for them. The emphasis here is on the transfer of wisdom through actions, creating a dynamic interplay between the observed and the observer. This learning and emulation serves as a gateway to understanding the impact by example in character development, transcending personal relationships, and echoing across the broader canvas of societal values.

In the realm of self-development, the influence wielded by guidance and discipline is akin to a sculptor shaping clay into a masterpiece. This intricate process involves providing a moral K-rail, a solid steady guide, to aid in navigating the labyrinth of ethical discourse. Through judicious discipline administered with love and fairness, fathers craft a tool for imparting essential life lessons and instilling self-discipline in their sons. It is a harmonious influence between correction and instruction, building not just adherence to rules but the internalization of moral Biblical standards guiding ethical conduct.

In this loving narrative, fathers become architects of character, offering a moral architecture sculpting the ethical familial framework of Godly living. As this guidance continues, it becomes a consolidated legacy, fortified, and based on principled ideals transcending the living. This realization serves as a poignant reminder of the significant role fathers play in the personal development of their progeny. It is a beckoning call to embrace the lessons imparted and the ideologies ingrained, acknowledging the forthright impact of fatherly directives on the intricate substance of character formation. The echoes of fatherhood and its influence reverberate beyond the immediate, weaving a narrative of Godly living standing as a testament to the lasting impact on the father-son bond.

The lessons, absorbed through the subtle art of guidance and discipline, become the threads stitching a moral fabric throughout the relationship. The reminder embedded in this chronicle is an invitation, a call to recognize the valuable role in fashioning character and contributing to the endless narrative of ethical living. Within the portrayal of building character, the instilled essence transcends the immediate; it becomes an integral constituent of the legacy, akin to an enduring heavenly melody persisting through the notes of time.

Thus, its movement is not a haphazard compilation of deeds but rather a manifestation of the merits meticulously woven into the essence of their sons. This emphasis is a vital part of the familial legacy, bringing forth a thorough understanding: it extends beyond material possessions and worldly achievements; instead, it is an ethereal composition of integrity, values, and meaningful ethical statutes.

In the orchestration of legacy-building, the perpetuation of values and precepts serves as the resonating theme. The torchbearers of this heritage carry forward the harmonious cadence of righteousness instilled by their fathers. In this continuum, testimony becomes a living entity, pulsating with the values echoing through the passageway of time, an invitation to become stewards of not just a familial heritage but guardians of a delicate composition, a legacy enriching the human experience with timeless truths.

As fathers engage in the intentional act of influencing the legacy's character, they step into the role of a privileged designer. This entitlement lies not in material bequests but in the nuanced artistry of sculpting a history standing as a testament to trustworthy living. Their testament is not a static relic but a dynamic creation, an ever-evolving, crafted masterpiece for those who recognize the immense responsibility bestowed upon them. This privilege involves stewardship, not dominion, acknowledging the character infused into their heritage as a sacred trust, an everlasting flame eternally handed down.

Nurturing a Legacy of Virtue

In the intricate weaving of human influence, the role of guiding, mentoring, and instructing transcends fatherhood, taking on the essence of moral architecture. Within this abstract realm, the concept of fathers fashioning the character of those who follow them emerges as a nuanced interplay between instruction and a loving impact. It is a contemplation of the way individuals, positioned as designers of morality, mold the very fabric of virtue and principle, defining subsequent generations.

The responsibility bestowed upon these architects extends beyond the realm of leadership and into the foundational construction of honesty. This abstract responsibility involves not just imparting lessons but sculpting the very core of ethical existence. In this conceptual landscape, the notion of nobility serves as the elemental building blocks, carefully laid to withstand the perils ahead. These values, once instilled, echo through the hallways of generations, becoming an inseparable thread woven into the legacy of combined human history.

The continuing nature of righteousness becomes pivotal in understanding the intricate role between guidance and legacy. The virtues, similar to the elements reverberating through the seasons, contribute to the ongoing story of human character. They become integral fragments in the larger circuitry of a concerted Biblical understanding, perpetuating a familial legacy surpassing individual lifetimes.

In this conceptual framework, the influence of these moral designers extends far beyond the immediate, reaching into the vast expanse of the future, where integrity persists as an enduring monument in the landscape of humanity. The wisdom encapsulated transcends the mundane, evolving into luminous beacons on the path of righteousness. In the stretch of ancient wisdom, an intricate gyration unfolds, shedding light on the significance of rectitude within the domain of ethical considerations. This abstract exploration contemplates the intrinsic value bestowed upon virtues, likening them to celestial bodies steering the course of moral enlightenment.

CHAPTER FOUR

In the nuanced space of Biblical wisdom, an intricate communion unfolds, echoing the sentiments found in Daniel 12:3, which declares: *"Those who are wise will shine as bright as the sky, and those who lead many to righteousness will shine like the stars forever."* This metaphorical radiance, akin to celestial bodies guiding the trajectory of ethical enlightenment, finds resonance in Matthew 5:14-16, *"You are the light of the world, like a city on a hilltop that cannot be hidden. No one lights a lamp and then puts it under a basket. Instead, a lamp is placed on a stand where it gives light to everyone in the house. In the same way, let your good deeds shine out for all to see, so that everyone will praise your heavenly Father."* Here, believers are likened to the light of the world, a beacon on a hill, illuminating the path with their good deeds.

Furthermore, in James 3:17-18, *"But the wisdom from above is first of all pure. It is also peace-loving, gentle at all times, and willing to yield to others. It is full of mercy and the fruit of good deeds. It shows no favoritism and is always sincere. And those who are peacemakers will plant seeds of peace and reap a harvest of righteousness,"* contributes to this rich alignment of metaphors, portraying heavenly wisdom as pure and peace-loving, clustering a harvest of righteousness.

The conceptual landscape deepens as emphasis is placed on the living embodiment of values, transcending the limitations of verbal expression. This exploration navigates the idea of virtues, woven into the fabric of actions, becoming an immersive experience. It invites recognition, emphasizing the resonance of values is most evident when observed in the silent ballet of ethical conduct. The transformative power lies not in spoken discourse but in the seamless integration of morals into the rhythm of life, where they become an inseparable thread in the design of ethical existence.

Exploring the intricate fabric of moral and spiritual dimensions, one discovers a rich tapestry woven with timeless insights. It transcends the surface of individual experiences, inviting contemplation on universal principles influencing character and values. This search, devoid of the explicit mention of fathers and sons, becomes a journey into the gathered consciousness, where the essence of righteous living is a reservoir of knowledge.

A FATHER'S LEGACY

In emphasizing this postulate, the focus remains on the underlying and universal principles forming the foundation of Godly living, transcending individual efforts and familial relationships. It is a narrative extending beyond the slim confines of personal anecdotes and resonating with the broader human experience. Within this conceptualization, the joint contemplation of fathers and their sons becomes an integral part of the discourse. It is not simply about the relationship between specifics but rather a collective reflection on the moral and spiritual underpinnings of God's commands.

Stripped of personal narratives, the discourse navigates through the broad landscape of ethical considerations, transcending the boundaries of specific family ties. The focus shifts from themselves to the universal principles they grapple with, emphasizing responsibility in contemplating and embodying uprightness. This exploration serves as a powerful reminder regarding the meaningful influence of their predecessors on character and values. The emphasis here is on the lasting legacy, which extends beyond the immediate interactions.

By avoiding the explicit mention of individuals, the tale broadens its scope, portraying the intergenerational transmission of values as a continuum beyond the confines of familial connections. In this context, the quest for influence becomes a collective acknowledgment of the interconnectedness of the human journey in shaping the moral and spiritual landscape. The integration of Godly values into a legacy highlights their significance as an inherent component. It transcends the internalized account of fathers and their sons, evolving into a broader discussion on justice and other virtues as a timeless principle sewn into the fabric of their familial legacy.

The focus here shifts from individual connections to their unique nature, positioning them as an integral and perpetual thread within the larger fabric of human equity. This understanding allows for a more symbolic perspective, emphasizing the universality and timeless relevance within the context of legacy. Within this journey, their sons emerge as custodians of the moral directive initially provided by their fathers. The perpetuation of this compass goes beyond singular actions, becoming a collective responsibility to enrich the overarching family legacy.

This picture sidesteps specific familial dynamics, portraying the transmission of ethical values as a continuous process extending beyond their lifetimes. In this sense, those who become stewards of a moral history contribute to the ongoing chronicle without explicit reference to personal relationships. The nurturing of an inheritance centered on values brings into focus the long-lasting impact of fathers on building future generations through their moral teachings.

By deferring direct references to specifics, the portrayal broadens its perspective, depicting their lasting influence as a universal force in molding the ethical landscape. It emphasizes the collective responsibility to cultivate and pass on a legacy extending beyond the temporal, highlighting the exclusive and lasting impact of moral teachings in shaping future generations.

Continuity of the Legacy

The concept of continuity revolves around the family legacy formed by fathers who diligently teach God's commands, wisdom, and love, building an unbroken continuum of values and faith. This seamlessly emphasizes the lasting connection between fatherhood, spiritual guidance, and legacy-building. Recognizing this as part of a larger conversation, it operates similarly to those authors writing the initial chapters of a story and continuing through ages, leaving a living testament to the fidelity, devotion, and dedication held dear.

Contributors do not script the concluding chapter; they participate in a tale perpetuated by subsequent generations and their progeny. The guidance and principles conveyed are similar to threads intricately woven into the pages of a family's chronicle. Embedded within the teachings of Deuteronomy is a fountain of wisdom fortifying the notion of continuity. Communicating these directives transcends singular instructions, constituting integral components of a broader narrative encompassing belief and credence. Fathers can exemplify how these directives link them to a lineage of believers who have steadfastly upheld these principles over eons.

A FATHER'S LEGACY

In addition, the emphasis lies on the privilege of being a bridge between the past and the future. This connection to values and faith transcends time, molding the path for the upcoming heirs. It ensures the legacy left behind is not a relic but a living testament, evolving daily. This serves as an invitation to recognize their role as carriers, embracing the values and faith passed down to them.

The focus is on being part of a larger episode, becoming the authors of the next chapter in the ancestry, and continuing the story begun by those before them. In terms of legacy-building, it is not confined to one era; rather, it is a gift passed on, echoing through time and influencing descendants. When carried forward, this enriches the narrative with individual experiences and contributions.

When exploring the intricate web of responsibilities accompanying the role of parenting, it emphasizes the diverse aspects of caregiving, an interplay of responsibilities, and the collective impact on legacy-building. Fatherhood comprises not a singular role but an intricate weave of obligations. Wearing multiple hats and serving as guides, providers, mentors, and role models, these personal reflections intersect and overlap, creating a complex and interconnected web of influence.

It is important to recognize, their responsibilities interrelate rather than stand alone. Guidance, support, and role modeling are not separate facets but complementary elements collectively building development. Recognizing interconnectedness is vital to creating a positive impact on the next offspring. Within the teachings of Deuteronomy, guidance is found, reinforcing the idea of multifaceted responsibilities. These teachings emphasize the importance of God's commands residing in their hearts and being diligently taught. One can convey these commands, which provide a moral direction informing all aspects of life. The importance lies in fathers achieving a balance between instruction and allowing room for their son's growth and independence.

Providing support while also encouraging self-reliance becomes vital. Being a good example means living by the values and principles one wishes to impart and demonstrating them in their daily actions. Emphasizing the importance of comprehending these roles, one must be self-aware and

CHAPTER FOUR

intentional in their positions, acknowledging the way these actions and choices have an impact on growth. Understanding this interconnectedness allows for the creation of a harmonious and nurturing environment.

For those influenced, it serves as a reminder of the diverse ways they impact lives. It is an invitation to appreciate the complexity of caregiving and the many layers of support, guidance, and mentorship provided. In terms of legacy building, underscoring the fulfillment of diverse roles fashions the path left behind. This understanding becomes a part of their history, enriching it with a nuanced perspective on the varying nature of fatherhood. Conclusively, it explores the intricate roles, emphasizing their mutual dependence and their collective impact on development.

—— Guiding the Way ——

Pursuing the varied and invaluable responsibilities entailed in guiding through impediments and opportunities awaits the importance of mentorship, leadership, and direction in the process of building a lasting legacy through fatherhood. This acknowledges the value of assumed obligations beyond parenthood; fathers also serve as mentors and guides. Engaging in a spectrum of activities includes navigating the complexities of life, providing advice, offering moral direction, and serving as instructors who impart resilience, knowledge, and wisdom.

Tailoring guidance to the unique needs of a lifestyle involves the deliberate and thoughtful adjustment of deliverance and direction to accommodate the specific circumstances, characteristics, and challenges faced by each individual. Taking into account the distinct aspects of each person's journey while recognizing a personalized approach enhances the effectiveness and relevance of the guidance provided. This tailored approach reflects an understanding of their sons diverse nature and ensures the support offered is well-suited to address their unique situations.

Furthermore, these teachings emphasize the importance of God's commands residing in their hearts and being diligently imparted. Conveying these commands offer not just moral guidance but also a roadmap for navigating difficulties, since it highlights the concept, fathers are not just problem solvers but also cultivators of resilience and wisdom. Instilling the belief in viewing problems as opportunities for growth and learning, they can teach ways to overcome obstacles and grow through adversity. In the domain of meaningful intergenerational discourse, both can engage in enriching conversations marked by the exchange of advice, responsive elucidation of queries, and the provision of essential leadership.

These dialogues, beyond serving as a forthright platform for the transmission of wisdom, also act as furrows for the dissemination of values and principles from one generation to the next. Within this relational dynamic, father-son connections then find a medium through which they not only acknowledge their pivotal roles but also impart a meaningful understanding of their multifaceted identities.

The significance of these exchanges become evident as they internalize the imparted wisdom and advice, recognizing themselves not simply as distinct responsibilities but as valuable mentors offering loving support. This acknowledgment propels them to embrace the resilience instilled, thereby acknowledging the lasting impact of counsel on their personal development. The direction bestowed then becomes an integral and valuable component. Reflecting on the mentorship and counsel received, they gain a deeper comprehension of the virtues and principles underpinned in their upbringing. This introspective process enriches the family unit by infusing it with a subtle perspective on the intricate role fathers play as sage guides through the complexities of life.

Modeling Excellence in Fatherhood

The essential and influential role fathers embody as a source of inspiration and emulation seamlessly aligns with the diverse nature of fatherhood. Highlighting the way actions, attitudes, and values significantly impact character development and the history they leave behind, setting examples every day, whether consciously or not, goes beyond being just providers of information through words but also through decisions and behaviors. These examples build character development and deeply influence values and aspirations, conveying their commands are not theoretical ideologies but living values guiding the process.

Fathers have the privilege of demonstrating, living by one's values is not only admirable but also attainable. Focusing on the importance of consistency, they assert their actions, merits, and worth in aligning with the lessons they wish to impart, reinforcing the credibility of the teachings. For their sons, this serves as a reminder of their powerful influence as role models and an invitation to recognize they are watching and learning every day. They are encouraged to embrace the Godly examples set for them and to reflect on the ways these instances influence their own character.

For legacy-building, it brings into focus the integration of modeling excellence into the core of the family inheritance. When reflecting on these ideas and standards, it deepens a comprehension of the benefits formulating their upbringing. This understanding enriches the legacy with an appreciation for the role of active influencers through positive examples. Conclusively, it highlights the influential task of mentors through actions, attitudes, and values, emphasizing the importance of leading by example and the process these decisions create the character development and values of the next generation.

Although a constant, love's ever-changing fluidity provides emphasis on the varying applications, demonstrating when expressed through tangible choices, it becomes the very essence of building a strong, well-rounded, and lasting relationship between fathers and their sons. At its essence, the connection is not passive but dynamic, an ever growing bond lasting a lifetime. It is not limited to the momentary interruption of varied feelings but instead is expressed through resolute commitment. It is actively demonstrated throughout everyday life, and those actions form, mold, and build the quality of their relationships.

One key aspect to emphasize is the transcendence of love beyond elementary emotions to become a verb, demanding intentionality. Actively expressing this connection involves spending quality time, providing unwavering support, and consistently appreciating their qualities and efforts. Drawing inspiration from the instruction of the Mosaic passages reinforces the concept, noting the importance of God's commands residing in the heart and being diligently taught. Conveying this significant bond signifies more than a theoretical concept; it embodies a lived experience intricately ingrained into the relationship.

The understanding extends beyond verbal expressions, reaching toward the deep insights gained from the actions and gestures. In turn, the privilege of illustrating this as a continuous, tangible experience accentuates the importance of intentionality, urging purposeful pursuit in manifesting affection. Whether through meaningful conversations, mutual activities, or genuine acts of kindness, intentional expressions create a purposeful impact on their sons' hearts. It further serves as a recognition of the profound and abundant affection their fathers hold. Additionally, it encourages them to acknowledge love surpasses pure sentiment; it is a lived reality within their relationship, embracing and reciprocating this affection through both actions and words.

Living in the Present

In the realm of fatherhood, significant importance lies in actively engaging in the present moment. This narrative extends beyond creating a future legacy, encompassing the vital essence of being fully immersed in the lives of their sons. While the building of a lasting inheritance holds importance, equal emphasis is placed on being wholly involved in day-to-day occurrences. These moments form the foundational elements of a robust and enduring relationship. It is vital to recognize where the true impact lies; fathers wield the privilege of constructing the ongoing maturation process through real-time conversations and experiences. The efforts made in the present exert a direct and immediate influence on the quality of the relationship.

Derived from the insights of Deuteronomy, the inspiration unfolds, fortifying the significance of being present in the moment. Emphasis is placed on the nature of God's commands, which reside in the hearts of fathers and are meticulously imparted to their progeny. They grasp the conveyance of Biblical instruction delivered beyond abstract concepts, forming statutes actively guiding their everyday interactions. Opportunities arise to craft lifetime memories, nurture connections, and instill moral directives. Within this essence, bonds fortify, trust cultivates, and love finds expression. This highlights the importance of seizing present opportunities and encouraging the infusion of intentionality into interactions, whether through communal quality time, meaningful conversations, acts of love, prayer, or support. Each present moment becomes a chance to nurture the relationship and add to its lasting imprint.

During these times, a reminder of inherent familial values remains within their connection. This extends an invitation within the family unit to cherish everyday interactions, each conversational moment, and collective experiences in the shaping of their spiritual bonds. It is this divine prompting to actively engage in the father-son connection in the present, recognizing these valued moments, that lays the foundation for their relationship.

In terms of legacy-building, living in the present redefines heritage not solely as what fathers leave behind but as how they exist in the present. A reflection of this active presence shines as an immense appreciation for the daily investments made in upbringing. This understanding enriches the family history in real-time with an appreciation for the importance of being fully engaged in the present moment.

In retrospect, living in the present contemplates the significance of participating, even minute by minute. This highlights a path of fatherhood by the clock in a sense, as though each second counts in crafting a bequest for the future; it involves being fully present in the now, forming their sons' lives in the very echo of time and space, as the active engagement is less calculated and more inspired by the Spirit of God in becoming an integral part of the legacy they leave behind.

Nurturing Values for the Future

Intentionality takes center stage in instilling Biblical values. Encouraging meaningful conversations, sharing personal stories, and consistently modeling cherished principles becomes a deliberate practice. Each interaction becomes an opportunity to reinforce their importance. For fathers who engage in these conversations, it serves as a reminder of their significance, inviting active participation and reflection on how these precepts will guide their lives in the future. Encouragement is extended to embrace and carry forward the imparted ideals, serving as a testament to a lasting legacy.

In legacy-building, the mentorship provided is a guide, a reflection on the imparted ideals, and a way to gain a deeper understanding of the moral and ethical foundation carving their upbringing. This understanding enriches their lives with an appreciation for the role of Godly instruction in molding character and guiding life choices. In the unfolding journey of instruction, present values lay the groundwork for the future. The continuous nature of this attribute showcases its active engagement in framing a strong birthright.

The recognition of instilled morals significantly impacts the future; choices are made to impart indelible ethical beliefs, spiritual guidance, and timeless righteousness. This develops a foundational basis for leading descendants in the years to come. Actively nurturing these meritable concepts by modeling them daily and engaging in fruitful conversations concerning their significance ensures learning these notions not just through words but through actions.

Inspiration is found as reinforcement, which highlights the importance of instilling confidence in spiritual matters. These teachings underscore the significance of diligently modeling Godly precepts. Conveying this as a living truth supports the selfless decision-making process throughout life. Seizing the opportunity to provide a moral and ethical framework helps navigate mishaps. Therefore, the canon instilled becomes a source of strength and guidance for future commitments.

The ongoing importance of transmitting timeless values and wisdom through generations is magnified in these diverse and morally changing times. It centers on the continuity of counsel, emphasizing practical methods to convey valuable life lessons, ethical living, and spiritual direction to successive generations, wielding a lifelong impact. The knowledge, beliefs, and insights transmitted become the foundation upon which character is built and decisions are made throughout their journey.

CHAPTER FOUR

Those in the role of providing guidance have the privilege of consistently giving wisdom, life lessons, and ethical fortitude, acting as a supportive source in navigating complexities. Within these fatherly teachings, the emphasis is on reinforcing the importance of passing down insight, discernment, perceptivity, knowledge, and sagacity. These instructions accentuate the purpose of diligently teaching essential ideals, while conveying these attributes are not static but dynamic, growing within each passing generation.

When actions are emphasized, they are more than just a theoretical concept, but in fact, are a practical function of passing on the torch in virtuous living. This resonates with the discernment found in Ecclesiastes 12:13-14, emphasizing the conclusive nature: *"Fear God and obey his commands, for this is everyone's duty. God will judge us for everything we do, including every secret thing, whether good or bad."*

This Biblical passage underscores the timeless significance of imparting wisdom, insight, and the duty to follow God's commandments, reinforcing the value of passing forward essential attributes. The emphasis is then placed on the importance of open and meaningful communication. It encourages fathers to create an environment where their sons feel comfortable discussing daily hurdles, seeking advice, and learning from their experiences.

Each conversation becomes an opportunity to pass down valuable lessons. For some, this serves as a reminder of the significance in the acuity shared by others. It is an invitation to actively engage in these conversations, to seek enlightenment, and to reflect on how these lessons will define their own journey. Encouraged to embrace the foresight handed down as a valuable resource for life.

In terms of legacy-building, this emphasizes the method spiritual insights and values serve as the bedrock, upon which individuals construct their lives. When they reflect on the lessons imparted, they gain a deeper appreciation for the practicality and relevance of these teachings. This understanding enriches the legacy with an appreciation for the role of wisdom in influencing character and guiding decisions.

Conveyance of Spirituality

The impact of imparting knowledge and understanding within the context of a lasting imprint highlights the importance of emphasizing the generational spiritual legacy. This perspective reinforces the continuous nature of this vital role, clarifying the manner in which instruction can actively nurture personal growth and contribute to building a solid ethical framework. Acknowledging these spiritual principles is not just an external teaching but an integral component of one's character and moral foundation. These deeply ingrained beliefs transcend rudimentary existence; instead, they serve as a luminous guide, influencing the understanding of the world and one's place within it. This opportunity surpasses the process of casting abstract beliefs, extending a conveyance of personal significance and experiences, and contributing to character-building and molding in ongoing spiritual growth. Within this narrative, learning expands beyond the boundaries of intellectual understanding, encompassing a broader spectrum, including the richness and reflective insight accompanying those experiences. Inspiration is then found by reinforcing the importance of imparting spiritual prudence.

The conveyance of spirituality is not a set of rules but a way of life, a source of strength, and a moral endowment leading to a Godly and virtuous path. It is intimately connected to daily events, as guidance extends to the understanding of faith. This then embraces the mentoring and stewardship persona fathers possess in becoming the guide in sourcing resilience and moral clarity in adversity. It suggests the importance of open and meaningful conversations within the Biblical domain. Each conversation becomes an opportunity to pass down a belief system and a sense of oneness.

An invitation is extended to actively engage in discussions, seek understanding, and reflect on their beliefs and values aligning with those led by the Spirit. The end result is encouragement in embracing the spiritual legacy sustaining the family as a source of strength and moral understanding. When considering legacy-building as thematic, spiritual direction and values become integral to moral foundations. The reflection imparts a deeper appreciation for the richness and depth of belief, faith, and hope. This understanding enriches the familial legacy with a sense of adoration for the Biblical truths as a guiding force in molding character. The perpetual landscape of spiritual growth provides various pragmatic methods for nurturing trust, promoting open communication, and cultivating empathy within the father-son relationship.

This acknowledgment highlights the significance of these bonds as essential components of effective leadership, supporting the residence in legacy-building within the family. The trust, understanding, and empathy provided establishes a robust framework for compassionate listening and empathetic support. The process of building meaningful kindred involves recognizing these dependencies evolve through common experiences, heartfelt conversations, and a genuine interest in well-being. Inspiration is then found in reinforcing the importance of the connection. These teachings emphasize diligence in imparting virtues. The conveyance is, these bonds are not just a matter of sentiment but also a reflection of love and compassion.

Furthermore, this connection serves as a source of spiritual strength. Knowledge extends to understanding trust, and open communication creates a safe space for thoughts, concerns, and dreams. Learning involves understanding their alliance provides the support and encouragement needed to navigate life's interruptions. This refocuses on the importance of active listening, involvement, and empathy. Encouragement then exists to create an environment where everyone feels heard and understood. Each conversation becomes an opportunity to strengthen and reinforce the connection. An invitation is extended to actively engage in open and heartfelt dialogue, to seek understanding, and to cherish the trust and empathy underpinning relationships.

By reflecting on their emotional bonds, a deeper appreciation is gained for the depth and resilience of their relationship. This recognition enriches the legacy with a sense of connection as a guiding force in building character. The discourse moves beyond rituals or doctrines into the deeply personal and meaningful aspects of Godly conviction and moral fortitude. In doing so, this showcases a tangible and valuable relationship through the Spirit of God infusing an attachment with their earthly and Heavenly Father in all aspects of life.

A FATHER'S LEGACY

Within the father-son bond, opportunities arise to demonstrate ethical codes of conduct in a dynamic and evolving way, influenced by daily events and reflections. Spirituality extends past institutions, encompassing everyday life. Cultivating this idea traverses a path beyond imposing a specific ideology; it involves creating communal experiences, engaging in meaningful conversations, and encouraging self-reflection.

This lends itself to a dynamic and evolving process of establishing and nurturing this alliance, requiring active participation in discussions, especially within the scriptural boundaries of living a virtuous life. When sharing personal stories and reflections, humanizing spirituality becomes a means of making it relatable, placing the realness at the forefront where the "rubber meets the road." This process builds a robust foothold, serving as a source of strength and moral fortitude.

By investing in the father-son connection, their environment thrives in searching out both the visible and invisible aspects of belief, spiritual gifts, scriptural tenets, and the saving grace of the Gospel. Each of these conversations becomes an opportunity to fortify the connection and strengthen their bond. Through encouragement and active engagement in discussions, seeking understanding, and reflecting on varied milestones, their spirits begin to align with the precepts of the father-son bond.

Legacy-building takes on an energized status, as the connection holds paramount importance. Upon reflection, a deeper appreciation for the richness of their love exhumes, providing resilience, strength, and tenacity in solidifying trust. This enriches the heritage with an Agape sense of embracement as a guiding force in shaping character and moral direction.

—— Passing Down a Fathers Legacy ——

Passing down a father's legacy through the ages becomes an act of generational continuity, a tradition with its roots in the sacred texts of the father-son relationship. A wonderful and inspiring story is recalled, drawing from the tale of Eli and Samuel in 1 Samuel Chapters 1-4. It vividly illustrates the power of spiritual guidance passed from one generation to the next, a legacy of love sown from the seeds of Biblical forefathers to the birth of Jesus Christ. Eli, a significant patriarch in the Old Testament, served as both a high priest and a mentor to the young prophet Samuel. Their relationship exemplifies the ability of a father figure, whether biological or not, to impart faith, values, and wisdom to the upcoming generation, ensuring the continuity of a rich spiritual heritage. In a manner reminiscent of the venerable

Eli with the young prophet Samuel, fathers serving as mentors actively engage in imparting Godly instruction. This involvement aids in the growth of understanding of the doctrinal precepts of God and His divine ways, creating a strong foundation upon which spiritual journeys flourish.

Within this preview, essential facets crucial to nurturing a towering and lasting connection exist. One such aspect is the role of mentorship and leadership. Fathers are bestowed with the privilege and responsibility of mentoring and directing their sons in matters of faith, values, and Godliness. These confidants keenly recognize the unique mission and gifting they possess, mirroring Eli's guidance of Samuel's prophetic summons. Remaining attentive to spiritual destinies, encouragement, and wholehearted support helps shape the pursuit of distinctive journeys and divine callings, paving the way for embracing their unique roles in the grand scheme of belief, faith, and spirituality.

The narrative of Eli and Samuel, illuminates dilemmas emerging within families, even among those deeply devoted to religious service. Responsibility rests on embodying united integrity and moral values consistently within households, which is essential for safeguarding the family's spiritual legacy. This resolute dedication emphasizes the significance of disciplinary measures when warranted and the courageous undertaking of offering necessary correction in instances where Godly instructions may be compromised.

The account serves as a powerful reminder, emphasizing the struggles faced by spiritual authorities as they navigate family challenges and moral quandaries amidst the intricate and multifaceted nature of fatherhood. Eli's firm commitment to upholding moral values and integrity emerges as a constant amidst these complexities. In the face of intricacies and tribulations, maintaining a Biblical compass and ethical grounding becomes of paramount importance since the transmission of faith, values, and Godliness from one generation to the next emerges as an act of love, defining the essence of father-son relationships.

Attentive engagement in discussions regarding journeys of faith, the exchange of personal narratives, and the sharing of experiences integrate these elements into the family's True North. Through mentorship, recognition of divine callings, unwavering integrity, and a readiness to correct and instruct when necessary, fathers reinforce the bonds with their sons, ensuring the establishment of a lasting spiritual legacy.

In the intricate melody of Samuel's story and exchanges through mentorship, the timeless echoes of transmitting a father's legacy resonate and display a manifestation of faith that is transcribed onto the tablets of their hearts, connecting past, present, and future. This instructional dimension, while inherently personal, reverberates with resilient consequences.

It becomes more than a casual bestowal of knowledge; it harbors a thorough sense of connection to a spiritual lineage. Perception shifts, allowing for introspection as an integral thread in a broader narrative shaped by the faith and resilience of those who came before. This perception instills a resounding sense of continuity, reinforcing trust in the divine as not stationary but rather interwoven into a vast Godly network by the forebearers.

The narratives unfolded, the teachings imparted, and the values embodied evolved into an inheritance carried forward by subsequent generations. This transcendence travels beyond a simple transfer of knowledge; it constitutes an impartation of identity, values, and beliefs. It stands as a testament to the resilient influence of faith within the familial context, a legacy transcending time, crafting the lives of descendants. It is in the sacred realm of father-son relationships, engaging in open and candid discussions regarding matters of faith becomes a fundamental element for nurturing an understanding of Biblical spirituality.

CHAPTER FOUR

Fathers play a significant role in establishing an environment where there is a feeling of ease and encouragement, facilitating the opportunity to pose questions and seek guidance on the intricate facets of life. This atmosphere of openness lays the foundation for a more in-depth exploration of Scriptural and Godly virtues, promoting a mutual exchange of insights. The emphasis on the significance of active listening, acknowledging the importance of seeking understanding, and generating a place of meaningful inquiries further enhances the depth of these discussions, creating a domain where both fathers and sons advance in their spiritual pursuits.

Drawing from their own experiences and knowledge, thoughtful responses not only address immediate questions but also encourage deeper exploration. These dialogues become a two-way street where insights are exchanged. The significance of these conversations is manifold. First and foremost, they allow navigation of the complexities in a supportive and nurturing environment. Seeking answers to questions leads to a clearer understanding of spiritual concepts and the development of critical thinking skills.

Second, engaging in such discussions strengthens their bond. It communicates faith is not a solitary journey but an exploration binding family members together. Third, these conversations create a safe space to express doubts, uncertainties, and even times of disbelief. Rather than viewing these moments as hurdles, they can be recognized as opportunities for growth and understanding. Last, openly acknowledging the complexities encourages their peers to develop a nuanced and mature perspective on spirituality. In this way, open and honest exchange becomes an act of mutual learning and Christian growth. A testament to the richness of father-son relationships emerges, where faith undergoes not only transmission but also exploration, questioning, and deepening through heartfelt conversations.

In these conversations, the bonds of trust, respect, and faith are nurtured, ensuring the flourishing of the legacy of spiritual wisdom. At its essence, this instructional journey transcends a one-way street of teaching, evolving into a transformative process with multiple facets. It imparts knowledge, foundational beliefs, doctrines, and stories forming the basis of their Christian faith. Drawing from their spiritual journey, fathers hold the unique privilege of instilling these timeless events. This instruction extends beyond imparting superficial knowledge; it offers a sense of spiritual identity and becomes an integral part of trust. It transcends the acquisition of a belief system; rather, it is a process of becoming a person who believes in the message of the Gospel. This transformative aspect shapes a sense of purpose, providing guidance in understanding their role within the broader scope of God's divine plan.

The Scriptural message is not confined to a set of doctrines; it is a way of life. By nurturing their sons' understanding of salvation and grace, they prepare them to embrace a way of life with authenticity and conviction. This reaches beyond the routine of attending church services for just attendance sake; instead, it encompasses living out the teachings of Christ Jesus in everyday actions, decisions, and interactions.

Instruction grounded in belief and trust instills a lifelong, virtuous commitment. It is not a passing phase or a childhood belief; it is a life of spiritual growth, providing strength through the trials and difficulties of life and the tumultuous seas of existence while offering solace, wisdom, hope, and faith. Within this instructional journey, fathers assume a path extending beyond the temporal, becoming spiritual mentors and guiding through the labyrinth of faith with unwavering love and dedication. This sacred responsibility is weighty, carrying great significance.

Through instruction grounded in faith, they emerge as the architects of their spiritual foundation, laying the stones of knowledge, identity, purpose, and commitment to create a structure withstanding the howling winds of a storm. This foundation serves as the launchpad for their sons to embark on their own spiritual journeys, carrying the torch of redemption into the future. The impact of instruction grounded in the Word of God within father-son relationships is immense. It leaves behind a legacy of wisdom, love, and everlasting trust transcending centuries, ensuring their Godly empowerment remains a vibrant and integral part of the family's heritage. This stands as a testament to the power of love, Biblical direction, and a journey of belief, binding fathers and their sons together in a timeless and eternal connection.

CHAPTER FOUR

An Everlasting Legacy

Father-to-son instruction, rooted in Biblical teachings, is a method for transmitting an everlasting legacy. Through the sharing of Scriptural narratives and principles guiding generations, a connection is established, linking them to a heritage of deep significance. This highlights faith, not as an isolated occurrence but an integral part of a broader and continuing tradition. In turn, embracing their belief is then woven into a fabric extending across their lineage. The act of passing down these timeless teachings functions as an arch spanning through time, linking the experiences, challenges, and triumphs of ancestors with the present.

In recounting stories of Biblical patriarchs who faced adversity with fortitude, fathers provide a source of strength for their descendants, aiding them when confronting their own conundrums. This sense of continuity reinforces the understanding the journey is not solitary but part of a greater legacy. Recognizing the truths, values, and principles guiding their forebears remain just as relevant in the contemporary context, this awareness deepens appreciation for the timeless wisdom embedded in Scripture.

The teachings of Jesus, the moral lessons derived from parables, and the Biblical commandments are not bound to a specific era but are recognized as possessing eternal significance, and continue to hold prevalence in the shifting sands of humanity. In a world often undergoing rapid change, resistance to the adherence of Scriptural ideology, and the fluctuation of Gospel tenets, this continuity offers a stabilizing presence. It serves as a reminder, while social circumstances may evolve, these core principles remain steadfast.

There is solace in the knowledge their faith is rooted in something lasting, sustainable, and embraced by countless preceding eras. This awareness establishes a sense of security and trust in the teachings passed down through time. Encouraging the embrace and upholding of these truths, they recognize their participation in a Godly legacy lasting through the ages. Connecting descendants to a broader heritage reinforces the idea, faith transcends solitary endeavors, evolving into a mutual journey. This journey extends beyond the immediate family to include a vast Christian community spanning eons.

A FATHER'S LEGACY

The resulting sense of belonging becomes a spring of strength as recognition grows of involvement in something much larger than oneself. Engagement through the discussion of Biblical stories and parables becomes a potent means for nurturing spiritual maturation, emphasizing their transcendent nature, and shaping the lives of those who embrace the inspired writings of the Scriptures.

The continuity of the inspired teachings emphasizes faith as an integral part of a rich and lasting tradition, forming countless lives over centuries. Passed down through generations, it transcends rituals to become a collective tradition, influencing many.

This lineage serves as a source of strength, inspiration, and identity for those navigating their spiritual travels. Akin to a precious treasure handed down, it forms a legacy extending far beyond the present moment, reaching back through the annals of time. When tradition is handed down from one generation to the next, fathers are passing on a piece of this timeless treasure. The pages of Scripture hold stories of patriarchs, prophets, kings, and souls who encountered God in remarkable ways. These narratives transcend mere historical tales of the past, serving as living testimonies of the Divine's faithful promise.

As they recount these stories, the invitation stands for successors to walk alongside those of the distant past and witness their journeys. Scriptural precepts and instructions extend beyond specific eras and cultures; they are universal truths transcending the confines of time and spatial dimensions. In understanding values such as love, compassion, justice, and forgiveness, exemplified by Christ Jesus, provides a timeless depth of inspiration, offering inspired insights.

This heritage of faith serves as a source of truth when drawing strength from Biblical stories of those who faced insurmountable odds with a strong sense of courage, trust, and a belief in God's word. The accounts are numerous and pronounced, as evidenced by the courage of historical giants such as David facing Goliath or the perseverance embodied by those similar to the Apostle Paul in spreading the Gospel, who inspired others to confront their own hurdles.

CHAPTER FOUR

This acknowledgment is not isolated but part of a grand narrative of those who had tread a similar path before them, forming an integral understanding. Inheriting the legacy of saints and believers and significantly contributing to the growth and spread of Christianity throughout history adds depth to their sense of identity. In a world often emphasizing the transitory and fleeting, connection to a rich legacy offers a sense of rootedness. Understanding this faith transcends a passing vogue; instead, it becomes a Godly culture worth cherishing and preserving.

This connection instills a sense of purpose and direction, highlighting participation in an ongoing tale. As this rich heritage is transmitted, it bestows an immeasurable gift, something beyond material possessions and temporal pursuits. This gift, a vast reservoir of spiritual resources, becomes a lifelong source. The uninterrupted succession of Biblical teachings serves as a reminder, faith is integral to a rich and meaningful tradition. It is a heritage transmitted, imparting strength, inspiration, and a sense of identity. This legacy is a timeless treasure, connecting to stories of the past and the ongoing journey of faith ahead.

Faith's Underpinning

Guidance rooted in Biblical teachings furnishes a robust footing upon which to construct faith. It resembles the bequest of a well-constructed edifice, complete with a resilient structure and solid groundwork. To further enhance the bequeath received, picture a young architect inheriting a splendid, well-built house from generations past. The house is not simply a structure; it stands as a testament to the artistry, sagacity, and commitment of those who preceded. It boasts a sturdy foundation, resilient walls, and a roof which has withstood innumerable storms. This residence signifies more than just a dwelling place; it embodies a legacy of architectural eminence.

Similarly, when fathers transmit the tenets of the Bible, they provide a well-constructed groundwork for the journey. This foundation encompasses a fuller understanding of Biblical doctrine, familiarity with the Scriptures, a robust ethical orientation, and the pragmatic tools for manifesting their belief. Comparable to the sturdy structure of a house, this substructure imparts stability and support, particularly during moments of uncertainty and skepticism. Amidst the tempests of life inevitably encountered, faith stands unwavering, anchored by this solid underpinning. Similar to a well-built edifice standing strong against the elements, a robust spiritual cornerstone fortifies the crucible of life's trials. Yet a house, no matter its impeccable construction, lacks completion without the personal imprint of its inhabitants. Likewise, the inheritance of a Godly trust transcends a quaint reception of beliefs; it entails the assimilation of those beliefs into one's essence. Possessing the opportunity to infuse personal experiences, insights, and understanding into the cornerstone of faith received.

It is much the same as a designer renovating an inherited structure to express a unique style and preference, personalizing the journey in deepening the grasp of Christian doctrine, engaging with the Scriptures in a distinctive manner, and allowing the Holy Spirit to guide ethical choices. This customization changes a well-constructed foundation into a lived and dynamic righteous dwelling. The legacy transcends complacency, embodying a thriving and evolving inheritance. It surpasses the preservation of the past, serving as a dynamic force shaping the future. Honoring the enhancement of this legacy with distinct experiences and perspectives renders it more relevant and meaningful for subsequent generations. Conceptual analogies find expression in the relationship between a master craftsman and an apprentice. The apprentice absorbs the wisdom and skills of the master, subsequently crafting their own masterpieces. While the master lays the foundation, the apprentice's creativity and innovation breathe new life into the craft.

In the transmission of rich heritage, spiritual mentors assume the role, passing on knowledge and values sustaining their own journeys. This process urges exploration, questioning, and a deepening of understanding. The mentorship establishes a dynamic interplay between tradition and innovation, preserving the timeless truths of Christianity while allowing for growth and adaptation in a changing world. Instruction rooted in Biblical teachings furnishes a robust basis, comparable to receiving a well-constructed building. This understructure offers steady support during times of hardship and doubt. The privilege of infusing personal experiences and insights into this legacy ensures an ongoing interplay between tradition and innovation, maintaining the relevance and insightful meaning of the familial legacy.

Attributes of a Living Tradition

Transmitted through Biblical instruction, the legacy of the Christian walk is a vibrant and living tradition. It defies the notion of being a relic of the past; instead, it embodies a dynamic expression of the Godly Spirit, continuously molding the lives of those who wholeheartedly embrace it. Active participation in this living truth involves contributing to its ongoing development and relevance within contemporary society.

Consider the analogy of a river gracefully traversing a landscape for centuries, ensuring it flows and remains cohesive. This river, with its continuous current, has sculpted its path, enriched the land, and provided sustenance for countless generations. It is not a stagnant pool; instead, it represents a living and dynamic force capable of adapting to changing circumstances while consistently following its course.

This legacy, passed down through Biblical instruction, mirrors the nature of the ancient river. It is not preserved as a frozen idea of a forgone era; rather, it gracefully flows through the generations, alive and shaping the spiritual landscape and nurturing the souls of those who embrace it. Akin to the characteristics of a flowing river, this legacy exemplifies the adaptability inherent in Biblical relevancy. Navigating the ever-changing world terrain is a challenging task, requiring one to remain dedicated to timeless truths while embracing innovative approaches. This adaptability empowers the confrontation of unique struggles in each generation, avoiding the confines of rigid traditions and welcoming fresh perspectives and approaches in communion with God.

This inheritance is not solely a transient belief; it represents a continuum, a river of trust maintaining its course from one generation to the next. This river flows with vitality, promoting spiritual growth, offering guidance, and providing solace in times of need. Similar to the way rivers are shaped by natural forces and human interaction, the living tradition evolves through active engagement in alignment with God's plan.

A FATHER'S LEGACY

As fathers pass on not only their individual beliefs but also their collective lineage, they cultivate a sense of rootedness and belonging within the Christian community. By participating in meaningful discussions, exploring theological questions, and applying Scriptural constructs to contemporary issues, they ensure the Biblical tenets remain relevant and responsive to their evolving needs.

Within this living tradition, there are depths to explore, analogous to the congregating pools of a river holding hidden treasures, offering the opportunity to search the rich theological and spiritual insights found in Scripture, seeking an understanding of God, and embracing the sense of wonder and discovery inherent within the tradition. The legacy, transmitted through Biblical instruction, is not a token of the past but a dynamic, living moral path. It adapts to changing circumstances, maintains continuity with previous generations, exudes vitality, invites active participation, and offers considerable depths of spiritual insight.

A valuable perspective is the passage of the Christian faith through instruction in building unity within families. It establishes a special language, a common set of values, and a collective purpose centered around Godliness. This unity strengthens the bonds between fathers and their sons, connecting them not only by blood but also through commitment and its loving legacy. Imagine a fine linen woven with threads of different colors and textures, each representing a unique soul within a family. As these threads intersect and intertwine, they give rise to a beautiful and intricate pattern.

This metaphor illustrates the unity emerging within families when Godly beliefs are passed down through generations. Just as the threads are woven together to create a coherent design, the transmission through instruction establishes a shared language within the family. A common vocabulary exists between fathers and their sons, employing words and phrases with deep meaning and significance.

This personal language facilitates communication and understanding, enabling them to easily discuss matters of spirituality, prayer, and belief. Just as colors blend harmoniously, their legacy imparts common values within the family. Grounded in Biblical instruction, these values act as guiding maxims. Concepts such as love, compassion, forgiveness, and integrity become doctrines, molding their interactions with each other and the world. Similar to the threads working together to create a unified design, the transmission establishes a collective purpose. United in a fortified mission centered around their faith, efforts extend beyond individual goals to encompass a commitment to living out Scriptural beliefs in practical ways.

Whether serving the community, supporting charitable causes, or nurturing a spirit of kindness, the collective purpose serves as a catalyst for inspiration and motivation. This unity forged through the transmission strengthens their bonds. Similar to a cherished heirloom passed down through generations, the connectedness formed through this continuity becomes a powerful legacy. It is a gift fathers pass on to their sons, who in turn, pass it on to their own offspring. It transcends time, linking generations past, present, and future in a bond of Godly trust. Perpetuation through instruction strengthens cohesiveness within families by weaving a shared language, instilling common values, inspiring a collective purpose, and leaving behind a lasting legacy. As a work of art, it enriches the lives of those who embrace it, connecting them in a meaningful way.

Legacy of Faithful Living

The transformative approach of instruction grounded in Scriptural guidance manifests as evidence of devoted living. It is an embodiment of living out Scriptural beliefs, making an impact on the world, and leaving behind a record of the lasting power of family bonds. This evidence, resulting from instruction based in Biblical counsel, speaks to the impact of such an approach within father-son relationships.

The tale of devoted living is a multifaceted story weaving together a rich array of virtues, impact, endurance, testimony, and inspiration. It transcends words and memories, becoming a living example of the values and principles passed down through generations of instruction. Living evidence comes to life carrying forward these teachings, manifesting them in their daily lives, and becoming examples of transformative power. Their actions speak louder than any words and serve as an influence on others, including future heirs. This reach extends far beyond their confines, radiating its impact on the communities and more. These actions possess the potential to create a long-lasting effect, inspiring those in their spheres to embrace similar Godly values and principles. In this way, faithful living becomes a formidable example of positive social change, not limited by time and boundaries.

The longevity and nature of this legacy stand as a testament to the resilience of their trust. It reinforces the sayings of the inspired writings, which are not superficial but instead deeply rooted in the hearts and minds of families. This evidence, passed down, demonstrates the strength of their connection and its remarkable ability to persevere throughout the daily circumstances. This evidence becomes a source of inspiration and guidance. Those who inherit this legacy receive a blueprint for living a life filled with purpose, meaning, and integrity. They can draw upon the examples set by their fathers, continuing the tradition of faithful living and perpetuating a cycle of Godly influence within their families.

Their living testimony's impact on the world, endurance, and source of inspiration collectively influence the lasting evidence of living in the father-son relationship. The proof of faithful living resulting from instruction grounded in Biblical teachings is a witness, a source of impact, a testament to strength, and a fountain of inspiration for future generations. It embodies the essence of inspired values and serves as a shining light, extending its influence far beyond the immediate family unit. Living out familial beliefs significantly shapes the perception and application of its tenets, surpassing adherence to handed-down mere traditions or rituals. This practice emphasizes a liberated connection with a living God through the guidance of the Lord Jesus and the Holy Spirit.

The essence lies in translating faith into tangibles, exemplifying love, compassion, and forgiveness in worldly interactions. Embracing the role of ambassadors for these statutes involves a commitment to translating their instructions into practical guidelines for life. Rather than remaining abstract concepts, the advice becomes a tangible instruction, leading to the application of lives infused with faith, hope, joy, and love.

CHAPTER FOUR

Those who prioritize the practical application of these creeds actively bridge the divide between belief and practice, encouraging others to embody love and forgiveness in their daily interactions and serving as catalysts for interpersonal and dynamic cultural transformation. As these values are internalized, the natural progression leads to becoming conveyors of the Heavenly message through deeds and conduct, making a positive contribution. The focus on practical application enhances father-son relationships and extends its impact to the broader community, promoting the dissemination of Godly virtues. Mentors, leading the way in embodying these standards, collectively forge a legacy of faith, imprinting a lasting influence on the world through their commitment.

In fashioning faith and values, fathers play an integral role in influencing the future. Instilling strong Christian virtues ensures the transmission of these tenets to the next generation, creating an effect extending far beyond immediate relationships. Grounded in the teachings of Scripture, this approach cultivates a lasting connection, transcending the superficial and touching the spiritual. It forges a bond strengthened by mutual understanding, becoming a source of hope and love in an ever-changing world. At its core is a common journey where they walk together on the path of righteousness, facing its ups and downs in unison. This journey cultivates camaraderie beyond family ties, allowing them to support and encourage each other's spiritual growth. The basis of this connection is built upon values derived from Biblical guidance. Imparting moral and ethical guidelines ensures understanding and involves witnessing the embodiment of these values in their lives.

This commitment to Godly principles forms a robust basis for the relationship, guiding interactions and decisions. Probing into the emotional intricacies often overlooked in surface-level connections and engaging in meaningful discussions about their faith, life's challenges, and spiritual experiences establish a space for emotional intimacy. Trust serves as the foundation of the father-son bond, where they rely on guidance and wisdom rooted not solely in authority but in a genuine belief in intentional understanding. This trust becomes the foundation for building open communication and encourages the exchange of occasional doubts and miscues.

A FATHER'S LEGACY

Navigating this important connection, they recognize its significance beyond the present moment, evolving into a legacy of understanding and a perpetual source of strength and inspiration, propelling them to continuously nurture their bond. It establishes a starting point rooted in values, explores emotional depths, and builds trust, leaving behind a legacy of love. This alliance weaves a rich fabric into their relationship, offering more than a surface-level connection and a powerful source of support and meaning. Ultimately, it transforms into a guiding light of hope and love in a world constantly undergoing change.

—— Moving Forward ——

The core of a father's legacy is centered on the divine commandment encapsulated in Deuteronomy 6:6-9. This scriptural foundation highlighted the invaluable role fathers played in transmitting an inheritance rich in love and wisdom to their sons. Drawing inspiration from Psalm 78:4, the story unfolded the substantial importance of transmitting values through generations, emphasizing the essence of family viscidity and the responsibility of molding the character and faith of their descendants.

Built upon these foundational principles, the account resonated with the timeless instruction embedded in the passages. It intricately combined the sacred commandments and the intergenerational narrative, depicting the father as a pivotal figure in the perpetuation of a spiritual lineage. Guiding through a contemplative journey, the record invited reflection on the divine injunctions and the significant impact they wielded on interpersonal connections. Depicting stewards of a lasting legacy, it prompted meditation on the influence of their actions and teachings on subsequent generations, thereby reinforcing the theme of legacy as a foundation for familial continuity.

Concluding the exploration of a father's legacy in Chapter 4, the text promoted an understanding of the valuable role played by fathers in transmitting an inheritance enriched with love and wisdom. Anchored in the divine commandments of Deuteronomy and inspired by the ageless insights found in the Psalms. The text painted a vivid picture of family responsibility inherent in shaping the character and faith of descendants. Portraying stewards of a lasting legacy, individuals are prompted to contemplate the enduring impact of their actions and teachings, recognizing the theme of the legacy of love as a foundation for father-son cohesiveness.

Transitioning into Chapter 5, the story further peers into love and guidance, exploring the transformative power of embracing and imparting wisdom, as guided by the Scriptures in Psalms 25:10 and Proverbs 22:6.

CHAPTER FIVE

Embracing Love and Guidance

Guiding the picturesque father-son bond is the wonderful wisdom expressed in Psalm 25:10, proclaiming: *"All the ways of the Lord are loving and true for those who keep his covenant and his testimonies."* Within this discourse, a dedication unfolds to unconditionally lead, nurture, and care for those under fatherly instruction. Relationships find anchoring in sacred promises, transcending immediate connections. Pivotal to this pledge are fathers, who solemnly commit to lead, develop, and cultivate those entrusted to them without reservation. This promise, mirroring the example of God's covenant, captures the essence of an exploration into the bond of love and guidance.

Preceding these reflections, verses 8 and 9 express a heartfelt plea: *"Good and upright is the Lord; therefore, he instructs sinners in the way. He leads the humble in what is right and teaches them his way."* These verses serve as an influential prelude, providing context for understanding the nature of God's directive and the depth of the covenant fathers are called to uphold.

Examining these foundational verses illuminates the broader context of Psalm 25, shedding light on the significance of verse 10, in illustrating the love and faithfulness inherent in God's pledge. This scrutiny unfolds against the backdrop of divine instruction and direction, emphasizing the transformative impact of humility in aligning with the Lord's way.

In the realm of father-son relationships, the embodiment of selfless love, as emphasized in the passage, manifests itself in various nuanced ways. Practical manifestations create deep and lasting connections. A fundamental facet of this affection is patience and kindness. Demonstrating unyielding love by practicing calmness in interactions,

CHAPTER FIVE

attentively listening to concerns, and empathizing with emotions reinforces this concept as steady and ever-present. Additionally, forgiveness plays a crucial role in exemplifying this commitment. For example, pardoning mistakes or setbacks and letting go of grievances builds a landscape of trust and openness in the relationship, facilitating its growth. It establishes a haven where those who are protected feel shielded from harm and embraced with affection. Nurturing this safe and secure environment communicates love as a constant and reassuring presence.

Trust and hope are indispensable elements of this commitment. Cultivating trust through consistently aligning words with action establishes a robust benchmark for a resilient bond. Nurturing hope for the future acts as an effective catalyst, constructing a positive outlook and reinforcing the timeless truth, love surpasses limitations. Perseverance emerges as another distinguishing feature. Demonstrating support in the face of adversity and refusing to waver or forsake loved ones during challenging times, reinforces the unyielding nature of the commitment.

In addition, modeling serves as a sound tool. Leading by example and showcasing the qualities of endurance and selfless love, imparts invaluable lessons, with others often adopting these behaviors, making the expression of genuine affection a significant influence. Open and candid communication serves as a fundamental conduit through which love flows.

Creating a secure space for those in their circle to openly express themselves, free from judgment or criticism, further nurtures the connection. This open dialogue strengthens the relationship as they navigate life's complexities together. The investment of quality time becomes a tangible expression of deep devotion. Engaging in meaningful activities, sharing hobbies, and participating in heartfelt conversations solidify their bonds. This intentional connection-building reinforces the selfless nature of familial love. They can weave it through their daily interactions and intentional acts of kindness, forgiveness, protection, trust, hope, perseverance, modeling, communication, and quality time.

These practical demonstrations create a legacy enriching the lives of future generations. By consistently adhering to the guidelines and exemplifying a selfless nature, fathers can create a nurturing and supportive environment, promoting growth and building binding connections. Further exploration into the unyielding dedication required to uphold this promise reveals the provision of love, determined support, motivation, and sagacity. They highlight the impact such a commitment has on personal development, character refinement, and spiritual maturation, ultimately leaving behind a lasting and loving legacy.

Exploring the Covenant

Throughout the Psalms, the focus remains on the essence of God's enlightenment, characterized by constant commitment and devotion. The radiance of divine wisdom serves as a consistent reminder of genuine dedication at its core. Reflecting on these inspired words reveals a compelling message: those who uphold this commitment and follow the decrees experience endless faithfulness. Embracing God's ways and remaining dedicated to His teachings opens the gateway to meaningful relationships, a testament to its limitless theme. Psalm 25:10 reveals an extra assurance through complete dedication to upholding the covenant and steadfastly adhering to the decrees. This dedication grants entry into the profound aspects of God's unfailing love, truth, reliability, and righteousness. It demonstrates the transformative impact when individuals conform to His guidance, emphasizing the notion of fostering authentic connections by embracing His teachings and staying faithful in belief.

This connection is not fleeting or conditional; instead, it is firm and everlasting. It is a message holding significant relevance for fathers, urging them to find inspiration in the examples set before them. Just as God's commitment is endless and His faithfulness is boundless, they can nurture immense connections and bonds by leading their sons in accordance with His truths. Their role of tutorship is emphasized and extends beyond instruction; it encompasses a commitment to exemplify and instill lasting values. This serves as a guiding light, reminding caregivers of the transformative potential embedded in the divine undertaking of leadership they establish. The promise in this passage carries significant meaning, highlighting the opportunity and responsibility to model this example in their interactions. This agreement embraces the father-son bond,

CHAPTER FIVE

embodying a blessed promise and commitment transcending the ordinary dynamics of family relationships. It emphasizes a higher calling, underscoring the importance of providing and nurturing with genuine love and trust, mirroring the care God extends to His people.

The message conveyed reinforces the fatherly role in modeling compassion and loyalty after the divine example. Psalm 23:1-6, further illuminates the characteristics of God's nurturing provision: *"The Lord is my shepherd; I lack nothing."* This verse emphasizes the concept of God being the guide and provider, aligning with the idea of a father offering guidance and nurture to his son. *"He makes me lie down in green pastures; he leads me beside quiet waters...Surely your goodness and unfailing love will pursue me all the days of my life, and I will live in the house of the Lord forever."* Given this backdrop, the Psalmist denotes constancy, reliability, and unconditional support, reflecting God's attentiveness to His people despite their shortcomings.

Biblical guidance offers a practical example for applying a Godly covenant to both lives and relationships. Fathers can embody these principles by practicing patience and kindness, refraining from keeping records of wrongs, and consistently demonstrating traits such as protection, trust, hope, and perseverance in their commitment. This form of allegiance establishes a secure and nurturing environment, fostering personal growth, learning, and thriving. Ultimately, embracing these principles not only strengthens the father-son alliance but also leaves a lasting legacy of loyalty and love for one another.

Focused on God's path of trustworthiness, Psalms determine the tone for understanding the fundamental value underlying strong familial bonds, particularly within the dynamics of fatherhood. Emphasizing the covenant embraces these roles; it serves as a continuation of the divine attributes in exploring the essential pillars in the framework of binding and sustaining family relationships. As a basis for mastering these family connections, the fatherly tenderness of influence is not portrayed as an optional trait in cultivating these bonds. Instead, it is depicted as a foundational and indispensable component supporting and sustaining viable, lasting connections developed within the family.

EMBRACING LOVE AND GUIDANCE

This perspective draws attention to the inherent prominence exemplified by God's righteous pathway; since these attributes are not merely desirable in this union but are the very building blocks upon which such family relationships are constructed. Emphasizing a strong and lasting father-son bond must be grounded in unyielding love and devotion. These qualities are not ideals to aspire to but fundamental principles guiding fathers in their roles as caregivers, nurturers, and mentors. They serve as the cornerstone upon which meaningful connections are established, contributing to the overall strength, care, and resilience of the family relationship.

In addition, this establishment accentuates the significance of providing guidance, support, and protection. Just as the verse reveals the nature of certain paths, it illuminates the direction to be taken in their respective duties. It serves as a reminder, the journey is marked by these values, prompting contemplation of their fundamental nature in nurturing. This brings to light that these virtues are the pillars of robust and meaningful relationships, where such qualities manage a pivotal aspect in molding character, shaping growth, and promoting well-being.

It encourages an acknowledgment of the importance of these ideologies and an active cultivation of them, ultimately leading to a fuller and more robust union. This foundation guides an understanding of relationships while serving as a directive for action. It instigates a conscious reflection, encouraging their integration into the responsibilities, duties, and roles of caregivers, mentors, and nurturers, thereby contributing to the strength, vitality, and resilience of the partnership forged.

Drawing Divine Inspiration

Drawing inspiration from the divine example of covenant-keeping beautifully portrayed, directs attention to an unyielding commitment to love and loyalty as the ultimate wellspring of inspiration for the familial bond it represents. The inspired texts foretell of an unshakable adherence, offering a powerful image, contemplating the ways of endless adornment and devotion, and serving as a luminary for the dedication of fatherhood. Just as the Spirit of God cares for, supports, comforts, and cherishes those loved, fathers are called to guide, nurture, and unconditionally embrace their duties with a similar compassion. The passage example serves as a reminder of the family accord, mirroring its depth as illustrated by the sacrifice of Christ Jesus for humanity. It exemplifies the ultimate gift of love, supported in John 15:13, *"Greater love has no one than this: to lay down one's life for another."* Fathers can draw inspiration from this example to demonstrate sacrificial love within the father-son relationship. At times, this may involve making personal sacrifices to ensure the needs, dreams, and security of their sons are met, even when it demands personal dedication beyond the given.

Ultimately, it emphasizes the immense impact of sacrificial love in building a strong and eternal father-son bond. Mirroring this aspect involves being consistently present and offering endless teaching, mentorship, and a dependable presence. His love, often described as unconditional, embraces all, regardless of shortfalls and mistakes. Emulating this quality by extending unreserved compassion and acceptance and reassuring them they are cherished and valued, in spite of circumstances, adds to the cohesiveness of the connection. This framework of unlimited love creates a safe and nurturing space to flourish.

The Scriptures abound with God's teachings on forgiveness and reconciliation, and imparting these valuable lessons provides an opportunity to broaden the significance of these virtues in the family. Modeling behavior and interactions serves as a powerful example, promoting understanding and compassion. Fathers can exhibit their commitment to their heir's comfort in the present and for the long term.

This entails planning for their future, providing a stable and loving upbringing, and remaining a consistent and steady presence throughout their lives. In aligning its promise with the depth of the heavenly embrace, a legacy is perpetuated and fashioned, spanning generations, mirroring the example set by God himself. When these attributes are understood, they can reflect the depth of divine love and devotion in the covenant, which involves words and actions demonstrating sacrificial love, consistency, acceptance, forgiveness, and long-term commitment.

EMBRACING LOVE AND GUIDANCE

Exploring the significance of modeling covenants of love and guidance after the Godly example is uncovered, ensuring the father's role reflects the steady embrace of the Heavenly Father. Its contribution is essential in establishing the Biblical groundwork for the importance of a bond within these relationships, drawing direct inspiration from the powerful portrayal of the revealed attributes. One then understands the illuminated path: those adhering to this pledge and decree become blessed recipients of these virtues.

Reflecting on the Psalms as a benchmark for this revelation, a noteworthy understanding is gained regarding the fundamental importance of relationships, particularly within the sacred bond of fatherhood. This serves as an illuminating balefire, signaling the path towards building strong, resilient, and loving connections. Essentially, it highlights the essence of love and loyalty, the basis upon which father-son relationships are built. It reinforces the idea, these roles reflect a resolute commitment to His people, thereby emphasizing the transformative power in a covenant of love.

Drawing inspiration from the Godly attributes showcased, there is encouragement to craft their own accord, infusing them with affection and fidelity, echoing the divine example. This Biblical foundation proves pivotal in shaping the legacy of instruction and nurturing passed down through the generations, underscoring the importance of such a promise in these relationships. Its significance lies in being the cornerstone of the legacy imparted, emphasizing the provided direction, and building a lasting impact reverberating through time.

The covenant, influenced by God's love, forms the basis upon which fathers construct their relationships, a dedication to immediate needs, and the placement of values, wisdom, and tireless support. This foundation emphasizes these relationships extend beyond the present, shaping the character, beliefs, and values which, in turn, influence future generations. It underscores the importance of a bond as it forms the eternal legacy left behind, perpetuating instruction and devotion.

The exploration unveils the essence of dedicated promises, highlighting their significance in forging deep and passionate bonds. This involves reflecting on the idea of a father's role extending far beyond biological ties;

it encompasses a solemn faithfulness to guide, nurture, and love unconditionally. The commitment is underscored as akin to a sacred vow, a covenant not to be taken lightly. By rooting relationships in such pledges, the stage is set for a loving atmosphere where connections can bloom. The spiritual dimension of these promises is reflected, recognizing they are not just earthly commitments but also reflections of the divine love and guidance fathers should strive to embody. It serves as a reminder that love, counsel, and nurturing should be more than words; they should be solemn commitments creating unbreakable connections.

Significance of Sacred Promises

Moving forward, the importance of grounding the relationship in sacred promises surpasses the notion, these connections are solely based on biological inference. The emphasis lies in forging deep and meaningful commitments, beginning with a reflection on the idea, while blood ties are significant, they should not exclusively underpin a strong father-son bond.

Instead, the perspective presented advocates for a robust and enduring relationship founded on commitments. These encompass the vows made to guide, nurture, and unconditionally love. The Scriptures, emphasizing this tenet, underscore the significance of biological ties not solely constituting the foundation of a father-son relationship. The belief asserted is a truly everlasting and meaningful connection transcending mere blood relations. The importance is underscored in forging deep loyalty, encompassing the commitments made to guide, nurture, and unconditionally love. While biology may unite fathers and sons, their dedication to love, guide, and nurture forms the strongest alliance.

These organic ties may provide a starting point, but they are just the beginning of a lifelong journey of mutual experiences, integral support, and familial love. Through these commitments, fathers become mentors, role models, and lifelong sources of guidance and support. The conveyance of this relationship is not solely defined by a genetic code; rather, it is expressed by sacred promises and dedication made to build a fortified and resilient connection.

EMBRACING LOVE AND GUIDANCE

A parallel can be drawn from Matthew 12:46-50, emphasizing the significance of spiritual kinship: *"While Jesus is still talking to the crowd, his mother and brothers stand outside, wanting to speak to him. Someone tells him, 'Your mother and brothers are standing outside, wanting to speak to you.' He replies, 'Who is my mother, and who are my brothers?' Pointing to his disciples, He says, 'Here are my mother and my brothers. For whoever does the will of my Father in heaven is my brother and sister, and mother."* This passage serves as a reminder, the father-son relationship extends beyond the physical seed and is firmly grounded in the promise of their devotion, values, and trust.

Just as God's promises are trustworthy, so too is His allegiance. The aim is to inspire and encourage fathers to recognize the impact of these commitments and approach their roles with the utmost dedication and sincerity. In doing so, they strengthen these relationships and lay the foundation for a legacy of love, mentorship, and nurturing. It transcends familial duty and becomes a trust to provide support, encouragement, and wisdom, instilling values beyond the confines of kinship. This forms the foundation of a father-son alliance and serves as a powerful testament to their legacy.

As an affirming reminder, within the realm of fatherhood, there exists an immense sense of responsibility. Highlighting its depth, emphasizing the decisive significance of a solemn oath to guide, nurture, and wholeheartedly love their sons. Fathers are not passive observers; instead, they actively engage in their duty to provide persistent support, care, and affection. These connections are not to be taken lightly; they serve as the very substance upon which robust father-son relationships are constructed. They symbolize dedication to embodying divine love and mentorship.

As fathers, the willingness to embrace the role of being earthly representations of Godly love and leadership is paramount. This role transcends the biological ties noted; instead, it is a sacred and honorable duty requiring the provisions of resolute love, steadfast support, and invaluable inspired wisdom. In doing so, they reflect the heavenly example set before them, striving to embody the qualities of love, faithfulness, and guidance that are characteristic of their Creator. This allegiance goes beyond the ordinary and underscores the lifelong impact of caregiving, mentorship, and spiritual development through a steady presence and devotion. In Scripture, this passage sheds light on the significance of fathers mirroring the divine example noted in Ephesians 5:1-2, "*They are encouraged to follow God's example, therefore, as dearly loved children, walking in the way of love, just as Christ loved them and gave himself up for them as a fragrant offering and sacrifice to God.*" These verses emphasize the importance of fathers who are called to exemplify God's selfless love, serving as living examples of divine compassion and sacrifice.

To imitate the Heavenly example involves embodying love in its purest form, transcending conditions and circumstances. It becomes a bastion of security and acceptance, cultivating a robust sense of self-worth and emotional stability. God's guidance, based on principles of righteousness, truth, and moral values, is a model to follow, helping navigate life's complexities with integrity and discernment. This mentorship includes offering advice, leading by example, and demonstrating virtuous living through actions and choices. It encompasses faithfulness, meaning a consistent and reliable presence. Just as the Divine is a constant presence, being there to provide support, encouragement, and reassurance is integral. This consistency builds trust and a sense of security in relationships, allowing individuals to grow and develop with confidence.

Reflecting on this example involves loving unconditionally, offering wise and morally grounded guidance, and maintaining a strong and dependable presence. In doing so, while contributing significantly to character maturity, moral values, and spiritual growth, it lays the foundation for a strong relationship reflecting virtuous qualities. This commitment not only shapes the immediate alliance between the father and his son but also echoes the everlasting and divine principles embracing their relationship.

Fathers as Earthly Representatives

In their roles as the earthly embodiment of love and guidance, fathers hold significant influence in their understanding of essential virtues such as compassion, loyalty, and instruction. This influence is not confined to the realm of abstract ideologies, but instead extends to the tangible impact of lived experiences. Manifesting these virtues in everyday actions and interactions is a responsibility of immense weight, necessitating their

EMBRACING LOVE AND GUIDANCE

dedication. This duty surpasses the simple utterance of words; it is a call to exemplify these virtues through their deeds, creating a resonating example. In this way, fathers transform into more than just parental figures, becoming spiritual mentors, instructors, and guides, imparting moral lessons and the essence of a meaningful and spiritually enriched life. By assuming the role of earthly representatives of Godly qualities, the role played in character expansion, offering a concrete model to emulate, a guidepost begins to shape values, choices, and adjusting their viewpoint on life.

This connection, rooted in love and guided by trust, forms a connection extending beyond the temporal and into the realm of the eternal. The emphasis here lies in recognizing the transformative impact of upholding a covenant of love within their relationship. Such a covenant transcends the boundaries of the temporal and material aspects of life; it peers deep into the realm of spiritual maturity and character formation. This pledge, woven with the threads of wholeheartedness and devotion, instill a sense of security, trust, and an understanding of the values forming the very load-bearing stratum of their relationship. It is this secure foundation laying the groundwork for them to mature into solid Christian men who possess a well grounded moral compass and bear the responsibility of guarding the family legacy.

This eternal treaty ensures the timeless impact of a father's role as an earthly spokesman, persisting as a guiding force through the ages. It evolves into a legacy resonating within this relationship and extending its influence across the broader fabric of society, imbuing the hearts and minds of future heirs with these important values. It is an accord transcending generations, perpetuating the significance of a father's love and leadership. Highlighting a father's willingness to embrace the role of being an earthly embodiment of divine love and instruction holds immense significance. This role carries a tremendous responsibility, as they are tasked with exemplifying qualities closely aligned with the very essence of divinity. Compassion and mentorship, attributes often regarded as inherently Godlike, cease to be tangent abstract concepts; instead, they manifest as living realities in the intricate relationship between fathers and their sons.

CHAPTER FIVE

They become channels through which Godly love and guidance flow, creating an everlasting bond with sweeping implications transcending the earthly realm. It permeates every facet of the relationship, molding it into a transcendent and transformative experience. Those who embody these qualities in their interactions elevate the relationship to a higher plane. By providing a tangible model of upright living extending beyond theory and theology and aligning actions with these statutes, fathers can teach and demonstrate the power of these virtues in shaping character, building trust, and nurturing a sense of purpose. Their sons grow into personas of love, truth, and counsel, illuminating the path to a life enriched with spiritual and moral values. This embodiment of righteousness imparts wisdom and leaves a memorable mark on their hearts and minds, building a path to carry forward the legacy of love and mentorship.

Within this role, fathers serve as mirrors reflecting divine inspiration, allowing others to witness love and instruction in action. It is not just about preaching; it's about living out their Christian principles in daily life. The essence of serving as ambassadors of love and leadership lies not in sermonizing the outlines of doctrinal statutes but instead in embodying them daily. This transformative role transcends the spoken word since they become living examples, illuminating the path toward practicing these values of love, patience, kindness, selflessness, wisdom, steadfastness, and compassion.

Enlightenment becomes a lighthouse of wisdom in the hands of those who make decisions rooted in thoughtful consideration and moral postulates, revealing counsel is not arbitrary but is based on an understanding of what is right and just. By modeling steadfastness, guidance remains constant even in the face of challenges and embodies compassion by providing support and understanding in times of difficulty. When living out these principles, they create a tangible blueprint. Witnessing firsthand the manifestation and outpouring of instruction and advice can transform relationships, developing them into robust, meaningful, and loving bonds. Through their everyday actions, they contribute to the creation of a legacy rooted in wisdom and compassion, one enduring through generations as they pass on profound lessons learned from earthly representatives of divine principles.

EMBRACING LOVE AND GUIDANCE

The responsibility of embodying Godly advice and counsel on earth means possessing the potential to shape an understanding of these values and the character and moral orientation of those under their care. This is a transformative journey in which they assume a central role in nurturing those who embrace the significance of these ideologies and internalize them, thereby perpetuating the legacy.

Through faithfulness, they illustrate the significance of trust, reliability, and an unwavering commitment in managing a climate of security and dependability. Mentorship, provided with wisdom and empathy, becomes a tool to navigate life's challenges, building resilience and developing the ability to make ethical choices. This process forms a lasting legacy as lessons and principles are absorbed and carried forward. Witnessing the alignment of actions with Godly virtues brings an understanding of the significance of these values in shaping not just character but also approaches to life.

Their mutual alignment with spiritual ideals strengthens the alliance, creating a deep sense of connection rooted in common values. The significance of serving as examples of loyalty, faithfulness, and trustworthiness is a testament to its lasting influence. It is through this role they contribute to spiritual and moral growth, leading those who carry forward the legacy of trust and tutorship into the world and perpetuating the powerful impact of their responsibility as earthly representatives.

The pivotal influence of sustaining a love connection within the father-son bond is essential, transcending a symbolic notion to become a divine force sculpting the development and character of their offspring in dynamic dimensions. Upholding this covenant entails a relationship deeply embedded in unfaltering love, trust, and commitment. This substratum uniquely affects spiritual evolution, building feelings of security and belonging and facilitating the exploration of spirituality within a robust framework.

Within this intricate interrelation, the encouragement to explore queries of faith and morality is accompanied by sagacious guidance, steering them through their transcendent journeys. The basis of maintaining a promise of love within this connection indeed exerts a loving impact on their spiritual development. It creates a nurturing environment where one feels a deep sense of security and belonging. This sense of security is fundamental in facilitating the exploration of spirituality with confidence and curiosity, recognizing there is a robust support system in place. In the context of this connection, one is not solely a passive recipient of Godly teachings but an active participant in their own spiritual growth. They are encouraged to pose questions, seek answers, and embark on their own journeys of faith and morality. Fathers, as mentors and guides, have an intricate role in this process by providing wisdom and care. They offer insights into complex matters, sharing their own experiences, and their leadership is both nurturing and based on Biblical principles. This supportive and caring environment deepens an understanding of faith and morality and develops a sense of ownership over Godly beliefs.

Their guidance offered is marked by wisdom which goes beyond rules and dogma, emphasizing the importance of a genuine and authentic spiritual connection. The dedication becomes fertile ground for the exploration of spirituality. It cultivates a sense of curiosity, a hunger for understanding, and an appreciation for the moral and ethical dimensions of life. This process enriches their own lives and contributes to the legacy of compassion and mentorship passed on, ensuring its impact on Godly development endures through time.

Its influence extends to overall spiritual health, molding character by instilling values such as compassion, forgiveness, and empathy. Those raised in this environment learn the importance of treating others with kindness and respect, and they carry these standards in their interactions with the world. It encourages their sons to be morally upright in making ethical choices, not just because they have to, but because they understand the significance of doing so in the context of love and loyalty. They soon discover it is an understanding of love both active and transformative.

This has a deep-seated and lasting impact on spiritual growth and character evolution. It provides the tools needed to lead meaningful and righteous lives, grounded in love and guided by the examples of their earthly surrogates. This ensures the influence of fathers as mentors and guides extends far beyond the immediate relationship, leaving a legacy of love and spiritual maturity.

EMBRACING LOVE AND GUIDANCE

The keen impact of a loving and faithful relationship cherishes the transformative power of this relationship. This connection searches deep into emotional, moral, and spiritual dimensions, gathering essential elements for a healthy and well-adjusted life. When cultivated in an environment of empathy and compassion, their sons experience a sense of security and trust, molding their emotional safety. An understanding of unconditional love is gained, including the significance of trust and the reassurance fatherly support is a heartbeat away.

Through the example set by their fathers, their sons soon learn the importance of the moral values of integrity, honesty, and righteousness. Witnessing the embodiment of these values in action through practical demonstration instills a strong sense of ethics and responsibility. The spiritual dimension of this relationship nurtures a connection. When guided, they explore questions of faith, doctrine, and the greatness of the Holy Scriptures with a sense of reverence and inquiry.

This loving and faithful alliance serves as a crucible for emotional, moral, and spiritual growth. It provides a solid foundation to navigate the complexities of life with resilience, empathy, and a profound sense of purpose. This ensures the pertinent impact of an earthly archetype, leaving a legacy of love, moral values, and spiritual depth. The significance of worldly ambassadors in embodying divine love and guidance is vital, since this directs the focus towards the impact of their pivotal role on various dimensions.

The primary emphasis lies in the relational dynamics, where living examples of love, truthfulness, and counsel shape a bond characterized by trust, respect, and emotional connections. It plays a significant part in personal growth. The actions and guidance from mentors instill moral values, ethical principles, and a strong sense of responsibility. It is then, one acquires an understanding not only of what is right but also of its underlying significance, promoting the development of a robust character marked by compassion, integrity, and empathy. The role of fatherly guides extends into the spiritual realm, offering a platform for the exploration of spirituality, questioning faith and morality, and seeking deeper connections.

CHAPTER FIVE

Maintaining the Sacred Covenant

In the establishment and nurturing of a covenant of love, there is an important role actively played. This spotlight brings to sharp relief the significance of taking the initiative to create and sustain this pledge. Its emphasis extends well beyond the boundaries of the present generation, leaving a lasting impression on both the immediate relationship and the legacy passed down. The act of forging is not haphazard but rather an intentional and purposeful endeavor. These interactions become rituals, forming an institution of love, trust, and steadfastness. The intentional effort put into these interactions leaves a lasting impact, transcending the immediate relationships and shaping a legacy lasting a lifetime.

This effort, guided by a sincere sense of Godly purpose, serves as the pretext upon which a lasting and meaningful interaction exists. Within this, love is not an abstract concept; it becomes a living spirit, sustaining and nourishing the connection. Guidance then transcends advice; it becomes a formative source leading the way through life's challenges and uncertainties. It isn't just spoken of; it is ingrained in the very nature of the relationship.

Further, faithfulness is not a passive virtue; it is an active commitment to being there for one another through the good and bad times. This intentional act of forging is an investment in the future, both for the father-son relationship and the generations to follow. It is a Godly legacy in the making, a testament to the everlasting power of love, and a blueprint for meaningful and purposeful connections resonating through the ages.

Maintaining this alliance is equally vital. It signifies an ongoing agreement to upholding values. By consistently modeling these virtues through actions, reinforcing the relationship builds trust. They adapt to the changing dynamics of life, always confirming their bond remains strong and unwavering. Those who experience this depth of care and mentorship are more likely to pass it on to their own heirs. The abiding heritage of safekeeping and counsel becomes a powerful force for building character, values, and relationships. Remember, this pledge is not a passive agreement but an active and intentional effort, leaving an ingrained influence on the present relationship and paving the way for a legacy of caring connections extending far into the future. The act of building this begins with

EMBRACING LOVE AND GUIDANCE

acknowledging their vital role as counselors of a Godly origin. Understanding actions speaks louder than words, and a commitment to this sets the tone for the entire relationship. This recognition inspires the initiation of meaningful interactions, building trust, and cultivating an environment where the bond can flourish.

Encouragement to view fatherhood as an ongoing journey is present since the connection is not motionless but dynamic and evolving. As such, recognizing this continuous effort is required to maintain its vitality. This requires an adaptation to changing needs and circumstances, always prioritizing the principles of love in action. It calls for active involvement and intentionality in efforts, understanding this alliance has far-reaching effects on the immediate relationship along with the spiritual and moral legacy passed on. Their inheritance extends beyond the current moment, leaving a lasting impression shaping future generations. The influence ripples through time, affecting subsequent family members as well.

In actively nurturing this connection, fathers impart moral values, providing a template for constructing meaningful relationships. The inheritance positively influences succeeding generations by instilling in them the importance of moral Christian values, empathy, and compassion, while equipping them with the tools to navigate the complexities of life with integrity and a sense of purpose. As their birthright continues to unfold, it constructs a community built on fundamental beliefs, trust, and sincere interactions, making a positive impact on society. It serves as a motivator for taking action, organizing intentional allegiance to the Scriptural tenets, and understanding the impact created in constructing, molding, and leading a brighter and more harmonious future.

Counsel through Generations

The central focus remains steady in illuminating the lasting impact arising from the maintenance of affectionate counsel. This impact, stretching far beyond the boundaries of the present moment, emphasizes the effects transcending this relationship. It weaves through the generations to come, leaving a noticeable and transformative legacy in its wake. Carefully nurtured and unwaveringly upheld by mentors of the family history with

CHAPTER FIVE

intention and devotion, it serves as a powerful marker. It does more than just illuminate a path; it becomes a guiding light to follow. This path extends deep into their relationships, interactions with the world, and future roles as fathers.

Meticulously crafted and passed down through generations, this endowment serves as a guarantee the values of love, trustworthiness, and guidance endure as an unbroken chain, connecting one generation to the next in a canvas of Godly living. Extending beyond the immediate familial context, it reverberates throughout society, carrying these values into their diverse spheres they impact. Inspired by exemplary figures in their lives, they become beneficiaries and bearers of this bond of love, transmitting it to the next generation. This establishes an ongoing cycle of principled living transcending time and place.

Experiencing this depth within their connection urges them to uphold these truths in their own lives, evolving into fathers who lay hold of the immense influence on their descendants and are motivated to preserve this sacred link. This continuity assures the legacy remains a living reality, developing the character and values of numerous generations. The reflection serves as a powerful reminder of the significant influence fathers have in fashioning the present and future of their families. It goes beyond being a simple agreement; it becomes an extruding momentum for family connections and values for generations.

Within the family, this serves as the cynosure, guiding a deep sense of belonging and connection and emphasizing an individual's participation in a lineage marked by love, gratefulness, and tradition. The sense of belonging forms the foundation of strong family bonds, promoting closeness, trust, and a commitment to upholding these values. The heritage created through this extends beyond the confines of the family home, radiating outward and influencing family members in their interactions with others. Those members, inspired by the statutes embodied, become ambassadors in their communities, carrying forward the legacy into society.

In addition, the traditions created by this covenant serve as a testament to the lasting impact of their role as carriers of Godly virtue, underscoring their power to mold not just their own lifetimes but the lifetimes of their children, grandchildren, and beyond. Their inheritance becomes a testament to the uplifting power of love and guidance, echoing through the annals of time and leaving a memorable memory.

This reflection serves as a reminder of the fatherly influence on creating a family legacy extending far beyond their own lives. It highlights the bonds and values formed by the Godly morals upheld, with the impact of their role as delegates resonating through generations, an heirloom enriching countless lives. This spotlights the aspect of legacy-building in fatherhood, emphasizing the potential to leave a lasting and positive impact on both current and future generations.

However, the message is clear: fathers are not just participants within the family dynamics; they are the draftsmen of this bequeathal. By actively and intentionally nurturing the relationship, they create a basis upon which future generations can build. This is not just a theoretical idea but a tangible reality, influencing family members in their relationships with one another. It emphasizes the transformative power of actions, urging the proactive establishment of an atmosphere characterized by love and understanding.

In doing so, it paves a way for future descendants to experience the depth of these virtues and carry them forward into their own lives. This serves as a call to recognize the significance of the role as ambassadors of Godly love and instruction. It motivates a deliberate and intentional commitment; understanding the influence extends beyond lifetimes, shaping character, values, and relationships. This brings to light the substantial potential to leave a legacy enriching the lives of descendants and perpetuate a cycle of love and wisdom within the family.

Fathers Unwavering Commitment

The significance of commitment transcends the regular duties of fatherhood; instead, it emerges as the very essence of fatherly responsibility. This understanding is fundamental to grasping the depth of such dedication. The influence of this alliance permeates every facet of existence.

CHAPTER FIVE

It initiates with growth, where resolve and good health nurture an environment of security and stability. In this milieu, their sons can flourish and reach their full potential, assured in the preservation of manhood yet to be fully developed, with reliable support at every step.

Character maturity also takes center stage in this influence, as ethical firmness becomes a guiding force, imparting values, principles, and molding a moral directive. Through a father's example, a son gains insights into integrity, responsibility, and the importance of doing what is right, even when faced with adversity. This dedicated approach becomes foundational in solidifying their unbreakable connection. It serves as the fundamental underpinning upon which this closeness is constructed, and through this consistent commitment, dependability emerges as the mainspring of this formidable relationship.

Trust becomes an integral component, and one learns to place their faith not solely in verbal promises but also in consistent actions. Persistent dedication, regardless of circumstances, establishes a sense of security and reliability, nurturing this attribute between them. It forms the foundation upon which the entire relationship is established. Their expressions transcend words, finding manifestation in the continuous and steady presence within the familial relationship. The sense of being deeply cherished and valued permeates, acknowledging an embrace to goodness and development. This love operates as a Godly force, weaving an emotional connection and providing the substance for a strong kinship.

Reliability is another aspect of this lasting connection. This commitment ensures a consistent source for guidance, support, and a dependable pillar during life's challenges. Through consistent support and actions, a mentor becomes a reliable source of wisdom and strength, fortifying the depth of their relationship. The connection serves as the underpinning upon which an unbreakable bond is constructed. It forges trust, love, and reliability as the fundamental elements of a lasting alliance.

Through this relationship, character and values take shape, contributing to an interdependence transcending temporal and situational boundaries. The perseverance leaves an unforgettable imprint on growth and character. It conveys a potent message regarding the significance and necessity of

EMBRACING LOVE AND GUIDANCE

being dependable and responsible. Experiencing this support and internalizing these virtues molds character in positive ways. Since the consistent devotion within the love covenant serves as a linchpin in spiritual success, it offers a role model of commitment to moral and ethical principles, inspiring them to pursue their journey with a deep sense of purpose and devotion. Within this bond of love, it acts as a force shaping growth, character, and spiritual maturity in lasting ways, leaving a valuable impression for those following an embraced path.

It is important to note, this central idea emphasizes the significance of loyalty as the role model resting upon which the covenant of love and a father's pledge are constructed. This concept highlights the devotion offered is not a brief or conditional promise but rather a solemn and enduring vow forming the foundation of their relationship. Their allegiance transcends words; it becomes an inseparable part of the relationship's fabric, extending beyond the ordinary obligations of parenthood and signifying a strong commitment to the successful development.

Regardless of circumstances, this loyalty represents a lifelong promise to always be present, standing as a devoted support system, providing stability and strength to their relationship. The showcased resolve distinguishes a biological tie from a meaningful connection, emphasizing a presence not confined to moments of celebration but extending resiliently through life changing events. It is this determination nurturing trust, love, and emotional bonds, cultivating a deep connection.

Essentially, the core concept emphasizes a sturdy commitment as its essence, exemplifying the lasting and unbreakable nature of this relationship and molding it into a source of strength, guidance, and love relied upon throughout their lives. This highlights the depth undertaken, extending well beyond words. It symbolizes a resolute commitment and devotion to nurturing well-being, growth, and peace, representing a vow to offer consistent support, guidance, and affection during times of need, becoming a steadfast pillar.

This singular pledge carries a sense of responsibility and duty, signifying the roles of protector, mentor, and guardian, embodying the values of love, faithfulness, and instruction through their actions. It serves as a promise to

CHAPTER FIVE

nurture and uplift, aiding in the evolution of a strong, compassionate, and Christian life. It brings into focus the earthly representatives of divine qualities as one makes a commitment transcending words. It stands as a solemn promise, a wholesome vow, signifying sustaining resolve to always stand by, guiding through life's journey with love, wisdom, and support.

This pledge forms the foundation of the cherished relationship, emphasizing trust and affection. The concept assumes a central role in shaping and strengthening the emotional connections between them. It serves as the foundation upon which trust and emotional intimacy are meticulously established. Envision resolves as the sturdy and unyielding support of a bridge, connecting the two and enabling them to navigate hurdles and happiness together. This support remains resolute even in the face of life's storms, providing essential stability for trust and emotional devotedness to thrive.

Through their affirmation, fathers make a solemn pledge to maintain a constant presence in their sons' lives. This presence is not sporadic or occasional; it is consistent. It signifies being there in moments of triumph and celebration, but equally, standing firmly by their side during times of adversity and hardship. Their dedication extends throughout all aspects of life, embracing moments of joy and success as well as trials and setbacks. Providing a steady hand, a listening ear, and a loving heart, they reinforce this commitment who knows no bounds. This devotion is not a promise for the present but a legacy for the future.

Understanding their actions sets an example, and they are inspired to carry forward principles of love and guidance in their own lives and relationships. In this way, commitment becomes a powerful force, extending beyond the immediate relationship and echoing through generations. This illustrates a solemn pledge to always offer support, guidance, and love, forming a legacy influencing the values and principles passed down.

The dedication described here extends far beyond emotions, embodying a comprehensive resolve to provide long-lasting support, encouragement, and wisdom. As spokesmen of divine love and guidance, fathers become constant sources of these fundamental elements in their loved ones' lives.

EMBRACING LOVE AND GUIDANCE

The pledge is to be there through all phases of life, offering more than just words but instead a tangible presence to lean on. This support builds a sense of security and resolve, allowing individuals to manage difficulties with the knowledge of a loyal pillar of support. Additionally, there is a consistent provision of encouragement, motivating them to pursue dreams, overcome obstacles, and strive for excellence. Through words of encouragement and belief in the potential they possess, family members are empowered to reach for their aspirations without relenting.

Beyond providing support and encouragement, mentors as guides contribute visual examples, drawing upon life experiences to share invaluable insights and seek to instill discernment, integrity, and responsibility. Their dedication molds the relationship and influences the character and values of those under their instruction. Its comprehensive approach, encompassing long-term support, encouragement, and wisdom, serves as a guiding beacon.

As agents of divine qualities, fathers embrace the role of being perpetual and invaluable sources of these elements. Their dedication nurtures the growth, character, and spiritual progress for those they influence, leaving an everlasting legacy. Continuous support forms the foundation of this relationship, illustrating a commitment to maintaining a constant presence, irrespective of circumstances. It embodies the idea of standing together through every phase of life, whether during moments of joy and success or in times of difficulty and adversity.

Dedication encompasses the provision of reassurance and reliable support. This support becomes a source of security and trust, underpinning the very foundation of the relationship. The sense of security derives from the knowledge in knowing, no matter the dilemmas or uncertainties life may present, there is a consistent connection. Their commitment is comprehensive, offering an ear in every facet of life. It develops a nurturing environment where one can freely express thoughts, concerns, and emotions.

Fatherhood instills a sense of confidence and self-worth while offering peace and a moment of meditation aside God's word. There is purpose in abiding alongside the Spirit, receiving strength, resilience, and a lending hand to assist in overcoming dilemmas through a compassionate and understanding presence, easing the burdens of life's difficulties. Consistent support, in essence, encompasses the complete spectrum of a life journey. It signifies loyalty in nurturing growth and hospitality, serving as a constant source of comfort, guidance, and encouragement. This presence creates a strong and meaningful bond, marked by trust, love, and a deep sense of security.

Through thick and thin, fathers, mentors, and guides stand as pillars of support, ensuring no one walks alone. In these moments, encouragement reveals itself as a key component of the father-son bond. As the passage from Galatians 6:2, aptly states: "*Carry each other's burdens, fulfilling the law of Christ.*" This Biblical guidance aligns with the active and supportive role fathers play in the lives of their sons. By sharing burdens and offering mutual support, they contribute to the fulfillment of Christ's teachings, embracing a connection withstanding the tests of time.

During these instances of support, encouragement emerges as a vital and transformative element, reinforcing the inner strength of the father-son relationship. Within the cyclical times of life, fathers provide words of affirmation and motivation, instilling a sense of confidence and self-belief in their sons. This encouragement empowers them to pursue goals with determination and resilience.

Knowledge and wisdom are integral aspects of dedication as well. Drawing upon life experiences and the principles of love and guidance, they offer sound advice, imparting not just practical knowledge but also moral and ethical teachings. This aids in navigating complexities with discernment. It is seen as an integral part of perseverance in the active phase, manifested through persistent presence and involvement. By actively engaging in a supportive exchange, beneficiaries of this commitment find a limitless source of strength, aiding in growth, maturity, and the development of virtuous character in carrying forward the family legacy of love.

Spiritual Character Development

Within the resolute covenant of love, a nurturing environment reflects growth across diverse domains. This fertile terrain teems with the potential for abundant growth, especially when fathers showcasing their remarkable commitment, provide essential support and guidance for exploring varied interests and talents. Whether academic, artistic, athletic, or any other pursuit, their sons are emboldened to seek their goals and aspirations. This facilitates physical development and ensures intellectual, spiritual, and emotional maturation.

A covenant of love assumes an intricate role in forming their character. Consistent presence and support serve as a paradigm of integrity, compassion, and responsibility. Learning by example, through keen observation, facilitates the graceful navigation of their daily challenges. It is then, their practice of treating others with kindness and respect becomes an integral element in the constructive process. This instills a robust moral path, aiding in the discernment of right from wrong and building character by exemplifying virtues such as empathy, honesty, and resilience.

Beyond the realms of growth and character, it extends into the sphere of spiritual development. Standing as earthly representatives of God's forthright mission, fathers establish an environment wherein their sons explore godliness, the significance of Biblical teachings, and seek a deeper connection with God through Christ Jesus. This setting serves as a platform for inquiries on themes of faith, morality, and the meaning of life in light of the inspired text.

Through persistent and a fortifying loyalty to this covenant, fostering a heartfelt and personal understanding of spiritual beliefs within the family stands at the forefront of the bond. This spiritual growth transcends religious practices, encompassing a broader sense of purpose, an understanding of God's Word, and its practical life applications.

In the context of a staunch position, a nurturing environment shapes growth, character, and future prospects. Through this unwavering loyalty, they consistently provide support and encouragement, extending across the facets of life, daily routines, weekend ventures, church and family camps, group outings, and more. Assuming the roles of mentors and guides, fathers cultivate a sense of self-belief and self-worth. This tireless effort operates as a salient motivator, sparking the pursuit of aspirations with confidence and determination.

Imparting wisdom by suggesting setbacks are not failures but opportunities for growth encourages perseverance and the ability to rebound from adversity. A purposeful commitment to love establishes a robust foundation for future endeavors. This dedication empowers the pursuit of greatness by setting ambitious goals and diligently working to achieve them. It serves as the springboard for gaining confidence during the transition into adulthood, saturated with a clear sense of purpose. Within this nurturing environment, a daily array of actions and teachings accentuates the importance of honesty, integrity, and compassion. Observing firsthand the method by which mentors navigate life's complexities with grace and moral clarity, acts of kindness, selflessness, and responsibility become inherent traits of a maturing persona.

During the journey into manhood, these principles of moral and ethical conduct become internalized and seamlessly integrated into the understanding of how to live and engage with the world. The realization dawns: honesty is not just a policy but a way of life; integrity forms the basis of trust; and compassion propels meaningful connections with others. The received moral and ethical upbringing builds temperament in myriad ways, giving rise to mature souls imbued with strong moral values and principles and a persistent commitment to do what is right, even in the face of worldly temptations offering to compromise.

Integrity emerges as a defining trait, seamlessly carried into every facet, spanning personal relationships to professional endeavors. Compassion, grounded in the experience of God's love, becomes the guiding strength in their interactions. The inclination to extend a helping hand, offer a listening ear, and exhibit empathy and understanding toward those in need is deeply ingrained. This sense of compassion enriches their lives and positively impacts those around them. Character growth through spiritual maturity is not a passive process; it is an active and intentional molding of moral and ethical values. It results in a harmony within the covenant of love and constitutes a legacy of great influence on their son's spiritual headway and development.

Exploring Godly Spirituality

In offering a structured framework for exploring Godly spirituality, fathers provide a supportive process within the guidelines of Scripture, encouraging inquiries into matters of faith and morality, nurturing curiosity and reverence, and enabling their sons to cultivate a unique and personal connection with the Biblical tenets. The dedication within this pledge extends beyond the present, acting as a guiding stronghold in shaping future relationships and personal growth.

This commitment serves as an influential presence, nurturing development, fortifying character, and contributing to spiritual welfare. It lays the groundwork for a future characterized by meaningful connections and personal advancement. Recognizing the importance of trust, empathy, and open communication within the father-son dynamic, these invaluable lessons often become guiding principles in interactions with others.

The instilled virtues serve as a foundation for constructing healthy and positive relationships extending outside the family circle. This commitment reaches beyond immediate connections, positively impacting the broader community and society. Those embodying the values instilled by their mentors actively contribute to beneficial social outcomes, advocating for trust, empathy, and true communication.

The dedication within these significant alliances empowers them to pursue lively objectives while equipping them to become well-rounded and capable of building meaningful connections and maneuvering life's complexities with confidence. The resolve in these relationships serves as a guide, leading one towards a path of personal growth, enhanced interactions, a brighter future, and the world they impact.

It is within the father-son conversations, the presence of a steady alliance instills essential values and virtues as integrity, compassion, and resilience become integral aspects of trait progression. This internal expansion of character isn't a one-time event but an evolving process sustained by their lasting commitment. Integrity and honesty cease to be abstract concepts; instead, they become core standards guiding their path in the Christian walk.

CHAPTER FIVE

Beyond the material and emotional aspects, devotion carries a spiritual dimension, as noted, since this nurturing significantly contributes to overall success, developing a sense of purpose and connection. Opportunities arise for meaningful conversations regarding faith, contemplation of the universe's mysteries created by God, and the pursuit of a deeper understanding of the hidden meanings of Scripture.

In addition, this stance ensures the development of a holistic sense of fortune transcending the material world and encompasses a unique connection to a Godly spiritual realm. Philippians 4:6-7, suggests: *"Don't worry about anything; instead, pray about everything. Tell God what you need, and thank him for all he has done. Then you will experience God's peace, which exceeds anything we can understand. His peace will guard your hearts and minds as you live in Christ Jesus,"* emphasizing the importance of turning to God in prayer, seeking a spiritual connection, and finding peace beyond understanding. This concept is further supported in Colossians 3:2, *"Set your minds on things above, not on earthly things,"* suggesting humankind look beyond the material world and focus on spiritual matters of importance. In doing so, it enriches each life with purpose and a deeper knowledge of one's role in the universe as a son of God created in His own image (Genesis 1:27).

The commitment demonstrated in the present becomes a foundational template for the future. It serves as a powerful benchmark through which one models their own interactions with others. This aspect of the father-son bond extends beyond the family setting; it has far-reaching implications in the broader world of social and interpersonal dynamics. Observers are keen witnesses of these actions, and learn through their watchfulness, the way love should be expressed and received. In essence, they witness firsthand the significance of trust, empathy, and open dialogue within the father-son bond.

These lessons are not theoretical but practical in approach, ingrained in everyday interactions and experiences facilitated by love. The observation reveals trust is not bestowed casually but is earned through consistent, reliable, and honest conduct. Understanding loyalty forms the solid foundation for meaningful connections and becomes ingrained, shaping how they approach friendships, personal relationships, and professional pursuits.

EMBRACING LOVE AND GUIDANCE

Additionally, empathy emerges as another invaluable lesson learned. Through their actions and responses, they exemplify the capacity to comprehend and share in the feelings and experiences of others. Witnessing the way empathy builds deeper connections and nurtures emotional support and understanding, this lesson inspires others to become more compassionate and considerate in their interactions. They carry with them the firsthand experience of empathy's transformative power, applying it to their relationships with others.

Close discussions within the father-son bond sets the stage for healthy dialogue and the expression of thoughts and emotions. Recognizing this engagement through meaningful conversations, where both actively listen and honestly express themselves, leads to better understanding and the resolution of conflicts. This understanding extends to the broader context of interactions with friends, partners, and colleagues. As such, the commitment demonstrated today transcends the family unit and influences how individuals approach their future relationships. They become carriers of the legacy of love and guidance, equipped with the knowledge of how to convey and receive these essential qualities.

Faithfulness, trust, empathy, and open dialogue are the foundational elements for building meaningful and lasting connections. As a result, the personal commitment of fathers today shapes the father-son relationship for tomorrow. It informs them how they can engage with others, forming healthier and more fulfilling relationships in all aspects of their lives. This unyielding viewpoint becomes a model for personal growth, forming the internalization of virtues such as consistency, dedication, and responsibility. The exemplified values encourage recognition of a focus on reaching goals and aspirations, urging the pursuit of excellence in all endeavors.

Provided within the covenant of love, this devotion becomes a source of inspiration, propelling a trajectory toward a future marked by determination and purpose. Spiritual health is deeply influenced by this approach. Those who experience the nurturing of spirituality within the covenant of love are more likely to carry a sense of reverence and connection into their adult lives. They embark on journeys with an understanding of the importance of faith and morality, directed by wisdom, faithfulness, and guardianship instilled. The demonstrated commitment within the familial covenant extends well beyond the present moment, building approaches to future relationships, molding personal growth, and contributing to spiritual protection. It represents a warm and honest legacy, stretching into the future and leaving a lasting, meaningful impact on lives and the world they inhabit.

Dedication within Fatherhood

The dedication within fatherhood holds an important and invaluable role in parenting, extending far beyond basic verbal expressions. It embodies a solemn and firm promise extended to their sons, reflecting a commitment to always stand by them. This loyalty transcends spoken words, carrying substantial weight and significance through actions. At its essence, it entails maintaining a consistent and dependable presence, promising constant support, encouragement, and protection, regardless of circumstances.

This support surpasses material necessities, encompassing emotional and moral guidance. It is a defining attribute within the father-son relationship, providing a source of security and trust and instilling confidence in the very meaning of the bond. The element of encouragement encompasses the process of inspiring and motivating. These items nurture self-confidence and determination, encouraging the pursuit of dreams and goals with untiring belief.

Alongside emotional support, the sharing of wisdom derived from life experiences imparts valuable insights and lessons, guiding informed and principled decisions. This transmission is not an isolated event but an ongoing process of molding character and values over time. The importance of these elements holds considerable weight. They form the essence of relationships, serving as the cornerstone upon which trust, emotional bonds, and the development of these attributes are built. These factors form the present and future, influencing approaches to relationships, decision-making, and navigating the daily threads of life. They represent a sacred and solemn vow, impacting lives, creating loving connections, and nurturing personal growth.

EMBRACING LOVE AND GUIDANCE

Conscientiousness within fatherhood extends beyond passivity, embodying an active and resolute focus on their holistic welfare and creativity. This single-mindedness is an earnest pledge, involving a consistent provision of mentorship and benevolence, establishing a sturdy and dependable presence. It transcends a pure declaration, evolving into a promised manifest through ongoing actions and involvement. Recognizing the importance of a continuous presence and guidance, fathers extend their influence across various facets of their son's growth and development.

One key facet of this dedication lies in the consistency of fatherly mentorship, embracing the responsibility of offering insights, wisdom, and direction. Through mutual life experiences and providing assistance in managing opposition in favor of admirable choices, it sets an exemplified pathway to traverse the journey throughout the family legacy. This guidance through instruction is not confined to specific moments in time but remains a steady, enduring presence, ready to assist in the journaled moments, with a duty to nurture a culture of love within their relationship. In this context, love transcends mere emotion; it represents an immense expression of care, support, and affection.

Fathers can consistently manifest love through words and actions, ensuring their loved ones feel cherished and valued. This emotional connection forms the foundation upon which trust and a strong father-son bond are built. The commitment described is a mobile, ongoing, and relentless perseverance by fathers to be present, navigating through triumphs and adversities. It is a dedication embodying their role as stewards of divine love and moral protection.

Through their continuous mentorship and benevolence, they contribute significantly to growth, character, and overall vigor, leaving a lasting impression. This loyalty forms the very basis upon which love and deep emotional connections are meticulously constructed between fathers and their sons. It is the foundation for a sense of trust and the strong, lasting emotional alliance defining their relationship. These bonds are not constrained; since fathers zestfully nurture them through their dedication and energetic engagement. In the father-son relationship, the building blocks are not assumed; instead, it is a meticulously crafted integration through purposeful decisions and the fulfillment of promises. Resolute in

CHAPTER FIVE

their efforts, fathers pledge to be reliable and ever-present mentors in their sons' lives, extending this commitment across various facets of their partnership. Their sons witness the alignment of words with actions, ensuring the promises spoken are fulfilled. The intricate connection is linked to consistency, where their staying power and loyalty translate into a reliable presence, offering love, guidance, and daily support. This embracing presence cultivates a sense of dependability, reinforcing zeal as evidence of their actions.

Emotional connections, a vital dimension of this bond, flourish through active fatherhood and openly expressing love, care, and affection. Through both words and deeds, an environment is cultivated where feelings are emotionally secure and cherished. The exposition on spiritual development adds another layer of significance. In their continuous commitment, fathers assume the roles of mentors and guides in the spiritual odysseys of their progeny. They actively build an environment conducive to exploring matters of faith and morality, instilling a sense of curiosity and reverence.

This interplay serves as an intimate role in nurturing the spiritual interest of their sons, aiding in the establishment of a profound and personal connection with the Divine. It underscores the impact of faithfulness in the realm of fatherhood, portraying it not merely as a verbal commitment but as a sacred pack with implications extending far beyond words. Such faithfulness refines personal growth, shapes character maturity, and contributes to a spiritual relationship grounded in Godliness. Importantly, these connections transcend simple biological ties, flourishing through ongoing interactions and mutual life experiences.

A father's focus and active engagement act as catalysts for these emotional connections, evident in both celebratory and difficult moments, reinforcing the reliability of their relationship. The persistence in uplifting this bond forms the basis for the thoughtful construction of trust and personal emotional connections. It is a reminder, these elements are not left to chance but are continuously nurtured, recognizing their important role as embodiments of divine love and instruction.

EMBRACING LOVE AND GUIDANCE

Through persistent dedication, they establish a robust foundation of trust and emotional closeness, enriching lives and shaping lasting connections. This plays a central role in developing personal growth since it empowers the wayfinding of life's impediments with resilience and integrity, instilling in them a sense of responsibility and moral values.

—— Guiding with Wisdom ——

Empowering fathers with essential knowledge and inspiration to apply wisdom practically and through Godly love within the context of their father-son relationship is a straightforward endeavor. Proverbs 22:6, *"Train up a child in the way he should go; even when he is old, he will not depart from it,"* serves as a repository of insight, emphasizing the importance of nurturing in alignment with a destined course, a pathway of guidance leading them through the blessed experiences of fatherhood with wisdom, love, and grace.

Derived from the inspired writings of King Solomon, this sacred reminder encourages fathers to instill values, principles, empathy, and compassion as a moral compass, navigating the intricate journey of maturity in the Lord. The timeless nature of this directive offers valuable insights into applying Scriptural teachings to tangible actions within their respective roles.

In a domain promoting growth in learning and understanding, wisdom facilitates open dialogue, encouraging the exchange of knowledge and experience while building mutual respect and trust. These moments become opportunities for inspiration, prompting the pursuit of advice and instruction.

This acknowledgment highlights their understanding gained through life's problems, embracing both hardships and unforeseen twists and turns. The reflection esteems these attributes as an active influence, molding individual roles within the father-son bond. It embodies an influential and leading power rooted in divine principles and values derived from Scripture. The implications are limitless in application, remaining viable through the ongoing presence and impact of God's oversight, forming actions, decisions, and the overall approach to life. This influence is activated and propelled by the Spirit, significant in nature, and aligned with the very essence of God.

Emphasizing a connection to Scriptural tenets, the spiritual source becomes a dynamic element in the exchange between generations, fortifying their bonds and creating a rich fabric of common experiences and lasting values throughout their lifetimes. The pivotal duty of fathers to nurture their sons has a purposeful path. The term "pivotal duty" emphasizes the central and important role fathers have in their sons' lives, especially in their growth and development. This responsibility goes beyond mere caregiving; it encompasses the moral and spiritual education forming the foundation of their character.

The concept of "nurturing" further accentuates their supportive role. It implies they are not just providers of material needs but also mentors responsible for their emotional and intellectual maturity. This process is a mutual journey where they impart practical life skills, including values, principles, and a sense of purpose. The word "purposeful path" highlights the intentionality behind leadership. It signifies the importance of their task in guiding deliberate events in a meaningful direction. This path is not random; it is purpose-driven with a clear intent and direction.

In this passage, fathers are reminded of their pivotal role in extending a calling beyond caregiving, contributing to the understructure of character through the imparting of moral and spiritual education. Entrusted with actively molding the trajectories of their sons' pursuits, they find themselves serving as a source of insight, offering diverse perspectives. This emphasizes the importance of nurturing through fatherhood and provides a clear directive outlining the vital duty of guiding, instructing, and keeping a watchful eye. Called upon to instill values, principles, and wisdom as a moral compass for navigating life's journey, embodies a sacred responsibility as directed.

Entrusted with nurturing the next generation along a Godly path, fathers receive inspiration and a call to action, encouraging the embrace of roles as guides and mentors. This enriches the significance of influencing and

EMBRACING LOVE AND GUIDANCE

shaping the journey. As knowledge and wisdom empower generations to make informed choices, cultivate strong character, and live virtuous lives, the father-son relationship grounded in purposeful instruction and love becomes a beacon of hope and strength, revealing the way forward in life's intricate journey.

In the ongoing exploration, a compelling interpretation emerges, underpinning the significance of tailoring advice to their unique needs and inclinations. This perspective encourages discerning distinct qualities and potential, urging the provision of counsel to align seamlessly. By embracing this approach, it plays a valuable role in aiding the cultivation of a sense of purpose and direction. It is these lessons and values instilled during formative years that seem to leave an ingrained mark, molding character and choices throughout life. This brings into focus the weighty responsibility to guide during formative years and provide a moral directive serving admirably in adulthood.

Recognizing Individuality

The focus is on recognizing uniqueness and the impact of leading by example, offering insights into the roles of mentors, instructors, and guides. At the outset, two key points for discussion arise: The first brings to light the concept of nurturing individuality. Encouraging the acknowledgment of their uniqueness in possessing distinct qualities, talents, inclinations, and potential, this perspective emphasizes the significance of appreciating and nurturing, whether within their family, among mentees, or among those seeking counsel.

Second, it becomes important to find practical ways of actively identifying and celebrating the individuality of those they attend to and mentor, recognizing and uplifting their qualities and potential. To achieve this, strategies such as attentive and empathetic listening, asking thoughtful questions, and conducting strength assessments can be employed. Emphasizing the importance of observation, facilitating self-exploration, and celebrating achievements become integral components of this approach, including tailoring guidance to specific needs, promoting self-acceptance, supporting goal-setting, and maintaining regular check-ins.

CHAPTER FIVE

The goal is to create an environment where feelings are understood and valued, allowing them to flourish on their singular journeys. By applying these strategies, fathers enable their sons to discover and embrace their authentic selves, guiding them towards the fulfillment of their aspirations and potential. This approach highlights the importance of personalized objectives and support in nurturing originality within the mentorship relationship, promoting growth and self-realization.

Focusing on the timeless nature and impact of mentorship significantly influences fathers as guides. This insight underscores the lessons, values, and counsel, leaving a lasting impact on character and choices throughout life. For example, this perspective prompts them to recognize the long-term consequences of their guiding influence. It reminds them the way values and wisdom imparted during early development shape both immediate decisions and future outlooks and behaviors. Just as a stone creates undulations when cast into a pond, this influence has a similar effect, molding numerous aspects of the journey. This presses mentors to view their role beyond the temporal, recognizing it as a lifelong commitment.

Second, fathers bear the responsibility of nurturing character and values; understanding their impact continues well beyond youth. This viewpoint places an emphasis on consistency and dedication in mentorship efforts. In practical terms, it encourages mindfulness of the messages conveyed and the examples set. It reinforces the importance of modeling the values and principles they instill. This long-term mindset also encourages ongoing support and leadership, recognizing the continuous need to seek advice throughout their lives.

Further, highlighting the lasting influence of instruction, this passage establishes the very essence, nature, and enduring impact of its provision. In this setting, introspection and the assessment of emotional maturity play a crucial role, emphasizing the importance of consistency, dedication, and the resilient legacy of the values and wisdom imparted. Recognizing this, their approach aligns with a sense of responsibility, diligence, and commitment. Understanding this influence extends far into the future, shaping character and forming choices.

EMBRACING LOVE AND GUIDANCE

A substantial duty exists in the upbringing and molding of the future, facilitating spiritual and contemplative reflection on how guidance can create perpetual, creative effects in the journey under mentorship and fatherhood. A mental challenge arises concerning the prioritization of values and principles as moral guides while steering future generations. Building on authenticity and consistency forms the basis of effective guidance, establishing trust and credibility. This approach enables upcoming heirs to embrace trust and honesty as they navigate life.

Equally essential is an environment of open and empathetic communication, establishing a sense of safety for sharing thoughts and concerns, and facilitating personalized counseling. Leading by example reinforces these values and principles, serving as tangible embodiments of mentorship. Empowering critical thinking and independent decision-making cultivates autonomy and self-reliance, enabling the next generation to navigate complex situations confidently and building problem-solving skills. Establishing a supportive environment where making mistakes is seen as a valuable learning opportunity is paramount. Providing support during such times, whether they succeed or face setbacks, sustains resilience and encourages calculated risks, knowing there is a safety net to fall back on.

Faith and Spirituality

Basing fatherhood in faith and spirituality is a transformative decision. It entails aligning the instruction and moral directive with deeply held beliefs and a connection to something greater than oneself. Guided by their fathers' Biblical belief and his spiritual principles, their sons are bestowed with a sense of purpose transcending the ordinary pursuits of life. It adds meaning to their actions and decisions, connecting them to a higher calling or divine purpose led by the Holy Spirit, since trust and Godliness provide a sturdy moral footing. It serves as an anchor in the turbulent seas of life's moral dilemmas and ethical decisions. This moral essence is not arbitrary; it is rooted in the ageless Scriptural values and principles enduring the trials of time.

CHAPTER FIVE

In this space, a resolute and steadfast formation arises, providing a basis for shaping character and deciding in harmony with the teachings of the Scriptures. When counsel is firmly anchored in faith and divine inspiration, a beautiful sense of duty to live in alignment with convictions in Christ is instilled. This in turn, further encourages upholding ethical standards and virtuous behavior with Godly accountability, not as a casual obligation but rather as a natural expression of deeply held faith. The alignment develops a sense of inner peace and precious harmony as the understanding prevails.

Embedding instruction in belief and spirituality provides an emerging sense of purpose and moral direction. This alignment directs actions in accordance with deeply held views, offering a clear moral compass to navigate the complexities of life. It is a choice moving far beyond the temporal and situational, offering a timeless and meaningful starting point for ethical living and righteous character development.

Promoting and cultivating empathy and compassion within these moral standards is an important consideration with extensive consequences. These virtues form the fundamental basis of human connection and serve as catalysts for nurturing. Empathy, in its essence, entails walking in another person's footsteps, understanding, and genuinely sharing their feelings and experiences. The encouragement of empathy empowers individuals to transcend their own perspectives and embrace the viewpoints of others. This empathetic comprehension bridges gaps of misunderstanding, nurturing a sense of unity and shared humanity, grace, and love within the father-son relationship. It imparts the significance of attentive listening, not with the ears alone but with the heart, recognizing the emotions and struggles of those in proximity.

Compassion, on the other hand, arises from empathy. It is the heartfelt desire to alleviate the suffering or distress of others. Cultivating fatherly love involves developing a genuine concern for the health of those encountered, leading to acts of kindness, generosity, and support. It is the momentum driving a father's son to take action and improve the lives of others as well, whether through prayer, gestures of goodwill, or more significant acts of service.

This nurtures a culture of kindness and consideration where one naturally looks out for another. It builds a sense of community and supports feeling valued and understood. This reinforces the idea by suggesting each person's struggles and joys are interconnected, promoting a family sense of shared responsibility for the well-being of all.

In prioritizing and nurturing empathy and love within moral guidance, sowing the seeds of kindness and consideration is paramount. The invaluable lessons taught are a recognizable Godly presence led by the Spirit, improving their heirs and humanity. These choices enrich countless lives, strengthen Christian communities, and contribute to a more compassionate and empathetic understanding of the world.

Integrity and Honesty

Upholding integrity and honesty to the status of core values is a virtue of the highest order with far-reaching implications. These values form the nucleus of trust and character, serving as the energy upon which father-son relationships build their reputations and moral identities. Integrity is a commitment to uphold a set of ethical principles, especially when there is no watchful eye. It signifies consistency is in alignment with their actions and deeply held values and beliefs. When integrity is prioritized, fathers become known for their reliability and sturdy adherence to their Godly principles. This consistency creates a sense of trustworthiness others can rightfully depend upon.

Honesty, on the other hand, is the practice of truthfulness and transparency in all interactions, whether seen or unseen. Similarly, the Apostle Paul infers in 2 Corinthians 4:17-18, *"For our present troubles are small and will not last very long. Yet they produce for us a glory that vastly outweighs them and will last forever! So we don't look at the troubles we can see now; rather, we fix our gaze on things that cannot be seen. For the things we see now will soon be gone, but the things we cannot see will last forever."*

The essence of this passage lies in the recognition, current tribulations, though seemingly insignificant and fleeting, serve as an impetus for glory, far surpassing a transient nature and lasting an eternity. It urges a shift in perspective, steering away from the observable, momentary difficulties, and instead, fixing attention on the intangible and hidden aspects of existence. This invites contemplation on the impermanence of visible troubles, emphasizing their eventual evanescence, juxtaposed with the continuing and unseen elements carrying perpetual significance.

The central theme promotes a contemplative understanding, fostering a focus on the timeless and eternal rather than the fleeting and ephemeral aspects of this journey. It is honesty promoting candor and authentic communication, where the father-son bond can rely on the veracity of each other's words. In doing so, it builds an environment of trust where they feel safe sharing their thoughts and concerns.

Affirming trust as a core virtuous attribute has a lasting impact on temperament, becoming an integral part in principled behavior and sincerity. This in turn, fosters a sense of trustworthiness in personal and family relationships transcending selfish gain, representing a deliberate cognitive commitment to doing what is right, even in challenging or inconvenient circumstances. The commitment to ethical behavior builds character and sets a moral standard to follow. It creates a reverberating effect of integrity, reinforcing the importance of principled living.

Therefore, prioritizing and upholding these attributes as core values is a choice, building trust and character in the father-son relationship. It transforms their bond into beacons of reliability and authenticity, creating an atmosphere of love and ethical conduct in all facets of their lives. This becomes a commitment to doing what is right regardless, and in doing so, it enriches both father and son, their family, and the broader Christian community and fellowship.

Resilience and Perseverance

Instilling resilience and perseverance as essential values is a proper choice for providing the right set of equipment to confront life's inevitable curve balls and missed swings with strength and determination. However, resilience is the capacity to bounce back from bad calls and strike-outs. It teaches one not to kick the dirt up in the face of difficulties but to respond with flexibility, adaptability, and a spirit refusing to be defeated.

EMBRACING LOVE AND GUIDANCE

Resilience is about learning from failures and setbacks and using them as an opportunity to step into the batter's box again and hit the next home run. Perseverance, on the other hand, is the commitment to persist in the pursuit of one's goals and ambitions, regardless of the obstacles. It enhances the father-son relationship with value, determination, and grit, instilling the belief, effort and persistence are the keys to achieving success. It is about not giving up when faced with difficulties but pushing through when the path seems steep and daunting.

When fathers teach their sons to navigate hardships with resilience and diligence, it becomes an investment in their ability to thrive. This preparation empowers them for the unpredictable sway in life, instilling the necessary skills and mindset to withstand and overcome the seemingly major undulations. It imparts an understanding, these obstacles are not failures but opportunities for learning and fortification. At this juncture, resilience and perseverance emerge as invaluable assets carried with them through the entirety of their lives. These values also instill a sense of empowerment. It is the buoyancy to weather storms and the determination to pursue far-reaching goals tirelessly helping their sons become architects of their own destinies. They then learn they have the inner strength God provides to shape their lives while making a beneficial impact.

Teaching resilience and perseverance is a choice of empowerment used to face life's detours with strength and fortitude. It shores up their mindset and skills needed to thrive in the face of adversity, reinforcing their belief that they can overcome any obstacle on their journey to success. Elevating personal responsibility and accountability as core values is the right choice for instilling a sense of ownership for these actions and decisions. This responsibility is a primary motivator for life decisions and distilling a proper mindset. It signifies an acknowledgment, actions have consequences, and therefore, their sons are responsible for the outcomes of their decisions. Embracing personal responsibility, culpability, and a sense of onus are proactive choices shaping their lives in pursuit of lifelong goals.

Accountability goes hand in hand with responsibility, and involves taking ownership and embracing both the successes and the mistakes. Fathers in these times have a wonderful opportunity to teach these core values. Because accountability does not shy away from admitting when errors or misjudgments are made. Instead, these situations are confronted with honesty, integrity, and a commitment to making amends and learning from their mistakes. Emphasizing personal responsibility and accountability is a transformative choice in constructing a sense of ownership for actions committed on either side of the fence. It encourages critical thinking by providing an opportunity to reevaluate the choices they make and the impact those choices have on themselves and others. They can lovingly instill a sense of empowering ownership, as it reinforces the idea their sons have agency in their lives and the power to shape their Godly destinies through meaningful choices.

Enduring Parental Influence

The parental influence remains ever-present in the father-son relationship, extending far beyond childhood. It supports this bond through guidance, values, and lessons imparted during the formative years, leaving an everlasting trace on their psyche influencing the choices made throughout their lifetime. Fatherhood responsibilities, encompassing roles as a primary caregiver and mentor, carry significant importance in their development. Fathers take on the duty of being the initial educator, imparting fundamental and core values alongside moral and Biblical principles to steer their future choices and actions.

These early lessons become deeply embedded in the inner soul, shaping decision-making processes as they transition into adulthood. Continuous fatherly influence prompts them to be conscientious about the guidance they offer and the values they exemplify. It brings to light the responsibility inherent in the father-son dynamics of behavior and the virtues they aim to transmit. Interacting in the nurturing process involves upholding a culture of integrity, empathy, love, kindness, and forgiveness within their families; recognizing these qualities will persist and resonate throughout their lives.

The idea of devotion in caregiving underscores the nature of a father's influence, which persists indefinitely. Signifying an immovable interest in the security and development of the father-son relationship, this transcends their age or life stage. It goes beyond specific events, symbolizing a straightforward approach to building their bond, extending past daily tasks and routines, and embodying a solemn promise to consistently offer guidance, support, and love. This dedication is flexible, adapting to the changing needs arising from the maturation process. It encompasses qualities such as wisdom, guidance, and encouragement, providing a reliable presence and instilling a sense of security and reassurance.

The fatherly role, serving as a pathway of dedication throughout a lifetime, involves meaningful contemplation of mentor responsibilities, carrying extensive implications for this perpetual commitment. It becomes apparent the realm of parenting transcends specific life phases; instead, it constitutes an ongoing odyssey demanding a resolute, continuous endeavor. This recognition is a prompt to reflect on the strategies employed to sustain an active and meaningful role in influencing the character and values of those under their instruction. The task of molding their son's persona is a formidable undertaking, and acknowledging this influence extends well beyond formative years and childhood. It permeates every stage of life, from adolescence to adulthood and even into fatherhood. The values, principles, and guidance provided act as a beacon, aiding in the navigation of moral, ethical, and wise decisions.

Actions encompass more than the impartation of knowledge; they embody the demonstration of values. Leading by example not only communicates these values but also manifests the very character and principles one endeavors to instill. This engenders a heartfelt connection and resonance in the father-son relationship, allowing for the authentic experience of living out these concepts. It is a journey demanding continuous dedication, reflection, and active engagement, spanning across the various phases of growth. The pivotal moment arises when fathers recognize their integral role in guiding their sons toward Godliness, not merely through words but significantly through their own exemplary actions and the loyalty they emanate.

Core Values as a Moral Compass

The significance of instilling solid values and Scriptural tenets should not be underestimated. Serving as an ethical direction, these precepts offer insight into navigating life's intricate terrain. They lay the groundwork for decisions within the father-son relationship by influencing interactions with others and upholding integrity. Rooted in deeply held beliefs and ethical standards, essential values become a source of strength and clarity, aiding in discerning right from wrong. When guiding choices aligned with Biblical tenets, they maintain a sense of purpose and authenticity. This emphasizes the valuable impact transcending individual moments or decisions and shapes the course of life. As their sons carry these morals into adulthood, they rely on them as a directive, guiding actions, decisions, and relationships. By embodying these ideals, fathers teach and demonstrate the importance of integrity, compassion, honesty, and other virtues. This modeling reinforces the significance of Godly living as a guiding force in molding character and leading a mature Christian life. A virtuous pathway, forged by these foundational values, accompanies them, providing a sense of direction, purpose, and ethical clarity. Ultimately, these morals contribute to growth and development, making uplifting contributions to their communities and society as a whole.

Honesty is vital to cultivating integrity and trustworthiness. In encouraging fathers to teach the importance of truthfulness and transparency in actions and interactions, this virtue lays the foundation for building strong character and ethical behavior. Values similar to kindness and empathy are instrumental in developing compassion and consideration. This contributes to the development of moral uprightness and promotes harmonious relationships and an understanding of social responsibility.

Embracing an awareness of integrity and compassion then becomes essential, encouraging ethical choices and actions aligned with Scriptural teachings. This perspective underscores a father's pivotal role in molding his son's moral and ethical foundation and highlights the lasting influence of Godly guidance essential for leading them toward a life characterized by righteousness and Christian conduct. Self-discovery flourishes in a nurturing environment where interests, passions, strengths, and values are freely explored. Through open and non-judgmental conversations, the initial step is taken to facilitate the unveiling of innermost desires and motivations within the Christian walk.

EMBRACING LOVE AND GUIDANCE

Personal experiences passed down from fatherhood convey a path for self-discovery, including moments of realization serving as guides and sources of inspiration. Practical approaches, such as journaling, self-reflection exercises, and engaging in activities aligned with interests, offer empowerment opportunities in the quest for self-awareness. This holistic and Biblical approach helps shape a sense of consciousness and acceptance while also establishing the foundation for a lifelong commitment to personal growth. Embracing manhood deepens the father-son relationship, and finding self-worth in this journey is interwoven with fatherly love, understanding, and support.

The voyage is shared into maturity, evolving over time and creating an everlasting bond grounded in the principles of self-discovery and lifelong flourishing. The central focus lies in nurturing perpetual growth, transcending the confines of childhood and adolescence. The connection provides a scaffold for ongoing personal development throughout a lifetime. Consequently, instructional guidance unfolds as an unceasing learning process intertwined with the fabric of daily events. The essential essence directs attention to dialogue centered on the persistent evolution of mental, emotional, and spiritual dimensions into adulthood. This engagement sparks discussions of encouragement, inspiring the establishment of goals, active pursuit of novel experiences, and a perspective perceiving challenges as gateways to personal advancement.

Through the impartation of these values, the tools for steering life's ever-shifting landscapes persistently occupy the forefront. This marks the initial stride in an extensive journey to embrace the authenticity of a familial legacy. The imperative of instilling a growth-oriented mindset serves as a guiding principle in their immediate voyage of self-discovery and endures as a steady companion. This perspective envisions a future where their sons' mindset continuously unfolds, propelled by the lessons and values bestowed by their fathers, thus contributing to the foundational blocks laid since birth.

Highlighting the pivotal position held by their fathers in instilling a thoughtful and memorable love for knowledge, the pursuit of wisdom and understanding extends far beyond formal education, constituting a lifelong journey continually enriching their lives. Within this framework, discussions center on pragmatic strategies for nurturing a commitment to learning. Renowned for their erudition, they actively discuss the hidden meanings of Scripture while exploring its present-day application in creating an environment full of curiosity and intellectual exploration. Valuable insights are shared in facilitating access to ancient texts, educational resources, and opportunities for engagement.

This approach effectively plants the seeds of a lifelong passion for learning. Central to this effort is the encouragement of questioning, seeking answers, and the development of critical thinking skills. The dedication to lifelong learning enriches youthful experiences and contributes to the legacy they are building, a legacy founded on the everlasting pursuit of knowledge and wisdom within the context of a father-son bond. Beyond building a love for secular academia and street-wise learning, such knowledge resides beneath the surface in sacred fatherly duties. In comparison to leading exegetical studies, providing spiritual guidance and nurturing moral development with eternal rewards takes precedence. This dimension of their relationship focuses on instilling values, statutes, and a sense of purposeful design far beyond the present state of mortal mortality.

As fathers invest in guiding their sons toward learning and understanding, the wisdom of Matthew 6:19-21, resonates: *"Don't store up treasures here on earth, where moths eat them and rust destroys them, and where thieves break in and steal. Store your treasures in heaven, where moths and rust cannot destroy, and thieves do not break in and steal. Wherever your treasure is, there the desires of your heart will also be,"* echoing the eternal significance of a father's role, where the sustaining rewards transcend the temporal and earthly, building a legacy rooted in spiritual richness. Through heartfelt conversations and leading by example, imparting spiritual wisdom helps traverse life's moral complexities. This guidance often draws from a faith and belief system, emphasizing the importance of integrity, compassion, and empathy. By molding a strong moral directive and a sincere sense of Godly spirituality, fathers enable their sons to make ethical decisions, act with integrity, and cultivate empathy towards others. This moral foundation shapes their character and contributes to personal growth as they pilot the obstructions and opportunities life presents. The responsibility of guiding emphasizes a significant duty, highlighting a commitment to building character, values,

EMBRACING LOVE AND GUIDANCE

and future direction. The wisdom in Proverbs reflects this vision, placing the need for intentionality and purposefulness within the duties of mentors, guides, instructors, and caretakers.

This influence extends well beyond the initial stages of development, prompting fathers to recognize and appreciate the unique qualities and potential of their sons. It serves as a constant reminder of the responsibility to be dedicated and committed. This responsibility highlights the weight and significance of an active and dynamic role, drawing attention to its involvement in moral, ethical, and spiritual education. It entails providing physical care, emotional support, spiritual guidance, and a nurturing environment conducive to personal growth.

The Scriptural text shines a spotlight on the significance of advice, counsel, and instruction while bringing into focus their lasting impact. It becomes a primary influence in the lives of those they guide, tasked with the critical responsibility of fashioning their values, forming beliefs, and molding character. This character building relies on effective fatherly counseling, offering pointers, suggestions, and recommendations in a deliberate and purposeful endeavor. Encouraged to be intentional in their approach, the role of fatherhood extends far beyond the immediate needs of those they mentor.

The passage establishes the hierarchical structural requirements of familial responsibilities by placing the preponderance of weight on their shoulders in the moral and ethical education of their sons. They are seen as the primary source of leadership in matters of behavior, honor, and goodness. Encouraged to instill virtues such as integrity, kindness, and love, fathers guide the character of their sons by fostering a sense of Godliness. Proverbs magnifies the significance of Biblical guidance in one's development, positioning them as the central figures in their sons' lives, responsible for directing all facets of growth into manhood.

Practicality of Proverbs Wisdom

The Book of Proverbs unveils a wealth of practical and moral wisdom, presenting valuable insights into life, relationships, and Godly conduct. It serves as a timeless directive, providing a rich reservoir of principles and lessons to draw from in a fathers role. One of its remarkable qualities is its relevance to everyday life. Its knowledge is not abstract or detached, but deeply rooted in the realities of human existence, offering guidance on a wide range of topics, including honesty, diligence, humility, and wisdom, all of which are invaluable virtues to impart. Embracing this wisdom personally and sharing it builds growth and contributes to the enhancement of the familial bond. Composed of ageless truths and eloquent aphorisms, it encapsulates the distilled insights of generations. Its words are akin to those of a trusted friend, offering guidance through life's intricate paths. Through the vivid imagery of these verses, the illustrations contrast the outcomes of virtuous and non-virtuous living, allowing its disciples to comprehend the pervasive consequences of their choices.

The sage advice imparts moral lessons, encouraging self-reflection and introspection, instilling a sense of responsibility and the urge to weigh actions and decisions with discernment. This ancient repository of information transcends cultural and temporal boundaries, leaving a heartfelt impression on those seeking enlightenment. It provides an opportunity to actively implement this Biblical guidance by being intentional in parenting, setting positive examples, and providing consistent mentorship.

The inspired text offers insight into various aspects of life, relationships, and Godly living, making it highly relevant to everyday life. Among these key teachings is an emphasis on the value of diligence and hard work, using verses such as: "*Lazy hands make for poverty, but diligent hands bring wealth*" (Proverbs 10:4), encouraging families to develop a strong work ethic and responsibility. It underscores the importance of honesty and integrity: "*The Lord detests lying lips, but he delights in people who are trustworthy*" (Proverbs 12:22). These teachings lay the foundation for upholding truthfulness and integrity in their interactions.

Additionally, Proverbs advises on the importance of selecting friends wisely by suggesting: "*Walk with the wise and become wise, for a companion of fools suffers harm*" (Proverbs 13:20). The passage offers insights into peaceful conflict resolution, as shown in this verse: "*A gentle answer turns away wrath, but a harsh word stirs up anger*" (Proverbs 15:1). It promotes respect for others: "*Wisdom's instruction is to fear the Lord, and humility comes before honor*" (Proverbs 15:33), encouraging family members to embrace humility and respect in their relationships. It imparts wisdom on financial responsibility, as seen in this verse: *"The wise store up choice food and olive oil, but fools gulp theirs down"* (Proverbs 21:20). These teachings offer a straightforward toolkit to nurture their sons and their entire families with character and Godly values, preparing them to lead respectful and purposeful lives. By sharing the practical wisdom found in these passages, the impartation of valuable life skills extends far beyond immediate needs and contributes to the betterment of those they touch.

The discussions serve as a cornerstone for instilling ethical principles resonating within their own families and within the community at large. In the grand tapestry of this exploration, the multifaceted interpretation comes to light, emphasizing the ethos of guiding and mentoring. It serves as a reminder, this role extends far beyond providing for physical needs. Instead, there is an entrustment with the task of actively forming character and values, setting on a path characterized by distinct purpose and valued living. This in essence, is the heart of the mission: to empower and inspire those who seek Godly guidance and wisdom.

The verses, in their intricacy, provide a range of perspectives, elucidating a spectrum of meanings. Their significance transcends singular interpretations, transfiguring into sources of timeless wisdom reverberating in manifold ways. A pivotal aspect of embracing Proverbs lies in acknowledging their adaptability. The linguistic nuances within the text exceed fixed meanings, serving as a conduit for multiple layers of understanding. The exploration of these interpretations elevates an awareness of the profound richness of kept secrets embedded within these words to the forefront of contemplation. Moreover, this path underscores the dynamic nature of the inspired scrolls and its relevance to fatherhood.

It speaks to them in various life circumstances and stages, since the divine words are not rigid proclamations but vibrant inscriptions. They affirm the eternal essence of the Scriptural doctrines, offering enlightenment and applications across creation. Essentially, unraveling this passage invites those so inclined on a quest for discovery, a pursuit to unveil hidden truths. It serves as a reminder, the wisdom revealed becomes a provision for governance and inspiration, presenting varied vantage points to enhance understanding and balance virtuous daily living.

CHAPTER FIVE

—— Moving Forward ——

In Chapter 5, titled *"Embracing Love and Guidance,"* the intricate connection of the father-son bond unfolded under the timeless wisdom of Psalm 25:10. This chapter peered into the divine example of covenant-keeping, emphasizing an eternal commitment to love and loyalty as the wellspring of inspiration for the familial bond. It explored the significance of modeling covenants of affection and instruction after the Godly inspiration, transcending the seeds of a biological inference and grounding relationships in sacred promises.

In addition, fathers were portrayed as earthly stewards of love and guidance, wielding significant influence in crafting essential virtues such as compassion, loyalty, and instruction. It underscored the pivotal impact of sustaining a love connection within the father-son bond, transcending symbolism to become a divine force sculpting the development and character of their offspring in dynamic dimensions. It highlighted the transformative power of a loving and faithful relationship, cherishing the sustaining legacy of the covenant. The dedication within fatherhood emerged as a force upon which the accord and a father's pledge were constructed, building spiritual character development and a lasting impact on growth.

This chapter further explored the practical application of wisdom within the father-son relationship. Empowered with essential knowledge and inspired by Godly love, fathers were guided with wisdom, recognizing individuality, and promoting enduring core values. Basing fatherhood in faith and spirituality became a transformative decision, aligning instruction and the moral compass with deeply held beliefs. The narrative encouraged the cultivation of empathy, compassion, integrity, and honesty, instilling resilience and perseverance as essential values for life's hardships. The durable fatherly influence remained a guiding spirit throughout the father-son relationship, extending far beyond childhood, and the significance of instilling solid values as a moral directive was emphasized. The Book of Proverbs was presented as a source of practical and moral wisdom, offering valuable insights into life, relationships, and Godly conduct.

EMBRACING LOVE AND GUIDANCE

In the intricate tapestry of familial bonds, Chapter 6 embarks on an exploration of the *"Journey of Growth,"* a shared odyssey of learning and evolution for fathers and sons alike. Rooted in the wisdom of Proverbs 4:7, fathers assume the role of torchbearers, passing down the sacred legacy of wisdom to their sons. The chapter unfolds through various sections, delving into the mutual influence of generations, the transformative power of shared experiences, and the powerful impact of fatherhood on their sons' character, values, and self-identity.

It encapsulates the essence of a dynamic and ever-evolving relationship, where fathers and their sons surf life's waves together, directing each other's destinies through a continuous exchange of wisdom, moments, and lasting values. As one traverses the diverse seas of this upcoming chapter, the bond between fathers and their sons emerge as a resilient and transformative alliance, building not only individual lives but also the fabric of generations to come.

CHAPTER SIX

Journey of Growth

The relationship between fathers and their sons is rarely expressed in the journals of history, beyond the pages of the inspired Word of God. This connection is remarkably intricate, composed of several fundamental elements: love, respect, wisdom, and the mutual emotions of life experiences. Love forms the warp and weft of this weave, binding their hearts within the bond with everlasting affection. It is a Godly love expressed through the seed of humanity, derived from the very essence of creation and formed from the dust of the ground, with life's breath from the Heavenly Spirit.

This bond transcends words, as evidenced by a deep and unspoken understanding forming the foundation of their relationship. Biblical insights embraced by compassion serve as the compass, guiding them through the turbulent seas of daily adrift. Together, they seek to answer the call of adulthood's distant winds. This exchange of learning within the father-son bond is a lifelong pursuit of Godly directives, a path of growth and maturation. Wisdom is akin to a masterful artisan's hand, intricately whittling the splash patterns within this fabric of the father-son connection. It embodies the accumulated knowledge and divine guidance passed down from one generation to the next as a testament to the Scriptures, spoken by holy men as they were moved by the Spirit.

In the sacred text of Proverbs 4:7, resonance is found: "*The beginning of wisdom is this: Get wisdom, and whatever you get, get insight.*" In their roles as mentors and earthly examples, fathers carry the torch of this sacred wisdom, passing it down to their sons as a priceless legacy witnessed first-hand by the generations before them. Through guidance, knowledge is provided along with the moral direction necessary to navigate life's intricate and difficult paths.

Drawn from both ancient teachings and personal experience, wisdom becomes the steady hand on the rudder, enabling them to steer through the rough seas, offering insights and perspectives proving invaluable in the face of adversity. It is a defining element, bringing purpose, depth, and faith into their relationship as they navigate the high surf of life. This voyage comprises the memories, joys, struggles, and milestones they have faced together.

From the first steps taken as an infant to the achievements and setbacks throughout adulthood, their experiences create a unique and unbreakable bond. They are the stories binding them together, the laughter and tears helping them embrace their own destiny. Their connection is a masterpiece woven from the threads of love, wisdom, and the evolving history of their life experiences. It reflects the deep intertwining of their lives, forming a relationship of strength, resilience, and dedicated devotion defining the very essence of the father-son bond.

Exploring the Father-Son Journey

The Scriptural wisdom illuminates the central role of the father-son relationship as a divine process intricately involved in building and steering character development. It explores the nuanced dynamics at play when navigating the path of personal growth, instilling values, and nurturing aspirations. This connection elevates fathers beyond the conventional realms of parenthood, casting them as vessels of divine guidance and living examples. The multifaceted functions woven into this relationship highlight its distinctiveness, meticulously outlined and marked by a spiritual significance deeply etched in its records.

Fatherhood, as portrayed, transcends parental duties of providing, protecting, and caregiving. It evolves into a foundational role, encompassing responsibilities and extending beyond the tangible, reaching into the transformative realm of moral virtues. This mentorship underscores the influence fathers hold in directing their sons toward a virtuous path. Scripture serves as an encouragement to impart not only practical life skills but also to embrace and embody additional values contributing to the holistic development of character. Through this lens, the father-son bond becomes a journey of forming and managing temperament, guided by divine wisdom and exemplifying the eternal impact of righteous living.

Assuming the mentorship role involves a proactive and purposeful approach to leading through challenges and opportunities. This responsibility entails offering fundamental life lessons, wisdom, and insights drawn from personal experience tempered by the Scriptures. The mentorship commitment extends beyond the passing down of knowledge, involving a proactive dedication to nurturing personal growth, providing guidance, and serving as a wellspring of counsel.

In guiding, practical skills are shared, aiding in the development of critical thinking, decision-making, and problem-solving abilities. This instruction enriches the journey by offering a sense of purpose and direction amid life's complications and opportunities. When endeavoring to embody these qualities and virtues, fathers aim to instill values such as integrity, kindness, resilience, and empathy.

By setting these noteworthy examples, they enhance lives and inspire the emulation of these qualities, thus playing an integral role in molding personal growth and championing ethical development. This proactive mentorship becomes a strobe, guiding the way through life's complexities and shaping individuals with a strong foundation built on eternal values and virtues.

The enrichment of this relationship flourishes when seamlessly incorporated into their roles and responsibilities. Its integration signifies an extension, moving beyond the basics of bonding and actively investing in growth, maturity, and development. Enrichment is characterized by meaningful interactions, common experiences, and a profound awareness of togetherness.

Consequently, as the bond is nurtured, it makes a significant contribution to character maturation and self-discovery. The relationship transcends traditional dynamics, evolving into a deep and transformative bond founded on respect, guidance, and personal maturity. It becomes more than just a family connection, expanding into a dynamic partnership playing a vital part in building a sense of purpose and direction.

CHAPTER SIX

The seamless integration of duties and the commitment to active investment in growth create a foundation for a lasting and impactful connection, expanding into the realms of common experiences and mutual expansion. At the heart of this message lies a recognition of the immense impact it has on molding character, values, and dreams. It is a journey unveiling the strength of a father's devotion, transcending generations, and laying the foundation for the men their sons will become.

Within these words, the primary role played by mentors and role models is emphasized. Through love, patience, and continuous support, they guide their sons through the complexities of life, standing as exemplars of wisdom and strength, illuminating the path toward becoming honorable and compassionate men. This highlights the very importance of mentors and role models, showcasing the strength of their love and support.

In these intricate connections, the purpose of mentors as guides, stands as a testament to the endless legacy of wisdom and love. Through their accumulated life experiences and insights, they become head lamps of guidance and guardians of moral character. One valuable aspect of this mentorship is the transmission of accumulated wisdom. Noted for possessing a wealth of knowledge drawn from their journeys, encompassing both practical know-how and intangible insights, it forms a bridge between generations, allowing their sons to benefit from the lessons learned.

In guiding the maturation process, fatherly mentors play a vital role in instilling core values, principles, and a great sense of responsibility. These values often mirror the ethical and moral direction of the father, reflecting what he cherishes and deems significant in life. This instruction extends beyond simple moral lessons; it serves as a fundamental force in character development, enabling an understanding not only of the "what" of morality but also the "why." This deeper understanding involves grasping the rationale behind ethical choices. Leading by example in this pursuit, they manifest these values through their actions and decisions, and as observers witness their conduct, they internalize essential lessons on navigating the complexities of ethical decision-making.

JOURNEY OF GROWTH

At the heart of this mentorship lies the establishment of a foundation of inspired values and principles. With the tools and blueprints needed to construct a robust moral character, virtues such as integrity, honesty, perseverance, and compassion are actively imparted and celebrated. These values become integral to their identity, developing the way they perceive themselves and interact with the world. As Lamentations 3:25-26, suggests: *"The Lord is good to those who wait for him, to the soul who seeks him. It is good that one should wait quietly for the salvation of the Lord."*

This provides direction on the practical application of these principles in everyday life, preparing them to make ethical decisions with confidence and conviction. The values passed down are not motionless; they are dynamic and evolve over time, adapting to the changing circumstances. Empowering their sons to make ethical choices and helm life's complexities with integrity and resilience, this continual dialogue between generations reinforces the eternal nature of the father-son bond. This aspect of mutual influence is a testament to the lasting connection, rooted in values and a dedication to the postulates guiding their lives.

Within the intricate web of father-son connections, fathers play a pivotal role in nurturing their sons' perception of responsibility. This element is not just about teaching personal accountability; it extends far beyond to encompass a broader and more important notion of duty. They understand the weight of responsibility, emphasizing one's actions and decisions have consequences flowing through various spheres. This facet of mutual influence is about imparting a sense of ownership. It emphasizes each person has a role to play in contributing positively to their family, community, and society at large.

The awareness of responsibility is not bound by age; it grows and evolves as their sons mature and take on increasingly significant roles in these various domains. The mentorship extends beyond words; it is a practical demonstration of living with integrity and responsibility. Leading by example, they demonstrate what it means to be accountable for one's actions and to fulfill one's obligation. Through mutual experiences and life lessons, enlightenment is provided in developing a strong work ethic, which forms the foundation for shouldering responsibilities effectively. This extends to nurturing a commitment to making a positive impact on the world. It encourages them to recognize they possess the agency to effect change and improve the lives of those around them. Playing an integral role in developing their understanding of accountability and duty, fathers embark on a journey, guiding their sons to recognize the consequences of their actions and decisions. This awareness of responsibility extends beyond the individual to encompass the well-being of the family, community, and society. By empowering them to be responsible, ethical, and compassionate, fathers leave an impact on their sense of duty and commitment to making a positive difference.

Dynamic Generational Bond

Enriched by the process of common influence, this relationship experiences a dynamic exchange of wisdom, perspectives, and values forming a deeper understanding. The strengthening of their bond transcends family relationships and holds the potential to be a powerful force for personal and collective prosperity. Often built upon shared experiences, whether triumphs or challenges, it's a concept creating lasting memories and bridges, serving as the common ground for their relationship.

Their strengthened bond goes beyond family relationships; it becomes a friendship based on values and a commitment to each other's moral health. It extends beyond these roles, as it turns into an alliance founded on trust, respect, and love. Furthermore, the strengthened connection serves as a powerful element for personal and collective growth. It creates a support system in which both rely on each other for guidance and encouragement. This support enables them to face difficulties with greater resilience and determination, serving as a source of motivation to continually strive for self-improvement.

Importantly, the strengthening of their relationship is a lifelong process. It evolves as both learn and grow. It is not limited to a specific phase of life, but continues to deepen and mature with each passing moment. This partnership is a testament to their understanding of the relationship. Shared influence strengthens this alliance by creating a deeper understanding based on experiences, respect, and the acknowledgment both generations have something valuable to offer. The interplay in the father-son connection gives rise to a distinctive and continuously developing bond, marked by its adaptive and progressive nature. This connection, rather than remaining aloof, undergoes a perpetual state of adjustment.

Amidst the intricate canvas of life, the perspectives, priorities, and circumstances of both generations undergo shifts. This bond flexes and adapts, ensuring its pertinence and significance are maintained. The dynamic essence of these relationships mirror the evolving epochs in which they unfold. The challenges, opportunities, and societal norms characterizing different eras employ considerable influence on the dynamics of their interaction.

This adaptability equips them to engage with contemporary issues and meet the demands of the present moment. The evolution of this relationship becomes intertwined with personal development. Over the course of time, the accumulation of experiences, insights, and wisdom contributes to the development of their life perspectives. Through the journey of learning and growth, they introduce fresh viewpoints and knowledge into the relationship, thereby enhancing its depth and richness.

The lasting significance of the father-son bond is found in its ability to withstand temporal challenges. It remains pertinent not only to those directly involved but also extends its relevance to future generations. The wisdom and values transmitted leave a lasting imprint, establishing a legacy of abiding love and ageless sway. Its unique and evolving nature serves as a testament to its growth and adaptability. This underscores their capacity to learn from each other, embrace change, and govern encroaching difficulties together.

The resilience ensures their bond remains a viable source of strength and inspiration. The reciprocal impact between them sculpts their distinctive and continually developing connection. It is one characterized by adaptability, a reflection of changing times, and the ability to remain relevant and meaningful across the years. This serves as a testament to the growth, resilience, and purposeful love defining the father-son bond.

CHAPTER SIX

Strengthening the Relationship

Strengthening the father-son alliance through experiences is a central outcome of familial engagements. This reinforcement holds particular importance, emphasizing the concept partners in life learn to rely on each other, offer support and encouragement, and face both successes and setbacks together. Their connection extends beyond specific experiences, becoming a mindset influencing how they approach various aspects of their lives.

Deepening the relationship creates a history of moments spent together, serving as a source of emotional significance and a reminder of the love, support, and unity defining their bond. Reflection on these moments with fondness nurtures a sense of closeness and belonging. The strengthening of the relationship through experiences reinforces the idea, they are more than just connected by blood; they are lifelong companions and allies through the Spirit. These times together build a strong foundation for their bond, ensuring resilience and endurance. Experiences enjoyed within the father-son connection significantly impact character and values, guiding both generations profoundly. These instances serve as workshops for the development of fundamental virtues, providing a practical context for understanding the importance of core values. The lessons learned become part of the narrative, written on the tablets of their relationship and family history. This chronicle serves as a touchstone, reminding both generations of the wisdom and worth imparted.

Their stories and memories created become durable reminders of the importance of family bonds. During these times, core values essential for character development are reinforced; honor, responsibility, empathy, and perseverance are not merely discussed; they are lived. Navigating hurdles with integrity, understanding various perspectives with empathy, and pursuing goals with perseverance serve as firsthand lessons in the importance of these principles. The experiences of contributing to their sons' personal growth by teaching flexibility and adaptability provide a fuller understanding when setbacks occur, presenting them as natural aspects of life. The resilience to bounce back and adapt to change is cultivated. As a result, fathers witness their sons grow into responsible, compassionate, and resilient Christian men.

Essentially, shared experiences are not just opportunities for bonding and fun; they are moments for character building. These experiences forge a common narrative, reinforce core morals, strengthen family bonds, and impart lessons in resilience and adaptability. They leave a lasting impression on both generations, highlighting their loving bond and providing guiding statutes. The legacy of love, wisdom, and instructions passed down through these moments transcends generations, becoming a hallmark of the family's identity.

Character development stands as a fundamental and transformative process. Fathers manage an essential role in instilling important qualities such as integrity, honesty, resilience, and responsibility. This process initiates early in a child's life and continues to evolve throughout adolescence and into adulthood. Serving as powerful male role models, they exemplify the importance of respect, consistency, and moral uprightness.

Resilience and honesty are two valuable concepts often cultivated within these relationships. The idea of resilience revolves around facing hurdles with courage and determination. It is not simply about avoiding failure but embracing it as an opportunity for learning and growth. Resilience encompasses adaptability, problem-solving, and maintaining an optimistic outlook in the face of adversity. On the other hand, honesty stands as a benchmark for character maturity, emphasizing the importance of truthfulness and integrity in one's life. It extends beyond truth-telling, urging those to live authentically and with unyielding integrity. Discussions regarding ethical dilemmas and moral choices guide the navigation of complex situations with honesty and integrity.

These conversations facilitate the development of critical thinking skills and the cultivation of a strong moral conscience. Character development within their relationship involves fathers serving as role models, teaching responsibility through everyday actions, fostering resilience in the face of challenges, emphasizing the importance of honesty, and encouraging ethical choices through meaningful discussions. Through these processes, they contribute significantly to shaping their sons' views and helping them develop strong ethical Christian virtues guiding their choices and actions throughout life.

CHAPTER SIX

—— Transmission of Family Traditions ——

In the vital role of the delivery process, fathers play an indispensable part in transmitting family traditions, cultural values, and Biblical beliefs. This process becomes interwoven into the very essence of family life, leaving a valuable impact on cultural and moral growth. They often stand at the forefront, upholding and passing down cherished traditions, encompassing specific holiday celebrations, unique customs, and rituals defining the family's identity. These traditions, acting as bridges spanning the past, create connections instilling an understanding of meaningful continuity. They guide their sons in discerning the significance of historical values held dear by their family and community.

Whether these values emphasize collectivism, respect for the elderly, or the preservation of traditional practices, essential wisdom is imparted. Through the passing of stories, lived experiences, and the embodiment of cultural customs, they empower their sons, nurturing an appreciation for the family heritage and a deeper understanding of their place within the broader community. Fathers are pivotal in helping their sons develop empathy, compassion, and respect. These qualities are essential for building positive relationships and contributing to a harmonious society. They nurture empathy by modeling it in their interactions and encouraging them to consider the feelings and perspectives of others. Empathy is connecting on a deeper emotional level, understanding the joys and struggles, and offering support. Engaging in activities involving volunteering or acts of kindness exemplifies the importance of sensitivity in building a healthy Christian community.

Compassion, closely linked to empathy, is promoted as a significant asset. Through practical acts of benevolence, there is a conveyance of compassion evidenced by a tangible expression of goodwill. Respect for others is a fundamental principle and involves acknowledging the intrinsic worth of everyone, regardless of their background, beliefs, or perspectives. They guide by treating others with courtesy and consideration, exemplifying this value through interactions with those from diverse perspectives and instilling an appreciation for diversity and inclusivity with the family connections. Within the intricate canvas of family relationships, fathers play a pivotal role as mentors, aiding in discerning between right and wrong while establishing the fundamental principles building their moral character and routing ethical considerations.

It is central to actively engage their sons in discussions on moral dilemmas, critical thinking, and introspection. These conversations frequently explore scenarios involving honesty, fairness, and justice, delving into their ethical implications. Through their actions and choices, fathers lead by example, emphasizing ethical conduct more than rules; it is a lifestyle deeply rooted in lasting values exemplified by integrity, truthfulness, and accountability.

Nurturing the cultivation of virtues through self-reflection while providing consistent support stands at the forefront. This self-awareness becomes an internal compass, helping others to follow and navigate complex ethical situations. As conveyors pass down family traditions, cultural values, and Godly beliefs, they instill the significance of empathy, understanding, and respect. In this manner, support for moral discernment aids in the development of a strong directive and the refinement of skills in ethical and social interactions. This fatherly connection contributes to cultural and moral maturity, molding their sons into individuals who embody the values and principles transmitted through the ages.

In their mentoring roles, fathers encourage the act of dreaming big and envisioning a future filled with endless possibilities. They instill the belief, greatness can be achieved through diligence and determination. Sharing stories of dreams and aspirations often ignites a spark, inspiring sons to set their sights high. This empowerment to envision without boundaries enables transcendence of limitations, aspiring to make a substantial impact in multiple domains.

Instructing on the importance of setting specific and attainable goals underscores the value of breaking down grand aspirations into manageable steps. This guidance supports the establishment of both short-term and long-term objectives which harmonize with interests and passions. In the process of setting objectives, a deep sense of purpose is then instilled, aiding in maintaining focus on goals. As mentors embodying key values, fathers emphasize the importance of dedication and unwavering effort, highlighting achievement is not granted freely but attained through persistent focus and hard work.

Offering instruction in choosing paths aligned with personal passions, strengths, and values facilitates the exploration of diverse avenues in both career and education. Placing a premium on overall health and satisfaction, fathers nurture the pursuit of journeys resonating with passions and aptitudes. Nurturing ambition and determination, they emphasize ambition as the driving force propelling those toward the realization of objectives. The ability to surmount obstacles and struggles with resilience and perseverance serves as a vivid illustration.

As role models, they exemplify ambition, which when combined with dedication and integrity, paves the way to personal and professional achievements. Fathers epitomize the values and virtues they aim to transmit, moving beyond mere words to embody these ideals through actions and behaviors. Their sons often regard these role models as significantly influencing their understanding of character and integrity.

Through their actions, they demonstrate integrity by practicing honesty and trustworthiness in interactions with others, emphasizing the importance of truthfulness. Responsibility is also exemplified through the fulfillment of family and work obligations, instilling values of dependability and accountability. This approach to the resolution of problems constitutes a critical lesson, teaching resilience and problem-solving skills.

During difficult times, a valuable lesson emerges: examples of resilience in the face of adversity serve as markers. These challenges may manifest in a career or personal life, where they demonstrate unwavering determination and a positive outlook. This direct experience imparts a crucial life lesson: setbacks are a natural part of life, and perseverance is key to overcoming them.

Additionally, respect and empathy are exemplified in interactions with various individuals, such as family members, friends, colleagues, and the community. Keen observations are made of these displays of compassion, empathy, and trust. This model of empathy cultivates compassion and understanding, motivating to approach others with dignity and respect.

Objectives, working diligently, and persisting in the pursuit of goals are essential components of personal development. Whether these objectives are related to career aspirations, personal hobbies, or projects, the value of ambition and determination stands out prominently. The concept imparts the importance of setting clear goals, putting in consistent effort, and maintaining resilience in the face of dilemmas. This philosophy serves as an important source of motivation and inspiration, empowering one to confidently pursue dreams and aspirations. Their dedication contributes significantly to overall generational growth and fulfillment.

Shaping Character and Integrity

Character and integrity stand as central qualities in life. These virtues form the foundation in personal development and play a fundamental role in robust and ethically sound communities. In the endeavor to instill these guidelines, fathers act as powerful exemplars, with their conduct and ethics laying the groundwork for moral growth. Those who uphold the values such as honesty, responsibility, thoughtfulness, and reverence provide a concrete and discernible example of the way these virtues manifest in reality. Through the observation of these actions and ethics, their sons begin to grasp the practical application of these values.

Within the dynamics of moral understanding, a vital role exists in the father-son relationship. The ethical principles and values imparted serve as a solid point of reference for decision-making. They acquire an understanding of the concepts related to right and wrong, along with their practical applications. These virtues seamlessly integrate into their personal value systems, motivating them to embody traits such as truthfulness, accountability, respect for others, and kindness.

Disposition and uprightness are closely linked to resilience and responsibility. The next generation learns how to handle hardships, grow from mistakes, and develop resilience and responsibility. These lessons serve as building blocks for their development in different areas. The impact of this instruction on their descendants' character and integrity is not confined to the present generation; it extends to future ones as well. The upcoming generation, having learned values, is more likely to pass

CHAPTER SIX

them on to their heirs, creating a legacy of ethical morals enduring through time. The influence it has on shaping the character and integrity of these descendants extends beyond the individual level. As their sons grow into responsible, compassionate, and morally upright men, they contribute positively to their communities and society as a whole. The domino effect of instilling these values in their progeny leads to the creation of more ethical and harmonious leaders in society.

Their valued role exists in developing character and integrity within the father-son relationship. Through the consistent demonstration of behavior such as moral correctness, leadership, nobility, and dependability, a framework for moral development is established. These virtues serve as a guidepost for the adoption of such principles in one's life.

This generational transmission of character and integrity holds far-reaching implications, impacting the family unit and society as a whole and contributing to the cultivation of a more ethical and compassionate world. Life lessons persist over time, becoming intrinsic to one's identity and serving as guiding principles for decisions and actions. As they take on the role of guiding future generations, these lessons provide a valuable source of wisdom, ensuring a continual cycle of influence. The impact extends into adulthood, with the values learned shaping one's character and accompanying them through the complexities of life.

Confronted with ethical dilemmas, difficult decisions, and life-changing choices, they often reflect on the principles and behaviors witnessed in their fatherly mentors. This reflection serves as a compass, helping them make choices aligned with the virtues acquired. The influence of role models extends to their duties in fatherhood. As their sons become fathers themselves, they draw upon the lessons and experiences they have gained.

This generational transmission of these constructs is a testament to the powerful and lasting impact offered. Observing a commitment to family and community instills a strong likelihood these values will take precedence. Role models establish a lasting legacy transcending generations. This legacy extends to descendants, nurturing a culture of ethics and moral integrity within the family as a defining aspect of their identity and emphasizing the significance of these influential mentors. The influence fathers have on

JOURNEY OF GROWTH

their sons is not confined to childhood or adolescence; it extends far into adulthood and even into fatherhood itself. The values and aspirations instilled serve as a sustaining compass continuing to shape their lives, guiding them through the complexities of adulthood and beyond.

This long-term impact is a testament to the lasting influence of the father-son relationship. The guidance initiated during childhood and adolescence remains a lifelong endeavor. The qualities of integrity, honesty, resilience, and responsibility instilled in their sons continue to define their character through maturity. These values become the foundation of decision-making, ethical choices, and interactions with others. The promotion of aspiring for significant goals, setting clear objectives, and persistently working toward them resonate across generations.

In transitioning into adulthood, they draw upon a nurtured sense of ambition and determination to guide their chosen paths. The idea of aligning goals with personal interests and strengths continues to be a primary principle in career decisions and personal pursuits. The belief in one's inherent potential, cultivated by previous generations, becomes a propelling force toward achieving personal aspirations and success. The transmission of family traditions, cultural values, and Christian beliefs continues to be an influence as they grow older.

The sense of identity and belonging instilled by fathers through these examples remain a significant part of their lives. Serving as a constant source of guidance, this helps their sons navigate the complex moral dilemmas and make decisions aligned with their values. The principles of empathy, compassion, and consideration for others become not just ideals but a daily practice. Those who have witnessed consistent adherence to virtues during their formative years carry these impressions throughout their lives. Recollections of the way they faced challenges, exemplified kindness and respect, and pursued their ambitions served as the guiding goal.

The loving legacy of fatherhood in nurturing the next generation becomes apparent when their sons step into the role of fathers themselves. They purposefully draw upon the teachings, insights, and aspirations handed down. This cyclical process of influence underscores the perpetuity of the father-son connection. The transmission of character and principles becomes a cornerstone of the family's identity, connecting the past, present, and future. Character, guidelines, ambitions, and the transformative power of influence mold their lives as they transition into adulthood and fatherhood.

It is the fathers who leave an everlasting impression, leading their sons through the complexities of life and ensuring the legacy of love, wisdom, and learned values persists across generations. The nurturing process plays a pivotal role in personal development, laying a robust foundation for self-worth, self-esteem, resilience, and confidence. They are instrumental in this process, employing assurance, encour-agement, and a firm display of love and support. Through these actions, they construct a positive and resilient persona.

These bonds grant a unique capacity to provide a declaration of confirmation, significantly contributing to self-worth. Verbal and non-verbal cues become the tools through which they convey the message their sons are valued, loved, and capable individuals. Simple yet potent statements like, "I believe in you" or "You can do it" hold the power to instill profound self-confidence and assurance. These proclamations serve as a constant reminder, they are not only worthy of love but also fully capable of achieving their yearning.

The cornerstone of nurturing a faith in oneself lies in unconditional love. Within this supportive framework, there is room to explore interests, learn from mistakes, and undergo growth without the dread of rejection. This kindness builds security and affirmation, aiding in the development of a Godly self-image. It reinforces the notion, their true selves hold worth, ultimately fostering a strong and wholesome sense of self-esteem. Nurturing their character is closely tied to the cultivation of resilience.

When they demonstrate, setbacks and failures are intrinsic parts of life, it emphasizes the idea, adversities are part of the human experience. The support and encouragement offered during difficult moments convey the concept of possessing the inner strength to overcome adversity. This resilience, in turn, becomes a vital aspect of individuality, enabling one to rebound from roadblocks with confidence and determination.

Confidence plays a central role in cultivating a positive sense of self-trust. This empowerment develops a belief in one's capabilities and competence. Through guidance, mentorship, and opportunities for personal growth, those engaged in this process acquire the necessary tools to develop confidence in their own abilities. Whether it involves mastering new skills, pursuing passions, or confronting life's trials, discovering strength in sustaining support leads to a resilient identity.

When this quality is nurtured, it gives rise to a meaningful self-image. The perception one deserves love and respect, possesses the capacity to achieve aspirations, and is well-prepared to face life's impediments, gradually takes root. This viewpoint becomes the driving force behind choices and actions, guiding them towards success and personal maturity. A strong recognition of self-esteem serves as a reliable guide, assisting them in navigating life's interruptions, making important decisions, and cultivating meaningful connections.

The central role fathers play in fashioning their sons' emotional health is evident through the provision of affirmations, encouragement, and eternal love. This transformative process contributes to the development of resilience and confidence, molding a lasting positive self-view. The continuing impact of such comfort extends beyond childhood, influencing personal growth. Underscoring the significance of the father-son bond emphasizes its empowering and transformative nature. By instilling in their sons a strong belief in paternal capabilities, fathers establish a basis for a relationship built on trust and encouragement.

Fulfilling the roles of mentors and guides, fathers present invaluable opportunities for growth, learning, and self-discovery. These experiences, guided by support, instill a deep-rooted sense of confidence, fostering feelings of assurance and competence in various pursuits. Amid the intricate dynamics of family relationships, particularly those shaped by fatherly influence and expectations assume considerable importance.

These expectations, coupled with associated anxieties, trigger emotional shifts. Longings for parental approval, potential strains in relationships, and their impact on overall well-being introduce complexities into father-son dynamics. Navigating this delicate balance between personal goals and assumptions necessitates clear communication. This process often entails a quest for fatherly acceptance and a vital focus on character development and resilience within the mentorship journey.

Emotional Impact on Well-being

Fatherhood anticipations are a fundamental aspect of a son's upbringing, substantially influenced by societal, cultural, and familial dynamics. Within this framework, fathers as prominent mentors, convey a weighty impact in shaping these expectations. Self-esteem, the basis of an individual's psychological health, revolves around their perception of their personal emotional worth and capabilities. However, when these expectations remain unmet, self-regard becomes vulnerable, potentially triggering an adverse self-perception. This internal turmoil often prompts those to question their abilities and feelings of worthiness, creating a pervasive form of inadequacy.

The emotional disruption does not remain confined but extends into various facets of a son's life, impacting their relationships and career goals. Importantly, these early experiences have lasting reverberations well into adulthood, significantly influencing self-concept and personal worth, emphasizing the long-lasting impact of these dynamics. In this context, a fundamental human desire for validation and acceptance is a compelling force deeply rooted in the psyche. The fear of falling short in fatherly expectations often stems from this intense desire for approval.

The combination of doubt and anxiety permeates various emotional aspects, affecting confidence, decision-making, and overall spiritual strength. The failure to meet a father's goals also has a meaningful and multi-faceted impact on their son's self-esteem. This influence extends to emotional states such as worry and concern, affecting not only their perception but also their ability to navigate challenges within relationships.

The complex dynamics between the fear of disappointing a father and its consequences in the father-son bond, as well as other facets of life, can be substantial. Failing to meet these beliefs exerts significant strain, manifesting in various ways. The difficulties of disappointment indeed cast a shadow. This concern may lead to communication becoming strained, with family members often being hesitant to express themselves openly. The anxiety stemming from these unmet expectations result in a feeling of tension, further hindering healthy and candid interactions. This strain does not remain confined to the father-son relationship alone; its effects extend to other aspects of life. Those carrying this burden may find it problematic in maintaining an awareness of balance in their personal and professional connections, as well as in their overall mental health.

Performance anxiety, rooted in the concern of not living up to established expectations, is a common experience for many. In academic and professional contexts, the desire to meet or exceed these hopes is a double-edged sword. On one hand, it serves as a motivational force, pushing to strive for excellence.

On the other hand, it evolves into a significant source of stress and anxiety. The pressure to excel, often stemming from the desire to meet specific familial standards, becomes overwhelming. One may feel as though their entire self-worth hinges on their performance, leading to an unrelenting pursuit of perfection. This pressure is all-encompassing, affecting not only academic or professional performance but also mental, spiritual, and physical well-being.

The cumulative stress may culminate in burnout, a state of emotional, mental, spiritual, and physical exhaustion. This perspective brings to light the intricate relationship between the worry of not meeting certain benchmarks and performance anxiety. It illustrates just how the desire to excel evolves into a source of extreme stress and, if not managed, resulting in overall exhaustion. Understanding and addressing these dynamics is essential to maintaining a healthy balance between striving for success and safeguarding their overall wellness.

In response to the fear of not meeting the father-son goals, reactions manifest in various ways. Some may opt for rebellion, rebuff established norms and seek independence, often leading to conflicts, particularly with fathers, who may perceive it as a rejection of their values. Conversely, others may choose a path of compliance, diligently trying to meet or exceed these standards, sometimes at the cost of their own dreams. This compliance is often rooted in the pursuit of fatherly approval and can lead to harmonious relationships initially, but may result in personal dissatisfaction and a feeling of living a life that does not align with true desires. These responses, rebellion and compliance, reflect the diverse ways of coping with the pressure.

Striking a balance between asserting one's individuality while respecting family values is a delicate task. Understanding these contrasting reactions and their potential impacts is central in navigating the complex landscape of reaching certain goals, building personal fulfillment, and maintaining healthy relationships.

The persistent fear of not meeting a father's standards has a lifelong impact on overall health. It often leads to heightened stress levels, feelings of depression, and a constant state of anxiety, significantly affecting total body wellness. This chronic fear, particularly when it becomes an enduring preoccupation, results in heightened stress levels. An enduring struggle persists under the weight of incessant pressure to meet or exceed these set standards, resulting in an ongoing state of anxiety that looms over various aspects of life.

The burden of unmet expectations, coupled with the constant dread of disappointing one's father, fosters feelings of hopelessness and inner turmoil. This burden takes a toll on mental, emotional, physical, and spiritual well-being, often enveloping individuals in a pervasive sense of unease and distress. Within these sentiments lies a heightened apprehension toward falling short of the objectives, giving rise to elevated stress levels, depression, and persistent anxiety, collectively presenting formidable obstacles to mental, spiritual, and emotional fulfillment.

Recognizing and addressing these effects is integral to promoting personal fitness and emotional resilience. It is important to note, the theme of personal growth and autonomy within the context of overcoming the fear of not meeting familial expectations is a deeply transformative journey. It involves several pivotal steps aimed at cultivating a sensation of self-worth, setting boundaries, and making choices aligning with personal aspirations and values. Overcoming this persistent concern often commences with the establishment of healthy boundaries, allowing their sons to define their limits and assert their individuality.

The development of a robust recognition of self-esteem becomes central, enabling them to recognize their intrinsic purpose and capabilities independently of external expectations. In parallel, the pursuit of autonomy involves the deliberate choice to make decisions resonating with one's inner aspirations and views, even if they diverge from these standards. It signifies taking ownership, demonstrating an evolving consciousness of self, and having the capacity to lead an authentic life. This transformative journey towards personal growth leads to empowerment and deepens the connection with their unique identity and personal goals, ultimately building a fulfilling life aligned with a Godly authentic self.

Open and honest communication between fathers and their sons is fundamental for addressing the heartfelt anxiety associated with unmet goals. This type of dialogue serves as a bridge to mutual understanding, providing a platform for the expression of concerns and a space for discussing desires. Effective interaction plays an essential role in alleviating anxiety and nurturing a healthier, more supportive relationship. By engaging in this kind of discussion, both gain valuable insight into each other's perspectives, building empathy and a deeper appreciation of their motivations, fears, and aspirations. This understanding forms the foundation for building a stronger, more empathetic connection.

Furthermore, honest conversation provides a safe space to express their concerns and fears candidly, enabling them to articulate frustrations about meeting goals set while giving each other the opportunity to voice their hopes and concerns as well. This exchange of emotions stirs a deeper connection leading to mutual reassurance. Through this exchange, standards can be clearly articulated and discussed, aligning them more realistically and allowing room for adjustments and compromises when necessary.

Embracing Mental Perseverance

The concept of mental perseverance is a powerful and transformative principle imparting integral skills for navigating adversities with resilience and determination. At its core, this teaches individuals to maintain unwavering resolve in the face of adversity, emphasizing the importance of mental strength and resilience. It involves standing firm when confronted with surmounting circumstances and not allowing adversity to deter one from their path or goals. Mental fitness offers effective strategies for managing stress, enabling one to handle the pressure and anxiety often accompanying adversity. It also instills the art of maintaining focus on the goals, ensuring that objectives remain in sight even when the road becomes rocky.

Those fathers who are able to embrace a broad perspective in understanding the concept of mental grit in modern times will sit at the forefront of helping their sons grasp the world around them, while providing a strong Biblical launch point. It is a focus enabling them to stay on course and work steadily towards their dreams. A key aspect of mental toughness is the commitment to one's goals, even when faced with steep difficulties. This dedication fuels the perseverance needed to overcome adversity and achieve long-term success. The principle of cognitive persistence serves as a comprehensive guide to developing the inner strength and resilience required to confront and conquer adversity. It empowers personal focus in the face of trials with strength and determination, creating a mindset thriving in the midst of tough decisions.

Their devotion and determination in effective communication helps identify common ground, as both explore values and dreams, creating a foundation for a more harmonious and supportive relationship and bridging the gap between differing objectives. Oftentimes, there is the appearance of a divide in the open connection between generations. Yet, during these moments, fathers may ponder the mental toughness of the next generation and the temptation for alternative viewpoints within the family dynamics as a reason for this disconnect.

To the contrary, such fortitude may be misunderstood in light of the ever-evolving societal norms. While cognitive decisiveness on its face seems to be in a weaker state within the upcoming generation, this is not the case. There is a valuable role to play in seeing their sons through the next hurdle, which is dissimilar to the past. Times have changed over the previous decades, especially as it relates to technology. Discussions, opportunities, and the various life nuances are moving at the speed of light, as it is much faster and far more reaching than those beforehand.

JOURNEY OF GROWTH

Finding resoluteness within the Word of God will provide an anchor for the emotional, spiritual, and mental strength sought after. When the divergence of modern-day emotional ruggedness seems to collide with father-son connectedness, seeking support from professional counseling can be an invaluable resource for addressing the intricate and often overwhelming anxieties within father-son relationships.

These professionals serve as compassionate guides, offering a range of benefits in the journey to effectively manage these fears. Therapists and Christian counselors provide a safe and non-judgmental environment to explore issues, offering streetwise, educated, and Biblical guidance in navigating the emotional terrain of these concerns. They work through apprehensions methodically, dissecting their root causes and providing strategies for management and resolution.

This process often involves self-reflection through a Godly application, which leads to increased self-awareness and emotional resilience. These professionals can provide coping strategies to deal with the anxiety and stress stemming from unmet or unrealistic expectations. Their strategies also encompass stress management techniques, communication skills, and self-care practices which promote mental, spiritual, and emotional wellness. Essentially, the therapeutic setting provides a supportive space to express fears, frustrations, and hopes candidly. This cathartic release enables both to unburden themselves of emotional baggage and work towards healing and personal development.

Additionally, therapists and Christian counselors offer an objective perspective on the challenges faced, providing insights and alternative viewpoints contributing to a more balanced thinking and better decision-making. In essence, seeking support from professionals plays a pivotal role in navigating and eventually overcoming complex fears, frustrations, and disappointments, promoting personal growth, emotional resilience, and healthier father-son bonds.

In this quest thus far, the previous discussion centered on the Biblical insights of Proverbs 4:7, highlighting the primary role of this unique bond in guiding and shaping lives. The discussion unveiled the intricate dynamics at play in guiding character development, values, and aspirations, transcending traditional roles into divinely-inspired mentorship and exemplification outlined in the Scriptures. Moving forward and expanding on this foundational concept, emotional intelligence, an essential aspect of personal growth, thrives within the nurturing dynamics of meaningful relationships. Proverbs 16:32, conveys this principle, noting it is better to be a patient person than a warrior and greater to have self-control than to conquer a city. Discovering equilibrium is akin to navigating obstacles along a winding path, where emotions surge and self-discipline may waver.

This brings to light the extraordinary strength required to manage internal emotions and behaviors compared to external challenges. At various stages of personal growth, emotions may momentarily eclipse the pursuit of serenity, emphasizing the significance of inner resilience, self-discipline, and self-control. This theme unveils the intricate interplay of emotions, restraint, and Godly revelations within the father-son connection, adding another layer of depth to the understanding of this heartfelt alliance.

—— Nurturing Emotional Intelligence ——

Capturing the essence of a father guiding his son, who learns through example the virtues of self-awareness and control, assumes profound significance. These paternal duties and responsibilities extend beyond the realms of limited instruction, guidance, and affection; they necessitate a heightened understanding of self-awareness, humility, and adaptability. As Proverbs 16:32, wisely conveys: "*It is better to be patient than to be a warrior. It is better to have self-control than to conquer a city.*"

This Biblical wisdom punctuates the central role guiding mentors play in setting a model for their sons to follow. Called upon to embody emotional intelligence in all facets of self-improvement, fathers serve as advocates for ongoing learning and the pursuit of excellence. Actively participating in self-reflection, seeking wise counsel, and honing their coaching skills signify a determined commitment and unyielding resilience.

JOURNEY OF GROWTH

It is key to acknowledge this journey represents a collaborative effort in cultivating emotional maturity, offering invaluable guidance, and strengthening the sacred bond between fathers and their sons. Woven into the narrative with love as its overarching theme, the storyline emphasizes the intrinsic requirement to engage in self-assessment, aligning a father's standards with those of fellow Christians who epitomize the authentic essence of Biblical teachings within fatherhood. In doing so, one does not solely depend on intuition since this reveals itself as a precarious path fraught with the potential for missteps in guiding the subsequent generation.

Within the contemporary landscape, dilemmas arise as social influences occasionally clash, creating complexities in sustaining the father-son relationship. This reality becomes particularly evident when leadership and guidance lack the forefront of preparedness. Understanding the different roles fathers wholeheartedly take on in personal growth and mentorship, wrapped in the concept of love, is more than just a choice; it becomes a vital necessity. This commitment ensures the guidance of the next generation, characterized by a harmonious blend of love, wisdom, and strength.

Foundation of Fatherly Mentorship

Seeking the prerequisites for adept mentorship reveals the significance of self-awareness and preparedness. Fatherhood, bestowed upon man as a noble and gratifying blessing from the Divine, requires acknowledgment. Simply holding the title of father, whether through biological connections or otherwise, does not inherently bestow the integral skills and qualities necessary for effective tutoring. Similar to the way a warrior meticulously trains and prepares before entering the battlefield, the standard for embarking on a preparatory journey is set.

Fathers prepare themselves with the necessary skills for guiding, surpassing the confines of a biological relationship. This evolves into a sustaining commitment to nurture and fortify the growth of those under their care. Resembling a challenging trek, effective mentoring demands an ongoing dedication to refinement and enhancement. The exercise of self-control stands as a commendable attribute intrinsic to fathers when leading by example. This quality seamlessly aligns with a personal understanding of emotions, reinforcing an expedition into fundamental life skills passed down through successive generations.

These proficiencies encompass adept conflict resolution and stress management, providing invaluable counsel for skillfully navigating through emotionally charged situations. The significance of these skills extends beyond momentary resolutions; they serve as a centerpiece for traversing intricate emotional terrain constructively. When embodying self-control, fathers lay the foundation for resolving conflicts with a blend of respect and empathy, establishing the groundwork for the cultivation and sustenance of wholesome relationships throughout one's lifetime.

This indispensable skill set becomes a reservoir of resilience, equipping them with the capacity to confront and overcome adversities with efficacy. In addition, the perpetuation of emotional intelligence across generations empowers the forging of meaningful and harmonious connections. It not only fortifies interpersonal bonds but also cultivates self-regulation, awareness, motivation, social skills, and compassion while adapting to the complex and intricate landscape of human sentiments. The development and inheritance of such emotional quotients prove to be an enduring legacy, comprehensively preparing fathers for the nuances of human interaction and the complexity of affective responses.

In this intricate journey of fatherhood and mentorship, it is prudent for fathers to actively seek training advice and guidance. Much like a warrior honing their skills through training, fathers benefit from intentional preparation and learning. This proactive approach not only equips them with the necessary tools for effective leadership but also serves as a safeguard against the tendency to over-correct without proper training. Recognizing the importance of continuous learning and seeking mentorship resources becomes pivotal in navigating the complexities of guiding the next inheritors.

Guidance assumes a central role within the father-son relationship, surpassing simple knowledge transfer and emphasizing its delivery. At its core resides love, a personal affection expressed through compassionate advice and care-rooted direction. This form of leadership does not assert control or authority but emanates from a deep yearning for their welfare and success, establishing a sturdy foundation of trust and open discourse. Acknowledging the inevitability of mistakes and the emergence of difficulties, they embrace patience in their mentorship, forging a space for learning from experiences, decision-making, and occasional missteps. This patience creates a sanctuary where their sons can seek advice without trepidation.

Through the seamless fusion of love and understanding, instruction assumes a nurturing and supportive role, facilitating the navigation of life's intricacies, the shaping of values, and the making of choices. Counsel builds character, instilling virtues along with empathy, resilience, and integrity, creating a sincere understanding of trust, and reinforcing the significance of the bond. Amidst the intricate nature of these relationships, steadfastness, often referred to as firmness, unshakable, and a sense of doggedness, emerges as a foundational virtue, wielding substantial influence when these bonds encounter hurdles. It transcends the act of suppressing frustration; instead, it embodies an active commitment to understanding and showcasing resilience.

This perspective accentuates its value, elevating it beyond a passive trait to a purposeful choice to engage with difficulties in a constructive and intentional manner. Within the framework of father-son relationships, self-restraint assumes a multifaceted role. It serves as a catalyst, encouraging both fathers and sons to cultivate this virtue as a pragmatic approach to confronting the inevitable strains. Essentially, it functions as a protective shield within this dynamic, enabling them to maintain composure and fortitude when confronted with life's obstacles. A pivotal duty is evident in creating a conducive space for open dialogue and effective problem-solving. By actively embodying restraint, fathers and sons can navigate the intricacies of their relationship without hastily jumping to conclusions or overreacting to contrasting situations.

It becomes the footing, enabling an environment where understanding flourish and conflicts can be resolved with thoughtful consideration rather than impulsive reactions. This deliberate cultivation serves as a linchpin in the delicate dance of father-son relationships, ensuring a supportive and resilient basis for navigating the complexities of life together. Support within this relationship transcends material or emotional aid; it embodies a commitment to the growth and well-being of the younger generation. It acts as a motivator for nurturing aspirations, be they in the realms of education, profession, or personal development. This backing provides a stable foundation from which their sons can boldly explore and achieve their ambitions.

Consistency in this encouragement is of paramount importance. It entails maintaining a constant presence in the lives of family members, participating in significant events, and celebrating milestones. This dedication imparts safety and belonging, reinforcing the importance of the familial bond. In times of adversity, this reinforcement manifests as reassurance and wise guidance. It serves as a model for resilience, teaching the way to gracefully confront setbacks and adversity. Such encouragement empowers individuals to cultivate confidence and the ability to surmount obstacles. This approach encompasses the art of active listening, creating an environment conducive to open communication where thoughts and feelings are freely expressed. It builds emotional intelligence and empathy, highlighting the utmost value of listening and understanding. Support within the father-son connection embodies an intense commitment to nurturing growth and development. This support transcends material or emotional assistance, representing a consistent, resilient presence in their life.

It is a relationship built on trust and understanding. Biblical teachings influence this alliance by providing moral and ethical guidance, emphasizing values such as love, respect, and forgiveness. These guidelines help build a strong, faith-based understanding and navigate issues. As their heirs mature into adulthood, the father-son dynamic undergoes a natural transformation. Fathers balance this by transitioning from the role of primary authority to a trusted adviser, respecting their son's growing independence while offering guidance as needed. When providership is no longer the primary focus, the relationship shifts toward a more equal partnership, with both learning from one another.

Life's Profound Companionship

The concept of self-discovery and personal development emerges as a forerunner for nurturing a unique companionship. It highlights the idea within this path, when undertaken, serves as a stimulus for growth and the exploration of one's inner identity. As this duo encounters a diverse array of experiences, they engage with a spectrum of situations molding character, values, and dreams. Through these collective experiences, lessons are drawn not only from achievements but also from mishaps.

Fathers offer wisdom and guidance, helping their protégés navigate dilemmas and learn the essence of resilience, determination, and ethical choices. Their sagacity and support form a steady foundation as the next generation embarks on their unique paths of self-discovery. This journey of experience deepens mutual understanding and nurtures companionship. Mentors become not just sources of wisdom but trusted guides on the walk of life.

In turn, their relationship is infused with fresh perspectives and renewed vitality, enriching their outlook. Ultimately, the concept of self-discovery and personal growth within this unique relationship creates a nurturing environment where both generations thrive. As lessons are drawn from one another's experiences, a companionship is cultivated transcending conventional ties. Through this collective pursuit of growth, a powerful and long-standing understanding is formed, forging a lifelong kindred holding immense meaning.

The idea of lifelong companionship highlights a lasting and deeply meaningful relationship. This lasting alliance extends beyond various life stages, including adulthood and old age, emphasizing family members are not merely relatives but also steadfast companions on a journey of personal and developmental growth. As they maneuver through life's complexities together, they evolve and grow, drawing strength from their loving bond. This lifelong relationship is characterized by mutual influence and support. The elderly generation continues to offer guidance and provide wisdom, drawn from experience. Simultaneously, the younger generation brings fresh perspectives and vitality, enriching their elders' outlook and experiences.

CHAPTER SIX

Family bonds have remained a source of support and understanding throughout their lives. During moments of triumph and challenge, they offer each other a reliable and comforting presence. This relationship becomes a fountain of emotional strength and resilience, enabling them to face difficulties together. Additionally, family ties leave a lasting imprint on personal growth and development. Through the journey of life, they exchange insights, shaping their character, values, and aspirations. This ongoing exchange of wisdom and understanding deepens their connection and mutual appreciation for each other.

Understanding the reciprocal nature of growth and change within the father-son bond provides valuable insights. The real-life stories and experiences serve as windows into the dynamic exchange of influence and transformation within the relationship. The narratives exemplify the significant impact this unique bond has on personal growth and development.

When examining such stories, one gains tangible examples of the potential for positive change. This further highlights family bonds involving a journey of mutual growth and transformation where both generations learn from each other. Reflecting on these experiences invites an appreciation of the transformative power of these connections. It encourages recognition of the potential for change and personal growth, molding a meaningful companionship and unity in these cherished relationships.

In the context of exploring father-son connections, it is essential to begin by acknowledging and introducing the concept of complexity. While these relationships are undeniably profound and meaningful, they are not without their hurdles and intricacies. This introductory step is vital because it lays the foundation for a more holistic perspective on the dynamics within these bonds. First and foremost, recognizing the existence of complexities is a testament to their depth and significance. It underscores the idea, these bonds are not one-dimensional but are instead rich with variation and depth. This recognition invites an approach to the subject matter with curiosity and openness; understanding the journey of fatherhood and sonhood is multifaceted.

In addition, by acknowledging the presence of issues and intricacies, it validates their experiences. It is a reminder, struggles, misunderstandings, and conflicts are a part of the journey, and they should not diminish the value of the relationship. This acknowledgment creates empathy and understanding, allowing a personal connection to the legacy.

Embracing the complexities within these relationships is a step toward growth and improvement. By understanding these problems are ever evolving, it encourages one to seek solutions, enhance communication, and navigate these variations with grace and patience. It sets the stage for the exploration of specific strategies for building deeper connections within these relationships.

The introduction to complexities serves as a crucial first step in the journey of understanding and strengthening their bonds. It highlights the richness of the connection, validates the experiences of both fathers and their sons, and encourages a proactive approach to addressing obstacles. By acknowledging and embracing these twists and turns, one travels on a path towards molding an allegiance grounded in empathy, understanding, and growth.

Bridging Generational Divides

Within the intricate tapestry of these connections, a noteworthy aspect to explore is the presence of generational gaps. The chasms are not simple abstract concepts but rather tangible elements influencing the dynamics between generations. It is imperative to peer into this topic, as it sheds light on the complexities emerging within these relationships. Generational divides, in essence, stem from differences in age, upbringing, and life experiences. They often find themselves belonging to different eras, each marked by its own set of historical, social, and cultural contexts.

The disparities in life experiences and the worldviews they engender are at the heart of these segregations. The significance of understanding these differences lies in recognizing they are not indicative of a lack of love or affection. Instead, they are a byproduct of the passage of time and the evolution of societal norms, values, and technology advancements. By acknowledging their existence, they are encouraged to view them as

CHAPTER SIX

opportunities for growth and understanding rather than sources of division. Generational differences have the potential to lead to disastrous misunderstandings and conflicts. The variations in perspectives and values create fertile ground for tension. Shaped by their experiences and traditions, fathers may have certain expectations and beliefs about the way things should be done, while younger generations, influenced by their own era, may have contrasting viewpoints. These disparities manifest in various aspects of life, from communication styles to career choices to lifestyle preferences.

However, it is essential to underscore these differences, while challenging, are not insurmountable. In fact, they offer a unique opportunity for mutual learning. The older generation can provide valuable insights, wisdom, and historical context, while the younger generation can bring fresh perspectives, innovative ideas, and a contemporary outlook. When approached with openness and a willingness to understand, generational divides become bridges for deeper connections.

The discussion of these gaps within family relationships is significant because it acknowledges the complexities inherent in these bonds. By understanding how differences in age, upbringing, and life experiences contribute, they are better equipped to appreciate the nuances of the relationship. Furthermore, it underscores the importance of approaching the disparities with compassion, open communication, and a common commitment. Ultimately, navigating generational separations lead to a more profound connection, transcending the boundaries of time and change. The presence of their differences is a natural and often enriching aspect of the relationship.

To truly harness the potential for growth and deeper connections, it is essential for fathers to explore and employ strategies bridging these differences. The significance of these strategies lies in their power to foster understanding and create stronger bonds. Therefore, promoting open and honest communication is paramount in this context. It serves as the cornerstone upon which understanding is built. When both express their thoughts, feelings, and perspectives without fear of judgment, it creates an environment where authenticity thrives. This honesty is a pathway to mutual insight and understanding.

Additionally, attentive listening plays a vital role. Fathers and their sons should respectfully express themselves and actively listen to each other's viewpoints. This involves giving undivided attention, asking clarifying questions, and showing an interest for the emotions and experiences conveyed. Active listening paves the way for sincere understanding and connection. One of the variables in these strategies is the value of respecting each other's differences. Embracing these disparities with respect and without judgment establishes a place where both feel valued, heard, and accepted.

A central aspect of these strategies involves a commitment to educating oneself about each other's peer group. Learning the historical, social, and cultural context that has influenced each generation's values and beliefs builds sincerity and understanding. It provides a framework for comprehending why certain perspectives exist. To bridge these differences effectively, it is important to emphasize empathy and perspective-taking. This exercise in sensitivity transcends the boundaries of one's own generation and fosters compassion.

Fundamentally, the proposed strategies entail a substantial commitment to nurturing a sense of camaraderie between fathers and their sons. Grounded in transparent communication, mutual respect, and a sincere readiness to comprehend each other's individual perspectives, this course of action effectively closes divides and embraces the depth diverse viewpoints contribute to their relationship. Through active participation in these strategies, they forge a deeper connection by recognizing and valuing the distinct qualities each brings to the connection. This approach builds understanding, intimacy, and a companionship treasuring each other's uniqueness.

Strong Father-Son Communication

Addressing communication challenges is integral to building the father-son bond. Effective discourse serves as the basis of healthy relationships and should be a top priority. However, discussion hurdles such as emotional misalignment, a scarcity of open discourse, and divergent conversational styles can pose interrelational perplexities. The significance of reviewing these hurdles lies in recognizing the vulnerability of human connectedness and the importance of deliberate and empathic dialogue. Misalignment is one facet of this challenge, where fathers and their sons find themselves out of sync. Misunderstandings stemming from differing interpretations of words, phrases, or intentions erode trust and create chasms. The inability to convey thoughts, emotions, and expectations then leads to an absence of depth and mutual cohesiveness.

The absence of open dialogue is another facet. Both may struggle to engage in meaningful and transparent conversations, resulting in a lack of connection. With distinct ways of expressing themselves, listening, and resolving conflicts, this creates tension and hinders understanding. The potential consequences of conversational barriers within these relationships are multi-fold.

Misunderstandings sow seeds of mistrust, while unresolved conflicts lead to emotional distance. Addressing these dilemmas is vital, as effective conversation enables both to express love, concerns, and goals. Flourishing these interactions acts as a channel, connecting hearts and minds to navigate challenges together. The introduction of obstacles in the relationship is inevitable, emphasizing the central role of successful engagement in managing deep and meaningful interactions. It highlights the fragility of human emotional bonds when exchanges falter, underscoring the need for proactive efforts to improve these skills. Addressing these challenges minimize misinterpretations, conflicts, and emotional distance, nurturing a bond thriving on open, honest, and empathetic exchange.

Discussion breakdowns and an absence of candid dialogue severely affect the father-son relationship. When communication falters, disagreements surface, giving rise to mistrust and emotional distance between the two. As these interactions go awry, they find themselves talking past one another, leading to bewilderment and frustration. Differences stemming from misinterpretations of words and intentions breed doubt, conflict, and mistrust. Over time, these false impressions accumulate, nurturing resentment and emotional detachment. When they lack meaningful conversations, the chance to convey emotions, concerns, or dreams is missed, resulting in a lack of depth and mutual understanding.

This leads to fathers and their sons feeling unheard, ultimately generating emotional distance and a sense of disconnection. As trust erodes, the bond between both strains. They become less willing to share their thoughts or feelings with their fathers, while fathers become less supportive and understanding of their sons' needs. These challenges spiral into a breakdown, exacerbating the stress in the relationship. Miscommunication and the scarcity of candid dialogue exert a significant impact. It is important both actively dedicate themselves to enhancing their skills, comprehending each other's perspectives, and nurturing open, honest, and empathetic dialogues to prevent trust erosion and emotional distance. Within this realm, where the conduit for understanding and connection is imperative, it is important to provide both actionable insights and practical solutions for enhancing their dynamics.

Effective verbal conveyance not only prevents misunderstandings but also deepens their bond and promotes familial growth. The significance of offering solutions lies in their transformative potential. Fathers and their sons often struggle with these hurdles, which, if left unaddressed, stunt the growth of the relationship. By empowering them with practical tools, they navigate these hurdles with greater ease and reap the rewards for their efforts.

Promoting effective conversation stands as a fundamental element in nurturing strong connections. It provides a platform for them to express their thoughts, feelings, and expectations, grasp each other's viewpoints, and to traverse conflicts and disagreements jointly. Building strong communication skills is essential for molding healthy father-son relationships. Encouraging active listening, empathetic communication, and clear expression helps deepen the connection.

Conflicts are a part of these relationships, but understanding how to resolve them is essential to effective dialogue. Preparing them with conflict resolution skills, such as learning to stay calm during disagreements, focusing on issues rather than personal attacks, and seeking common ground for resolution, helps limit conflicts from escalating while turning them into opportunities for growth. This approach creates a healthy exchange and promotes an emotionally safe environment.

CHAPTER SIX

Stressing the importance of building an open dialogue and practicing self-restraint deepens the bond between them. Creating a safe and non-judgmental habitat for honest and ongoing exchange is key. Improvement is gradual and requires patience. This allows for growth and learning, helping to develop a stronger alliance over time. By emphasizing these pillars, they build a strong, trusting, and fulfilling relationship. Effective discourse is a central aspect of any healthy bond, and the unique connection between them requires developing robust communication skills. By offering insights and practical solutions, they can be equipped with the tools to address the transmission challenges in their relationships.

The straightforward strategies viewed, including empathetic discussion, clear expression, conflict resolution, openness, and patience, establish a solid foundation for effective interactions. Engaging in active listening, showing empathy and understanding, expressing thoughts and emotions clearly, resolving conflicts effectively, developing open dialogue, and practicing patience are pivotal to building deeper and more meaningful connections. These practices create a safe and understanding space for both to communicate, understand each other's perspectives, and pilot the course ahead.

A healthy bond founded on trust, empathy, and openness provides a source of support. These types of relationships contribute to positive emotional development, character building, and growth, all of which enhance overall peace and well-being. Therefore, it is vital to nurture effective discussions as a cornerstone for a strong and meaningful connection. Understanding generational differences is inherent in comprehending relationships between individuals of different age groups.

Recognizing distinct eras shape values, beliefs, and cultural norms is fundamental to acknowledging potential hurdles in communication. These disparities result in misunderstandings and a sense of disconnect. Nonetheless, it is essential to highlight such differences should not be viewed as insurmountable. The focus is on actively bridging these distinctions with empathy and open-mindedness.

Offering personal experiences and providing context for one's upbringing offers insights into the world in which each generation came of age. These meaningful dialogues encourage a deeper understanding, valuing the wisdom of the older group while appreciating the fresh perspectives of the younger generation. This open and respectful exchange builds understanding, strengthens connections, and facilitates navigating the complexities of these differences with grace and respect.

By actively addressing these disparities and promoting empathy, they bridge generational divides, building mutual understanding, growth, and harmonious relationships transcending the boundaries of time and age. It is through embracing these distinctions and engaging in open and respectful communication they can then navigate generational gaps and build lasting, timeless bonds.

Successful conversation is integral for any robust relationship, and in the realm of the father-son alliance, it holds immense significance. Communication complications arise in diverse forms, necessitating a thorough exploration and understanding. Expressing thoughts and emotions can be complex, with additional difficulties stemming from distinct interaction styles and struggles to find common ground. Acknowledging these impediments is valuable as it paves the way for proactive solutions that can transform their dynamics. Effective conversation requires a two-way exchange, with both parties actively participating in understanding each other's viewpoints.

This process involves asking questions, seeking clarity, and practicing empathy. Spending quality time together, participating in activities, and demonstrating genuine interest in each other's experiences further enhance interaction and connection. Interactions create a deeper sense of bonding and provide fertile ground for meaningful conversations. This approach is the basis upon which the entire structure of a father-son alliance rests. It is the language through which love, guidance, concerns, and aspirations are exchanged.

Acknowledging the difficulties arising in communication is not a sign of weakness but a testament to the commitment to nurturing a strong and meaningful alliance. The realization of these challenges offers a road map for growth and improvement. By recognizing the potential pitfalls, they gain the insight to traverse these hurdles more effectively. This awareness is the first step towards lasting change and a stronger bond. The practical strategies provided offer a tangible path to improvement. As a result, fathers and their sons are not left grappling in the dark but are equipped with a blueprint needed to enhance their interconnectedness.

Patience, proactive listening, empathy, and a commitment to creating a safe space become guiding principles. Developing open dialogue and understanding becomes the foundation of a thriving connection. It is the bridge spanning any differences in perspective or experience, connecting hearts and minds. This open interchange is a passageway for empathy, trust, and mutual growth.

Addressing discourse dilemmas not only enhances the quality of the relationship but also fortifies it for the long haul. Their dialogue plays a pivotal role in nurturing a thriving relationship; recognizing their misunderstandings or a dearth of straightforward conversations hindering the connection between the two. Encouraging the practice of active listening fosters a sphere of mutual understanding where both parties experience being heard and esteemed.

Another valuable verbal deliverance technique underscored is the utilization of "I" statements. This method enables both to express their sentiments and thoughts without passing judgment or assigning blame, promoting personal accountability for emotions and creating more constructive exchanges. Embracing this approach empowers them to navigate delicate subjects with greater effectiveness.

Prioritizing dedicated time for meaningful discussions holds great importance. In the hustle and bustle of today's fast-paced world, it is easy to underestimate the value of personal moments together. This intentional effort to enhance communication and strengthen their connection signifies a commitment to their relationship. It indicates a conscious decision to set aside the frenetic pace of modern life and the many external pressures in favor of engaging in sincere and open interactions. In doing so, it demonstrates the bond between them is of the utmost importance and deserving of dedicated time and attention.

These purposeful discussions serve as a means to bolster communication and foster deeper connections. They provide a secure environment for lending thoughts, emotions, and experiences. In these moments, fathers impart wisdom, guidance, and support, while their sons express their concerns, ambitions, and inquiries. This exchange of ideas and emotions nurtures a meaningful understanding of each other and reinforces the bedrock of trust and intimacy within their relationship.

In a world where distractions and the relentless pace of life jeopardize the quality of their interactions, the act of setting aside time for meaningful conversations serves as a deliberate counterbalance. It breathes vitality into the father-son relationship, ensuring it remains vibrant, resilient, and continually evolving. This is a conscious choice to honor and invest in one of life's most precious connections, one capable of transcending generations and leaving a lasting legacy of love, mutual respect, and understanding.

Graceful Relationship Resolutions

Grace assumes an integral position in nurturing understanding and acceptance, aligning with the guidance of Ephesians 4:32, urging recognition of shared humanity and the inevitability of making mistakes: *"Be kind and compassionate to one another, forgiving each other, just as in Christ God forgave you."* This acknowledgment, further illuminated by Colossians 3:13, cultivates an environment where they are encouraged to: *"Bear with each other and forgive one another if any has a grievance against someone."*

The essence of forgiveness, noted in Matthew 6:14-15, constitutes the heart of grace. It symbolizes an atmosphere characterized by kindness, forgiveness, and empathy by stating: *"For if you forgive others when they sin against you, your heavenly Father will also forgive you. But if you do not forgive others their sins, your Father will not forgive your sins."* Through grace, the capacity to release grudges and judgments, in accordance with Luke 6:37, *"Do not judge, and you will not be judged. Do not condemn, and you will not be condemned. Forgive, and you will be forgiven,"* creates room for a more open and accepting alliance. It is grace which serves as a healing balm for wounds occurring in the relationship.

CHAPTER SIX

1 Peter 4:8, highlights the importance of: "*Love each other deeply because love covers over a multitude of sins.*" Love, as an expression of grace, facilitates the process of healing and reconciliation. This attribute, as reflected in the Scriptures, is not simply a concept but a transformative Godly power nurturing a unique understanding and acceptance, paving the way for a more harmonious and loving connection between those involved. Inevitably, conflicts and disagreements arise, and without grace, these wounds fester and create distance. However, when grace is present, it enables both to forgive and move forward. It rebuilds trust and strengthens the bond by showing them, despite the challenges, love and understanding prevail.

Reconciliation is the process which transforms conflicts into opportunities for growth and deeper connections. Instead of avoiding conflicts or allowing them to escalate, reconciliation encourages fathers and their sons to confront issues head-on, seeking resolution and common ground. It requires both to listen actively, express themselves honestly, and work towards a solution. This enhances communication skills, making it easier to navigate future challenges. It is through reconciliation, those in the relationship learn to speak their minds and to truly hear and understand each other.

Grace and reconciliation are essential to fortifying the relationship. By addressing conflicts with composure and actively pursuing an understanding, the bond is empowered with the emotional tools needed to navigate future issues more effectively. This resilience becomes the benchmark of a lasting and profound alliance, developing personal growth and learning. It enables them to reflect on their actions and make amends when necessary, promoting personal development. Reconciliation facilitates learning from conflicts, aiding both in their evolution as individuals and as a unit. The commitment to growth ensures their relationship continually deepens and matures. This serves as the building blocks of a healthy, loving companionship. When kindness is extended and a settlement is actively sought, conflicts migrate into opportunities for growth, wounds are healed, and trust is fortified. These elements cultivate understanding, acceptance, and effective communication, ultimately ensuring the relationship remains resilient and meaningful over time.

An entry-level approach to conflict resolution involves the practice of mindful attentiveness. Full attention, eye contact, and the demonstration of empathy constitute this decisive strategy. When fathers and their sons experience a sense of being heard and understood, conflicts gain a pathway for more effective resolution. Beyond attentive mindfulness, the cultivation of compassionate communication emerges as an imperative. The endeavor to comprehend each other's perspectives takes center stage, encompassing the reception of spoken words and an understanding of the emotions and intentions underlying them. Empathy acts as an agent, nurturing a sense of connection and contributing to the de-escalation of conflicts. The art of conflict resolution further demands both master the skill of expressing themselves with efficacy.

The ability to articulate feelings, concerns, and needs in a clear and respectful manner stands as a central aspect of this process. In navigating problems, it is beneficial to identify common ground and mutual goals. Collaboratively finding areas where their interests align provides a foundation for compromise and collaboration. It is important to note, in discovering common ground does not mean giving up one's own values but rather finding solutions respecting both perspectives.

Problem-solving is a key aspect of effective resolution. Encouraging them to approach differences as challenges can be solved together is significant. This involves brainstorming solutions, considering different options, and evaluating the pros and cons of each. Productive resolve addresses immediate issues and contributes to relationship strengthening by showcasing the ability to collaborate seamlessly. Sometimes, situations escalate, and emotions become intense. In such instances, it's essential to take breaks as needed. Those involved can agree to step away temporarily to regain composure and gather their thoughts. The emphasis is then placed on the importance of returning to the discussion table with a calmer mindset and a commitment to finding a resolution.

The practice of forgiveness and the release of grudges prevent lingering issues from obstructing the solution of present tasks. This highlights the healing potential of forgiveness in mending relationships and moving forward. Considerations regarding interpersonal dynamics encompass more than just resolving disputes; they also offer moments for growth and learning. Encouraging reflection on personal struggles and deriving insights from them becomes vital. These situations serve as opportunities to deepen their understanding of each other and strengthen their bond.

In review, practical strategies are essential tools for fathers and their sons to manage differences and maintain a healthy relationship. These approaches include active listening, empathetic communication, effective expression, seeking common ground, problem-solving, taking breaks when necessary, third-party mediation when needed, forgiveness, and the ability to learn and grow from disagreements. By employing these strategies, they address complications constructively and mold a stronger and more active allegiance. To proactively navigate roadblocks within their relationships, employing strategies such as setting clear boundaries, managing expectations, and practicing active appreciation becomes paramount to reducing the likelihood of misunderstandings and conflicts.

However, in instances where difficulties prove more intricate, external assistance may be necessary. Seeking professional support, such as Christian counseling and therapy as previously noted, emerges as a constructive step in addressing deeper issues embedded within the relationship. Encouragement stands as an available option, providing valuable guidance when needed. Constructively working through the hurdles demands patience and persistence, recognizing not all obstacles can be promptly resolved and some may require ongoing effort. The commitment to collectively overcoming conflicts, differences of viewpoints, and personal opinions becomes a testament to the strength of their bond.

Effective communication is the basis of any healthy connection. Fathers and their sons can benefit from techniques such as attentive listening, assertive communication, and conflict resolution strategies. These empower them to express thoughts, emotions, and concerns openly and respectfully, nurturing a deeper understanding and unity. Bonding methods encompass activities allowing them to engage and create lasting memories, reinforcing their togetherness. Goal-setting techniques involve identifying shared objectives related to personal growth, family values, or mutual interests, offering purpose and direction to the relationship, and encouraging collaboration.

Empathy-building exercises prompt both to view situations from each other's perspectives, promoting understanding and compassion and fostering a deeper fellowship for each other's joys and heartbreaks. Conflict prevention tools encompass proactive measures to sidestep misunderstandings and disputes, such as setting boundaries, managing expectations, and practicing active appreciation to maintain a harmonious relationship. Creating emotionally safe spaces within the relationship is vital, involving guidelines for open and non-judgmental communication and ensuring both feel at ease expressing thoughts and emotions without the fear of criticism or rejection. The resources build trust and vulnerability. Reflective approaches encourage fathers and their sons to periodically assess and strengthen their bond. These methods involve journaling, self-assessment exercises, or regular check-ins to gauge the state of the relationship and identify areas for improvement.

Embracing Family Differences

It is valuable to emphasize the concept of embracing differences and dilemmas. The essence lies in recognizing the variations and quandaries intrinsic to any relationship, regardless of its nature. These variances, whether in thoughts or external pressures, are part and parcel of the connection. When approached with a balanced perspective, they become opportunities for growth and understanding.

The core of effective communication plays a central role in this process. Fathers and their sons are encouraged to express their thoughts, feelings, and concerns openly but respectfully. Differences often lead to conflicts, and having concrete resolution techniques in place is invaluable. The relationship then benefits from strategies using compromise, negotiation, and finding common ground. These techniques ensure conflicts are approached as opportunities for growth and understanding rather than as destructive forces. Father-son relationships possess unique qualities, with differences in personalities, values, and interests being entirely natural. Navigating complexities involves embracing these distinctions rather than viewing them as hurdles. These differences can be harnessed by both to complement each other's strengths and enrich the relationship. Empathy then serves as a valuable tool for addressing these intricacies. Practicing empathy entails trying to understand each other's feelings and perspectives, even during disagreements.

Practical strategies encompass placing themselves in each other's space, asking open-ended questions, and actively seeking to see the situation from the other's viewpoint. When faced with emotional obstructions, identifying common ground often proves helpful. Collaboratively finding solutions aligned with values and goals develops a sense of partnership and unity in addressing life's intricacies. These intricacies inherently offer opportunities for growth and learning. Viewing these as valuable lessons allows them to reflect on the insights gained from past experiences and apply the knowledge gained to future situations.

Meaningful strategies involve engaging in regular discussions to assess the relationship's strengths and areas for improvement. This facet of effective communication emphasizes the significance of clear, honest, and transparent conversations forming the foundation upon which all other aspects of their bond thrive. This process involves articulating thoughts, emotions, and intentions with clarity, ensuring both fully understand each other and reducing the chances of misunderstandings and misinterpretations.

Expressing true thoughts and feelings without fear of judgment and reprisal promotes trust and emotional intimacy, allowing for a deeper and more meaningful union. Their dialogue is not just about speaking; it also involves active and empathetic listening. Actively engaging in conversations by attentively listening to each other's perspectives creates a sense of validation and understanding, making both feel valued and heard. Within this relationship, open dialogue serves as a tool for problem-solving.

When conflicts arise, fathers and their sons can engage in constructive discussions to address these issues. They can collaborate on finding solutions acceptable to both, strengthening their ability to navigate difficulties together. Sharing thoughts, feelings, and experiences builds emotional bonds. It allows them to connect on a deeper level, creating a sense of emotional closeness and empathy. This emotional intimacy is valuable for building a supportive and nurturing environment.

Roundtable discussions play an important role in managing conflicts. Instead of allowing differences of opinions to fester or escalate, fathers and their sons can use structured conversations to address the root causes of disagreements. By approaching dissension with understanding and a willingness to find common ground, they can reach resolutions enhancing their alliance. A fundamental aspect of such dialogues is mutual respect, where both treat each other's viewpoints and feelings with consideration, even if they don't always agree. This mutual respect reinforces the idea they are partners and have valid perspectives to share.

Clear communication, honesty, active listening, problem-solving, emotional bonding, conflict resolution, and mutual respect all contribute to creating an environment where communication is open and real. This type of dialogue forms the basis for a flourishing bond, enabling them to navigate the complexities of life together with understanding, trust, and mutual support.

Empathy is the backbone of nurturing and fortifying these connections. It underscores the valuable role that understanding and compassion play in deepening their bond. This aspect is characterized by an empathetic attitude and an ability to perceive and resonate with each other's emotions and experiences. It involves the capacity to understand and appreciate each other's perspectives, feelings, and experiences.

Striving to put themselves in each other's views and seeing the world through the other's eyes builds a sense of unity, as both feel genuinely acknowledged and valued. It extends to providing emotional support, being attuned to each other's emotional needs, offering comfort and encouragement when needed, and celebrating each other's successes.

Nurturing Dynamic Growth

Compassion and kindness are fundamental components of empathy. Acts of kindness, whether small gestures or significant displays of support, contribute to a warm and nurturing relationship. When disagreements and conflicts arise, they can utilize empathy to de-escalate tense situations. By understanding each other's perspectives and emotions, they find common ground and work toward mutually beneficial solutions.

CHAPTER SIX

This approach limits conflicts from causing lasting damage. Approaching conversations with empathy builds an atmosphere of trust and openness. Their sons feel comfortable conveying thoughts and concerns, knowing their fathers will respond with understanding and compassion. This improved communication deepens their attachment, allowing them to connect on a profound level, sharing their joys and sorrows, fears, and dreams. The emotional connection forms the core of a supportive and loving bond, reinforcing the idea they are not just family but confidants and allies.

By modeling a loving behavior, fathers demonstrate the importance of compassionately understanding, setting a powerful example they carry into their own interactions with others. The rapport serves as a fundamental element in managing comprehension, emotional support, compassion, and improved communication.

This empowerment enables them to gracefully navigate their challenges, cultivating a relationship marked by deep emotional trust and mutual respect. Prioritizing empathy ensures their bond remains strong and enduring, enriched by common experiences and genuine care for one another.

Another element is the concept of growth, which suggests the father-son bonds are dynamic and evolve efficiently over time. This aspect of their alliance acknowledges they are continually changing and developing and encourages them to actively contribute to their mutual growth. Doing so helps them learn from each other's experiences, perspectives, and journeys, building a sense of humility and openness to new insights. Growth requires adaptability and the willingness to embrace change. Being open to evolving roles and responsibilities as they transition through different stages is important.

For example, as one transitions into adulthood, the father-son dynamic shifts from a more paternalistic one to a more egalitarian alliance. To promote developmental maturation, they can explore goals and aspirations, set objectives related to personal progress, family values, or interests, and provide a sense of purpose and direction in the relationship. Pursuing these goals together strengthens their mutual commitment to support and growth. This support involves offering guidance and encouragement when needed, being a source of inspiration, and facilitating advancement through effective communication and self-reflection.

Engaging in meaningful conversations about their journeys and reflecting on their experiences, difficulties, and aspirations allows them to gain valuable insights and refine their paths forward. Evolution within this bond requires resilience and adaptation when faced with these conundrums. Demonstrating a commitment to working through difficulties together, learning from hardships, and using them as opportunities for growth is vital.

Prioritizing personal development is a means of contributing to their maturity. This involves self-awareness, self-improvement, and a commitment to becoming the best versions of themselves. By actively participating in each other's development, they ensure their bonds remain vital, relevant, and deeply meaningful throughout the various stages of life. It encourages commitment to continuous learning, adaptability, shared goals, support, effective communication, resilience, and personal development. Through active contributions to each other's maturation, fathers and their sons ensure these connections remain vibrant and enriching, reflecting the evolving nature of their relationships as they mature over the years.

—— Moving Forward ——

In this chapter, the exploration led into the heart of father-son connections, revealing the intricate insight of challenges and complexities and the perpetual significance of their journey together. Shared influence remained a core theme, and a constant interchange of wisdom shaped their perspectives, values, and life outlook, much like the insights found in Proverbs 4:7. It forged an enduring and ever-evolving bond. Fathers, in their roles as mentors and role models, carried the torch of this sacred wisdom, passing it down to their sons as a priceless gift witnessed first-hand by the generations before them. Common experiences emerged as catalysts for learning and personal growth, and the role of

CHAPTER SIX

fathers as living embodiments of the values they sought to impart was of paramount significance. This influence extended beyond childhood, shaping their sons' lives into adulthood and fatherhood.

In addition, emotional intelligence was expounded upon as a fundamental aspect of personal growth, as echoed in the wisdom of Proverbs 16:32. Through this process, fathers nurtured their sons' self-identity, instilled core values and principles, and formed confidence and a positive self-concept. Additionally, stressing the importance of embracing disparities and hardships as opportunities for growth and enlightenment was emphasized as a key role of effective communication.

In Chapter 7, the eternal legacy of love and wisdom within the intricate father-son relationship comes into focus, as found in Psalm 103:17-18. This final chapter brings to the forefront the invaluable task of passing down essential teachings and affection, perpetuating a chain of influence extending across generations. Drawing inspiration from both Biblical and historical ancestral legacies, the path toward a manageable future is navigated.

Ending with 2 Timothy 2:2, the discussion considers the weighty responsibility of acting as torchbearers, entrusted with the wisdom and virtues handed down through the annals of time. This narrative artfully paints a vivid tableau of the timeless connection, enriched by wisdom and love, a touching reminder of life's most cherished and imperishable treasures emerging within this sacred bond. Their relationship is not merely an alliance, as the father-son relationship transcends into an allegiance inseparable for eternity.

CHAPTER SEVEN

Everlasting Bond

Through countless generations and within the seamless passage of the familial legacy, integral roles begin to unfold as bearers and conveyors of invaluable instruction and affection take their place. Guided by the wisdom woven into Biblical teachings and the timeless force of divine love, the everlasting connection shines beyond the far-reaching influence of those who lead. This horizon yields a profound insight into the majestic beauty of love in understanding the foresight of a Godly empowered bond, transcending time to shape the generations ahead, and resonating throughout entire family lineages.

Significant in its source, the transition emphasizes the central weightiness of these relationships in the unfolding fabric of life's connections. The ageless understanding in the legacy of fatherhood extends past the present, reaching across generations, and finds affirmation in the words of Psalm 103:17-18, proclaiming: *"But from everlasting to everlasting the Lord's love is with those who fear him, and his righteousness with their children's children, with those who keep his covenant and remember to obey his precepts."*

This abiding birthright is not a relic of the past; instead, it possesses the potential to form the lives of descendants. It reflects core values, beliefs, and the boundless love cultivated over epochs. In this conclusive exploration, the dynamic nature of the legacy is unveiled, persistently influencing future inheritors. Recognizing this accentuates the importance of their roles and the impact it creates. Carrying both dual responsibility and divine privilege, fathers shape a legacy enriching the lives of their sons, serving as a guiding luminary for their offspring and subsequent heirs.

CHAPTER SEVEN

Inspired by a deeper look into the book of Psalms, this exploration delves into the concept of a father's legacy as an eternal gift transcending boundaries through the unfolding eons. The sacred text serves as a spiritual link for this understanding, a testament to the eternal nature of love and righteousness, forming the basis for discussion.

In the context of fatherhood, the impact of love and wisdom passed on to their sons is contemplated. The inheritance a father creates is not bound by the constraints of a single age; instead, it extends across the continuum of time. It is a provision transcending earthly limitations, carrying with it the essence of timeless fundamentals. Venturing into this concept reveals the responsibility mentors hold in shaping the lives of their progeny. The gift they offer, through the display of affection, dedication to Godly essentials, and provisions by example, is not just for the present, but a precious heirloom passed down through the family patriarchs.

This notion inspires reflection on the values instilled throughout the endowment, recognizing these statutes will continue to influence their children, grandchildren, and beyond. The understanding empowers them to craft legacies standing as beacons of love, righteousness, and wisdom, enriching the lives of their offspring. Their responsibility carries a sense of purpose and significance in considering the values and ideals to impart, becoming purveyors of a legacy extending far beyond their own lifetimes. It is a reflection on the importance of hard work, perseverance, and the pursuit of knowledge as essential elements for a thriving lineage, often striving to inculcate strong moral and ethical values, emphasizing honesty, compassion, and a commitment to moral justice.

As designers of this inheritance, these role models recognize their actions today shape tomorrow. Pondering the impact of this influence, they understand the love nurtured within these relationships with their protégés serves as a foundation. Their aim is to be exemplars of virtue, fashioning the values they wish to pass on, including demonstrating the importance of empathy by showing kindness to others and generating a domain of mutual respect and understanding.

Fathers see themselves as custodians of a legacy extending far beyond their own lifespan. This contemplation inspires them to strive for excellence in character and to leave a lasting imprint of love, righteousness, and wisdom enriching the lives of their descendants. Their awareness instills a sense of purpose, love, and intention in their actions, as they know the virtues cultivated today will serve as the guiding light for others to follow.

At the core of a father's legacy resides the immeasurable influence of love, a spirit transcending words and gestures. It encompasses a warm embrace, words of encouragement, and a sturdy support through example. This Agape love, expressed through these various forms of embrace, creates an emotional sanctuary for their successors, nurturing feelings of security and self-worth resonating throughout their lifetimes. Within this nurturing sphere, courage is discovered as their sons explore their hidden potential, cultivate resilience in the face of adversity, and develop empathy in their relationships with others.

Furthermore, it stands as the cornerstone of character development. Guidance finds expression in the fundamental values of kindness, compassion, and respect. The younger generation witnesses these virtues embodied in their fathers' interactions with the world, serving as an example for their own ethical guide. As the linchpin, love molds the character of the next generation, instilling in them a sense of responsibility, empathy, and moral integrity extending well beyond their own lives. In this way, the legacy they construct becomes an unending bequeath, enriching the lives of future inheritors and illuminating the path to a life imbued with meaning and purpose.

Echoes of a Virtuous Heritage

Love possesses a remarkable quality, transcending the boundaries of time. It is not confined to the moments shared between a father and his son during their lifetime but has the remarkable capacity to echo through generations. Endurance lies in the memories it creates and the values it imparts. Those who receive this embrace carry within them the indelible impressions of a deep connection, and they in turn, pass it forward to their own heirs. This impact is akin to an undulation in a vast pond. It begins with the initial touch, spreading outward to encompass the lives of their sons and future heirs. As each generation experiences and embraces this legacy, it becomes an integral part of their family's identity, a living testament to the loving connection.

The influence is not bound by the constraints of a single era; rather, it extends its reach across the continuum of time, offering solace, guidance, and a sense of belonging to descendants who may never have had the opportunity to meet their forefathers. In this way, the legacy of love is an endless gift, nurturing the hearts and souls of those who follow in their father's footsteps. Similar to a well-honed cornerstone, wisdom forms the bedrock on which the ethical and moral framework of future generations is constructed. As guardians of insight, fathers embark on the noble pursuit of imparting knowledge and the priceless understanding gained from life's journey.

This reservoir of experiences, life lessons, and profound guidance extends beyond the confines of textbooks and classrooms. It serves as a guiding light, illuminating the path toward informed decision-making and ethical conduct. The collective knowledge of past generations is a treasure trove of insights, empowering those who embrace it to navigate life's complexities with discernment and integrity. Their legacy is dynamic, evolving with each generation and adapting to the changing tides of the world while remaining firmly rooted in ageless values. The understanding extends an invitation for introspection and critical thinking.

It encourages contemplation of the consequences of choices, not only on an individual level but also on a broader scale, encompassing communities and the world at large. It creates a sense of responsibility, inspiring the continuation of ethical standards and positive contributions to society. In this way, the heirloom shapes the ethical compass of future generations, empowering them to make decisions reflecting not only personal gain but also contributing to the greater good. It is a holistic approach to passing down knowledge ensuring it remains relevant and impactful. Comprehension becomes a dynamic force, propelling their engagement with the complexities of the world while upholding valuable principles. Through this intergenerational transmission, the familial transfer becomes a living testament to the strength of character, resilience, and ethical fortitude guiding individuals through the intricate tapestry of life. The birthright, embodying knowledge and values passed from one to the next, is distilled from life's experiences.

Those entrusted understand it to be more than a set of instructions; it represents a living reservoir of accumulated knowledge and insights derived from life's journey. This generational gift, serving as a beacon of guidance, illuminates the virtuous path and encourages the resilience to confront life's obstacles, the discernment to approach dilemmas, and the ethical integrity to navigate the complexities of the world. Inheritors of the heritage bear both the bounty and the responsibility to pass it forward, preserving its depth for the future.

The concept emphasizes its dynamic nature, capable of evolving with the times while retaining its foundational values. It instills in descendants a sense of continuity, connecting them to the insights of their forefathers and reminding them of the principles guiding their family for eons. In this way, it transcends individual lifetimes, becoming a timeless source of inspiration, guidance, and a moral compass for those who follow in the path of their fathers. Within the intricate fabric of a legacy, love and wisdom stand as intertwined elements, each enhancing and strengthening the other.

Love, as the emotional core, provides essential nurturing for growth and the flourishing of connections. It is the foundation upon which values are built and rooted in a deep sense of understanding. Alongside this, mutual insight imparts valuable life lessons and equips them for the navigation of challenges. Wisdom acts as a wheel, steering through the complexities of life, and as a lamppost, enlightening the path to ethical and meaningful choices. It embodies experiences, offering discernment into the art of leading a purposeful and virtuous life.

The coexistence of understanding and foresight is where the true spirit of a father's endowment unfolds. This infusion of knowledge with compassion ensures the guidance provided is not just pragmatic but also deeply empathetic. Prudence in turn, reinforces the ethical dimensions, directing it toward nurturing values, encouraging empathy, and inspiring each to be compassionate and just. Together, these elements create a lasting impact, weaving a legacy encompassing both the emotional, intellectual, and spiritual realms of human existence. This harmonious coexistence becomes a source of strength, empowering them to lead purposeful lives enriched by both heartfelt connections and ethical choices.

—— Legacy of Living Wisdom ——

Cultivating the growth of wisdom is a foundational aspect of nurturing the path for the next generation. Extending beyond the transfer of knowledge, this concept highlights the responsibility to instill values, principles, and affection in the hearts and minds of descendants. Stewards of these invaluable seeds tend to their development with care and intentionality. Even as a gardener tends to the soil, providing optimal conditions for seeds to mature into thriving plants and creating an environment where values such as integrity, empathy, and compassion can take root and flourish becomes paramount.

This legacy must be continuously nourished, with guidance and instructions adapted to the changing times and needs of future successors. It ensures the inheritance remains relevant, resonating with the hurdles and opportunities of the present and the future. Essentially, this process emphasizes the impact on the development of those members next in line. By nurturing values, principles, and affection, it empowers future descendants to lead purposeful, ethical lives, enriching not only their individual journeys but also the broader texture of humanity.

Instilling principles highlight the central role fathers play in forming their family's moral and ethical stronghold. It serves as the ethical compass guiding future heirs toward virtuous living. These values build the foundation of a legacy of wisdom. They uniquely bear the responsibility of imparting qualities such as integrity, empathy, honesty, and compassion, along with statutes of justice, responsibility, and humility. These elements are essential for a well-rounded character, and they are the primary source of their vital life lessons. The legacy is not just a collection of wise sayings or knowledge; it is a deep reservoir of values and principles informing every decision, action, and interaction. As mentors, fathers model values through their own behavior, teaching practical applications of Godly living in daily life. The legacy is not confined to one family member; it has a cascading effect extending to the broader good of the Christian community and society. By passing on these essential elements, they ensure their history is not simply intellectual but deeply rooted in a moral and ethical foundation, improving the lives of those who follow in their footsteps.

Its continuity, rather than being a relic of the past, remains a dynamic and evolving momentum guiding and enriching the lives of the future. This responsibility entails several key aspects. First and foremost, there is an active engagement in passing down knowledge through the university of life. This transmission extends beyond the sharing of practical skills; it involves the imparting of experiences garnered from both successes and failures. Their tutorship surpasses formal education, offering invaluable insights sporadically found on the collective sheets between the dust covers of a text.

In addition, the creation of an environment encouraging critical and independent thinking is valuable. An open space for discussions, questions, and the exploration of ideas empowers the forthcoming generation to build upon the foundation provided. Flexibility characterizes the approach to addressing the differences and opportunities of each era. This adaptability ensures the relevance and significant resonance of the legacy. Wisdom encompasses not only knowledge but also values and principles. The emphasis is founded on an ethical basis, with values such as honesty, kindness, and respect integrated into the traditions, providing moral direction.

Therefore, presenting wisdom with love capable of guiding and enriching the lives of future generations is vital. This continuity is essential, involving the active transmission of knowledge, the modeling of sagacity, the encouragement of critical thinking, adaptation to change, and the highlighting of core values. Through these efforts, the bequeathal remains vibrant and significantly relevant, leaving an impact on the lives of descendants. Transmitting a heritage of love and affection encourages reflection, emphasizing the everlasting idea this emotion surpasses mere gifting; it becomes an ageless tradition. This suggests passing on the familial warmth to upcoming generations, creating a meaningful family tradition interwoven into the very fabric of time. This narrative, not a tangible bequest but rather a divine and emotional inheritance, transcends both temporal and spatial confines. It signifies an intangible yet deeply influential connection, bestowed and grounded in love, care, and a sincere sense of personal belonging.

Serving as a reminder, this point of view extends beyond the present; its influence reaches into the future. Nurturing the family heritage creates a duration of emotional wealth enriching the lives of their sons. Their tradition becomes a source of wisdom, with comfort, strength, and resilience, cultivating a profound sense of rootedness and stability while developing emotional wellness and creating strong family bonds. Imparting lessons on empathy, compassion, and the value of developing meaningful relationships, the legacy perpetuates its essence through time.

Essentially, the endowment of affection is not simply a brief sentiment but a cherished legacy, entrusted to be carried forward to the inheritors who follow. It stands as a beautiful testament to its power, connecting generations and enriching the lives of all who are embraced by its lasting presence. The idea becomes clear when reflecting on love and wisdom passed down, transforming into a cherished family tradition transcending boundaries. This tradition forms a bond, binding families together in a grand tapestry of affection and collective experiences. It stands as a testament to the everlasting emotional bond and strength within the family, extending beyond a single generation and becoming a continuous thread weaving through the ages.

Signifying a feeling of continuity and belonging, it reminds each generation of their place within the larger family story. The importance is magnified within the context of this lineage; emphasizing their love is more than a personal emotion; it is a bequest passed forward. Through actions and examples, the significance of love, care, nurturing relationships, and instilling wisdom underpinning this cherished gift is highlighted. In a changing world, the family tradition of love and compassion offers stability and comfort, reinforcing the bonds connecting members and emphasizing the need to cherish and preserve this tradition to ensure it enriches the lives of those who follow.

Legacy Narratives Past and Present

References and anecdotes act as vibrant colors, painting a vivid canvas of understanding through authenticity and relatability. Reconsider the impact of 1 Corinthians 13:4-7, which offers an ageless and universal perspective on love as a legacy. Drawing from sacred texts revered across cultures and generations, this reference transforms the abstract concept of a father passing down love into something transcendent and divine.

Within these sacred Scriptures, stories of love, compassion, and selflessness deeply resonate, offering glimpses into the immense influence within the context of faith. In the same spirit, it is also the personal remedies breathing life into this discussion. Drawing inspiration from ancestral legacies is a practice deeply rooted in the idea, the wisdom of the past can illuminate the path to a brighter future. This concept highlights the significance of encompassing both Biblical tales and historical accounts as valuable sources of guidance and wisdom.

When exploring this inheritance, the stories of fathers and their sons who bravely navigated life's trials and bequeathed lasting values to their inheritors are uncovered. Within the narratives, notable examples arise, including Abraham and Isaac, Jacob and Joseph, and David and Solomon. The stories unveil not only the complexities of father-son relationships but also the immeasurable impact of love, faith, and moral principles passed down.

Consider the account of David and his son Solomon, as told in 1 Samuel 16:7, and the story of Samuel's guidance in 1 Samuel 7. David, a father renowned for his unwavering love, instilled in his son the commitment to carry forward his father's legacy. These anecdotes take the abstract idea of love and anchor it in the tangible and relatable experiences of individuals and families.

Together, these two storytelling elements weave a rich and diverse fabric of chronicles enriching the exploration of love as a sustaining legacy. Through these instances, love is witnessed in action, transforming lives, fortifying family bonds, and leaving a lasting influence on the hearts of those touched by its embrace. In retrospect, these references and postulates become windows through which a glimpse of the real-world significance of

CHAPTER SEVEN

love within the context of a father's history is obtained, rendering it a concept reverberating deeply. Finding guidance from leaders, thinkers, and others, spanning various eras and cultures, who have bequeathed legacies of resilience, courage, and societal transformation, helps provide insights into the uniqueness of their tails.

These legacies serve as a reminder of the lasting influence of values, not only within the family but also in a wider social context. Assimilating these ancestral stories into one's life offers a moment to glean inspiration from timeless lessons and principles having steered preceding generations. This reinforces the idea, their journey of companionship is not isolated but part of a broader narrative, a recital woven with threads of love, wisdom, and experiences extending far beyond the present.

In exploring these endowments, they are not only an inspiration but also a sense of continuity, connecting these stories to the design of human history. The concept of learning from ancestral wealth represents a treasure trove of knowledge for contemporary fathers aspiring to craft a personal inheritance of love and wisdom for their sons and the future. For example, highlighting the lives of Thomas Aquinas and John Calvin reveals valuable lessons transcending time, offering profound insights.

One lesson can be drawn from these theological giants is their canny commitment to their faith and the pursuit of knowledge. Both devoted their lives to the study of theology and the dissemination of Christian teachings. Their intellectual rigor and dedication serve as a reminder that a mentor's commitment to imparting wisdom and values should be steadfast. Understanding this footprint is akin to planting seeds in fertile soil and producing a harvest of values, principles, and beliefs guiding and nurturing the hearts and minds of descendants.

When revisiting the posits of Thomas Aquinas and John Calvin, both revered Christian theologians, their systematic dedication to theological scholarship and their profound insights into matters of faith continue to resonate through the annals of history. Their written works, such as Aquinas' "*Summa Theologica*" (1274), and Calvin's "*Institutes of the Christian Religion*" (1536), remain foundational texts in Christian theology. These writings have not only shaped the views of their contemporaries but have also left a benchmark for successive generations of theologians and believers to consider. In a broader sense, when exploring the stories of fathers and their sons in Scripture, such as Abraham and Isaac or David and Solomon, their legacies of faith and righteousness have influenced the trajectory of their families. These narratives highlight the sustaining power of faith and virtue to guide not only one generation but many to come. The statutes and values instilled by these patriarchs continue to illuminate the path of righteousness.

In contemporary times, as fathers seek to leave a lasting heritage of love and wisdom for their sons, they can draw inspiration from these ancestral legacies. This serves as a reminder the impact of actions and the values upheld extend far beyond their own lifetimes. Just as the faith of patriarchs and the virtues of Biblical figures have influenced generations, the love, wisdom, and principles passed down can serve as beacons of light, brightening the path and enriching the lives of their families.

The lives of these Christian role models highlight the significance of cognitive and spiritual growth, as drawn from their inspirational and intellectual journeys. These men were not content with superficial knowledge but sought out the mysteries in matters of faith, ethics, and philosophy. The impact of the historical elders prompts consideration of the eternal nature of the inheritance yet to be created. Much like the influence of Aquinas and Calvin's teachings on Christian thought through the centuries, the aspiration is for fathers to leave legacies of lasting love and wisdom.

This endeavor involves imparting values and principles used to maintain their relevance. The concept of drawing wisdom from ancestral legacies underscores the timeless pertinence of faith and love. It inspires a purposeful and dedicated approach to the endeavor of creating a lasting inheritance, finding motivation in the footsteps of those who have gone before. By weaving these lessons into the narratives and passing them on, there is a collective contribution to the ongoing tapestry of ancestral gifts shaping the hearts and minds of the future. There is great richness in drawing inspiration from these Biblical and historical examples. They serve as powerful accounts transcending time and cultural boundaries, offering valuable insights for fathers and sons in their own journeys.

CHAPTER SEVEN

Within the Christian context, Biblical examples with the story of Joseph and his father Jacob highlight themes of forgiveness, reconciliation, and the strength of family bonds. Joseph's pardon of his brothers and the ultimate reunion with his father illustrate the impact of love and faith within a family. The chronicles of Jesus and Joseph emphasize the importance of fatherly guidance and the divine legacy of love and sacrifice.

Beyond the Biblical realm, historical examples of notable theological scholars, provide additional layers of inspiration. They reflect and demonstrate the ways individuals carried forward the teachings of Christ Jesus and left indelible marks on Christian tradition. By learning from these various examples, families within a Godly environment find relatable and impactful stories resonating with their faith. The portrayals offer guidance on love, belief, resilience, and the everlasting legacy of family values, serving as a reminder, their lineage extends back through history. This heritage carries forward a legacy of righteousness, compassion, and knowledge continuing to build future lives.

—— Passing the Torch ——

The essence of continuity and legacy building lies ahead as a guiding light in drawing inspiration from the ageless wisdom of 2 Timothy 2:2, *"And the things you have heard me say in the presence of many witnesses entrust to reliable people who will also be qualified to teach others."* The Apostle Paul imparts an insightful directive to Timothy: the immense truth emerges regarding the knowledge, values, and love inherited from fathers should not remain idle but rather vibrant, evolving, and passed forward.

At this crossroad, the solemn responsibility of the torchbearer comes into focus, serving as a moving reminder for those who are entrusted with a precious gift, symbolizing the teachings, values, and familial legacy handed down. It issues a resounding call to nurture the flame of wisdom and love, perpetuating a heritage transcending the confines of the past to brighten the path for the future.

In this ongoing exploration, clarity emerges during the transition: wisdom is not a stagnant entity but a living, evolving, Heavenly residence. The torchbearers of this wisdom are entrusted with the sacred duty of building it and sharing it with their own heirs. This realization is enlightening, emphasizing the legacy of love and wisdom is not confined to a single era but holds the potential to transcend time, leaving an indelible impression on the design of family tradition.

As the journey progresses, the intricacies of this legacy and the integral role each generation plays in nurturing, teaching, and loving the next come to light. It is an unfading cycle of inheritance where the flames of love and wisdom are carried forward, ensuring the torch remains ablaze for generations. As this text is traversed, immersion occurs in a narrative speaking to the very heart of father-son relationships. It is a tale of continuity, of passing down not just knowledge but a torch representing the values and love defining a family's identity.

"Passing the Torch" invites reflection on the roles as both bearers and recipients of this flame, recognizing actions today have an important impact on the legacy left behind. The torchbearer's responsibility, the nurturing of wisdom, the continuation of love, and the essential task of teaching the next generation will be further explored. Through these insights, a sense of purpose and commitment in fathers and their sons alike is kindled as they embark on the journey of passing the torch of love and wisdom.

Torchbearer's Responsibility

The torchbearer's responsibility is a central theme. This duty falls squarely on the younger generation as they carry forward the legacy of love and wisdom from their forebears. It's more than the transfer of knowledge; it is a Godly task to ensure values, principles, and love flourish in future generations. The foundational responsibilities of the role can be highlighted as follows: First, understanding the weight of this significant duty is essential. They inherit not just facts and teachings but a rich registry of family values, traditions, and love. This task extends beyond knowledge transmission; it encompasses preserving a family's identity and perpetuating core principles. As future gatekeepers of their family's history and heritage, they make their role powerful and meaningful. They are not just heirs to family values but custodians of a rich cultural wealth.

Beyond the weight of duty lies the responsibility to safeguard and celebrate the unique cultural aspects embedded in their family history. This involves preserving customs, rituals, and language, ensuring the traditional tapestry remains vibrant for generations to come. Their duty is not confined to a motionless preservation; it extends to adapting and navigating the family legacy through an ever-changing world.

Their sons must discern how age-old statutes resonate in contemporary contexts, ensuring the essence of their heritage remains relevant and applicable in the face of societal evolution. Their role is not merely about the present; it transcends generations. They carry the torch not only for themselves but for their children, grandchildren, and more. This perspective underscores the influential impact of their choices and the deep-rooted legacy they contribute to shaping, echoing through time.

Second, recognizing the gravity of this responsibility is important. It is not just being recipients of a legacy; it's actively participating in its renewal. The emotional weight lies in the realization their actions, choices, and commitments directly impact the history passed on. Neglecting this duty results in the loss of valuable observances and the dilution of core family values. Recognizing the importance of their responsibility entails not simply acknowledging it but actively participating in its continuation.

They are summoned to actively contribute to the unfolding story, making intentional choices molding the course of the family history. Each action and decision they undertake sends wavelets through the legacy they bear, emphasizing the interwoven nature of the family through generations.

This showcases the way individual decisions echo through time, shaping the collective identity of the family. They take on the role of guardians, ensuring the preservation of valuable traditions. It involves a commitment to not only pass down their history but actively nurture and protect them. The responsibility extends beyond casual awareness to a proactive role in safeguarding the rituals and customs defining the family.

They are tasked with safeguarding these values, acting as stewards who protect the essence of the family's beliefs against potential erosion over time. Third, this responsibility carries a significant impact on the posterity. The commitment to carry forward the legacy influences not only their own lives but also the lives of their progeny. Their dedication to preserving the family's values and passing on the wisdom they have received shapes their character and moral directives.

The lineage they leave behind becomes a guiding force for succeeding heirs. The responsibility goes beyond the present moment; it intricately connects their lives with those of future descendants. This interconnectedness underscores the far-reaching impact their commitment has on the unfolding tapestry of family history. The dedication to preserving family values and passing on wisdom is not just a duty but a legacy akin to planting seeds for the fullness of time. They earnestly contribute to the character development of their sons, imprinting a lasting influence shaping the moral compass of successive waves.

The legacy left behind becomes a guiding force for the future. It serves as a source of wisdom, offering insights and principles that navigate the challenges and choices faced by their offspring. This guiding force becomes an anchor in times of uncertainty. Their sons, in carrying forward the inheritance, instill qualities of resilience and adaptability. The resolution to preserving values in the face of changing times equips future lineages with the strength to manage challenges while staying true to the Godly core principles handed down through the family legacy.

Fourth, beyond the conveyance of knowledge, this responsibility involves the cultivation of character. They are expected to embody the values and statutes instilled in them by their fathers. This involves personal growth, self-awareness, and a resolve to living out these beliefs. Individual development is at the heart of carrying forward the legacy, as it ensures the values are not just spoken but lived.

Their sons serve as living testaments to the values and truths instilled in them. Choices made become a tangible expression of the family, transforming abstract concepts into lived experiences resonating through generations. The cultivation of a son's disposition involves the continuous journey of personal growth and self-reflection. Torchbearers are not static entities; they evolve and develop, mirroring the dynamic nature of the family legacy. This ongoing process contributes to the richness and depth of the beliefs they carry forward. Beyond embodying individual values, they engage in an interplay of virtues.

The harmonious integration of qualities such as integrity, compassion, resilience, and humility forms a cohesive and comprehensive temperament. This interplay becomes a model for future heirs to emulate. At the heart of carrying forward the inheritance, personal growth emphasizes the importance of teaching values through action. They not only verbalize beliefs but actively demonstrate them in their daily lives. This experiential learning becomes a powerful method of transmitting ideologies to their next successors.

It is essential to emphasize this role is far from subdued. They must diligently engage in this responsibility because it goes beyond the custodial possession of knowledge; they are stewards who actively nurture, protect, and propagate the endowment. This adherence involves making choices aligned with Biblical values, teaching them to the next-in-line, and safeguarding the traditions of the family history. The role extends beyond being a custodian; it requires earnest stewardship and leadership.

Conveyors of this gift are not docile recipients but dynamic individuals who take charge of nurturing, protecting, and guiding the legacy. This fervent engagement elevates their responsibility to a leadership role. Active involvement in the responsibility of carrying forward the ethos involves intentional decision-making.

They make choices aligned with the family's values, ensuring each decision contributes to the preservation and enhancement of the birthright. This deliberate approach distinguishes their role from a mere inheritor. Teaching values to the next generation is not a theoretical exercise but a practical one.

They intently demonstrate the application of values in real-life scenarios, providing tangible examples for the younger members. This experiential learning reinforces values and principles in a way transcending abstract teachings. The spirited commitment includes safeguarding traditions and history. This involves a proactive role in preserving rituals, customs, and the narrative of the past. By doing so, they ensure a continuum of identity and heritage remaining intact for future successors.

Last, this responsibility deepens the bond between fathers and their sons. It is a commitment strengthening their connection. Fathers play a vital role in guiding and supporting their sons in fulfilling this responsibility. Their wisdom, guidance, and encouragement empower them to carry the torch with honor and dedication, building a sense of unity and purpose.

The responsibility is truly substantial, encompassing a multifaceted role extending far beyond the transmission of knowledge. It creates a shared commitment spanning across generations. It is not only a connection between fathers and their sons but also a legacy binding family members together. This mutual commitment serves as a sense of unity and continuity, reinforcing the intergenerational connection.

In their role as guides, fathers become pillars of strength for their torchbearers. Their guidance is not just practical advice; it serves as a moral directive, providing a foundation upon which their sons navigate the challenges of their responsibility. This guidance becomes a source of strength, wisdom, and stability. The wisdom passed down is an empowerment to carry the familial message with honor and dedication.

It is not just about knowledge transfer; it's about instilling a sense of purpose and commitment. Their wisdom becomes a guiding light, illuminating the path as they navigate their multifaceted role. Their responsibility contributes to building a culture of unity. Through commitment and the guidance of fathers, a sense of togetherness is cultivated. This unity becomes a cornerstone for the family's resilience, fostering an environment where each member actively contributes to the preservation of the inheritance.

As entrusted stewards, they serve as guardians of their family's identity. Beyond the transmission of factual teachings, they actively preserve the essence of their history, values, and traditions. This guardianship involves a sincere commitment to maintaining the unique identity defining their legacy. Responsibility goes beyond mere preservation; it includes the active perpetuation of fundamental ideologies. They are not passive recipients but

CHAPTER SEVEN

dynamic agents, ensuring the core principles shaping their lineage are not only preserved but actively instilled in succeeding generations. In holding the role of narrators, they become storytellers of their ancestry's evolution.

It is more than just recounting the past; they actively contribute to shaping the ongoing account. This storytelling role involves an awareness of the kindred's journey, acknowledging both triumphs and challenges, and providing a meaningful context for the present. The duty as a new advocate for the inheritance carries the weight of maintaining a legacy continuing through the ages.

This eternal heirloom becomes a precious jewel for future beneficiaries, offering a connection to their roots and a source of inspiration. Torchbearers become architects of a heritage transcending time, influencing the values and decisions of those who will follow. To grasp the depth of this mission, internal fortitude is called upon to manage its emotional and practical weight. On an emotional level, it involves recognizing their actions and choices will directly influence the inheritance passed on to their future heirs.

In practical terms, it requires active engagement in preserving traditions, teaching values, and safeguarding the descendants identity. The commitment to this obligation vibrates throughout time, affecting their lives and the lives of their offspring. Internal fortitude becomes a pillar of strength for the new family advocate. This is not just a vague concept but a tangible quality of gaining empowerment to face the emotional and practical trials inherent in their responsibility. Their fortitude serves as a reservoir of resilience, allowing them to navigate the complexities of this duty.

Recognizing actions and choices directly influence this role passed on underscores the interconnectedness across generations. They realize their present decisions undulate through time, shaping the narrative for themselves along with their children and heirs. This awareness creates a unique sense of responsibility. Active engagement in preserving traditions, teaching values, and safeguarding the family's identity is not a one-time effort; it is a continuous commitment.

By actively preserving ancestral values and passing on inherited wisdom, the upcoming figureheads assume the role of their own architects of the lineage's legacy. Their dedication shapes the character and conscience of the next generation, serving as a guiding light for heirs yet unborn. The choices made today resonate through the years, influencing the values and decisions of those who will follow in their footsteps. This responsibility encompasses more than the transmission of knowledge; it necessitates embodying the morals and statutes passed down by their forebears.

Through their commitment, they become architects not only of their family's legacy but also of cultural continuity. They play a pivotal role in ensuring cultural richness endures and evolves, becoming a living testament to the values defining their heritage. This dedication goes beyond a mere duty; it actively shapes the character and moral pathway of the next beneficiaries. Their sons serve as role models, exemplifying the principles they hold dear and becoming a transformative force influencing the ethical foundation of those who follow.

The moral and ethical estate left behind becomes a timeless reference point, offering insights which navigate the complexities of life for those who come after. They understand the lasting impact of their decisions, creating an undulating effect extending far beyond their own lifetime. This awareness adds immeasurable depth to their sense of responsibility.

Personal growth lies at the heart of this duty. Each must strive to live out these beliefs in their daily lives, not simply as words but as a way of being. This entails cultivating qualities such as integrity, compassion, resilience, and humility. A virtuous character serves as the passage through which the legacy is transmitted, ensuring values are not simply articulated but actively embodied. Through their actions and behaviors, their sons become living testaments to the valuable wisdom passed down from their fathers.

The focus on personal development extends beyond a checklist of virtues; it is a holistic approach to molding individuals into embodiments of their heritage. They are tasked with seeking a mode of existence mirroring the fundamental spiritual righteousness passed down, surpassing mere compliance with rules, and embracing a complete set of ethical and moral values. Cultivating a quality such as integrity becomes a daily commitment, where actions align with principles even in the face of difficulties. This responsibility is not fulfilled through occasional displays of fortitude but through consistent and persistent adherence to these values. Integrity becomes a beacon for guiding decisions, ensuring they align with the ethical foundation laid by previous generations.

Compassion, another cornerstone of personal maturity, encompasses more than empathy; it requires active participation in promoting understanding and support within the household. By embodying love, they establish an environment where every member feels acknowledged and appreciated, strengthening a culture of togetherness and mutual care.

Resilience emerges as a vital attribute in maneuvering life's intricacies. Custodians of legacy, by prioritizing character development, foster resilience as a reaction to obstacles. The capacity to recover from adversity transforms from a personal characteristic into a shared asset, bolstering their bond during troubling times.

Humility, often overlooked but integral, shapes the sentinels' interactions. By acknowledging the contributions of previous generations and recognizing the collective wisdom molding the legacy, family leaders build an environment where humility becomes a binding force, promoting shared respect and appreciation. In addition, temperament is an active, ongoing process transforming the younger generation into a living testament of the values and wisdom passed down. It is not just about adopting virtues but becoming a reflection, ensuring each action contributes to the preservation and enhancement of the ethical foundation.

This role demands an active commitment, as they are not just recipients of their fathers' legacy. Instead, they serve as stewards tasked with actively nurturing, protecting, and propagating it. They engage in this responsibility by making deliberate choices aligned with their values, teaching these ideals to the next generation, and safeguarding the traditions defining their family. This devotion requires effort, dedication, and a genuine belief in the importance of preserving their heritage.

Loyalty extends beyond the passive reception of a legacy; it transforms into active stewardship. As a caretaker, they play a dynamic role in the ongoing narrative. This stewardship involves a proactive approach to ensuring the inheritance not only endures but flourishes through deliberate and mindful actions. Making deliberate choices aligned with their values is a cornerstone of the torchbearer's allegiance. This involves a thoughtful consideration of the ethical and moral principles defining the generations, ensuring each decision resonates with the values upheld by those before. This conscious decision-making becomes a mechanism for steering the trajectory of their ethical foundation.

Teaching values to the next generation is not a one-time event but an ongoing process, recognizing the importance of instilling values through consistent and intentional guidance. This involves practical demonstrations of virtues in everyday life, providing tangible examples serving as a foundation for the younger members. Safeguarding traditions is a multifaceted task requiring both preservation and adaptation. Torchbearers actively engage in maintaining rituals, customs, and the tales of the past. At the same time, they navigate the challenge of aligning these traditions with the contemporary context, ensuring their relevance and continuity in a changing world.

This responsibility demands effort and dedication. Understanding the preservation of their heritage is not a nonchalant duty but an ongoing endeavor. The dedication required involves a deep sense of responsibility, where the torchbearer's actions become a testament to the belief in the importance of preserving their identity and traditions. The role of a custodian is an undertaking requiring conscious choices, continuous effort, and a heartfelt dedication to the task. It is through this active engagement they contribute to the vitality and relevance of future generations.

Their function also deepens the bond between fathers and sons. It is a mutual arrangement strengthening their connection, nurturing a sense of unity and purpose. Fathers play a valuable role in guiding and supporting their sons in fulfilling this responsibility. Their wisdom, knowledge, and encouragement empower them to carry the torch with honor and dedication. Through this commission, both preserve their legacy and cultivate a deeper and more meaningful relationship rooted in a common purpose and a love for their family. The mutual promise in the father-son relationship extends beyond a scant duty; it becomes a powerful initiative, deepening the bond between them. In their valuable role, fathers become mentors and guides, providing not only practical advice but also imparting the wisdom coming from a profound understanding of their history. Their guidance is a source of stability and direction, empowering them to navigate the complexities of their torch-bearing trustworthiness with honor and dedication.

The wisdom, direction, and encouragement provided serve as foundational pillars. This support is not only practical but also emotional, creating a place of empowerment and enabling their sons to carry the torch with a sincere sense of province. Fathers become the cornerstone of strength, creating an environment where the torchbearer's obligation is met with encouragement and understanding. Through this resolve, both actively contribute to preserving their traditions. The responsibility becomes a collaborative effort, reinforcing the intergenerational connection.

In essence, cultivating a deeper and more meaningful relationship is rooted in their common efforts to honor and perpetuate their heritage. The commitment to preservation becomes a unifying force, strengthening their connection. Being torchbearers not only preserves the essence but also serves as a catalyst for building a wholesome and affectionate relationship. Through their dedication, they contribute to the continuity and vitality of their ancestral roots, establishing a narrative characterized by love, purpose, and harmony.

Wisdom's Eternal Flame of Love

Within the family legacy, this torch serves as a powerful representation, embodying the teachings, values, and love transmitted through generations. It signifies not only practical knowledge but also the Godly guidance and Scriptural nuances passed down. This emblem becomes the focus of enlightenment, symbolizing the instructions and illuminating their family's path. Just as its light dispels darkness, the knowledge and values it encapsulates, disperses ignorance and confusion.

It stands as a tangible reminder of the powerful legacy fathers bestow upon their descendants. In the spirit of Psalm 133:1, "*How good and pleasant it is when God's people live together in unity!*" This echoes the beauty found in familial unity, emphasizing the shared wisdom and values to create a

EVERLASTING BOND

harmonious foundation for generations, a testament to the strength derived from family unity. The lineage embodies the teachings and values passed from one generation to the next. It is a vessel carrying the accumulated wisdom of ancestors, captured in the form of lessons, moral principles, and ethical guidelines.

For instance, these values may symbolize traits such as integrity, compassion, resilience, and a commitment to kinship. Each time this legacy is passed down, it signifies the transmission of these valuable teachings, contributing to the broader wealth of their familial wisdom. Thematically, this symbol represents the heartfelt and everlasting love passed through generations within the father-son connection, transcending mere object status; instead, it stands as a representation of the emotional bond uniting their lineage.

This love serves as the vital fuel sustaining the flame, binding generations across time with an unbreakable emotional bond. The torch stands as a perpetual symbol, a touchstone reflecting the profound affection fathers hold for their descendants, carrying the enduring significance of love through the ages.

It serves as a reminder this path encompasses not only wisdom but also the everlasting affection and nurturing care provided to the next generation. The symbolism emphasized goes beyond the confines of the past, highlighting the timeless essence of the teachings, values, and love bestowed. This crest epitomizes the continuity of love and wisdom, stretching seamlessly from the past into the future.

The conveyed message is a living, evolving spirit remaining relevant across the divide. It continues to carry the flame forward, ensuring it illuminates the path for those who come after, entrusted with a precious representation and carrying a tremendous responsibility. They are more than just recipients of their fathers' bestowment; they are guardians tasked with caring for and preserving it. This responsibility encompasses the protection of the teachings, values, and love encapsulated by this lineage. It involves actively nurturing the legacy, guaranteeing its vibrancy and ongoing relevance. Safeguarding this torch from being extinguished is vital, as it symbolizes not only the family's history but also its future. The duty of care extends to preserving this birthright in its entirety for those to follow, ensuring the undiminished radiance of the flame of wisdom and love. The act of passing on this torch is a touching gesture of sharing the legacy with their own children and descendants. It represents the transition of knowledge, values, and compassion from one generation to the next.

When a father entrusts this symbol to his son, he is not only delegating the responsibility, but also affirming his belief in his son's ability to carry the legacy forward. This act is a ritual signifying the continuity of the inheritance and the commitment to ensuring the flame never extinguishes. In some cultural or historical contexts, this torch may hold additional layers of significance.

For example, in Biblical history, fire often represented purification and transformation, as demonstrated when God appeared to Moses in the burning bush (Exodus 3:2-4). In the broader context of the torchbearer's responsibility, interpreting this suggests, carrying the emblem becomes a transformative act, impacting not only individuals but also the entire family. It signifies a purification of values and a commitment to upholding the highest moral standards.

This crest may also have associations with courage, as it often lights the way in times of darkness, symbolizing the courage required to uphold family traditions and values. In the spirit of Joshua 1:9, which says: *"Have I not commanded you? Be strong and courageous. Do not be afraid; do not be discouraged, for the Lord your God will be with you wherever you go,"* reflects the proven courage demonstrated by those in the Biblical narratives.

By understanding the rich depth of this representation, one can grasp the breadth of their responsibility and the significance of the legacy they carry forward. It is not merely a representation; it's a symbol of wisdom, love, and long-lasting connections.

Honoring the Torch's Legacy

Embracing familial honor encompasses a deep and eternal reverence for the values, teachings, and traditions handed down through the legacy. In this sacred endeavor, torchbearers acknowledge the inherent value of this inheritance, elevating it to its utmost importance. Acting with honor is a testament to an unshakable loyalty to the principles defining a family's identity. Such respect involves upholding these values, even in the face of divisive temptations, and exemplifying a dedicated devotion to the responsibilities entrusted to them. Loyalty, within the task of carrying forward the legacy, refers to wholehearted devotion and dedication and is more than just a casual response. In this noble responsibility, those who embody loyalty do so with a sense of purpose and perseverance. They are steadfast in their resolve to protect, nurture, and propagate the legacy of love and wisdom.

This steadfastness is not merely a superficial undertaking but a deep-seated determination to ensure the torch burns brightly and endures. It involves a willingness to invest time, effort, and energy into the preservation and enrichment of their lineage. Committed heirs are proactive in seeking ways to pass on the teachings and values, knowing this duty requires ongoing attention and care.

This sustainable commitment is rooted in the recognition, the legacy is a sacred trust provided by God. Within the auspices of the Gospel, torchbearers safeguard its integrity with devoted honesty and moral rectitude. The Biblical message serves as the guiding light, shaping their ethical principles and influencing their decisions. It is not simply a set of rules but a source of profound inspiration, infusing their actions with the divine wisdom inherent in the teachings.

Embracing this responsibility becomes an act of faith, intertwining familial honor with the spiritual guidance found in the Scripture. Through this sacred trust, torchbearers affirm their belief in God's providence, ensuring the torch of love and wisdom not only endures but shines ever brighter for future generations. Loyalty and dedication are fundamental to preserving the authenticity of the legacy. They ensure the teachings and values transferred, deeply rooted in a family's history and culture, remain true and undistorted during transmission and are not forgotten or neglected. These qualities are essential in preventing it from losing its original essence and meaning. Its virtues ensure the seamless continuity, recognizing wisdom is not silent but a living, evolving entity. Loyalty acknowledges its importance and relevance, treating it with respect.

Dedication actively seeks to enhance and expand upon this virtue. Without such commitment, the family lineage and its historical value may stagnate, risking the loss of valuable insights over time. The presence of these virtues in the torchbearers significantly influence future generations. Those who embody these values set a powerful example, showcasing the importance of preserving and cherishing the endowment. These qualities create a groundswell effect, building the character and moral compass of the next generation.

Active engagement and seeking to understand and embody its values create a lifetime of enrichment. Their experiences and insights enhance the knowledge passed down, making it more dynamic and valuable. Without such proactive engagement, the family legacy may stall and fail to adapt to modern, changing times. They ensure its faithful passage, treating it as a sacred trust and passing it on with integrity and without compromise.

These values create a sense of responsibility and prevent it from being lost or forgotten. Honor and dedication are indispensable qualities for torchbearers, safeguarding authenticity, continuity, and enrichment. They set a positive example for the future and ensure a faithful passage. Without these virtues, the legacy risks losing its essence and significance.

Influence on Future Generations

The embodiment of faithfulness and trust within the legacy itself exerts a profound influence, setting a powerful precedent for those who come after and building a positive effect within the family's traditions. Allegiance and commitment manifest as a living demonstration of the core values and principles deeply revered within their inheritance. This embodiment becomes a visible testament to the fundamental beliefs. Observing this embodiment allows future generations to internalize and appreciate the significance of these values.

Actions often resonate more effectively than words, serving as a potent means of conveying the essence of the family's heritage. Consistent demonstrations of fidelity and zeal not only pass on knowledge but also encapsulate its practical application. This experiential approach to teaching imparts a deeper and more lasting understanding.

The lineage, steeped in justice and truth, inspires a sense of responsibility in those it touches. Witnessing the commitment required to uphold their principles encourages the next generation to embrace their roles earnestly. They understand their obligation to protect and nurture the timeless values encapsulated within their birthright. An inheritance infused with these attributes cultivates a sense of unity and purpose. It provides a foundation upon which the family can rally, forming a collective identity tied to timeless principles. This mutual endeavor strengthens the bonds between generations and deepens their emotional connection to the essence of their ancestry.

The impact of an inheritance steeped in integrity extends far beyond its familial borders, reaching into the wider community. Those endowed with such legacies often emerge as guiding lights within their neighborhoods, illuminating the Godly principles of respect, integrity, and responsibility. The propagation of these divine ideals encourages the advancement of society as a whole. Rooted in the very essence of the family, virtue and nobility guarantee the ongoing vitality and significance of the values and customs it upholds.

As successive generations embrace these principles, they are more likely to perpetuate and adapt the traditions and values instilled by their forebears. This heartfelt transmission is the hallmark of their family's legacy. The embodiment of virtue and goodness holds a far-reaching and eternal influence on future generations. It sets a powerful precedent for the next torchbearers, allowing them to grasp the essence and application of their lasting ideals.

This influence serves as a linchpin in ensuring the continuity and impact of these values on the lives of their descendants. Carrying forward the torch of a generational legacy is not without its hurdles and enticements. Embracing the responsibilities of inheritors involves encountering various obstacles along the way.

However, relatability and steadfastness are essential virtues serving as the guiding lights to navigate these challenges and resist temptations which could compromise the historical traditions. One of the primary challenges is the pressure to compromise on values and principles when confronted with adversity or societal expectations. Nobleness, acting as a moral compass, reminds bearers of their commitment to the core values of the legacy. Confronted with hardships, one can draw upon these qualities to make principled decisions aligned with Godly teachings. Despite the evolving nature of Scriptural views and traditions, the temptation to modify them for contemporary acceptance can be strong. True dedication, however, is a compelling force designed to resist such temptations and uphold the legacy defining their identity. Recognizing these traditions as integral to a family's makeup, their preservation becomes crucial.

Balancing personal aspirations and ambitions with the responsibilities of the torchbearers is another hurdle. Dedication motivates individuals to prioritize their role as the next entrusted conveyor, ensuring the inheritance remains at the forefront of their decisions and actions. Family dynamics can sometimes be complex, leading to conflicts threatening their unity. Those embodying these virtues are better equipped to navigate these differences with wisdom and grace; understanding the importance of maintaining harmony is essential for its preservation.

Temptations may arise in the form of short-term gains or shortcuts which seem attractive but could compromise long-term integrity. Adherence and purity of purpose are driven by a sense of responsibility and a commitment to the legacy's unrelenting impact. They resist the allure of immediate gratification in favor of long-term benefits for future generations. At times, doubts may arise regarding the ability to fulfill the role, or discouragement may come from other sources.

Tenacity and pledgement provide the inner strength needed to persevere through moments of doubt. One can draw on these qualities to remain focused. Sincerity and resolve act as armor for their heirs, protecting them from temptations. These virtues serve as a constant reminder of the responsibility they have undertaken and the importance of preserving the family's values and teachings. When their sons embrace these virtues, they are more resilient in the face of adversity and better equipped to pass on the familial legacy faithfully.

A Brief Reflection

Encouraging personal reflection on the concepts of honor, dedication, loyalty, and steadfastness is a powerful way to engage and inspire meaningful introspection. Prompting self-examination invites a pause to ponder the experiences and dynamics of familial perspectives. It encourages consideration of the way these characteristics manifest themselves in the interactions and influence of family bonds. By exploring past events and memorable experiences, one can identify instances where these traits may have been demonstrated or lacking.

Reflecting on specific moments allows for a deeper understanding of the impact of these qualities on relationships and family fluctuations. Recognizing strengths and growth areas becomes possible through contemplation. It allows for the identification of moments of resilience, integrity, and commitment. Simultaneously, areas where further enhancement of these qualities may be needed can be recognized. Assessing assumptions and patterns in relationships is encouraged through reflection. It prompts questions about whether certain behaviors or attitudes align with Biblical values and principles held dear and whether adjustments are needed to better embody these virtues.

Inviting consideration of the manner in which these qualities can be more fully embodied encourages proactive thinking about their roles, which is a first step. This involves contemplating actions, decisions, and behaviors conducive to honoring responsibilities and strengthening dedication to preserving the family legacy. Drawing on one's experiences serves as a catalyst for open and meaningful dialogues, providing an opportunity to discuss insights leading to a deeper connection and understanding.

The ultimate goal of encouraging this introspection is to inspire personal growth and transformation. This process encourages taking deliberate steps toward embodying Christian virtues more fully, thereby enriching their bonds with loved ones and contributing to the unflagging legacy of love and wisdom. Encouraging individual contemplation of these fundamental attributes, the material empowers their sons to interact with it at a profoundly personal level, nurturing introspection, drawing wisdom from experiences, and purposefully enhancing these roles.

CHAPTER SEVEN

The concepts noted are not simply abstract ideals; they are living statutes profoundly inspiring fathers and their sons on their journey of love and wisdom. These qualities extend beyond the pages of this writing, infusing life into their relationship and enriching it in ways transcending words. Their transformative potential lies in their ability to shape not only individual lives but entire legacies. They infuse this bond with a sense of purpose and unity, enabling families to navigate the complications of life with grace and resilience.

When both embrace these qualities, they become torchbearers of love and wisdom, illuminating the path for the future. The narratives emphasize honor and dedication are not theoretical ideals but practical, transformative forces, when embraced and practiced, have the power to form the dynamics and conversations of father-son relationships. Through these qualities, fathers and their sons can build a legacy founded on love, understanding, and the continuous pursuit of wisdom. The torch of honor and dedication, once lit, burns brightly across generations, leaving a memorable impression on the fabric of family and society.

The midway point of Chapter 7 encapsulated the theme of passing the torch and the torchbearer's responsibility, rooted in the Biblical guidance from 2 Timothy 2:2. It particularly focused on the younger generation's duty to carry forward the legacy of love and wisdom. Attributes highlighted were honor, dedication, loyalty, steadfastness, and others as essential elements in preserving the authenticity of the father's legacy, with an influence on future generations and a consequential effect within the family's heritage.

It acknowledged the challenges and temptations of carrying the torch of a family legacy and emphasized the importance of personal reflection. In addition, it underscored the attributes were not abstract ideals but living principles inspired by the Biblical passage, guiding fathers and their sons on their journey of love and wisdom. In the culmination of this book, the father-son legacy is solidified in the "*Final Journey of Love*," where the focus rests on the reflective assessment of the lasting connections. The teachings of 1 Corinthians 13:13, echo throughout this journey, affirming that the greatest gift is love.

——— Final Journey of Love ———

In concluding this exploration with a heartfelt reflection on the father-son bond, enriched by Biblical wisdom and love, the narrative affectionately turns to 1 Corinthians 13:13, *"And now these three remain: faith, hope and love. But the greatest of these is love."* Scripture declares the greatest gift is love, encapsulating the essence of the path fathers and their sons have traversed, a journey marked by compassion, guidance, and faith, leaving a lasting impression on the hearts and lives of the eternal connection. It serves as the building block in their relationship and remains the driving spirit behind the journey explored.

As this final chapter moves towards closure, it is vital to highlight the important role love plays in shaping and sustaining these remarkable bonds. This virtue is not merely a conceptual idea; it's a dynamic, transformative, Godly momentum weaving through the intricate fabric of their relationship. It embodies the essence of shared experiences, cherished memories, and the tireless connection moving through the very spirit of their existence.

Since it serves as the bedrock on which trust, understanding, and closeness are built, this compassion is the pathway embraced to move beyond the darkest moments, a source of strength in times of adversity, and a repository of unshakable support. Through love, both learn to navigate life's complexities with compassion, respect, and care. Serving as the adhesive binding their hearts and enriching their lives, it is not a modest sentiment but a dynamic, ever-evolving spirit breathing life into their connection.

Reflecting on the significance of this powerful bond, it's important to recognize it goes beyond the ordinary, since it forms their understanding of one another, deepens their trust, and stirs a connection transcending words. It is a Godly movement empowering them to confront life's challenges with resilience, navigate the complexities of the world with integrity, and approach dilemmas with discernment.

CHAPTER SEVEN

As the central theme, love embraces the essence of their journey, leaving a lifetime image in their hearts and lives. It serves as a timeless source of inspiration, guidance, and a moral compass for those who follow in the footsteps of their fathers. In all its forms and expressions, it plays a crucial role in these relationships, serving as the spiritual essence uniting them and providing essential guidance and faith needed to navigate life's complexities.

Approaching the culmination of the steps toward the summit, it is imperative to reflect on the significance of this cornerstone in father-son relationships. Love transcends mere affection; it is a dynamic and ever-evolving spirit breathing life into their bond. Its importance is noted: First, it serves as the foundation of the trust fathers and their sons place in each other, allowing them to embrace a deep understanding of one another's thoughts, emotions, and aspirations. This mutual understanding forms the basis of their relationship, enabling open and honest communication.

Second, it creates a closeness transcending the normal conduct of speech, allowing them to share their joys, sorrows, and dreams on a more personal level. This emotional, physical, and spiritual connection is the heart of their bonding, making them more than just family in a father-son relationship; they become lifelong companions, allies, friends, and partners in an exclusive manly image of God.

Third, it is this love which acts as a guiding light during their darkest moments, offering unwavering support as fathers and their sons traverse adversities as part of the everlasting support system in male bonding. In doing so, they can align themselves and mimic many of the precepts emulated by the Biblical patriarchs. Fourth, it is rooted in compassion and respect and teaches the importance of treating each other with kindness and consideration. These values, instilled by the deep affection they share, create a nurturing Scriptural environment for growth and mutual support, seemingly contrary to modern skewed norms.

Fifth, and closely related, love plays a vital role in shaping their values and principles, providing an ethical benchmark guiding their actions and decisions in the hierarchy of responsibility and ownership. The profound affection they have for each other significantly influences the ethics they live by and pass down. Finally, one of the most remarkable aspects is its dynamic and ever-evolving nature. It doesn't remain still but continues to evolve and grow as life unfolds. The bond between fathers and their sons deepens, and their connection takes on new dimensions, becoming a key factor in their relationship.

In essence, the significance of love as the cornerstone of these bonds lies in its multifaceted role. It is the foundation of trust, the source of emotional closeness, the guiding light in difficult times, and the Spirit empowering them to face challenges with compassion and respect. This embracement directs their values and principles, serving as an ethical guide. It's not a motionless concept; it continually evolves as their journey progresses, ensuring the unswerving nature of their bond. Throughout this exploration, love has been a guiding light, leaving a durable mark on their hearts and lives. The culmination of this journey serves as a reminder, within these connections some of life's most immense and cherished treasures have yet to be uncovered.

Reflecting on a Lifetime of Love

The lifelong journey of love transcends the expressions of chronological progression, evolving into a tapestry intricately woven with the threads of memories and milestones. Memories serve as the stepping stones across the endless creek forming the foundation of their connection. These are not just recollections, they embody the unbroken laughter, unfeigned conversations, tireless support during difficult times, and the jubilant celebrations of achievements. Revisiting these cherished events of the past provide a unique opportunity to relive those special fragments in time and to acknowledge the deep significance hidden within those seemingly ordinary experiences. Each shared laugh and supportive gesture contributes to the resilience and strength of their relationship, creating a tapestry of love moving with the pulse of eternity.

As their souls meditate on life's awe, it is heartfelt to recognize the value of these memories lies in their individual significance and the collective impact they have had on the father-son bond. Every conversation, every shared joy, and every supportive gesture weaves a narrative of embrace, connecting the core of their relationship.

CHAPTER SEVEN

Ordinary experiences, often overlooked, play a decisive role in fortifying the energy cord between fathers and their sons. Therefore, it is not surprising as they reflect on a lifetime of love, it becomes evident, the richness of their connection is intricately tied to the depth of their common experiences. By delving into the details of these moments, a more enlightening understanding of the journey emerges, revealing the true essence of their loving bond.

Milestones, in contrast, stand as significant waypoints on the expansive canvas of their lifelong journey. The incremental junctures encompass a spectrum of celebratory events, ranging from momentous birthdays and graduations to career achievements and various other key moments, father and son have joyfully shared.

Each turning point etches itself as a testament to the complex nature of their bond, signifying the prevalence of their abiding love navigating them through the intricate complexities of life. Reflecting on these common experiences, memories, and milestones serves not only as a trip down memory lane but also as a powerful reaffirmation of their importance in shaping the fabric of their relationship.

In providing a more nuanced perspective, it is essential to recognize milestones are not simply markers set alongside the road to measure the distance in time; instead, they are pivotal chapters in the ongoing chronicle of the father-son connection. Birthdays and graduations, for instance, are not only celebrations of personal achievements but also collective triumphs strengthening familial ties. Career attainments, in their own right, represent victories, emphasizing the collaborative spirit defining their journey together.

By peering into the experiences encapsulated within each marker, the roots of their bond grow deeper, weaving a narrative traveling beyond the surface-level significance of these events. It is within these mutual experiences one finds the guiding spirit of love becomes palpable, molding their lives in influential and lasting ways.

Love emerges as a formidable connection with the transformative power to frame lives and relationships in life-changing ways. Through this corridor, their sons begin the task of learning the valuable lessons of life, cultivating empathy, and forging their persona. This guidance extends beyond a list of casual instructions; it serves as a living example, offering a virtuous model to emulate and impart the essential values designed for growth.

Assuming the role of confidant, fathers become the designers of understanding, influencing the paths their sons tread in life. This influence goes beyond the tangible, lacing its way into the emotional, spiritual, and psychological welfare, becoming a repository of comfort, security, and persistent support especially during times of need. Recognizing the deeper impact of this guidance, it is vital to understand, love operates as the foundational bedrock upon which trust is meticulously built.

Trust is not merely an abstract concept but a tangible outcome of the enduring love fathers bestow upon their sons. This trust, in turn, serves as the foundation for encouraging open and honest expression, creating a space where thoughts, emotions, and aspirations are freely shared.

It is in this environment of trust and transparent dialogue that the father-son relationship thrives, becoming a sanctuary where both can navigate the complexities of life with resilience and mutual respect. The impact of love extends far beyond the emotional realm, influencing the very dynamics underpinning their connection.

Unveiling the transformative influence of the divine gift, love emerges not merely as a word but as a living tenet, intricately enriching the connection between fathers and their sons. The invaluable importance is to recognize, love transcends the limitations of language; it is a dynamic Godly impetus, an unrelenting and transformative movement extending beyond the means of verbal expression. This love is not confined to the fading presence of time; instead, it stands as an unyielding spirit, reaching far beyond the boundaries of the immediate and surpassing the constraints of the moment.

The love shared between fathers and their sons becomes a perpetual source of comfort, providing a sanctuary in times of tribulation. Its influence extends through the spirit of family history, offering a continuous stream of guidance and inspiration. It becomes a legacy, an unbroken thread woven into the lives of generations, building the character and

CHAPTER SEVEN

virtues of descendants. This exceptional love, handed down from one generation to the next, stands as a solid pillar of strength and a continuous source of sustainable support.

The act of guidance and mentorship in the father-son relationship transcends a vague process of simply passing on knowledge; it is fundamental to the creation of a thoroughly rooted legacy. This relationship goes beyond the transfer of ideas; it transforms into a source of enlightenment, revealing the path for the family's core values. The lasting love within their bond forms a legacy, serving as a guiding pathway to embrace foundational beliefs and a moral sphere, molding the essence of their being.

This legacy guarantees the loyal persistence of their values, offering a dependable source of guidance for succeeding generations as they navigate complexities. Family traditions and values serve as the channels through which love and guidance gracefully traverse into the future. Traditions, in their various forms, provide a sense of belonging and a robust identity, acting as the connective tissue binding families across generations. Whether manifesting as a cherished ritual, a collective celebration, or the observance of particular values, these traditions become more than a routine; they are a powerful means of transmitting a living inheritance.

Expanding on the significance of traditions, they offer more than just a link to the past; they are active contributors to the continuity of an impregnable love within their bond. Family rituals, for instance, become sacred moments, echoing highlighted memories of history and reinforcing the embrace defining their connection. Celebrations become joyful occasions, contributing to the waypoints marking the perpetuity of familial ties.

The observance of specific historical benchmarks serve as a compass, guiding family members through the intricacies of life with the wisdom and love inherited from their fathers. By actively nurturing and upholding their traditions, they become tangible expressions of love, etching it into the fabric of daily life. The intentional preservation of these rituals and values becomes a conscious effort to uphold the inheritance, making it a vibrant and integral part of the family's collective identity.

Wisdom gained through life experience is a treasure fathers possess. By dispersing this wisdom, they ensure their sons are better prepared to travel the future ahead. The guidance and values they impart extend beyond the familial sphere; they have a trickle-down effect, influencing their communities and society at large. Passing on this wisdom is not just transactional; it's a testament to their powerful legacy of love. The impact reverberates through generations, leaving an unfading impression on the lives of their family and beyond.

In considering the broader impact, fathers are not just mentors to their own sons; they become role models and guides to others within the greater community. As they lead by example, these actions embody the values and Christian morals they wish to instill. This leadership role extends beyond the familial bond and contributes to the development and wellness of those around them.

The concept of mentors and role models showcases the profound significance of their influence on a wider scale. As this role is explored, it encourages fathers to recognize the positive impact they have on their communities and inspires them to pass on their wisdom, love, and guidance, enriching the lives of those they encounter. When gazing ahead toward the future, the journey of love unfolds with infinite possibilities and opportunities. It is an open canvas, awaiting the brushstrokes of new memories, experiences, and lessons.

Hearing the tick on the clock of life with hope serves as an inspiration to anticipate the evolving dynamics of these relationships. It is a reminder, the journey of love is not confined to the past or the present; it's an ever-unfolding daily story. This message of love rekindles enthusiasm for what lies ahead, reaffirming the value of these connections and the potential for new milestones and memories that will continue to enrich their lives. The wealth of wisdom accumulated through experiences becomes a precious resource fathers keenly possess. This is not merely a personal asset but a treasure meant to be generously shared.

By imparting this legacy, fathers equip their sons with a reservoir of insights they can only dream of acquiring alone. This process fortifies their confidence by helping them navigate the myriad decisions yet to unfold. It extends beyond the confines of the father-son relationship to have far-reaching effects resonating throughout the moments of influence on a broader scale.

The guidance and values provided become a lantern, illuminating paths for others to follow. By positively influencing their communities, they contribute to the collective well-being and development of society. This impact is not confined to the immediate family but radiates outward, creating a formidable effect shaping the fabric of the entire community. The mentorship and guidance offered become integral threads in the social tapestry, weaving a narrative of common values and communal support. This role transcends family confines, emphasizing the interconnectedness of individuals within a society. As fathers pass on wisdom and a sense of responsibility toward Godly goodness, they contribute to the creation of a harmonious and thriving community.

The process of passing on experience, hope, and fortitude stands as a touching testament to the everlasting legacy fathers strive to create. It transcends a scant transaction of knowledge; it becomes a deliberate and meaningful way of preserving the accumulated wisdom and virtues that have shaped their own lives. This intentional act of gifting is a bridge connecting the past with the present and extends its influence into the future.

Passing on sagacity is akin to preserving a cultural heritage, a legacy encapsulating the personal experiences along with the collective ethos of a family, and by extension, a broader neighborhood. It is a conscious effort to ensure the knowledge and values cultivated over time remain vibrant and relevant for eons to come. This preservation becomes a living archive, an invaluable resource enriching the lives of their family and contributing to the cultural tapestry within community circles.

The impact of a father's wisdom and love reverberates through the corridors of time, leaving an ingrained influence on the lives of their children and the succeeding generations. This legacy is not confined to a faithless existence; it is dynamic, evolving, and adapting to the changing human landscape. As fathers pass down knowledge, they offer a unique insight into the understanding of life's intricacies, and they bestow upon their descendants a timeless gift, an inheritance ringing with the wisdom, love, and eternal values of generations past. Transcending their roles as mentors solely to their own sons; they emerge as indispensable role models and guides within their communities. Operating on the concept of leading by example, fathers embody the very essence and values they aspire to instill in their family and the wider community. This embodiment goes beyond verbal articulation; it manifests in their actions, becoming a tangible testament to the ethical and moral standards they champion.

The mentoring role undertaken extends far beyond the fence of the familial bond. They become a carrier of guidance, offering their wisdom and support to those who seek it. This outreach is not a resident contribution; they actively contribute to the development and well-being of those around them. Their impact, formed by a foundation of love and wisdom, becomes a reason for active change, fostering a sense of unity and communal support.

Fundamentally, fathers assume a dual role: one within the sanctity of their family, where they nurture and guide their own, and another in the broader circle of influence, where they extend their mentorship to contribute to collective growth. Through this multifaceted role, they become agents of spiritual influence, enriching both the microcosm of their family life and the macrocosm of the larger community. Their commitment to mentorship extends the cascading effect of love and wisdom, shaping not only the destinies of their progeny but also leaving a lasting imprint on the fabric of the society they inhabit.

The deep-rooted concept of fathers as mentors and role models has unfolded to reveal the expansive significance of their influence on a wider scale. As this role is summarized, it serves as a spark, inspiring others to recognize the transformative impact they can have on their domain. In assuming the mantle of mentors, tutors, and role models, fathers become the designers of familial well-being and agents of positive change in a broader societal context. This highlighted overview ignites an undulating effect, encouraging fathers and sons to acknowledge the potential they possess to mold and uplift their communities. It becomes a call to action, inspiring individuals to reflect on their own capacities for imparting wisdom, love, and guidance.

CHAPTER SEVEN

In doing so, it creates a collective recognition of the power each person holds to make a Godly difference in the lives of those they encounter. The cycle of inspiration set in motion becomes a testament to the formidable nature of their influence. It is not confined to the immediate impact on their own families but extends outward, encouraging a communal spirit of sharing, learning, and mentorship. By inspiring others to pass on their wisdom and love, they create a network of Christian influence transcending personal spheres, generating a tapestry of interconnected relationships enriched by the values and guidance passed down from one generation to the next.

The journey of love, an ongoing tale, unfolds as a canvas yet to be adorned with the hues of new memories, experiences, and lessons. The future presents itself as a blank canvas, a realm brimming with possibilities and opportunities. Approaching this unwritten chapter with hope becomes not just an optimistic outlook but a profound inspiration, urging them to eagerly anticipate the evolving dynamics directing their relationships.

This forward-looking perspective serves as a valuable reminder, the journey of love is not confined to the constraints of the past or the limitations of the present; rather, it is an ever-unfolding chronicle. The unwritten chapters of the future hold the promise of new beginnings, deeper connections, and uncharted territories of growth. It is a call to rekindle enthusiasm, prompting them to look ahead with anticipation, reaffirming the immeasurable value of their connections.

As they stand at the threshold of what lies ahead, this message becomes a directive, guiding them to embrace the unfolding narrative of their relationships with optimism and eagerness. It reinstates the potential for forging new milestones, creating fresh memories, and continuing the enriching journey of love. Ultimately, this is an invitation to approach the moments ahead not just as an unwritten chapter but as a canvas awaiting the strokes of affection, mutual experiences, and the ever-evolving tapestry of relationships that will undoubtedly add vibrancy to their lives.

——— Closing Thoughts ———

The legacy of love and wisdom is not limited to the present; it is also about preparing the ground for stronger relationships in the coming years. Methods to nurture and promote the strength and significance of these relationships were explored. Practical guidance was offered on ways to cultivate their connections, and these father-son relationships are now empowered to pass on the legacy of love and guidance. This included fostering open dialogue, maintaining a supportive and loving environment, and being actively engaged in one another's lives. It was a clarion call to action, motivating active participation in ensuring the familial legacy is passed down to future generations.

Further strategies were explored, equipping each with the knowledge and tools to continue the journey and ensure it remained a cornerstone of their family for years to come. The exploration peered into the unique interplay of love, guidance, and faith within the intricate dynamics of father-son relationships. These words explored love as the lifeblood of the family, guidance as the heart of fatherhood, and faith as the strong foundation on which these bonds were built.

The preceding chapters have shed light on the multifaceted nature of the father-son relationship, and it is fitting to briefly revisit them to set the stage for these closing reflections. In this context, love was not a passive sentiment but a dynamic and essential force. It was the driving spirit breathing life into the father-son bond, redefining the very essence of fatherhood. The exploration has shown the ways in which love transcended sentimentality and became a living truth, a presence molding the connection and defining what it meant to be a father.

Guidance, as explored, was the heartbeat of fatherhood while leading their sons on a path of wisdom, character development, and a deeper understanding of life's complexities. Fathers have been portrayed as mentors, tutors, and role models, imparting invaluable lessons and virtues extending far beyond the immediate family bonds.

CHAPTER SEVEN

Faith, the unwavering trust in the journey, has been a steadfast companion, illustrating even in the face of challenges and uncertainties, the legacy of love has remained a constant source of strength and that love isn't just a word; it's a living fruit of the Spirit enriching their connection.

As the conclusion of this journey approaches, it is important to focus on a message of continuity, highlighting the legacy explored does not end here. This heritage was meant to endure, to stretch across generations, and to leave an everlasting impression on the tapestry of family history. The love, guidance, and faith discussed were not confined to the pages of this book. They are living principles continuing to shape the lives of fathers and their sons today, as they have throughout history.

The message is one of encouragement, a call to action, and for those to take the lessons learned, the love experienced, and the wisdom they have gained and pass these on to future generations. This legacy was not just an idea; it is a living propulsion enriching the lives of countless fathers and their sons yet to come. It is a reminder, the impact of love and wisdom is not bound by time but is, in fact, timeless. As they embark on the next chapters of their own father-son journey, each has the opportunity to ensure the familial legacy thrives and flourishes for generations.

Their legacy is a gift that keeps on giving. It offers a message of hope, encouraging the inheritance of love and wisdom to flourish. The lessons learned, the values instilled, and the love shared between fathers and their sons serve as a pillar of light extending beyond the present. This bequeathal shapes the lives of their family and beyond. It leaves a permanent footprint on their sons, families, communities, and society as a whole. All are invited to take the lessons and knowledge shared and actively participate in preserving and enriching their own heritage.

By doing so, each ensures the bond between fathers and their sons remains a source of inspiration, guidance, and strength for the countless chapters yet to be written in the book of their lives. Love, as the foundation of fatherly relationships, played a vital role throughout the narrative. It was important to emphasize the significant role love played in forming and sustaining their remarkable bonds.

Beyond an abstract concept, love is a dynamic and transformative spirit weaving the intricate fabric of these relationships. It embodies the essence of common experiences, cherished memories, and the connection deeply interwoven into the texture of their existence. A deeper exploration of love's essence and its role in father-son relationships took place. Love served as the glue binding their hearts and enriching their lives. It was not just a casual sentiment but a dynamic, ever-evolving spirit, breathing life into their connection.

The significance of love went beyond negligible affection; it shaped their understanding of one another, deepened their trust, and embraced an emotional bond transcending words. It empowered them to confront challenges with resilience, to navigate the complexities of the world with integrity, and to approach dilemmas with discernment.

The significance of love in father-son relationships could not have been overstated; it was the foundation on which trust, understanding, emotional closeness, and a whole host of attributes, virtues, values, and statutes were built. It acted as a lighthouse, shining in the darkest moments, sounding its fog horn on the cliff's edge, and alerting their relationship in times of adversity. Through love, both learned to sail through life's complexities with compassion, respect, and care. Love, as the central theme, encapsulated the essence of this voyage. It has left an indelible impression on the hearts and lives of fathers and their sons alike, serving as an ageless source of inspiration, guidance, and a moral compass for those who followed.

In 1 Corinthians 13:13, this timeless declaration still resonates: "*The greatest... is love.*" This essence encapsulated the very heart of the journey. Love was not just one element among many; it was the ultimate Godly Spirit binding fathers and their sons together, providing the guidance and faith needed to navigate the complexities of life. As this concluding chapter began, it was essential to remember love, in all its forms and expressions, was the bedrock of father-son bonds. It had led them through this exploration, leaving a lifetime impression on their hearts and lives.

In the previous chapters, reflections would center on the lasting bond it had created, enriched by Biblical wisdom and faith. The culmination of this journey serves as a reminder: in the bond between fathers and their sons,

CHAPTER SEVEN

some of life's most profound and cherished treasures were discovered. The exploration of evolving alliance illuminates the dynamic nature of love, a force constantly changing along life's journey of growth.

The father-son relationship mirrors this evolution, deepening and transforming through new challenges and diverse phases. This connection serves as a testament to its resilience. The acknowledgment of its evolving nature serves as a reminder, there is perpetual room for growth, understanding, and connection. This realization sparks curiosity and anticipation for the future, envisioning the relationship continuing to flourish in unforeseen ways.

As this journey concludes, the guidance is to seek God in all endeavors, and following His ways becomes paramount. In these closing words a notable reminder emerges, there remains a scarcity of written accounts exploring the intricacies of the father-son bond. Despite this void, the unmistakable significance of this connection remains clear: there exists no greater love for a son than that of his father.

Perhaps there will be those who come to this enlightenment, seize this torch, and carry it into the future, passing on its wisdom and love to subsequent generations. May it be accompanied by the timeless blessing from Numbers 6:24-26:

"The Lord bless you and keep you; the Lord make his face shine on you and be gracious to you; the Lord turn his face toward you and give you peace." Amen.

God Bless you...

Dr. David R. Blunt

EPILOGUE

We find ourselves at the crossroads of a transformative expedition in finishing these pages of the *"Legacy of Love: Biblical Wisdom for Father-Son Relationships."* As the ink settles and the resonance of the chapters linger, these concluding thoughts serve as a heartfelt embrace, extending gratitude to those who have traversed the corridors of wisdom and love within the Scriptural teachings.

It was the very essence of this connection, acknowledging the shared experience of delving into the rich tapestry of fatherhood, and guided by the timeless principles gathered from the life-changing events written within the Biblical accord. This was a testament to the collective journey undertaken and a path transcending the pages, resonating in the lived experiences of those who engaged with the wisdom woven into the narrative.

As we conclude this step in the *"Legacy of Love,"* the invitation to reflect upon the everlasting impact of the lessons learned settles. It serves as a call to action, urging fatherly mentors to embrace the torch of love and wisdom in their unique journeys of fatherhood. This writer, with humility and gratitude, contemplates the reflections on the profound process of crafting this literary work. Unveiling the motivations that ignited the desire to illuminate the sacred connection between fathers and their sons, this concluding passage encapsulates a meaningful journey of sharing wisdom and fostering meaningful legacies.

In the quiet moments yet to follow, this serves as both a conclusion and a commencement, a final invitation to integrate the teachings into the fabric of daily life. It is a closing chapter opening the door to a legacy of love, inspiring all to write their own narratives infused with the external wisdom found within the Biblical passages.

—— AFTERWORD ——

In this moment of reflection, one recognizes the profound odyssey woven throughout the tapestry of *"Legacy of Love: Biblical Wisdom for Father-Son Relationships."* Herein lies an intricate interplay between the spoken word and its palpable resonance. The author's intent becomes clear as each chapter unfolds, offering panoramic vistas of wisdom and insight. It is a juncture where the revelations intersect with the reader's contemplation, forming a nexus of shared understanding.

The text meticulously explores the enduring reverberations of its core theme, the dynamic fusion of love, wisdom, and the myriad emotions defining the father-son dynamics. By beckoning all to internalize these teachings and weave them into the fabric of their lives, the script illuminates the transformative potential encapsulated within these pages.

It beckons forth an imperative to action, a summons to perpetuate a legacy of love transcending generations, leaving an indelible imprint on the hearts and minds of those who partake. As the final words find their resting place, it serves not only as a concluding meditation but also as a commencement, a rallying cry to embark on the ongoing voyage of crafting meaningful legacies infused with love within the father-son familial bond.

SCRIPTURAL REFERENCES

The Scriptural references presented follow the New International Version (NIV). However, numerous verses cited in the text are creatively expressed to enhance the coherence of the supported content.

INTRODUCTION: Preparing for the Journey Ahead

1 Corinthians 16:14 *"Do everything in love."*

Matthew 3:17 *"And a voice from heaven said, 'This is my Son, whom I love; with him, I am well pleased.'"*

CHAPTER ONE: Legacy of Love

John 13:34-35 *"A new command I give you: Love one another. As I have loved you, so you must love one another. By this everyone will know that you are my disciples, if you love one another."*

1 Corinthians 13:4-7 *"Love is patient, love is kind. It does not envy, it does not boast, it is not proud. It does not dishonor others, it is not self-seeking, it is not easily angered, it keeps no record of wrongs. Love does not delight in evil but rejoices with the truth. It always protects, always trusts, always hopes, always perseveres."*

James 5:7-8 *"Be patient, then, brothers and sisters, until the Lord's coming. See how the farmer waits for the land to yield its valuable crop, patiently waiting for the autumn and spring rains. You too, be patient and stand firm, because the Lord's coming is near."*

Galatians 5:22-23 *"But the fruit of the Spirit is love, joy, peace, forbearance, kindness, goodness, faithfulness, gentleness, and self-control. Against such things there is no law."*

Jeremiah 31:3 *"The Lord appeared to us in the past, saying: 'I have loved you with an everlasting love; I have drawn you with unfailing kindness.'"*

Proverbs 4:1-4 *"Listen, my sons, to a father's instruction; pay attention and gain understanding. I give you sound learning, so do not forsake my teaching. For I too was a son to my father, still tender, and cherished by my mother. Then he taught me, and he said to me, 'Take hold of my words with all your heart; keep my commands, and you will live.'"*

Psalm 139:14 *"I praise you because I am fearfully and wonderfully made; your works are wonderful, I know that full well."*

CHAPTER TWO: Building a Strong Foundation

1 John 4:7-8 *"Dear friends, let us love one another, for love comes from God. Everyone who loves has been born of God and knows God. Whoever does not love does not know God, because God is love."*

Genesis 1:26 *"Then God said, 'Let us make mankind in our image, in our likeness, so that they may rule over the fish in the sea and the birds in the sky, over the livestock and all the wild animals, and over all the creatures that move along the ground.'"*

Psalm 78:4 *"We will not hide them from their descendants; we will tell the next generation the praiseworthy deeds of the Lord, his power, and the wonders he has done."*

Proverbs 8:17-21 *"I love those who love me, and those who seek me find me. With me are riches and honor, enduring wealth and prosperity. My fruit is better than fine gold; what I yield surpasses choice silver. I walk in the way of righteousness, along the paths of justice, bestowing a rich inheritance on those who love me and making their treasuries full."*

Solomon 8:7 *"Many waters cannot quench love; rivers cannot sweep it away. If one were to give all the wealth of one's house for love, it would be utterly scorned."*

Romans 13:7 *"Give to everyone what you owe them: If you owe taxes, pay taxes; if revenue, then revenue; if respect, then respect; if honor, then honor."*

1 Peter 2:17 *"Show proper respect to everyone, love the family of believers, fear God, honor the emperor."*

Leviticus 19:32 *"Stand up in the presence of the aged, show respect for the elderly and revere your God. I am the Lord."*

Genesis 1:27 *"So God created mankind in his own image, in the image of God he created them; male and female he created them."*

Galatians 3:28 *"There is neither Jew nor Gentile, neither slave nor free, nor is there male and female, for you are all one in Christ Jesus."*

Colossians 3:12 *"Therefore, as God's chosen people, holy and dearly loved, clothe yourselves with compassion, kindness, humility, gentleness, and patience."*

Proverbs 27:17 *"As iron sharpens iron, so one person sharpens another."*

Matthew 22:39 *"And the second is like it: 'Love your neighbor as yourself.'"*

1 Corinthians 16:14 *"Do everything in love."*

Psalm 127:3 *"Children are a heritage from the Lord, offspring a reward from him."*

Philippians 4:6-7 *"Do not be anxious about anything, but in every situation, by prayer and petition, with thanksgiving, present your requests to God. And the peace of God, which transcends all understanding, will guard your hearts and your minds in Christ Jesus."*

CHAPTER THREE: Lessons from Scripture

Colossians 3:21 *"Fathers, do not embitter your children, or they will become discouraged."*

Proverbs 13:24 *"Whoever spares the rod hates their children, but the one who loves their children is careful to discipline them."*

Proverbs 22:6 *"Start children off on the way they should go, and even when they are old, they will not turn from it."*

Hebrews 12:11 *"No discipline seems pleasant at the time, but painful. Later on, however, it produces a harvest of righteousness and peace for those who have been trained by it."*

Proverbs 3:12 *"Because the Lord disciplines those he loves, as a father the son he delights in."*

Psalm 103:13-14 *"As a father has compassion on his children, so the Lord has compassion on those who fear him; for he knows how we are formed, he remembers that we are dust."*

Romans 11:33 *"Oh, the depth of the riches of the wisdom and knowledge of God! How unsearchable his judgments, and his paths beyond tracing out!"*

Ecclesiastes 11:1 *"Ship your grain across the sea; after many days you may receive a return."*

2 Timothy 3:14-15 *"But as for you, continue in what you have learned and have become convinced of, because you know those from whom you learned it, and how from infancy you have known the Holy Scriptures, which are able to make you wise for salvation through faith in Christ Jesus."*

Matthew 7:12 *"So in everything, do to others what you would have them do to you, for this sums up the Law and the Prophets."*

Matthew 6:14-15 *"For if you forgive other people when they sin against you, your heavenly Father will also forgive you. But if you do not forgive others their sins, your Father will not forgive your sins."*

Philippians 2:3-4 *"Do nothing out of selfish ambition or vain conceit. Rather, in humility value others above yourselves, not looking to your own interests but each of you to the interests of the others."*

Micah 6:8 *"He has shown you, O mortal, what is good. And what does the Lord require of you? To act justly and to love mercy and to walk humbly with your God."*

Proverbs 12:22 *"The Lord detests lying lips, but he delights in people who are trustworthy."*

Matthew 5:37 *"All you need to say is simply 'Yes' or 'No'; anything beyond this comes from the evil one."*

Matthew 22:39 *"And the second is like it: 'Love your neighbor as yourself.'"*

1 Samuel 17:45-47 *"David said to the Philistine, 'You come against me with sword and spear and javelin, but I come against you in the name of the Lord Almighty, the God of the armies of Israel, whom you have defied. This day the Lord will deliver you into my hands, and I'll strike you down and cut off your head. This very day I will give the carcasses of the Philistine army to the birds and the wild animals, and the whole world will know that there is a God in Israel. All those gathered here will know that it is not by sword or spear that the Lord saves; for the battle is the Lord's, and he will give all of you into our hands.'"*

Job 1:20-22 *"At this, Job got up and tore his robe and shaved his head. Then he fell to the ground in worship and said: 'Naked I came from my mother's womb, and naked I will depart. The Lord gave and the Lord has taken away; may the name of the Lord be praised.' In all this, Job did not sin by charging God with wrongdoing."*

Proverbs 25:2 *"It is the glory of God to conceal a matter; to search out a matter is the glory of kings."*

Philippians 2:3-4 *"Do nothing out of selfish ambition or vain conceit. Rather, in humility value others above yourselves, not looking to your own interests but each of you to the interests of the others."*

John 8:12 *"When Jesus spoke again to the people, he said, 'I am the light of the world. Whoever follows me will never walk in darkness, but will have the light of life.'"*

John 14:6 *"Jesus answered, 'I am the way and the truth and the life. No one comes to the Father except through me.'"*

Romans 1:20 "*For since the creation of the world God's invisible qualities, his eternal power and divine nature, have been clearly seen, being understood from what has been made, so that people are without excuse.*"

Proverbs 14:15 "*The simple believe anything, but the prudent give thought to their steps.*"

CHAPTER FOUR: A Father's Legacy

Deuteronomy 6:6-9 "*These commandments that I give you today are to be on your hearts. Impress them on your children. Talk about them when you sit at home and when you walk along the road, when you lie down and when you get up. Tie them as symbols on your hands and bind them on your foreheads. Write them on the door frames of your houses and on your gates.*"

Psalm 78:4 "*We will not hide them from their descendants; we will tell the next generation the praiseworthy deeds of the Lord, his power, and the wonders he has done.*"

2 Timothy 2:2 "*And the things you have heard me say in the presence of many witnesses entrust to reliable people who will also be qualified to teach others.*"

Proverbs 20:27 "*The human spirit is the lamp of the Lord that sheds light on one's inmost being.*"

Galatians 5:22-23 "*But the fruit of the Spirit is love, joy, peace, forbearance, kindness, goodness, faithfulness, gentleness and self-control. Against such things, there is no law.*"

John 14:26 "*But the Advocate, the Holy Spirit, whom the Father will send in my name, will teach you all things and will remind you of everything I have said to you.*"

Romans 12:2 "*Do not conform to the pattern of this world, but be transformed by the renewing of your mind. Then you will be able to test and approve what God's will is, his good, pleasing and perfect will.*"

Daniel 12:3 "*Those who are wise will shine like the brightness of the heavens, and those who lead many to righteousness, like the stars forever and ever.*"

Matthew 5:14-16 "*You are the light of the world. A town built on a hill cannot be hidden. Neither do people light a lamp and put it under a bowl. Instead, they put it on its stand, and it gives light to everyone in the house. In the same way, let your light shine before others, that they may see your good deeds and glorify your Father in heaven.*"

James 3:17-18 "*But the wisdom that comes from heaven is first of all pure; then peace-loving, considerate, submissive, full of mercy and good fruit, impartial and sincere. Peacemakers who sow in peace reap a harvest of righteousness.*"

Ecclesiastes 12:13-14 *"Now all has been heard; here is the conclusion of the matter: Fear God and keep his commandments, for this is the duty of all mankind. For God will bring every deed into judgment, including every hidden thing, whether it is good or evil."*

CHAPTER FIVE: Embracing Love and Guidance

Psalm 25:8-10 *"Good and upright is the Lord; therefore he instructs sinners in his ways. He guides the humble in what is right and teaches them his way. All the ways of the Lord are loving and faithful toward those who keep the demands of his covenant."*

Psalm 23:1-6 *"The Lord is my shepherd, I lack nothing. He makes me lie down in green pastures, he leads me beside quiet waters, he refreshes my soul. He guides me along the right paths for his name's sake. Even though I walk through the darkest valley, I will fear no evil, for you are with me; your rod and your staff, they comfort me. You prepare a table before me in the presence of my enemies. You anoint my head with oil; my cup overflows. Surely your goodness and love will follow me all the days of my life, and I will dwell in the house of the Lord forever."*

John 15:13 *"Greater love has no one than this: to lay down one's life for one's friends."*

Matthew 12:46-50 *"While Jesus was still talking to the crowd, his mother and brothers stood outside, wanting to speak to him. Someone told him, 'Your mother and brothers are standing outside, wanting to speak to you.' He replied to him, 'Who is my mother, and who are my brothers?' Pointing to his disciples, he said, 'Here are my mother and my brothers. For whoever does the will of my Father in heaven is my brother and sister and mother.'"*

Ephesians 5:1-2 *"Follow God's example, therefore, as dearly loved children and walk in the way of love, just as Christ loved us and gave himself up for us as a fragrant offering and sacrifice to God."*

Galatians 6:2 *"Carry each other's burdens, and in this way, you will fulfill the law of Christ."*

Philippians 4:6-7 *"Do not be anxious about anything, but in every situation, by prayer and petition, with thanksgiving, present your requests to God. And the peace of God, which transcends all understanding, will guard your hearts and your minds in Christ Jesus."*

Colossians 3:2 *"Set your minds on things above, not on earthly things."*

Genesis 1:27 *"So God created mankind in his own image, in the image of God he created them; male and female he created them."*

Proverbs 22:6 *"Start children off on the way they should go, and even when they are old, they will not turn from it."*

2 Corinthians 4:17-18 *"For our light and momentary troubles are achieving for us an eternal glory that far outweighs them all. So we fix our eyes not on what is seen, but on what is unseen, since what is seen is temporary, but what is unseen is eternal."*

Matthew 6:19-21 *"Do not store up for yourselves treasures on earth, where moths and vermin destroy, and where thieves break in and steal. But store up for yourselves treasures in heaven, where moths and vermin do not destroy, and where thieves do not break in and steal. For where your treasure is, there your heart will be also."*

Proverbs 10:4 *"Lazy hands make for poverty, but diligent hands bring wealth."*

Proverbs 12:22 *"The Lord detests lying lips, but he delights in people who are trustworthy."*

Proverbs 13:2 *"From the fruit of their lips people enjoy good things, but the unfaithful have an appetite for violence."*

Proverbs 15:1 *"A gentle answer turns away wrath, but a harsh word stirs up anger."*

Proverbs 15:33 *"Wisdom's instruction is to fear the Lord, and humility comes before honor."*

Proverbs 21:20 *"The wise store up choice food and olive oil, but fools gulp theirs down."*

CHAPTER SIX: Journey of Growth

Proverbs 4:7 *"Wisdom is supreme; therefore get wisdom. Though it cost all you have, get understanding."*

Lamentations 3:25-26 *"The Lord is good to those whose hope is in him, to the one who seeks him; it is good to wait quietly for the salvation of the Lord."*

Proverbs 16:32 *"Better a patient person than a warrior, one with self-control than one who takes a city."*

Ephesians 4:32 *"Be kind and compassionate to one another, forgiving each other, just as in Christ God forgave you."*

Colossians 3:13 *"Bear with each other and forgive one another if any of you has a grievance against someone. Forgive as the Lord forgave you."*

Matthew 6:14-15 *"For if you forgive other people when they sin against you, your heavenly Father will also forgive you. But if you do not forgive others their sins, your Father will not forgive your sins."*

Luke 6:37 *"Do not judge, and you will not be judged. Do not condemn, and you will not be condemned. Forgive, and you will be forgiven."*

1 Peter 4:8 *"Above all, love each other deeply, because love covers over a multitude of sins."*

CHAPTER SEVEN: An Everlasting Bond

Psalm 103:17-18 *"But from everlasting to everlasting the Lord's love is with those who fear him, and his righteousness with their children's children, with those who keep his covenant and remember to obey his precepts."*

2 Timothy 2:2 *"And the things you have heard me say in the presence of many witnesses entrust to reliable people who will also be qualified to teach others."*

Psalms 133:1 *"How good and pleasant it is when God's people live together in unity!"*

Joshua 1:9 *"Have I not commanded you? Be strong and courageous. Do not be afraid; do not be discouraged, for the Lord your God will be with you wherever you go."*

1 Corinthians 13:13 *"And now these three remain: faith, hope and love. But the greatest of these is love."*

Numbers 6:24-26 *"The Lord bless you and keep you; the Lord make his face shine on you and be gracious to you; the Lord turn his face toward you and give you peace."*

DISCUSSION QUESTIONS

CHAPTER ONE: Legacy of Love

1. In Chapter 1, the concept of love as a divine commandment is emphasized, drawing from John 13:34-35. Reflect on your understanding of this commandment and its implications for cultivating meaningful relationships, particularly in the context of father-son dynamics. How can the principles of selfless love guide your interactions with family members and contribute to a lasting legacy?

2. The chapter explores the idea of enduring love and transformation through the stories of John and Mark, Richard and Robert, and Michael and Ben. Consider these narratives and share your thoughts on the different aspects of enduring love portrayed in each story. How do these examples resonate with your own experiences or observations of fatherly love? What lessons can be drawn from these stories to nurture enduring and transformative relationships within families?

CHAPTER TWO: Building a Strong Foundation

1. Reflect on the role of love as the lifeblood of the family, as discussed in Chapter 2. How can a deep understanding of love as a foundational force shape the dynamics within a family? Share personal examples or observations that highlight the impact of love on family bonds.

2. The chapter emphasizes the significance of recognizing children as precious gifts. In what ways can fathers actively acknowledge and appreciate the uniqueness of each child? How does this recognition contribute to the nurturing of a strong foundation in the family?

CHAPTER THREE: Lessons from Scripture

1. Chapter 3 delves into the importance of Biblical teachings in enriching the father-son relationship. Explore the concept of flexible instructional discipline and its application in modern parenting. How can flexibility in discipline align with Scriptural principles while nurturing a child's growth?

2. Discuss the role of spiritual teachings in building a strong father-son bond. How can fathers impart spiritual guidance in a way that aligns with their beliefs while fostering a sense of understanding and connection with their sons?

CHAPTER FOUR: A Father's Legacy

1. Reflect on the divine commandment discussed in Chapter 4, emphasizing the role of love in building a lasting legacy. How can fathers integrate this commandment into their daily lives, ensuring that love becomes a guiding force in shaping the future generations of their family?

2. Explore the attributes of a living tradition and how they contribute to the continuity of faith within a family, as discussed in Chapter 4. Share examples from your own life or observations of families that have successfully passed down a legacy of faith and values.

CHAPTER FIVE: Embracing Love and Guidance

1. Delve into the exploration of the covenant in Chapter 5. How can fathers draw divine inspiration to create meaningful covenants within their families? Share insights on the significance of sacred promises and their impact on growth and character.

2. Discuss the transformative power of guiding with wisdom, as highlighted in Chapter 5. How can fathers apply the principles of wisdom in their guidance, recognizing the individuality of their sons? Share practical examples of wise guidance that fosters spiritual, emotional, and moral growth.

CHAPTER SIX: Journey of Growth

1. Explore the concept of the father-son journey in Chapter 6. How does the interplay of love, wisdom, and mutual emotions shape this journey? Share personal experiences or observations that highlight the intricate dynamics of the father-son relationship.

2. Reflect on the importance of nurturing emotional intelligence, as discussed in Chapter 6. How can fathers actively contribute to the emotional well-being of their sons, and how does emotional intelligence strengthen the bond between them?

CHAPTER SEVEN: An Everlasting Bond

1. Consider the echoes of a virtuous heritage discussed in Chapter 7. How do narratives of living wisdom contribute to the understanding of an everlasting bond between generations? Share your thoughts on the role of wisdom in shaping a lasting familial legacy.

2. Reflect on the responsibility of passing the torch, as emphasized in Chapter 7. How can fathers honor this responsibility and ensure that the flame of wisdom and love continues to illuminate the path for future generations? Share examples of families where the torch has been effectively passed, leaving a lasting impact.

DISCUSSION QUESTIONS
INSIGHTS FOR MODERATION

CHAPTER ONE: Legacy of Love

1. The concept of love as a divine commandment, rooted in John 13:34-35, highlights the profound nature of selfless love. This commandment serves as a guiding principle for cultivating meaningful relationships, especially within father-son dynamics. Selfless love involves prioritizing the well-being of family members above oneself, fostering a connection built on care and understanding. Embracing these principles in interactions contributes to a lasting legacy by creating a foundation of love that transcends individual actions, leaving an indelible mark on future generations.

2. The narratives of John and Mark, Richard and Robert, and Michael and Ben illustrate enduring love through different lenses. John and Mark's story reveals patience and perseverance, Richard and Robert exemplify strength and commitment, and Michael and Ben showcase the weightiness of separation and eventual reunion. These stories resonate with the diverse facets of fatherly love, demonstrating resilience, sacrifice, and transformative growth. Drawing lessons from these narratives, one can learn the importance of patience, commitment, and navigating challenges with unwavering love to nurture enduring and transformative relationships within families.

CHAPTER TWO: Building a Strong Foundation

1. Love as the lifeblood of the family, explored in Chapter 2, underscores its foundational role in shaping familial dynamics. A deep understanding of love as a foundational force creates an environment where relationships flourish. Love fosters connection, trust, and support within the family, acting as a unifying and sustaining factor. Personal experiences affirm that a family rooted in love exhibits resilience and cohesion, navigating challenges with a shared sense of purpose.

2. Recognizing children as precious gifts, as highlighted in the chapter, involves actively acknowledging and appreciating their uniqueness. Parents can foster a strong foundation by celebrating each child's individuality, encouraging their strengths, and guiding them with personalized attention.

This recognition contributes to a nurturing family environment, where children feel valued and understood, laying the groundwork for a supportive and harmonious family foundation.

CHAPTER THREE: Lessons from Scripture

1. The exploration of flexible instructional discipline in Chapter 3 brings attention to its relevance in modern parenting. Flexibility in discipline, when aligned with Biblical principles, becomes a guiding framework for nurturing a child's growth. It emphasizes adapting disciplinary approaches to suit individual needs while maintaining a foundation rooted in the values derived from these teachings.

2. The role of Spiritual teachings in building a strong father-son bond, as discussed in the chapter, highlights the importance of imparting guidance in alignment with beliefs. Fathers can foster understanding and connection with their sons by integrating these teachings into daily life. This approach involves sharing values, principles, and practices that shape a shared Spiritual foundation, creating a bond strengthened by a shared sense of purpose and faith.

CHAPTER FOUR: A Father's Legacy

1. The divine commandment of love, highlighted in Chapter 4, prompts reflection on its integration into daily lives for building a lasting legacy. Fathers can embody this commandment by making love a guiding force in their actions and decisions. This involves consistently demonstrating love through intentional choices, fostering an environment where future generations can thrive in the embrace of love.

2. The attributes of a living tradition, explored in the chapter, contribute significantly to the continuity of faith within a family. Successful examples involve families passing down legacies of faith and values through lived experiences. By modeling excellence in fatherhood and actively engaging in the present, fathers contribute to the shaping of a living tradition that transcends generations, creating a lasting impact on the family's Spiritual foundation.

CHAPTER FIVE: Embracing Love and Guidance

1. The exploration of the covenant in Chapter 5 invites fathers to draw divine inspiration for creating meaningful covenants within their families. This involves reflecting on common values, fostering sacred promises, and recognizing their impact on the growth and character of each family member. Fathers can actively seek inspiration from divine principles to shape these covenants, ensuring a foundation built on love, trust, and mutual values.

2. Chapter 5 emphasizes the transformative power of guiding with wisdom. Fathers are encouraged to apply these principles in their guidance, considering the unique individuality of their sons. Practical examples of this guidance could involve recognizing and respecting the individual strengths and challenges of each son, fostering growth not only in Spiritual aspects but also in emotional and moral dimensions. Through thoughtful guidance, fathers contribute to the holistic development of their sons.

CHAPTER SIX: Journey of Growth

1. Chapter 6 delves into the intricate dynamics of the father-son journey, where love, wisdom, and mutual emotions intertwine. This journey is molded by the interplay of these elements, creating a dynamic and evolving relationship. Sharing personal experiences or observations that highlight the complexities of the father-son relationship allows for a deeper understanding of these dynamics.

2 . Reflecting on the importance of nurturing emotional intelligence, fathers can actively contribute to the emotional well-being of their sons. Emotional intelligence strengthens the bond between fathers and sons by fostering open communication, empathy, and understanding. Fathers can explore practical ways to encourage emotional intelligence, creating a supportive environment for their sons to navigate their emotional landscapes.

CHAPTER SEVEN: An Everlasting Bond

1. Chapter 7 reflects on the echoes of a virtuous heritage, where narratives of living wisdom contribute to the understanding of an everlasting bond between generations. The role of wisdom becomes a guiding force in forming a lasting familial legacy, and sharing personal or cultural examples of wisdom being passed down through generations adds depth to this understanding.

2. Reflecting on the responsibility of passing the torch, fathers play a crucial role in ensuring that the flame of wisdom and love continues to illuminate the path for future generations. By honoring this responsibility, fathers contribute to the preservation of familial values. Examples from families where the torch has been effectively passed, leaving a lasting impact, provide insights into the practical aspects of fulfilling this crucial role.

BOOK CLUB GUIDE

CHAPTER ONE: Legacy of Love

1. Explore the metaphor of love as a divine commandment in Chapter 1. How does this concept resonate with your personal beliefs or experiences? Consider the impact of viewing love as a guiding principle in your own relationships.

2. Reflect on the storytelling approach used to illustrate enduring love in the narratives of John and Mark, Richard and Robert, and Michael and Ben. How does the power of storytelling enhance the message of fatherly love in these examples? Share your own stories or experiences that align with the themes presented in this chapter.

CHAPTER TWO: Building a Strong Foundation

1. In Chapter 2, the role of love as the lifeblood of the family is discussed. Consider how this metaphor shapes your understanding of familial bonds. How can recognizing love as a foundational force impact the dynamics within your own family or community?

2. Delve into the idea of recognizing children as precious gifts. How can acknowledging the uniqueness of each child contribute to building a strong foundation in a family? Share insights into the ways parents can actively foster a sense of appreciation for the individuality of their children.

CHAPTER THREE: Lessons from Scripture

1. Explore the concept of flexible instructional discipline in Chapter 3. How can this approach be integrated into modern parenting practices while aligning with Biblical principles? Share your thoughts on the balance between discipline and flexibility in nurturing a child's growth.

2.. Consider the role of spiritual teachings in building a strong father-son bond. How can fathers effectively impart spiritual guidance in a diverse and changing world? Discuss the challenges and opportunities of incorporating spiritual teachings into the modern father-son relationship.

CHAPTER FOUR: A Father's Legacy

1. Reflect on the divine commandment of love as a cornerstone for building a lasting legacy, as discussed in Chapter 4. How can fathers actively embody this commandment in their daily lives to build the future generations of their family? Share practical examples or strategies for infusing love into family legacies.

2. Discuss the attributes of a living tradition and their contribution to the continuity of faith within a family. How can families ensure the preservation of faith and values across generations? Explore the ways in which living traditions strengthen the familial legacy outlined in this chapter.

CHAPTER FIVE: Embracing Love and Guidance

1. Dive into the exploration of the covenant in Chapter 5. How can families draw inspiration from divine covenants to create meaningful agreements within their dynamics? Share your perspectives on the significance of sacred promises and their impact on familial growth and character.

2. Reflect on the transformative power of guiding with wisdom highlighted in Chapter 5. How can fathers apply principles of wisdom in guiding their sons, considering the unique individuality of each? Discuss examples of wise guidance that goes beyond imparting knowledge, contributing to spiritual, emotional, and moral growth.

CHAPTER SIX: Journey of Growth

1. Explore the intricate dynamics of the father-son journey in Chapter 6. How do love, wisdom, and mutual emotions mold this journey, and how can book club members relate these elements to their own experiences or observations? Share diverse perspectives on the complexities of the father-son relationship.

2. Reflect on the significance of nurturing emotional intelligence, as emphasized in Chapter 6. How can fathers actively contribute to the emotional well-being of their sons, and how does emotional intelligence strengthen the bond between them? Discuss the ability to manage the overall growth and development of individuals within a familial context.

CHAPTER SEVEN: An Everlasting Bond

1. Consider the echoes of a virtuous heritage discussed in Chapter 7. How do narratives of living wisdom contribute to the understanding of an everlasting bond between generations? Share personal or cultural examples of wisdom being passed down through generations, and discuss the ways in which these legacies endure.

2. Reflect on the responsibility of passing the torch, as emphasized in Chapter 7. How can fathers honor this responsibility to ensure the flame of wisdom and love continues to illuminate the path for future generations? Discuss the challenges and rewards of being torchbearers in your own families or communities.

—— BOOK CLUB GUIDE ——
INSIGHTS FOR MODERATION

CHAPTER ONE: Legacy of Love

1. The metaphor of love as a divine commandment deeply resonates with their personal beliefs, aligning with the idea that love is not just an emotion but a foundational principle guiding actions and decisions. This concept influences their relationships by emphasizing the importance of selfless and intentional love, creating a lasting impact on the bonds they share with others.

2. The storytelling approach in Chapter 1, showcasing narratives of John and Mark, Richard and Robert, and Michael and Ben, brings a powerful dimension to the message of enduring love. Storytelling adds a personal and relatable touch, making the principles of fatherly love more tangible. In their own experiences, stories have been instrumental in understanding and conveying complex emotions, creating a bridge between theoretical concepts and real-life application.

CHAPTER TWO: Building a Strong Foundation

1. Chapter 2's exploration of love as the lifeblood of the family resonates with their understanding of familial bonds. Recognizing love as a foundational force enhances the dynamics within their family, fostering a sense of unity, support, and unconditional care. This perspective also extends to the broader community, emphasizing the interconnectedness of relationships.

2. Acknowledging children as precious gifts is crucial for building a strong foundation in a family. Recognizing and appreciating the uniqueness of each child contributes to a nurturing environment where individual strengths are celebrated. Fathers can actively foster appreciation by embracing the distinct qualities of their children, encouraging self-expression, and promoting a sense of belonging within the family unit.

CHAPTER THREE: Lessons from Scripture

1. Chapter 3 introduces the concept of flexible instructional discipline, aligning with Biblical principles. Integrating this approach into modern parenting practices involves balancing structure with adaptability. Discipline, rooted in love and wisdom, can be flexible to meet the unique needs of each child, fostering growth while maintaining a solid foundation.

2. The role of spiritual teachings in the father-son bond is essential in a diverse world. Fathers can impart guidance by connecting timeless Biblical principles with contemporary challenges. Navigating these challenges provides opportunities for growth and understanding, strengthening the father-son relationship through shared values and a sense of spiritual connection.

CHAPTER FOUR: A Father's Legacy

1. Chapter 4 emphasizes the divine commandment of love as foundational for a lasting legacy. Fathers can embody this commandment by integrating love into daily actions and decisions. Practical examples, such as expressing affection, prioritizing family well-being, and fostering a nurturing atmosphere, shape a legacy of love that transcends generations.

2. The attributes of a living tradition play a crucial role in maintaining faith and values across generations. Families can ensure preservation by actively practicing and passing down traditions rooted in faith. Living traditions become a cornerstone, reinforcing the familial legacy outlined in the chapter and creating a continuum of shared beliefs and values.

CHAPTER FIVE: Embracing Love and Guidance

1. Chapter 5 delves into the exploration of covenants within family dynamics. Families can draw inspiration from divine covenants to create meaningful agreements, fostering growth and character. Sacred promises play a significant role, impacting familial dynamics and contributing to the overall development of family members.

2. Reflecting on the transformative power of guiding with wisdom, fathers can apply these principles by recognizing the individuality of each son. This guidance goes beyond imparting knowledge, extending to spiritual, emotional, and moral growth. Examples of such guidance contribute to a holistic development that enriches the father-son relationship.

CHAPTER SIX: Journey of Growth

1. Chapter 6 explores the intricate dynamics of the father-son journey, shaped by love, wisdom, and mutual emotions. Book club members can relate these elements to their own experiences, providing diverse perspectives on the complexities inherent in the father-son relationship.

2. Reflecting on the significance of nurturing emotional intelligence, fathers can actively contribute to the emotional well-being of their sons. Emotional intelligence becomes a cornerstone, strengthening the bond between them. Discussing the impact of emotional intelligence within a familial context sheds light on its role in overall growth and development.

CHAPTER SEVEN: An Everlasting Bond

1. Chapter 7 delves into the echoes of a virtuous heritage, exploring how narratives of living wisdom contribute to understanding an everlasting bond between generations. Sharing personal or cultural examples of wisdom being passed down enhances the discussion on enduring legacies.

2. Reflecting on the responsibility of passing the torch, book club members can discuss how fathers honor this duty to ensure the flame of wisdom and love continues illuminating the path for future generations. Exploring the challenges and rewards of being torchbearers in their own families or communities adds depth to the conversation.

INDEX

Love, Divine Commandment: Exploration of the concept of love as a divine commandment, discussed in Chapter 1.

Enduring Love Narratives: Narratives of enduring love explored through the stories of John and Mark, Richard and Robert, and Michael and Ben in Chapter 1.

Love as Lifeblood: Discussion on the role of love as the lifeblood of the family in Chapter 2.

Recognizing Children as Gifts: Emphasis on recognizing children as precious gifts and its significance in building a strong foundation, discussed in Chapter 2.

Flexible Instructional Discipline: Exploration of flexible instructional discipline in parenting, as discussed in Chapter 3.

Spiritual Teachings in Father-Son Bond: Role of spiritual teachings in building a strong father-son bond, explored in Chapter 3.

Divine Commandment in Legacy Building: Reflection on the divine commandment of love as a cornerstone for building a lasting legacy, discussed in Chapter 4.

Living Tradition Attributes: Qualities of a living tradition and their contribution to the continuity of faith, explored in Chapter 4.

Exploration of the Covenant: Delving into the exploration of the covenant in Chapter 5.

Guiding with Wisdom: Reflection on the transformative power of guiding with wisdom, highlighted in Chapter 5.

Father-Son Journey Dynamics: Exploration of the intricate dynamics of the father-son journey in Chapter 6.

Nurturing Emotional Intelligence: Significance of nurturing emotional intelligence, discussed in Chapter 6.

Virtuous Heritage Narratives: Echoes of a virtuous heritage discussed in Chapter 7.

Passing the Torch Responsibility: Reflection on the responsibility of passing the torch, emphasized in Chapter 7.

―― **PUBLISHER RESOURCES** ――

With sincere gratitude, the **CHURCH JUNCTION FOUNDATION** has graciously provided financial and loving support for this book. Their online church located at website: ChurchJunction.com provides weekly Sunday sermons, including blogs, discussion forums, and personal testimonials. It is an endeavor designed to fill a gap in reaching lost souls through salvation via the internet. Your tax donations to help their volunteer staff is greatly appreciated.

A portion of their statement of faith reads: We are dedicated to fostering a vibrant online community that celebrates and spreads the love, teachings, and principles of Christ Jesus. Our purpose is to provide a safe and inclusive digital space where Christians can come together, grow in faith, and find encouragement on their Godly journey and walk with Jesus.

We are more than just a virtual gathering place; we are a foundation grounded in faith and guided by the timeless teachings of the Scriptures. As believers united by an unwavering devotion to our Lord and Savior, we have created a space that goes beyond the boundaries of physical locations, connecting Christians from all corners of the world in a common pursuit of spiritual growth and meaningful fellowship.

Tax deductible donations can be accessed online or by mail:
CHURCH JUNCTION FOUNDATION
1207 Delaware Avenue #3535 Wilmington, Delaware 19806-4743
Non Profit 501(c)(3) Christian Organization SR20273122732
ChurchJunction.com

ABOUT THE COVER

The book cover, meticulously crafted, serves as a poignant representation of a deeply cherished aspiration, a longing for those precious moments of fatherly bonding with my beloved sons. The carefully chosen color palette symbolizes various facets of fatherhood and the journey of growth, with warm oceanic tones evoking an endless sense of nurturing love, and subtle contrasts reflecting the complexities inherent in father-son relationships.

Each hue and inflection contributes to the visual narrative, mirroring the richness found within the pages of this book. Intricate scenery woven into the cover design holds symbolic significance. The depiction of a father and his sons, engaged in moments of creating milestones along the sandy dunes of the beachfront, conveys the vision of fostering genuine connections and creating lasting memories within the landscape of God's earthly creation. The creative process involved drawing inspiration from personal experiences and reflections on the impact of fatherhood. Each element, from the chosen fonts to the placement of every image, was purposefully selected to resonate on a profound level.

This hands-on approach in designing the cover speaks to the commitment, authenticity, and genuine expression in conveying the core themes of this book. "I wanted to be the best dad... I never had," displays a heartfelt message, expressed in the cover, encapsulating the sincere desire to cultivate meaningful connections toward the journey of adulthood, and during the profound responsibility of fatherhood. This visual narrative not only reflects the content, but also highlights a personal journey, inviting all to join in the universal quest for enriching eternal and loving familial legacies.

NOTES

NOTES

www.ingramcontent.com/pod-product-compliance
Lightning Source LLC
Chambersburg PA
CBHW020937180426
43194CB00038B/217